The Caribbean before Columbus

The Caribbean before Columbus

WILLIAM F. KEEGAN AND
CORINNE L. HOFMAN

OXFORD

UNIVERSITY PRESS

Oxford University Press is a department of the University of Oxford. It furthers
the University's objective of excellence in research, scholarship, and education
by publishing worldwide. Oxford is a registered trade mark of Oxford University
Press in the UK and certain other countries.

Published in the United States of America by Oxford University Press
198 Madison Avenue, New York, NY 10016, United States of America.

© Oxford University Press 2017

Library of Congress Cataloging-in-Publication Data
Names: Keegan, William F., author. | Hofman, Corinne Lisette, author.
Title: The Caribbean before Columbus / William F. Keegan and
   Corinne L. Hofman.
Description: New York, NY : Oxford University Press, 2017. |
   Includes bibliographical references and index.
Identifiers: LCCN 2016019899 (print) | LCCN 2016021992 (ebook) |
   ISBN 9780190605247 (hbk) | ISBN 9780190605278 (UPDF) |
   ISBN 9780190605261 (EPUB) | ISBN 9780190605254 (pbk)
Subjects: LCSH: Excavations (Archaeology)—West Indies. |
   West Indies—Antiquities. | Indians of the West Indies—Antiquities. |
   Archaeology—West Indies.
Classification: LCC F1619 .K44 2017 (print) | LCC F1619 (ebook) |
   DDC 972.9/01—dc23
LC record available at https://lccn.loc.gov/2016019899

CONTENTS

FIGURES AND TABLES

Figures

Tables

The islands of the Caribbean are remarkably diverse in terms of both environments and cultures. They range from low limestone islands barely above sea level to volcanic islands with mountainous peaks; from large islands to small cays; from expansive shallow banks, to near shore reefs, to deep-water passages; from rivers, to tidal creeks, to salinas; from sand beaches to rocky shores and steep cliffs; from mangrove swamps, to blue holes, to freshwater ponds; from desert habitats, to whitelands vegetation, to tropical dry forest, to rainforest; from trees stunted by wind and salt spray to giant Ceiba trees more than 30 meters tall. We could go on and on discussing environmental differences alone. To complicate matters further, many of these differences can be observed on the same island or within a small group of neighboring islands.

Caribbean islanders today have diverse culture histories. Beginning with a mosaic of indigenous communities; Spanish, French, Dutch, English, Swedish, Danish, Irish, African, East Indian, Chinese, Syrian, Seminole, and other nationalities settled on these islands during historic times. In some cases they were transported against their will, while in others, they sought a better life. In all cases, they encountered and melded with those who preceded them. Every island and every community has unique combinations of individuals: individuals who trace their island ancestries back hundreds of years, and individuals who count their residence in hundreds of days.

Today, the Caribbean Islands are being homogenized. The goal is to attract tourists who expect a standardized product—call it the "Sandals resort experience." The hotel is on a sand beach, the vegetation in the gardens is imported from other tropical isles (e.g., coconut palms, Casuarinas, bananas, bougainvillea, bird of paradise), and the staff is appropriately servile. The last thing these tourists, or the hotel staff, want is for the guests to wander outside of the compound and mix with those who actually live on these islands. No hair-braiding, necklace-selling, trinket-vending itinerants are allowed on the grounds. A classic example is the Royal Caribbean Cruise Line, which advertises a stop at their "private island" of Labadee. The reality is that Labadee is not an island; it is attached to the country of Haiti (what tourist would want to go to Haiti?). The result is that, even in benign destinations, tourists go away from these experiences thinking that they were on "Turquoise Island," when in fact they were on Providenciales in the Turks & Caicos. The mantra is "homogenize, sanitize, and commoditize."

There is a similar attempt to homogenize the Caribbean past. The initial frame of reference viewed every new wave of immigrants as displacing those who arrived before. During the Ceramic Age, it was assumed by archaeologists that every new culture had developed out of the culture that preceded it. We now know that far more complicated processes of migration, transculturation, and accommodation were going on. Moreover, in the professional community, the entire region had come to be viewed in relation to the "Classic Taíno Culture" of Hispaniola, Puerto Rico, and eastern Cuba (Keegan 2013; Rouse 1992). Any indigenous community that was not classified as "Classic Taíno" was defined by what they lacked, rather than what they had.

The popular press has followed this dichotomy. The distinction between "good Indian" and "bad Indian" is still emphasized. For example, distinguishing between the "peaceful Arawak" and "cannibal Carib" forms the structure for James Michener's historical novel *Caribbean* (Michener 1988), with the notion of good versus bad reifying this simplistic view that dominates popular notions of precolonial Caribbean societies (Hofman, et al. 2008). We cannot fault most students (and we consider ourselves students) of Caribbean archaeology for adopting a simple, fail-safe perspective. Yet simplistic categories and stereotypes mask enormous variability.

Archaeologists have used a bewildering assortment of names: Saladoid, Ostionoid, Troumassoid, la Hueca, Island Carib, Island Arawak, Taíno, Lucayan, Agroalfarera, Ciboney, and so on. The challenge is to make sense of these various names, some of which even we are not sure what they really mean. For this reason, we are very careful in how we define and use specific terms. Moreover, most Caribbean archaeologists have worked on only one or a few Caribbean islands or sites and then have used their experiences to generalize to the entire region. These perspectives tend to lack what David Watters (1997) has called an "archipelagic view." This perspective is changing as information becomes more widely disseminated in comprehensive publications (e.g., Keegan, et al. 2013; Reid and Gilmore III 2014).

Nevertheless, there are significant lacunae in the regional coverage. At some sites, faunal preservation, burials, evidence for structures, and other cultural features are more common than they are at others. Syntheses have tended to treat every site from a particular time period as equal, and in writing such syntheses, the information from one site is used to define general characteristics for the cultural history of the entire region. We have illustrated this practice by highlighting important sites in the text. We have done so because there remains a gap between the reality of practice and the generality of theory. In this regard we recognize our limits, while still seeking a clearer understanding of precolonial Caribbean societies.

In this book, we document the diversity and complexity that existed in the Caribbean prior to the arrival of Europeans, as well as a bit of what happened after they arrived. This diversity results from different origins, different histories, different contacts between the islands and mainland, different environmental conditions, and shifting social alliances and ideological beliefs. The islands of today are a metaphor for the islands in the past. Understanding the Caribbean, past and present, is like looking through a kaleidoscope—every time you change your view, even slightly, you see a different image.

ACKNOWLEDGMENTS

Over the past thirty-five years. we have had the good fortune to supervise archaeological research projects in Antigua, Commonwealth of the Bahamas, Cuba, Curaçao, Dominica, the Dominican Republic, Grand Cayman, Grenada, Guadeloupe, Haiti, Jamaica, Martinique, Puerto Rico, Saba, St. Eustatius, Saint Lucia, St. Martin, St. Vincent, Turks & Caicos Islands, and Trinidad. We greatly appreciate the permissions granted by island governments, collaboration with local researchers, local communities, and the hospitality extended to us. We cannot adequately express our debt, and it would require an entire book if we tried to acknowledge everyone to whom we are indebted. We have also visited most of the other islands in the Caribbean, and have benefited greatly from the generosity of our colleagues. They are a special group of multicultural individuals whom we have the good fortune of seeing at least every other year at the biennial meeting of the International Association of Caribbean Archaeologists. Rather than risk not acknowledging someone by name, we have decided that the best way to acknowledge their contributions is by citing their publications.

Funding for these projects has come from the European Research Council (Nexus 1492 research project grant nr. n° 319209), National Science Foundation (NSF), Humanities in the European Research Area (HERA/ Carib project), Netherlands Organization for Scientific Research (NWO), American Philosophical Society, National Geographic Society, Bijvanck Fund (the Netherlands), Wenner-Gren Foundation for Anthropological Research, Nova Albion Foundation, Center for Field Research (Earthwatch), Caribbean Research Foundation, University of Florida, Florida Museum of Natural History, Foundation for Anthropology and Prehistory, Faculty of Archaeology at Leiden University, Leiden University Fund, French Ministry of Culture; and from numerous private contributions. Reed and Barbara Toomey, Grethe Seim, and Michael Dion have contributed to an endowment for Caribbean Archaeology at the University of Florida, and numerous others have provided funds for specific projects.

We would like to recognize a number of individuals and institutions that have made our research possible. They include: Eric Branford in St. Lucia, Tony Clarke in Jamaica, André Delpuech and Henry Petitjean Roget on Guadeloupe, Jean-Claude and Kathy Dicquemar in Haiti, Peter O'B. Harris in Trinidad, Michael Jessamy, Angus Martin, Cleopatrice Andrew, La Potterie community, Dolton Charles and Neil and Colin Willcox in Grenada, Will Johnson on Saba, Bruce Larson at Guantanamo Bay, Kathy Martin, the National Trust, the Garifuna association and the St. Vincent and the Grenadines International Airport Company LTD., on St. Vincent, the Museo del Hombre Dominicano in the Dominican Republic, especially Jorge Ulloa Hung and Glenis Tavarez Maria; National Archaeological - Anthropological Memory Management (NAAM) on Curaçao, Archaeological Museum Aruba (AMA) on Aruba, Desmond Nicholson and Reg Murphy on Antigua, Benoit Bérard and the Service Régional de l'Archéologie on Martinique, Association Archéologique Hope Estate on St. Martin, Brian Riggs in the Turks & Caicos Islands, Drs. Gail Saunders and Keith Tinker in The Bahamas, St. Martin Archaeological Center (SIMARC) on St. Martin, Saba Archaeological Center (SABARC) on Saba, St. Eustatius Center for Archaeological Research (SECAR) on St. Eustatius, Roberto Valcárcel Rojas in Cuba, and Reniel Rodríguez Ramos and Jaime Pagán Jiménez in Puerto Rico.

Menno Hoogland provided invaluable contributions throughout. He offered critical comments, reviewed much of the text, and was invaluable in preparing and assembling the figures. We cannot adequately express our appreciation for all of his contributions. Lisabeth Carlson, Joost Morsink, Joshua Torres, Jorge Ulloa Hung, and Roberto Valcárcel Rojas read and offered comments on drafts of particular chapters. Lisabeth Carlson, L. Antionio Curet, John de Bry, Kathleen Deagan, Michael Heckenberger, Peter Siegel, Joshua Torres, Jorge Ulloa Hung, Roberto Valcárcel Rojas, and David Watters graciously contributed figures.

Our research could not have been conducted without the assistance of our colleagues and students at Leiden University and the University of Florida. More than 200 students from the Faculty of Archaeology at Leiden University either participated in a field school, or conducted fieldwork for their BA, MA, or PhD research. A very special team that calls themselves "Keeganites" made major contributions over the past ten years. Finally, there are two individuals who have made major contributions to our study of Caribbean archaeology; they are Drs. Menno Hoogland and Lisabeth Carlson.

None of this would have been possible without the support of our families. Lorie, Dan, Lindsay, and Caroline Keegan; and Menno and Yann Hoogland.

The Caribbean before Columbus

CHAPTER 1 | Caribbean Kaleidoscope

TAKE A VIEWING TUBE, add some colored shapes to a chamber at one end, and hold it up to the light. From a material culture perspective, we might describe the kaleidoscope as a 15-centimeter hollow tube with a clear eyepiece at one end, a larger, translucent lens at the other, six yellow triangles, five blue squares, eight red octagons.... But this view does not capture the dynamics of this instrument. Rotate the tube slowly, and you are entertained by a seemingly infinite combination of colors and shapes. The kaleidoscope is a classic example of chaos in action. It has a fixed structure, but as conditions change, even slightly, the result is unique and unpredictable. This is how we view Caribbean archaeology. The precolonial cultures of the Caribbean are not simply a collection of different materials arranged in a particular order. Indigenous Caribbean societies were dynamic combinations of elements that are constantly in motion.

The perspective of the observer also leads to different and sometimes distinct views of the same phenomenon. Archaeologists often see only the end product and lack insight into the dynamic processes that produced a particular outcome. For example, surface scatters of artifacts often do not accurately reflect the original size of a site (Versteeg, et al. 1993), and middens arranged around a central space may reflect sequential episodes of deposition and not contemporaneous features (Keegan 2009). The final outcome is the *product* (in the mathematical sense) of long-term processes. Short-term behaviors (synchronic) and historical contingencies (diachronic) are played out in n-dimensional "timespacescapes."

Furthermore, the observer influences the outcome by adding a fifth dimension to three-dimensional space and time. Different theoretical perspectives approximate this fifth dimension. Caribbean archaeology is the product of historical processes that are refracted through the different perspectives of the archaeologists who work there. The islands of the Caribbean have been referred to by several other names, including "the West Indies" and "the Antilles." Although these names often are used interchangeably, they can denote very different geographical and historical landscapes. The name "West Indies" is mainly a British and American term that does not include all of the islands discussed in this study. This term is the product of the British colonial enterprise. It was introduced to distinguish the Caribbean colonies from British colonies in the Indian subcontinent ("East Indies"). Its history can be traced to Columbus's confusion regarding the geographical (hemispherical) location of the islands he visited. The name "Antilles" has a mythical origin (Rainbird 1999). It is used today in reference to two archipelagoes (i.e., the Greater Antilles and Lesser Antilles). The term is used here to denote modern geographic nomenclature. However, "Antilles" is not general enough to cover all of the islands that are included in Caribbean cultural geography.

Even the name "Caribbean" is not completely satisfactory, because it can be interpreted in several ways. In a strict sense, "Caribbean" refers to all of the land areas (mainland and islands) bordering on the Caribbean Sea. In practice, the Bahama archipelago is considered to be part of the indigenous Caribbean, although these islands do not touch on the Caribbean Sea and are actually located in the southern North Atlantic. The cultural heritage of the precolonial inhabitants of the Bahama archipelago is closely related to that of other Caribbean societies. For our purposes, we will distinguish a circum-Caribbean region, which is bounded on the south, west, and north by the coastal zones of the mainland (South, Central, and North America) (see also Hofman and Bright 2010). The mainland extends in a roughly semicircular shape from the Guianas around to the Florida peninsula. The eastern boundary for this region is the islands extending from the South American mainland (Lesser Antilles) to the southeast coast of Florida (Bahama archipelago).

We use the name "Caribbean Islands" to describe the subject of our study. The Caribbean Islands extend over 4,000 kilometers between the South, Central, and North American mainlands (Figure 1.1). The islands exhibit a

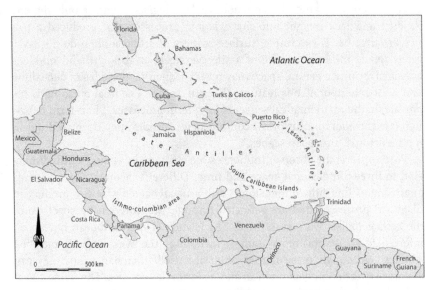

FIGURE 1.1 Map of the circum-Caribbean (courtesy of Menno Hoogland).

bewildering diversity in landforms, geology, and history. For example, all but the northernmost Bahamas fall within the tropics; all of the islands fall within the North Atlantic hurricane belt, but some are more susceptible to hurricanes than others; all of the islands are influenced by persistent trade winds, while variations in topography and rainfall create landscapes that range from steep mountain peaks to depressions below sea level, and from rainforest to desert. There are also issues of long-term changes in geomorphology, volcanism, sea-level fluctuations, climate change, and distributions of marine and terrestrial fauna. Dividing Caribbean landforms into six archipelagos and continental islands captures some of this diversity (Table 1.1).

TABLE 1.1 *Sizes and Elevations of the Caribbean Islands*

ISLAND GROUP	ISLAND AREA (KM²)	COASTLINE (KM)	COASTLINE/ AREA (M/KM²)	MAX. ELEVATION (M)
Southern Caribbean	2,071			
(1% land area)				
Margarita	1,150			920
Bonaire	288			193
Curaçao	443			241
Aruba	193	69	357	167
Trinidad and Tobago	5,128	362	71	
(2% land area)				
Trinidad	4,828			941
Tobago	300			572
Lesser Antilles	6,520			
(3% land area)				
Guadeloupe	1,702	307	188	1,467
Martinique	1,090	350	318	1,397
Dominica	790	148	196	1,422
Saint Lucia	603	158	261	951
Barbados	440	97	225	338
St. Vincent	389	84	215	1,179
Grenada	345	121	352	840
Antigua	280			403
Barbuda	161			22
St. Kitts	176			1,156
Nevis	130			1,156
Anguilla	88	61	598	55
British Virgin Islands	153	80	523	
Montserrat	84	40	392	742
St. Martin	34	59	1,093	742
St. Eustatius	21			549
Saba	13			884

(continued)

TABLE 1.1 Continued

ISLAND GROUP	ISLAND AREA (KM²)	COASTLINE (KM)	COASTLINE/ AREA (M/KM²)	MAX. ELEVATION (M)
Greater Antilles (89% land area)	208,312			
Cuba	110,922	3,735	34	1,972
Hispaniola	75,940	3,059	40	3,175
Haiti	27,560	1,771	64	
Dominican Republic	48,380	1,288	27	
Puerto Rico	8,897	501	56	1,065
U.S. Virgin Islands	344	188	543	465
Cayman Islands	241	160	611	15
Bahama Archipelago (5% land area)	10,500			
The Bahamas	10,070	3,542	352	63
Turks & Caicos Islands	430	389	905	48

Starting in the south, there are two archipelagos with modern Dutch and Venezuelan affiliations. To the west are the islands of Aruba (190 km²), Bonaire (288 km²), and Curaçao (443 km²). The Los Roques archipelago is situated to the east and is composed of about 50 very small, low-lying limestone cays. Indigenous fishermen from the mainland exploited the rich marine resources in the shallow banks surrounding these cays, but never established permanent settlements (Antczak and Antczak 2006). They did, however, deposit an abundance of ceramic figurines that reflect a spiritual association between mainland settlements and offshore camps. The largest Venezuelan islands of Margarita (1020 km²), Cubagua (22 km²), and Coche (61 km²) are the easternmost of the Southern Caribbean Region. Cubagua was the site of an early Spanish colony called "Nueva Cádiz" that was first established in 1502 to exploit the pearl fisheries in the area. The ABC (Aruba, Bonaire, and Curaçao) and Venezuelan islands are of volcanic origin. Their surfaces are characterized by predominantly limestone lithofacies, although metamorphic rocks are exposed on Margarita (Watts 1987). This Southern Caribbean Region comprises less than 1% of the land area of the Caribbean Islands (Haviser 1987:11; Watts 1987:4).

Recent investigations of the Los Roques archipelago and the Venezuelan islands (Antczak and Antczak 2006), along with studies conducted on Aruba, Bonaire, and Curaçao (Antczak, et al. in press; Boerstra 1982; Dijkhoff and Linville 2007; Haviser 1987, 1991; Hoogland and Hofman 2015), have demonstrated that their precolonial histories reflect a close association with cultures of the South American mainland. There has been some research to date on potential interactions with the inhabitants of the Lesser and Greater Antilles (Ayubi 1990;

Haviser 1997; Dijkhoff 1997; Versteeg and Rostain 1995), and their connections are currently being reinvestigated in the context of the broader Antillean-Isthmo-Colombian interaction spheres (Hofman and Bright 2010; Rodríguez Ramos 2010). In this book, we do not further interrogate these islands or the Caribbean coasts of northern South America and Central America; we concentrate on the Lesser and Greater Antilles and the Bahamian archipelago.

Trinidad is an extension of the South American mainland, and has been portrayed as the "gateway" to the Caribbean (Boomert 2013; Rouse 1992). It is the sixth-largest of the Caribbean Islands (4,828 km²) and was connected to the mainland until the Holocene epoch (c. 7000 BC). It has a more continental flora and fauna than the other Caribbean islands, and its Pleistocene land-bridge facilitated the movement of numerous animals that are typically not found in the Antilles. Except for the Miocene-age "Andean folding and faulting" that forms the rugged northern coast (Watts 1987:12), most of the relief is low hills with poorly drained lowlands (West and Augelli 1976:185). Tobago (300 km²) and Barbados (440 km²) are built on the same Andean geological structures, but being farther from the mainland, they have a more insular flora and fauna and are considered part of the Lesser Antilles archipelago. It is possible that Grenada, southernmost island of the Lesser Antilles, was "visible" from Tobago, which may have encouraged voyages of exploration to the north.[1]

The islands of the Lesser Antilles account for about 3% of the insular land area (7,164 km²). The islands are arranged in a double arc "along an arcuate zone of instability which roughly coincides with the Atlantic edge of the Caribbean tectonic plate" (Watts 1987:11). The inner arc is built around high volcanic cones, while the discontinuous outer arc is limestone islands built on older volcanic or crystalline bases (Watts 1987:11–12; Watters, et al. 1992). In addition, Antigua, St. Martin, and Guadeloupe are best described as composite islands that combine volcanic and limestone facies.

Traditionally, the Lesser Antilles has been divided into the Windward and Leeward Islands. These designations originated as British colonial administrative units that describe the sailing directions by which the islands were approached (into and away from the trade winds; West and Augelli 1976:194–195). The Windwards are the islands from Dominica to the south, with the Leewards (pronounced "Loowards") including all of the islands to the north. We mention these colonial designations because archaeologists have tended to use them as shorthand for describing differences observed in precolonial material culture. However, archaeologists often use the term "Leeward" to refer to the islands from Guadeloupe north. There is a fuzzy relationship between geographic, geological, modern political, and indigenous boundaries.

The Greater Antilles archipelago comprises 88% of the land area in the insular Caribbean (207,968 km²). Cuba (110,922 km²), Jamaica (11,424 km²), Hispaniola

---

[1] By "visible," we mean all of the signs that may have indicated the presence of islands to the north. These include cloud formations, reflections on the horizon, and bird migrations.

(76,484 km²; today shared by Haiti and the Dominican Republic), and Puerto Rico (8,897 km²) are the largest islands. These volcanic islands formed around northern and southern sections of mountain ranges that originate in northern Central America. The southern range forms the Blue Mountains of Jamaica and the Sierra de Baharuco on Hispaniola (Watts 1987:9; West and Augelli 1976:31–32). One of the northern ranges rises in southernmost Cuba as the Sierra Maestra, forms the Cordillera Central of Hispaniola and the central range of Puerto Rico, and ends in the Virgin Islands. Here we see the complications in relating geography and culture. The Virgin Islands archipelago begins geologically as an eastward extension of the central mountain range of Puerto Rico. The main islands have modern geological and political divisions between the high volcanic U.S. Virgin Islands of St. Croix (215 km²), St. John (51 km²), and St. Thomas (31 km²); and the low, limestone British Virgin Islands of Anegada (38 km²), Virgin Gorda (21 km²), Anguilla (91 km²), and Tortola (56 km²).

The second, lower mountain range is the Cordillera Septentrional, which runs along the northern coast of the Dominican Republic. The highest mountain in the Antilles, Pico Duarte (3,175 meters), is a huge gold-bearing batholith, which was uplifted into the Cordillera Central in the Dominican Republic (Watts 1987; West and Augelli 1976:31). Despite volcanic foundations, the surfaces of these islands are mostly weathered limestone, as well as sedimentary and metamorphic rocks. Puerto Rico is a microcosm of the natural diversity found in the Caribbean: it has a high central mountain chain covered by dense rainforest, a narrow, but well-watered, north coastal plain, and a rain-shadowed, xerophytic, broad south-coastal plain. Narrow, deeply dissected river valleys extend from the central cordillera. Lastly, the three small (*c.* 241 km²) carbonate Cayman Islands are also in this group. Recent archaeological surveys in the Cayman Islands failed to uncover evidence of any that the islands were occupied prior to the arrival of Europeans (Scudder and Quitmyer 1998; Stokes and Keegan 1996). It is likely that their small size and isolated location precluded their discovery and settlement until historic times.

The final major archipelago is the Bahamas, a chain of calcareous islands stretching over 1,000 kilometers, from 100 kilometers east of West Palm Beach, Florida, to within 100 kilometers of Haiti and Cuba (Sealey 1985). Today composed of the Commonwealth of the Bahamas and the Turks & Caicos Islands, these islands occupy about 5% of the land area in the island Caribbean (11,826 km²). These carbonate (limestone) islands were never volcanic. Rainfall increases from south to north, with the climate of the southern Bahama archipelago considered arid. The vegetation across this archipelago is dry tropical to subtropical woodlands.

It is impossible to investigate the precolonial history of the Caribbean without also considering cultural developments on the surrounding mainland. Although we will not discuss these in detail, we will refer to interchanges between the islands and the South, Central, and North American mainland. It is important to remember that the Caribbean islands were never isolated landscapes. Their history is a story of mobility and exchange across the Caribbean

Sea, Gulf of Mexico, and Florida Straits (Curet and Hauser 2011; Hofman and Bright 2010).

Different Ways of Seeing

We divided the Caribbean into a series of six archipelagoes. There are, however, other ways to "see" the Caribbean islands (Keegan, et al. 2013). The first shows these archipelagoes as stepping-stones with a Y-shape configured to connect South, Central, and North America. The islands are pointed at the coastal hearts of the continental mainland. Biogeographers have viewed the islands as "stepping-stones" in order to explain the distribution and movement of plants and animals among, between, and across regions (Woods 1989; Woods and Sergile 2001). An interpretive problem arises when geographical proximity becomes the only way of seeing (Ammerman and Cavalli-Sforza 1973). We avoid the description of Caribbean Islands as "stepping-stones" because this perspective has contributed to the belief that all movements of animals, people, and goods necessarily followed a straight line with each step taken in turn. As we will show, this was not the case.

Second, the sea was a highway (Callaghan 2013; Watters 1982). When the region is mapped with regard to the distance at which the next island is visible on the horizon, the image created is what Joshua Torres and Reniel Rodríguez Ramos (2008) have described as a "continent divided by water" (Figure 1.2).

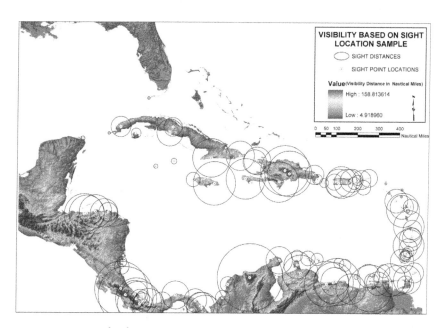

FIGURE 1.2 Inter-island viewscapes (courtesy of Joshua Torres).

The map shows that there are only four water gaps across which one cannot see another land mass. These are the Grenada passage in the south (c. 120 km), the Anegada passage east of Puerto Rico (65 km), the passage between Hispaniola/Cuba and the southern Bahama archipelago (c. 100 km), and the passage between northern Cuba and the central Bahamas (200 km). Yet movement between the islands is not always easy, due to shifting winds and currents. Richard Callaghan (2007) has commented on the difficulty in reaching Jamaica during the earliest episode of migration to the islands, and similar difficulties in the Guadeloupe passage during later times (Callaghan 2013). Somewhat surprisingly, he suggests that direct movement from South and Central America across the Caribbean Sea was the optimal path to reach the islands of the Greater Antilles (Callaghan 2001).

Third, modern maps are drawn with North at the top. This practice reflects the development of a compass that points to magnetic north (thus providing the most specific point of reference), and the practice of representing Europe in the northern hemisphere as geographically dominant. Yet many cultures perceive the world as oriented toward a different cardinal direction (cf. Wilson 2007). Most often this direction is east, the direction of the rising sun. The Spanish friar Ramón Pané reported that Hispaniola was seen by its indigenous inhabitants as a giant female beast with its head to the East and anus in the West (Harris 1994). Moreover, east was the direction of their mythical islands called "Matininó," "Guanín," "Soroya," and "Carib" (Stevens-Arroyo 1988); and east was the direction of travel attributed to the mythical Caribes (Keegan 2007). If we rotate the map 90° so that East is at the top (Wilson 2007), we gain an entirely different perspective of the relationships between islands, and between the islands and surrounding mainland (Figure 1.3).

Fourth, perspectives that better reflect the way indigenous communities conceptualized space can be based on indigenous networks defined by marriage, exchange, polity, and ceremonial obligations (Keegan 2004). In these cases, kinship trumps geographical distance. An additional dimension is time reflected in cyclical, seasonal differences in rainfall, winds, agricultural cycles, fishing, and opportunities for long-distance voyaging.

Finally, the spatial perspective employed in archaeological practice has strongly influenced interpretations (Fewkes 1907, 1922). For example, the size attributed to an island is influenced by one's vantage point. Someone on Hispaniola may see Puerto Rico as a small island, while someone on Puerto Rico will see their island as large and Guadeloupe as small, but someone on Guadeloupe may see their island as large and La Dèsirade as small, and so on. Also, an archaeologist working on only one island will have a different perspective from someone who conducts research on many different islands. Political and social forces (e.g., notions of cultural patrimony and *patria*) also have shaped the manner in which the past has been interpreted (Curet, et al. 2005; Siegel and Righter 2010).

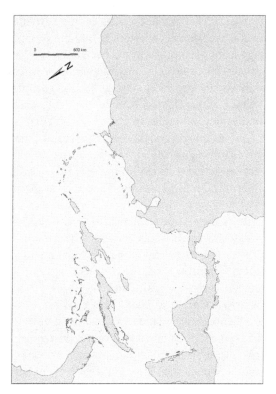

FIGURE 1.3 Map of the Caribbean with east at the top (courtesy of Menno Hoogland, after Wilson 2007).

Far Tortuga

Efforts to describe Caribbean culture history typically adopted linear temporal and spatial perspectives. Time is progressive (e.g., radiocarbon years), versus seasonal cycles of farming, fishing, foraging, exchange, and ritual. Space has been represented as a linear geography with movement constrained to a single path (Rouse 1992). The historical path begins in the Upper Amazon and progresses eastward along the Orinoco River. From the Orinoco River delta and Trinidad, the path turns abruptly north, and continues island by island through the Lesser Antilles to Puerto Rico, where further movement to the west and north ceased. Because the original question was framed in terms of how tropical-forest horticulturalists from South America reached Puerto Rico (Rouse 1953), it has been explicitly *assumed* that indigenous communities left South America with the *goal* of reaching Puerto Rico. Puerto Rico then became the homeland for all subsequent cultural developments (Siegel 1991, 2010).

But what if, like the characters in Peter Matthiessen's (1975) novel, we begin our voyage in Jamaica? What change in vision does this new perspective bring? For the earliest time period, beginning around 5000 BC and extending to the first centuries AD, there is no evidence that anyone visited or settled on Jamaica. The absence of material remains can be attributed to the failure by archaeologists and avocational collectors to find the earliest sites. The possible reasons range from geomorphic transformations to a lack of systematic archaeological surveys, but none of the justifications are particularly satisfying. Private collectors have engaged local laborers to find and procure objects of interest, and academic archaeologists have conducted research on the island for over 150 years (Keegan and Atkinson 2006; Wesler 2013). The most valued raw materials for the Archaic Age (5000 to 200 BC), including high-quality chert, are widely available on the island, and there are no obvious reasons why Jamaica would not be settled if it had been discovered. The best explanation is that Jamaica was not discovered at this time due to maritime conditions (Callaghan 2008).

We need to address the fact that Jamaica was not visited by humans until around AD 500 (Atkinson 2006; Wesler 2013). Furthermore, the neighboring Cayman Islands were not visited by humans until Columbus sighted them in 1503 (Scudder and Quitmyer 1998; Stokes and Keegan 1996). These observations are significant because Jamaica and the Cayman Islands cast a giant voyaging shadow across Cuba and Haiti. This shadow restricts the possible voyaging corridors between the islands and mainland during the 5000 years before Jamaica was settled. In other words, none of the voyages from the mainland to islands, or islands to mainland, apparently crossed the Jamaican or Cayman viewscapes before AD 500. The absence of sites in Jamaica is a significant detail in reconstructing the earliest history of voyaging in the Caribbean.

After Jamaica was settled, it again affects the ways we view cultural developments throughout the Greater Antilles. The earliest Jamaican settlers made redware pottery that reflects an episode of human migration. The source of these colonists has yet to be determined. Nevertheless, Jamaican redware appears at the same time, and possibly earlier, than redware pottery in Puerto Rico, with both classified as belonging to the same Ostionoid pottery series (Howard 1950; Rodríguez Ramos, et al. 2013; Wesler 2013). The traditional view is that redware pottery originated in Puerto Rico and spread West after AD 700. However, the simultaneous appearance of redware pottery in Jamaica contradicts this view.

A second, and very distinct, type of pottery appeared suddenly in Jamaica about 400 years after the appearance of redware. The paste is darker in color, and decorations are executed as incised lines. There is virtually no overlap between these pottery styles (Wesler 2013). Pottery made with linear-incised decorations represents a second, separate migration into Jamaica. Again, the prevailing model is one of linear pottery series genealogies: Saladoid begat Ostionoid begat Meillacoid begat Chicoid. In Jamaica (and elsewhere), Ostionoid and Meillacoid reflect separate migrations to the islands, with little evidence of interaction and overlap. These styles are not the product of evolutionary transitions; they are discrete representations of agency and practice.

We will return to these issues. For the moment, they serve to highlight two important dimensions of this book. First, there are lacunae in the archaeological record that result from actual absence. In other words, it is not that we have failed to find the data; *the data never existed*. The absence of evidence for humans in Jamaica prior to AD 500 is not simply an empty box in the time-space systematics. These voids are not "negative evidence," they are factors that need to be accounted for. Second, broadly defined pottery styles are assigned an origin and affiliation, with distinct "peoples and cultures" associated with different styles. In this regard, they are much more than the linear progression of styles. These styles were created and used to capture expressions of identities; identities that must be socially constructed in historical space.

The Name Game

The first task involves making sense of the names (Figure 1.4). History begins with names. It is impossible to communicate about the past without generally recognized and accepted names for the societies about whom history is written. However, names denote a variety of meanings. Anyone familiar with the Caribbean has heard the names "Ciboney," "Arawak," and "Carib." These names have become conventions for denoting three different cultures. The Ciboney have been characterized as Stone Age societies that lacked pottery and agriculture, and who are assigned to the Lithic and Archaic ages of Caribbean archaeology. The Arawak-speakers supposedly arrived somewhat later from lowland South America and introduced pottery and agriculture to the region

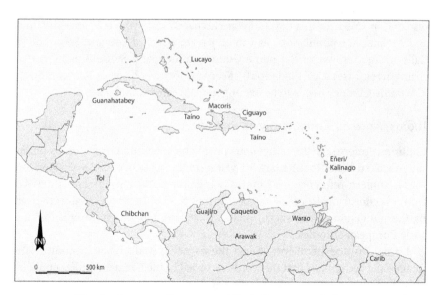

FIGURE 1.4 Distribution map of names used for indigenous societies (courtesy of Menno Hoogland).

and evolved into what has been called "Taíno" by anthropologists in the twentieth century. The Carib were the last immigrants who arrived from South America and colonized the Lesser Antilles in the century prior to the arrival of Europeans. In addition, anyone familiar with the Bahamas will know that the name "Lucayan" has been used to denote the indigenous inhabitants of these islands. But where do these names come from, and what do they really mean?

Ciboney and Guanahatabey

Bartolomé de las Casas was the first to use the name *Ciboney* (also *Siboneyes, Cibuneyes* or *Exbuneyes*; see Lovén 1935:80–81). He accompanied Columbus on his second voyage, and was the first priest ordained in the Americas. During the conquest of Cuba in 1510, he had a crisis of faith, and declared himself "Protector of the Indians." In his 1516 memorial to Cardinal Cisneros, Las Casas noted that there were four societies in Cuba whose souls should be saved. These were the *Guanahacabibes* (*Guanahatabey*) of the Cape of Cuba (see Lovén 1935:3–24), and three other societies that shared similar characteristics: the inhabitants of the small islands along the north and south coasts of Cuba (Jardines de la Reina), the Lucayans of the Bahamas, and the *Ciboney* who were kept as servants by the other Cuban Indians. Las Casas was very clear in his use of Ciboney to denote a Ceramic Age ("Arawak") culture in central Cuba.

Confusion regarding the use of the name Ciboney began with Jacques Roumain in 1912, who associated the stone-tool assemblage at the Cabaret site near Port-au-Prince, Haiti, with the Ciboney (Roumain 1943). Misuse of the name continued with Mark Harrington (1922) who used the name Ciboney for the Stone Age material culture he encountered during his archaeological research in Cuba. To this day, there are archaeologists who still refer to Lithic and Archaic Age populations as Ciboney (e.g., Dacal Moure and Rivero de la Calle 1996). Yet, use of the name Ciboney to denote a Stone Age culture is clearly wrong (see Coscullela 1946; Keegan 1989a; Rodríguez Ramos 2008). The name Ciboney needs to be expunged from our vocabulary.

Indios, Arawak, Taíno, Lucayan, and Igneri

Columbus referred to the indigenous people he encountered as "Indios under the mistaken belief that he had arrived near the east coast of Asia" (Morison 1942). Modern reference to "American Indians" or "Amerindians" is derived from his confusion. There is no specific mention of the names that were used by the indigenous local, social, political, or ceremonial communities in the early European chronicles.

Daniel Brinton (1871) introduced the name Arawak. Brinton studied languages and recognized that the words recorded in the Greater Antilles could be classified as part of the Arawak language family. He suggested that Caribbean islanders should be called "Island Arawaks" to distinguish them from the diverse Arawak communities of South America (Noble 1965). The Arawak language family is widespread in South America and is more diverse than the Indo-European language family. In other words, the Arawak languages of the Caribbean may have been no more inter-intelligible than Hindi is to English! Justifiably, the use of language to create cultural boundaries has been challenged by anthropologists (e.g., Boas 1940; Welsch, et al. 1992).

A significant complication occurred when the "Island" prenom was dropped. Because the Arawak of the Caribbean were different from the Arawak of South America, the name "Taíno" was promoted, following the practice of Hispanic colleagues who had been using this name for years (Rouse 1986, 1992). The name Taíno comes from Columbus's second voyage when he was greeted by the words "Taíno, taíno," which has been translated as meaning *noble* or *good*. The first use of this name as a cultural designation is attributed to Constantine Samuel Rafinesque whose 1836 essay used linguistic criteria to classify the indigenous population of the Greater Antilles. This time the Taíno language was the basis for classification.

The name game has not stopped here. When one name is applied to the inhabitants of a large territory, the assumption is that everyone spoke the same language and shared a common culture. This assumption was reified by the Spanish chroniclers' assertion that these were all one culture (Las Casas 1951). Yet Jamaica, central Cuba, the Virgin Islands, and the Lesser Antilles all had material expressions that were interpreted as less developed than those observed in eastern Cuba, Hispaniola, and Puerto Rico. Irving Rouse (1986) used material evidence to distinguish the later as "Classic Taíno" and the former as "sub-Taíno." Without meaning any disrespect, the prefix "sub-" nevertheless carried a pejorative connotation. The sub-Taíno were next transformed into "Western and Eastern Taínos," while those who possessed a "superior" material culture continued to be known as the "Classic Taíno" (see Keegan 2013; Rouse 1992). As a result, the cultures of Jamaica and central Cuba are now referred to as "Western Taíno," the cultures of the northernmost Lesser Antilles and Virgin Islands are called "Eastern Taíno," and the culture of the Bahama archipelago is called "Lucayan" (Taíno). The latter is based on the Spanish name for the Bahama archipelago—"Las Islas de los Lucayos."

It would seem that the naming of cultures in the northern Antilles during initial encounters was resolved. Yet again, the name "Taíno" assumes a level of homogeneity that is unwarranted (Hulme 1993). For example, Bartolomé de las Casas (1951) reported that three mutually unintelligible languages were spoken in Hispaniola. One was "Taíno," which was described as the general language, a *lingua franca* or *lingua jural* (Granberry and Vescelius 2004). There also was "Macorix de Arriba" and "Macorix de Abajo," with "Macorix" translated in Taíno as "foreign tongue." In addition, Columbus called the inhabitants of the Samaná peninsula (northeastern Dominican Republic) "Ciguayo" to distinguish them from other inhabitants of the island, based on a single hostile encounter. These hostilities have been interpreted erroneously as evidence that "Carib" had begun to invade the island. Turning to the northern Lesser Antilles, there is abundant evidence for influences from the Greater Antilles.

The island of Saba, for example, shows clear affinities with Chicoid modes of pottery decoration after AD 1200 (Hofman 1993; Hofman and Hoogland 2011; Hoogland 1996; Hoogland and Hofman 1999). Similar influences are recognized on St. John (Wild 2001), St. Croix (Faber Morse 2004), and St. Martin and Anguilla (Crock 2000).

The name "Igneri" has been used to distinguish the indigenous inhabitants of the southern Lesser Antilles. Rouse described Igneri as an Arawak language that was different from, yet related to, Taíno (Rouse 1992). In fact, it is a non-ethnic name (meaning "people"), given to the indigenous peoples the Island Carib believed they had defeated in their mythical account of the conquest of the Windward Islands when they ate Igneri men and married Igneri women (Boomert and Hofman 2016). Most archaeologists have not adopted the name Igneri, the notable exception is Luis Chanlatte Baik (1981) who refers to the Igneri culture when speaking of the Early Ceramic Age (Saladoid or Agro-II). Igneri also has served to distinguish the initial Ceramic Age colonists from the Carib who later invaded the islands

In summary, it is important to recognize that names based on reconstructed languages mask the cultural diversity expressed in these islands when Europeans arrived (Wilson 1993, 2007). Singular names give the impression that the Caribbean was a homogeneous cultural landscape. In order to expose this diversity, we need to look more closely at the material evidence.

Carib and Kalinago

The first mention of "Carib" comes from the *diario* of Columbus's first voyage. The manuscript that has survived is a transcription written by Bartolomé de las Casas (Dunn and Kelley 1989; Fuson 1983, 1987). Columbus was looking for an audience with the Grand Khan, who he thought was the ruler of this region (possibly based on the writings of Marco Polo; Morison 1942:64). According to the *diario*: "And thus I [Columbus] say again how other times I said, he says, that Caniba is nothing else but the people of the Grand Khan . . ." (Dunn and Kelley 1989:217). Further, "[there] was some talk about the men of Caniba, whom they call Caribes, who come to capture them . . ." (Dunn and Kelley 1989:285). It is apparent that the inhabitants of the Bahamas and Columbus had similar names for different beings (Keegan 2015). It was Columbus's repeated reports of a race that consumed human flesh that were used to create a "Culture of Cannibals" (Davis 1992).

The present understanding of "Carib" is an amalgam of four distinct concepts:

1. "Caribes," which Columbus thought were real, when in fact they were creatures that existed only in the indigenous mythology;
2. "Caniba," by which Columbus meant "the people of the Grand Khan";
3. "Cannibales," meaning indigenous communities characterized as idolaters and consumers of human flesh who could not be converted to Christianity and were therefore suitable for enslaving; and

4. "Carib," which is a modern anthropological construct used as the name for indigenous communities in lowland South America and the Windward islands of the Caribbean (Keegan 1996a).

It has been suggested that the names "Island Kalina" or "Kalinago" are more appropriate monikers because these names are associated with indigenous communities in South America with whom the Carib expressed kinship (Allaire 1996, 2013). Hulme and Whitehead (1992:108) quote the French missionary Raymond Breton as stating that on Guadeloupe they called themselves

> *kallinago* following the language of the men and *kalliponam* following the language of the women; although, for some distinction among themselves and those of the mainland, they call the latter *Balouðouri*, from the word *Ballouð*, which means mainland.... We call those from the mainland *Gallybis* and our savages *Caraïbes.*"

Both Carib and Galibi are reported as living in Grenada at the time of European encounters (Holdren 1998; Martin 2012), and numerous ethnic groups are reported for Trinidad and South America at this time.

Adding to the confusion is the fact that the language of the Lesser Antilles was Arawak. Yet "Carib" communities living today in lowland South America speak a Cariban language. Arawak and Cariban are very different families of languages. The "Island Carib" use of an Arawak language, combined with Spanish attempts to enslave them, have led some to suggest that the Carib are the terminal phase of Arawak cultural development in the southern Lesser Antilles (Davis and Goodwin 1990).

That conclusion follows interpretations that associate the Carib with the terminal Suazoid series pottery of the southern Lesser Antilles (Bullen 1964). However, vessel shapes from the Suazoid series do not match those known for the ethnohistoric Kalinago of the mainland (Allaire 1991, 1996). A very different style of pottery, called the "Cayo complex," appears in late precolonial and early colonial contexts (Bright 2011; Hofman and Hoogland 2012). Arie Boomert (1986, 2000; 2011) has suggested that the Cayo complex is evidence for the arrival of new influences and immigrants from South America. The most recent archaeological investigations indicate that Carib emerged in the islands through a new synergism of island and mainland societies (Hofman and Hoogland 2012; Hofman, et al. 2015). Self-identified Kalinago still live today on several islands of the Windward Islands, notably on Dominica, St. Vincent, and Trinidad.

Caribbean Archaeology in Practice

The practice of archaeology on different islands often has proceeded independently, and various alternative frameworks for characterizing the past have been proposed (see Hofman, et al. 2008). These approaches developed from different theoretical perspectives and are complicated by differences in language. Thus, one can identify a Marxist frame of reference in which *modo de vida* or mode of life is emphasized (Ensor 2000; Veloz Maggiolo 1976); a framework based on French (Paleolithic) archaeology (Petitjean Roget 1970); cultural sequences framed by local interests (e.g., Chanlatte Baik 1981; Dacal Moure and Rivero de la Calle 1984); and a variety of different models for classifying material culture (e.g., Hoffman 1967, 1979; Sears and Sullivan 1978). Language is a major factor. English-speakers have dominated the debates, while papers published in Spanish and French have received far less consideration. We feel that it is worth examining some of the ways that archaeologists have classified the material remains. The diversity and complexity of Caribbean archaeology are a reflection of its practitioners.

There are rare moments on the time–space continuum when one individual comes along and completely transforms a field of study. "Ben" Rouse developed a taxonomy that has dominated the study of Caribbean culture history, at least from a North American perspective (Roosevelt and Siegel 2007), for more than sixty years (Figure 1.5). Rouse introduced the scientific method to archaeology thirty years before it became fashionable (cf. Rouse 1939 and Watson, et al. 1971), and his systematic methodology provided the foundation for the Classificatory/Historical School of American Archaeology (Willey and Sabloff 1974).

One of Rouse's final papers was an overview of the history of Caribbean archaeology (Rouse 1996). He identified four levels of interpretation in the sequential development of Caribbean archaeology. His lived perspective is worth repeating. The first level was called "artifactual research." It involved the discovery, description, and identification of archaeological materials that often had been removed to private collections and public museums. Such activities began in the late eighteenth century and continue today, but they reached their acme in the early twentieth century. Rouse reports that by the 1920s, attention had shifted to a second level—organizing known assemblages in chronological order. It is worth noting that radiocarbon dating was not developed until decades later. Chronologies were based on stratigraphy and seriation. Coincident with chronology was the spatial distribution of material remains. The third level commenced in the 1950s. It involved using material remains to define "cultures," which in turn defined the "peoples" who are the subject of culture-historical inquiry. Rouse (1972) developed elaborate systems of classification and nomenclature, and expressed a feeling of kinship with similar efforts by David Clarke (1968). The fourth level emerged during the 1980s and was called "sociocultural research." It involved a shift of attention from the individuals who produced the local cultures to the societies who used the material culture (Watters 1976:6). Rouse was uncomfortable with this change in perspective. He believed that chronology, spatial distributions, and economic activities had to be determined before sociological studies could commence (Rouse 1977).

Most Caribbean archaeologists have adopted Rouse's systematics and then have labored to arrange "peoples and cultures" in time-space diagrams (cf. Agorsah 1993). The main emphasis of Rouse's approach was artifacts, especially pottery, because potsherds constituted up to 90% of the artifacts in most Ceramic Age sites. The basic organization of his taxonomy has *time* on the vertical axis and *space* on the horizontal axis (see Curet 2004). Stratigraphic relations determined temporal positions, and calendar years eventually were obtained by radiometric dating.

Until recently, relatively few radiocarbon dates were available. The tendency has been to cross-date assemblages by reference to the few dated deposits. However, several issues have plagued this approach. These include the selective reporting of dates (Haviser 1991:64; Rouse and Alegría 1990:56), the potential for mis(cross-)dating burials because older potsherds were mixed in the fill (Siegel 1992:196–243), uncorrected dates from marine mollusks, the dating of potentially contaminated samples (Keegan 1989a:377), and an over-reliance on mean dates to the exclusion of standard deviations (Davis 1988).

Of more general importance is the fact that carbon isotope $^{13}C/^{12}C$-corrected and calibrated dates significantly alter the interpretation of cultural sequences (Fitzpatrick 2006; Rodríguez Ramos 2010). Calibrated dates between AD 750–950 can be offset by more than a century, and uncorrected dates on marine shells often are 400 years too old (Davis 1988, 1992; Keegan 1997). When Dave D. Davis (1988) calibrated the dates from Antigua, he found that there was a substantial overlap in the dates for the Mill Reef, Mamora Bay, and Freeman's Bay complexes. These complexes previously were arranged in a discrete chronological sequence. The same is true for other islands (Haiti: Keegan 2001; Puerto Rico: Rodríguez Ramos 2010; Rodríguez Ramos, et al. 2013).

Island, island group, and water passages organize space in Rouse's chart. The emphasis on water passages reflects the observation that archaeological complexes that face each other across water passages are more similar than those on opposite ends of the same island (Watters and Rouse 1989). Names within the body of the chart distinguish *peoples* and *cultures*, which are classified "by comparing their ceramic styles and associated traits and grouping together peoples that resemble each other most closely in their styles and in other diagnostic traits" (Rouse 1992:33). In the absence of ceramics, other elements of material culture were substituted. The classification was made hierarchical by grouping local *styles* into regional *series*, (ending in -oid), and by dividing series into sub-regional *subseries* (ending in -an).

Rouse's taxonomy was based on his background in the Linnaean classification system. He received his bachelor's degree in plant science from the Sheffield Scientific School at Yale University in 1934, and believed that this approach represented a "mature field of study" (in Siegel 1996a). He was further constrained by the fact that he never excavated a stratified site (in Siegel 1996a), and had to rely on potsherds (versus whole vessels) to evaluate cultural changes through time. Despite these limitations, he developed a model for the classification of Caribbean material culture that is still in use today.

Changing Frames of Reference

Two main approaches have dominated Caribbean archaeology (Keegan and Rodríguez Ramos 2004). The first focuses on the classification of material

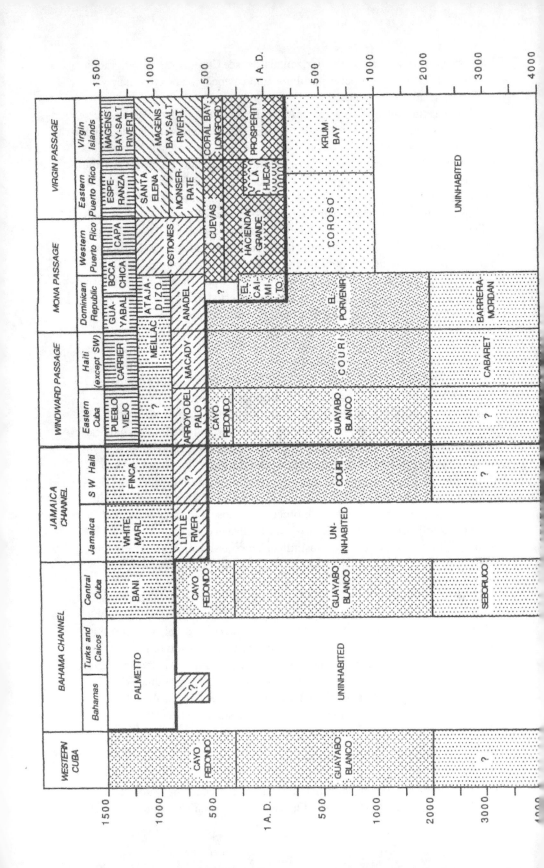

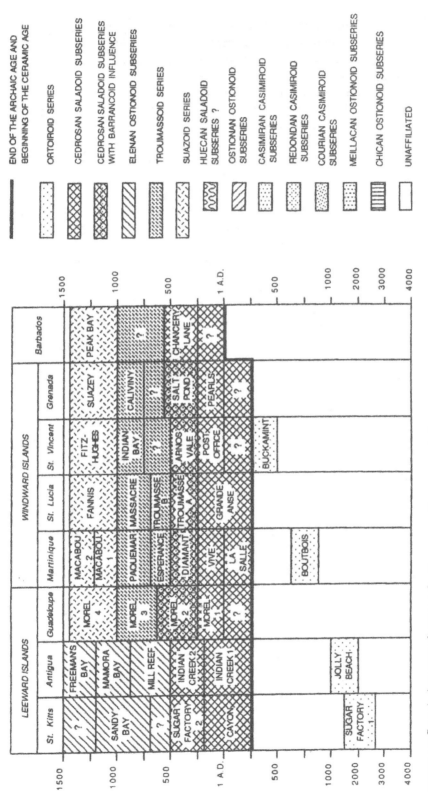

FIGURE 1.5 Rouse's time-space diagram (after Rouse 1992: Figures 14 and 15).

remains during particular time periods. The various forms of time–space systematics employed are important because they focus on distinguishing classes of material remains observed at different sites and at different times. During the initial phases of research, classification systems provide a useful method for identifying and naming distinct cultural expressions. Yet the identification of "peoples and cultures" (Rouse 1972) tends to emphasize general similarities and ignore differences (Curet 2004). The boundaries between time–space groupings often are represented as hard and fast, and differences between the boxes are explained as due to migration, diffusion, and/or independent invention. Under this approach, we have a Lithic Age defined by flaked-stone tools, an Archaic Age defined by ground-stone tools, and a Ceramic Age defined by the occurrence of pottery. These ages are explained as the outcome of three separate migrations into the Caribbean. Yet flaked-stone tools are a significant component of Archaic and Ceramic Age sites throughout the region, and pottery is present in all three. The boundaries between these Ages are becoming increasingly hazy.

The second approach has focused on cultural systems. Practitioners of the second approach have emphasized *modo de vida* or ways of life in developing their classifications. This second approach is characteristic of research conducted by archaeologists in Cuba, the Dominican Republic, and Venezuela, where their scholarship has been influenced significantly by Marxist theory. The product of this approach was socioeconomic stages of development that progressed through a sequence of dialectical transformations.

Both approaches have reached the limits of their usefulness. Certainly we need to continue to name types of material culture and the societies they have come to represent. In addition, general portraits of *modo de vida* are useful in looking at different ways of life at different points in time. However, the similarities by which such groupings have been made mask significant differences between groupings, even to the level of individual sites. For these (and other) reasons, a third approach has emerged in the past decade.

This third approach emphasizes differences and diversity. The goal is not to create increasingly finer boxes into which archaeological sites can be grouped, but rather to recognize that everything was in flux all of the time. Thus, nothing is ever really the same at any time or any place. This chaos approach makes it difficult to assign names and characteristics, yet it is more realistic in recognizing that nothing in life is ever exactly the same (Keegan 2004). In this regard, we have intimated that the indigenous populations of Lithic and Archaic (and we will soon add Ceramic) ages were not necessarily different; they just used different means to achieve the standard of living that they sought. The challenge for the future is to look more closely at the diversity inherent in living systems and explain the processes by which societies developed and changed through time.

Underlying Structure

Our primary objective in writing this book is to present a new way of looking at the past. Caribbean archaeologists recently have begun to appreciate the diversity and variability of the precolonial societies (e.g., Wilson 2007, 2013; Hofman and Carlin 2010). The situation is chaotic at the moment; however, as recognized in chaos theory, there is an underlying order (Keegan 2004, 2007). The order we impose emphasizes culture, place, and time. In this regard, it employs the principles used in other culture-historical studies. For the purposes of this book, we accept Rouse's (1992) opinion that pottery styles and series reflect "peoples and cultures." We assume that vessel forms, manufacturing techniques, and decorations reflect traditions that express social identities, albeit their specific meanings are still being decoded. We, therefore, use pottery series (Saladoid, Huecoid, Ostionoid, Meillacoid, Troumassoid, Suazoid, and Chicoid) to represent the distribution of these socially defined identities across large geographical areas. Whenever possible, we use style names to distinguish spatially restricted social units that share meanings with one of the larger identities (distinguished by the "-oid" suffix; see Rouse 1972). We fully expect that this taxonomy will be transformed in the coming years, but for now, it provides a means to communicate with other Caribbean archaeologists while operating in a transitional stage.

In Chapter 2, we discuss the first inhabitants of the Caribbean Islands. Here we collapse the Lithic and Archaic ages into one Archaic Age. Although flaked macroblades provide evidence for the first human exploitation of the islands, the clearest expressions of accommodation to the Greater Antilles (except Jamaica) and their diverse environments only become clear after about 3000 BC. Throughout the book, we refer to these diverse expressions as "the Archaic Age." We are not completely satisfied with the name, but Archaic Age it is (see Goodwin 1979).

In Chapter 3, we examine continuity and change as new migrants moved into the islands and interacted with those who preceded them. We again confront the issue of names, and have decided to use the names for pottery series. In doing so, we accept that pottery[2] and the way it was decorated reflect cultural norms and expressions of identity (see Meggers 1996; Rouse 1939). The first challenge concerns Saladoid and Huecoid. Because Saladoid also is strongly essentialized as a singular, long-term cultural manifestation, our efforts focus on deconstructing Saladoid.

Puerto Rico has been promoted as the heart (*corazón*) of precolonial cultural development in the Caribbean. Working from far more extensive and

---

[2] The terms *pottery* and *ceramic* often are used interchangeably. However, *ceramic* refers to the specific material transformation of clay that occurs at very high firing temperatures (Rice 1987). The low-fired earthenwares produced in the precolonial Caribbean are more accurately called *terracotta*, or in this book, *pottery*.

detailed systematic investigations, Puerto Rico has been used to model cultural developments leading to the emergence of "Taíno" (Rouse 1992; Siegel 2010). The Saladoid was the foundation on which developments in Puerto Rico were built, so it is logical to proceed to these before looking outside Puerto Rico. Our emphasis is on explaining these developments as they express themselves archaeologically, and not assume that that their final expression was something described by the Spanish and later christened Taíno. The consolidation of local polities as expressed in social and political transformations in post-Saladoid Puerto Rico is the subject of Chapter 4. One expression of these transformations is the development of a diverse range of pottery styles. In this case, there is sufficient attention to detail to use style names instead of series names to discuss the archaeology. Our discussion tracks developments that began around AD 600 up to the arrival of the Spanish in 1493.

Concurrent with post-Saladoid Puerto Rico, three pottery series developed in Hispaniola. They are the subject of Chapter 5. We employ the names "Meillacoid" and "Chicoid" to distinguish their distribution and articulation, but we do not propose these as monolithic cultural expressions. A number of distinct pottery *styles* are recognized for each of these series, but their inconsistent application makes them of limited use. Because Saladoid as a series never materialized on Hispaniola, Meillacoid and Chicoid represent the Ceramic Age colonization of the island. The communities that manufactured Meillacoid pottery were successful in expanding their influence across Hispaniola and into Cuba, Jamaica, and the Bahama archipelago. Chapter 6 resumes the examination of cultural developments in Cuba and initiates the sequence for the Bahama archipelago and Jamaica.

The Lesser Antilles are the subject of Chapter 7. These islands exhibit an enormous range of variability in size, geology, topography, climate, vegetation, fauna, and raw materials. First settled during the Archaic Age, and resettled during the Ceramic Age, these islands had unique historical trajectories. This chapter repeats some of our earlier discussions, but does so to emphasize diversity. The chapter concludes with a consideration of the Carib and Kalinago communities whose lives crossed the boundary of written history as the Caribbean became a colonial enterprise.

It is our opinion that archaeologists have placed too strong of a reliance on the European descriptions of life in the islands. The observations of untrained observers have been wrongly elevated to the status of ethnohistory. Chapter 9 addresses this issue by examining the articulation of archaeology and writing. In this final chapter, we summarize some of the images that emerged from particular readings of the documents. Our objective is to illuminate a more vibrant understanding of the indigenous Caribbean.

There are no other recent overviews of the Caribbean that articulate the specific precolonial histories of the entire region claimed by Caribbean archaeologists. We have attempted to stay close to the archaeology and avoid sweeping generalizations based on theoretical postures and historical documents.

THE FIRST HUMANS TO reach the Caribbean islands arrived in the fifth millennium BC. We know precious little about this time period; the reasons are multifaceted. First, most archaeological sites from this time period are located in Cuba and Hispaniola, where local archaeologists have conducted most of the investigations. Although their research is excellent, most of the reports are published in Spanish and often are not widely disseminated. Moreover, these archaeologists have emphasized historical materialism in the frame of reference associated with Latin American Social Archaeology (see Vargas Arenas 1995; Vargas Arenas and Sanoja Obediente 1999). Because language and theoretical orientations did not fit the dominant structures of North American archaeology, much of this work was never incorporated into their mainstream syntheses (see Keegan and Rodríguez Ramos 2004; Sued Badillo 1992).

Caribbean archaeologists have classified the earliest material expressions in the islands according to North American (Willey and Phillips 1958; Willey and Sabloff 1974; Rouse 1964) and/or Old World methodologies (Kozlowski 1974, 1980). Most archaeologists today recognize that these frameworks are outmoded. However, the general lack of interest in this time period has served to reify existing classification schemes. The first issue in this chapter is explaining the frameworks that form the basis of the basic literature for the region (Rouse 1992; Sued-Badillo 2003; Wilson 2007), and then explaining why they are no longer adequate.

The earliest inhabitants were first called "Paleo-Indians" (Casimiroid series in Rouse's taxonomy) and are placed in the Lithic Age. The tools are primarily flaked-stone blades that in continental settings are attributed to big-game hunting. In fact, Daniel Koski-Karell (2002) has likened these tools to Solutrian blades. The problem for the Caribbean is that there never was large game (with the possible exception of sloths, manatees, and sea turtles), and no remains from large game have been identified in any of the archaeological sites. In sum, the continental model does not fit the circumstances of the Caribbean Islands. Moreover, several of the principal architects of these classifications have stated that the current schemes are inadequate (Kozlowski 1974; Pantel 1988; Rouse

1992:55). To avoid the more specific connotations of "Paleo-Indian," we discuss the material evidence under the heading "flaked-stone complexes."

According to conventional wisdom, the Lithic Age was followed by a "Meso-Indian," Archaic Age, which began about 2,000 years later. The Archaic Age was assumed to reflect a separate migration from South America because its ground-stone technology was a significant departure from flaked-stone industries. It was proposed, based on ethnographic examples, that there was a stronger reliance on the gathering of plants and small-game hunting (this shift apparently occurred in other parts of the world due to the extirpation of large game). The transition was marked by the introduction of ground-stone tools to the flaked-stone tool kit. Because Meso-Indians were living in South America until modern times ("Marginal Tribes," Steward and Faron 1959), this framework was considered appropriate for characterizing the earliest inhabitants of the islands.

Most syntheses refer to all Lithic Age and Archaic Age assemblages as "aceramic" or "preceramic." These terms are no longer viable due to the discovery of pottery in sites with predominantly lithic technologies (Rodríguez Ramos, et al. 2008, 2013). Moreover, new analytical techniques, especially starch grain analysis, have demonstrated that they also practiced incipient forms of farming, and that most of the crops attributed to the Ceramic Age already were being cultivated during the Archaic Age (Pagán Jiménez 2011, 2013; Pagán Jiménez, et al. 2015). Again, the role of farming among communities previously characterized as hunter-gatherers merits careful consideration.

We begin this chapter by following the traditional framework, but with the goal of demonstrating that there was substantial diversity, and that pottery and farming were neither independent inventions nor separate migrations. A ground-stone technology may have been added to a preceding flaked-stone technology, but the former never completely replaced the latter (Rouse 1992:50). Flaked-stone technologies remained important throughout the entire precolonial history of the islands (Rodríguez Ramos 2010). Second, the fact that pottery was made and used up to 2,000 years before the beginning of the Ceramic Age challenges prior notions concerning the stages of cultural evolution based on technological innovations. Finally, we consider the status of the "aceramic" Guanahatebey who supposedly were living in southwestern Cuba when Christopher Columbus visited the island in 1493 (Keegan 1989a).

Flaked-Stone Complexes

The oldest archaeological sites in the Caribbean are radiocarbon-dated to the fifth millennium BC. These dates mark the beginning of the exploration and exploitation of Cuba, Hispaniola, and Puerto Rico. The oldest radiocarbon dates come from the Vignier III site in Haiti (4510–4350 BC; Moore 1998); the Angostura and Maruca sites in Puerto Rico, which date to about 4000 BC

(Rodríguez Ramos 2010); and the uncalibrated date of 3220 BC reported for the Levisa site in Cuba (Dacal Moure and Rivero de la Calle 1984:75–76). A number of other dates fall within the range of 4560–4400 B.P. (Rouse and Allaire 1978; Rouse, et al. 1985). A very early date was reported for the Caminar Abajo site (6460 +/– 140 B.P.), but recent investigations have shown that this date is centuries too early (Roksandic, et al. 2013). The number of dates is few, some sites provide contradictory dates, and undated sites often are attributed to this time period based solely on the presence of flaked-stone tools. In addition, many of these sites have tools that were ground through use. The Honduras del Oeste site in the Dominican Republic is a good example (Kozlowski 1974). Because these tools were created through use, and not the application of a stone-grinding technology, they have not been included, and have even been specifically excluded, from classification schemes (e.g., Rouse 1992:50). Nevertheless, they provide a precedent for the later ground-stone technology.

At present, there are very few archaeological sites known for this period, and all of them are located on Cuba, Hispaniola, and Puerto Rico. Jamaica, the remaining large island in the Greater Antilles, is an interesting case in that no sites from this time period have been identified, despite a substantial amount of archaeological prospecting (Callaghan 2008). A related issue concerns the likelihood that some early Caribbean sites have been displaced by tectonic activity and/or submerged by rising sea level (Cooper and Boothroyd 2011; Milne and Peros 2013; Watters 1982:6).

Origins

Four migration routes have been proposed (Figure 2.1). One route crosses mid-Caribbean chain of islands from Nicaragua to Jamaica (Keegan and Diamond 1987). Rising eustatic sea level has submerged these islands. This route is considered the least likely because Lithic Age sites have not been found in Jamaica, despite abundant raw materials for flaked-stone tools (Rouse 1992:56–57; Wesler 2013). In addition, Peter Drewett, and Anne Stokes and Keegan (1996), made independent archaeological surveys of Grand Cayman, one of the few remaining islands along the mid-Caribbean chain. They failed to find any evidence for human settlement on the island. Sylvia Scudder and Irvy Quitmeyer (1998) reached a similar conclusion following their investigations of caves and rock shelters on Cayman Brac. In sum, the now-submerged mid-Caribbean chain was not the route taken by the first colonists.

The second route crosses the Yucatan Channel directly to Cuba. The identification of a similar flaked-stone tradition in Belize was used to support this Central American origin (MacNeish and Nelken-Turner 1983; Rouse 1992:56–57). However, there are two problems with this route. First, the Yucatan Peninsula is closer to Cuba than Belize. Yet, the lithic industry in Belize has not been found on the Yucatan Peninsula. It is possible that the ocean current that runs

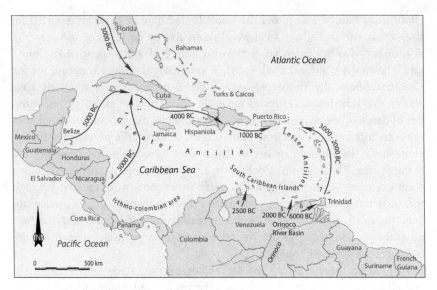

FIGURE 2.1 Map of previously proposed migration routes (courtesy of Menno Hoogland).

between the Yucatan and Cuba was so strong that human-propelled craft could not reach Cuba from the Yucatan due to the power of the Gulf Stream, and voyages with any chance of reaching Cuba had to start farther south (Callaghan 1990a, 2003).

Another problem concerns the artifacts themselves. Macroblades from the Sand Hill Site in Belize show the closest conformity to those from Cuba and Haiti. Yet the Sand Hill phase was dated to between 6000 and 7500 BC, which is considered too early to account for the lithic tools in the islands (Callaghan 1990a, 1990b). More recent studies have shown that the lithic industry at Colha, Belize, is similar to that at Sand Hill and Ladyville sites. Dated to around 3000 BC, it is roughly contemporaneous with the lithic industry in the islands (Wilson, et al. 1998). Nevertheless, the Cuban flaked-stone tool assemblage does not completely replicate the variety of tools identified in Belize. These differences have been explained as the result of "cultural drift," which recognizes that a colonizing population may not completely replicate the complete cultural (or genetic) repertoire of the source population.

Janusz Kozlowski (1974:68) observed sufficient differences in flaked-stone technologies to conclude that the Caribbean version did not develop out of the "Blade and Burin Tradition" found in Belize. He noted that ground-stone tools were being manufactured in Belize by the time of the earliest settlements in the Greater Antilles, and proposed a more southern origin, in the Catrú Culture of Colombia or the El Inga Culture of Ecuador.

Based on computer simulations of voyaging between Central America and the Caribbean, in concert with differences in the lithic industries in the two areas, Richard Callaghan (2001) proposed that Central America was *not* the source of colonists. He concluded that similar lithic industries in Central America were too dissimilar, and that northwestern South America was a more likely the source of Lithic Age colonists (Callaghan 2003). This conclusion is consistent with later evidence that a wide variety of materials and finished artifacts found in the Caribbean originated in the Isthmo-Colombian area (Rodríguez Ramos 2010, 2013).

Some Cuban archaeologists have equated the microlith industry in Cuba with the North American Western Lithic co-Tradition (Davies, et al. 1969) and have identified Florida or the southeastern United States as the source area for Lithic Age colonists (Rey Bettancourt and García Rodríguez 1988). However, the microlith industry appears after the macro-blade industry was already well established on the island. It is possible that the shift to small, expedient, flaked-stone tools and the introduction of pottery reflect a later arrival from the North American mainland. Recent simulations studies indicate that it is very difficult, if not impossible, for a vessel without sails to cross the Gulf Stream current from the southeastern United States to the islands (Seidemann 2001). Moreover, Dave D. Davis (2000) notes that the material culture of the southeastern United States was significantly different from that found in Cuba at this time.

We currently lack any physical evidence for the types of watercraft in use at this time. However, we can offer a conjecture. Callaghan (2001) concluded that oceanic conditions made it highly unlikely that simple rafts were the primary method of transport, because winds and currents would have carried rafts away from the islands. Moreover, when the Spanish arrived, they did not record the use of sails anywhere in the Caribbean (McKusick 1960). It is possible that the use of sails was abandoned at some time in the past, as was the case with seafaring in eastern Polynesia (Irwin 1992). However, unlike Polynesia, long-distance voyaging for the purpose of trade continued in the Caribbean until the time of European contact. If sails were present at any time, we would expect their use to have continued. Given the ubiquity of dugout canoes in the circum-Caribbean, it is likely that the earliest colonists also used this type of vessel and that the canoes did not have sails (Figure 2.2).

The widely accepted explanation is that explorers in dugout canoes paddled to Cuba from an Isthmo-Colombian source area, with Belize offering the closest material culture similarities (Wilson, et al. 1998). Both technological and oceanic conditions make the Yucatan Peninsula and the Gulf Coast United States unlikely sources. In addition, because the material remains are more typical of a later material assemblage, the arrival of immigrants from North America would have occurred after the islands already were settled. Lowland South America through eastern Venezuela and Trinidad remains an option, but a similar macro-blade technology is not known from this area. The issue of where the Lithic Age assemblage came from has not been resolved.

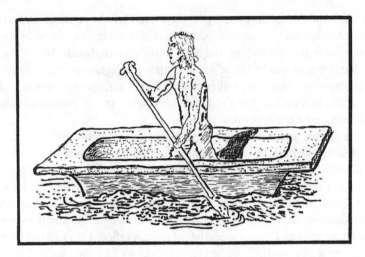

FIGURE 2.2 Dugout canoe based on drawing by Oviedo y Valdez (1959).

Cultural Characteristics

Various names have been used to describe Lithic Age assemblages. Rouse (1992:54) classified Lithic Age deposits as belonging to the Casimiroid series, which is named for the Casimira site in the Dominican Republic. Under this series, he distinguished a Casimiran subseries comprising three local "peoples and cultures": Seboruco in Cuba, Cabaret in Haiti, and Barrera-Mordán in the Dominican Republic. Veloz Maggiolo (1993) calls this culture "Barreroides." He named his series for the type-site at which the artifacts are most representative, while Rouse named his series for the first site at which the style was identified (Casimira). Kozlowski (1974) used the term "Seboruco-Mordán Culture" to recognize similarities between the tools found in Cuba and the Dominican Republic. The different names highlight the different objectives of the investigators. Rouse selected the first site, Veloz Maggiolo the most typical site, and Kozlowski the combination of two sites that reflected an inter-island distribution.

None of these early sites has been studied in sufficient detail to provide general conclusions regarding the economy, demography, sociopolitical organization, or other aspects of their culture. One problem is that the sites predominantly are lithic workshops that do not exhibit the full range of cultural activities. Archaeologists have turned to general ethnographic models of hunter-gather societies to describe what their lifeways may have been like. The two main sources of information are the "Marginal Tribes" of South America (Steward and Faron 1959), and the Marxist notion of *moda de vida* (see Ensor 2000; Veloz Maggiolo 1991).

In general, Lithic Age groups are described as living in small, mobile "bands" organized around extended families and including in-marrying spouses. Bands are flexible because individuals who share kinship relations join together and then split apart during different times of the year. This form of organization is not unusual in lowland South America, where communities assemble in villages during the wet season and then disperse during the dry season when travel is not constrained by the flooding of the forest (Steward and Faron 1959). It is worth noting that these modern South American societies practice a form of casual cultivation in which root crops are planted during wet season aggregations, and then left largely untended until the community reassembles at the end of the dry season. The notion of a band level of sociocultural integration is based entirely on evolutionary models that posit a "simple" form of social organization as typical of hunter-gatherers (Steward 1955; Service 1962). Because many of the early sites occur in caves and rock shelters, it was proposed that this was their favored settlement location (Osgood 1942). Caves and rock shelters were used as temporary shelters and for burials in Cuba, but they were not troglodytes, and the majority of sites occur in open-air settings.

Environmental Considerations

The islands on which the first colonists arrived were very different from the islands of today. Eustatic sea level had risen since the end of the Pleistocene and stabilized at near-modern levels about 5,000 years ago. When humans arrived, the coastal and near-shore marine habitats they encountered are best described as recently formed and transitional. The inland progression of the sea created chaotic conditions that affected the development of coral reefs, littoral rocky shores, tidal flats, and mangrove habitats (Watters, et al. 1992).

On land, the study of pond core sediments from Lake Miragoane, Haiti, showed significant changes in climate and vegetation over the past 10,300 years (Curtis and Hodell 1993; Curtis, et al. 2001; Higuera-Gundy 1991; Higuera-Gundy, et al. 1999). Between 10,000 and 8,600 years ago, the climate was cool and dry, and the vegetation was scrub and xeric. About 7,000 years ago, when humans first arrived, the Greater Antilles experienced a warmer and moister climate, and forests replaced the dry-adapted woodlands. Increased quantities of charcoal and changes in pollen profiles in core sediments provide evidence that natural habitats were being transformed into anthropogenic landscapes (Burney and Burney 1994; Higuera-Gundy, et al. 1999; Siegel, et al. 2005, 2015).

The coastal vegetation and the animals that inhabited these zones were a reflection of local environmental transformations. Many terrestrial and marine animals were more common due to the absence of large predators (Steadman, et al. 2005; Steadman and Stokes 2002). These animals included a giant flightless owl (*Ornimegalonyx oteroi*), tortoises similar to the Galapagos tortoise (*Geochelone* sp.), sloth (*Megalocnus rodens*), iguanas (*Iguana* sp. and *Cyclura* sp.), manatee (*Trichechus* sp.), marine turtles (*Chelonia mydas, Caretta caretta, Eretmochelys imbricata*), crocodile (*Crocodylus acutus*), a variety of rodents

(*Isolobodon* sp. and *Capromys* sp.), and possibly monk seals (*Monachus tropicalis*; cf. Baisre 2013).

Unwary of the newly arrived human predators, these species would have been easy prey, and the blade tools found in these sites are well suited to their capture and processing. It has been suggested that hunting caused the local extirpation of the sloth (Steadman, et al. 2005) and manatee (Veloz Maggiolo, et al. 1976), and Cunningham (1997) suggested that 90% of the fauna in the Greater Antilles went extinct shortly after humans arrived (also see Morgan 1993; Morgan and Woods 1986; Woods and Sergile 2001). Unfortunately, faunal remains are not preserved in most of the sites that have been investigated to date.

Barrera-Mordán Site, Dominican Republic (*c.* 4000 BC)

The most comprehensive studies of lithic technology in the Greater Antilles were conducted in Cuba by Kozlowski (1974, 1980) and Rives and Febles (Rives and Febles 1988); in Haiti by Davila (1978), Moore (1991), and Rouse (1941); in the Dominican Republic by Veloz Maggiolo (Veloz Maggiolo, et al. 1974, Veloz Maggiolo 1991); by Rodríguez Ramos (2005, 2010) in Puerto Rico; and by Pantel (1988) for the entire region (Figure 2.3). The flaked-stone tools from

FIGURE 2.3 Barrera-Mordan site, Dominican Republic (photo by Corinne Hofman and Menno Hoogland).

the Barrera-Mordán sites are the most widely recognized, and often are used as the "type" examples (Keegan 1994). Located in the south-central Dominican Republic, there are four named sites at this locale. Barrera and Mordán are in two different parts of the small modern community, and originally were identified as two different sites. It has since been recognized that they are part of a single large site. In addition, the Casimira site is located 100 meters to the north, and Las Alejandrinas is 75 meters to the northeast.

Marcio Veloz Maggiolo, Elpidio Ortega, José Cruxent, and Luis Chanlatte Baik were the first to investigate the sites in this area (Figure 2.4). Gus Pantel (1988) reinvestigated the sites in 1975 to provide a more complete definition of the assemblages. The problem he encountered was that the sites were disturbed by modern activities and were much eroded. Nevertheless, excavating in 25-centimeter levels, he encountered six strata that comprised the main deposit. Pantel (1976:254) noted that the frequency of blades increased with depth, which fit the prevailing notion that large blades gave way to microblades, flakes, and bone and shell tools through time.

Pantel's study illustrates the difficulties faced in assigning lithic tools to a particular age. These sites are lithic workshops or quarries that lack any evidence of permanent habitation and most other activities. Strata III, IV, and VI comprised the main lithic components (Pantel 1976:254), but strata III and IV also contained pottery. The first radiocarbon dates from the site were made on one charcoal sample at three different labs. Every laboratory obtained a slightly

FIGURE 2.4 Archaic Age flaked-stone blades from Haiti (courtesy of John de Bry).

different date: 2585 +/- 80, 2165 +/- 130, and 2425 +/- 170 B.P. (*c.* 500 BC). Yet new dates obtained by Pantel (1976:254) from stratum IV yielded radiocarbon dates of AD 1 +/- 300 and 625 +/- 80. These dates suggest that the quality of the raw material in this area proved attractive for hundreds of years. Furthermore, although the flaked-stone blades from the site are taken as representative of the earliest settlement of the islands, this is not confirmed by the dates.

Lithic Age Assemblages

Lithic Age assemblages contain a variety of flaked-stone artifacts and use-ground stones. The flaked tools tend to be struck from fine-grained cherts in Cuba and Hispaniola, and chalcedony in Puerto Rico (Pantel 1988). The diagnostic tool is unretouched macroblades stuck from prismatic cores. Although less common, these blades were sometimes backed and tanged, and exhibit secondary retouching along one face. At the Savanne Carree No. 2 site in the Ft. Liberté area of Haiti, Davila (1978:210) noted that 50% of the flaked-stone tools were blades, there was little evidence for cores or debitage, and that the stone was not typical of this coastal floodplain. His investigations indicate that blade preforms were being made at workshop sites and were obtained through exchange or possibly direct procurement, a situation that Kozlowski also emphasized (1974:69).

Tool production seems to have occurred in two stages. The first was procurement of unmodified blades from areas that had concentrations of the highest quality raw materials. Blade "preforms" were then modified at a later date to create a variety of tools, including side-scrapers, end-scrapers, knife-scrapers, burins, leaf-shaped points, notched implements, and retouched flakes and blades (Kozlowski 1974). The obvious conclusion is that flaked-stone tools were used for woodworking and the manufacture of other objects made from perishable materials (Veloz Maggiolo 1993). This suggestion is supported in part by lithic use-wear studies (Febles 1988). However, there are other variables that need to be considered. For example, Pantel's (1988) study of flaked-stone assemblages demonstrated that the same stone-working tradition was employed in Cuba, Hispaniola, and Puerto Rico. Moreover, "those attributes of 'style' which in the past have been ascribed to cultural variation in the Greater Antilles, may in fact be the result of local raw material variability" (Pantel 1988:169).

The issue of form versus function has not been adequately addressed. The main emphasis has been on classifying tools according to spatial and chronological distributions. The most widely used taxonomy is Rouse's (1992:51–62) classification of three subseries assigned to the Casimiroid series. He identified a Casimiran Casimiroid distributed from central Cuba through Hispaniola (4000–2000 BC), a Redondan Casimiroid for Cuba (2000 BC to AD 500, and possibly dating to AD 1500 in the west), and a Courian Casimiroid covering all of Hispaniola (2000 BC–AD 500). The dates were not based on established chronologies, but were selected to fill empty time slots in the taxonomy.

Janusz Kozlowski (1974:73–79) developed a different classification based on his identification of four distinct tool assemblages:

1. The Funche Culture was characterized by an "amorphic" technique and a poverty of other stone artifacts (e.g., hammer stones, grinders, and anvil stones). The sites are located in western Cuba and the Isle of Pines, and the type-site is in the Funche rock shelter in Pinar del Rios Province (Pino 1970). This assemblage was characterized as the "most primitive" (expedient), and Kozlowski speculated that the economy was based on hunting small mammals and land crabs, with minor contributions from mollusks and fishes.

2. The Damajayabo-Couri Culture was named for the Damajayabo site in Oriente Province, Cuba, and the Couri site near Fort Liberté, Haiti. The assemblage was represented by a poor-quality local set of chipped stone tools, the importation of Seboruco-Mordán blades, and a variety of tools made with pecking and grinding techniques (e.g., hammer stones, grinders, mortars, pestles, axes, stone balls, pseudo-daggers). The sites tended to be located on the coast near river mouths and on offshore islands. The lack of lithic raw material in the area justified the conclusion that chert blades were imported.

3. The Guayabo Blanco Culture was characterized by bifacial flaked-stone tools, side scrapers, and a variety of shell tools, and was named for the site on a swampy peninsula of Zapata, Cuba (also see Cosculleula 1946). The stone tools are very similar to those found in later cultures (called "sub-Taíno" by Rouse 1986). The sites typically are shell heaps, and there is evidence that fishing was an important component of the diet. In fact, other archaeologists have commented on their similarity to *sambuques* in Venezuela (Sanoja Obediente 1987).

4. The Carnero Culture was mostly microliths and pecked and ground tools. This is the latest of the assemblages and has the widest distribution. It is associated with Loíza Cave in Puerto Rico, Railroad Cave on the Samaná peninsula of the Dominican Republic, and Ortoire sites in Trinidad. Radiocarbon dates from the La Victoria site suggest that this culture developed in the first centuries BC and survived until the period of European encounters in western Cuba, where they were known as the Guanahatabey.

This study of Lithic Age assemblages has focused on stone tool classifications. There is some evidence for a decline in the production and use of macroblades and an increase in the use of microblades and flakes.[1] The shift from blades to flakes has been interpreted as resulting from new influences from North America (Rey Bettancourt and Garcia Rodríguez 1988). Alternatively, the

---

[1] There is inconsistency in the use of the terms *blade* and *flake*. Blades are defined as being at least twice as long as they are wide, while flakes are less elongate.

change may have resulted from changes in food procurement resulting from the local extirpation of large game, and local, perhaps seasonal, adaptations to the diverse environments of the Greater Antilles (Veloz Maggiolo and Vega 1982). The absence of mortars, pestles, and other grinding tools was used to distinguish these sites from later sites. This absence of grinding tools may signal a lesser emphasis on gathered roots, seeds, nuts, and fruits, or may reflect differences in the ways these foods were processed (Veloz Maggiolo 1991). However, the sites that have been excavated to date do not contain evidence for the full range of activities because most are lithic workshops. Investigators have drawn a hard-and-fast temporal line between the "Cultures" or "series" in which flaked-stone tools predominate, and those with a stronger reliance on ground-stone tools. This division is an artifact of classification schemes and the notion that the different technologies reflect separate migrations (Rouse 1986). There are too few well-excavated assemblages from this time period to draw definitive conclusions.[2]

Ground-Stone Complexes

The next phase in Caribbean archaeology is recognized by the appearance of formal tools produced by grinding (Figure 2.5). This period is commonly called the Archaic Age. In addressing what constitutes the "Archaic," R. Christopher Goodwin (1978) recognized three distinct and separate perspectives. First, the Archaic as an *age* is defined by the absence of pottery and the presence of ground-stone and/or formal shell tools (e.g., Rouse 1992). Second, the Archaic as a developmental *stage* is characterized by a marine-oriented subsistence that followed a terrestrial, hunting-based economy (e.g., Willey 1976; Willey and Philips 1958). Third, the Archaic as an *economic pattern* is defined by an emphasis on marine mollusk collecting (e.g., Davis 1982). We have already addressed problems with the first two definitions, in that pottery was made and used by at least some of them, and that big-game hunting was never a viable option in the Caribbean islands. Unfortunately, a more precise definition of the Archaic Age has not been proposed (cf. Terrell, et al. 2003), and our understanding of this period has advanced little since Goodwin's seminal musings.

The Archaic Age also dates to between 5700 and 200 BC, and thus overlaps completely with the Lithic Age. Archaic Age sites traditionally are distinguished by the use of ground-stone and shell tools and an abundance of marine mollusks. The almost complete absence of pottery resulted in the common use of the terms "aceramic" or "preceramic" to describe this

---

[2] The ubiquitous tool in the Caribbean today is the machete or cutlass. Our conjecture is that macroblades were hafted to create a machete-like tool for clearing and penetrating the dense bush that characterized island habitats at this time. In this regard, we shift the focus from big-game hunting to mobility through the forest.

FIGURE 2.5 Archaic Age ground-stone artifacts from Saba (photos by Corinne Hofman and Menno Hoogland).

period. However, these criteria are not always sufficient for differentiating early sites from later procurement sites. At Krum Bay (St. Thomas), for example, Lundberg (1991) demonstrated that some of the "aceramic shell middens" were actually later special-purpose sites, while others were natural collections of shells. A similar situation is reported for the Bahamas, where the radiocarbon dates showed that a supposed Archaic Age deposit was a natural accumulation of shells that dated to well after the Archaic Age ended (Bahamas Archaeology Team 1984). Accumulations of mollusk shells in which pottery is absent are being found in increasing numbers. In the absence of diagnostic tools, shell deposits cannot be assigned to a particular period or Age. We also need to consider the effects of the natural deposition of mollusk shells along the coast. In some cases these former beach deposits are well inland of their original location. Thus, some shell deposits are probably the product of natural forces (Watters, et al. 1992). A natural deposit of shells on Medio Cay, Guantanamo Bay, Cuba, has been described in detail (Serrand and Keegan 2004).

The distinction between an Age in which flaked-stone tools were predominant, and one in which ground-stone tools became more common, was compelling on technological grounds. Mapping the diffusion of ground-stone tools was based on efforts to identify *one* source area, based on the assumption that changes in technology had a single source from which they diffused (Rouse 1992). In this regard, South America appeared to be the best candidate because northeastern Venezuela is closest to the Lesser Antilles. The discovery of a predominantly ground-stone technology in Trinidad's St. John and Banwari Trace sites at a very early date seemed to provide the perfect source (Boomert 2000; Harris 1976; Pagán Jiménez, et al. 2015).

Banwari Trace Site, Trinidad (*c.* 5000 BC)

Dated to around 5000 BC, the Banwari Trace site on Trinidad is one of the two oldest Archaic Age sites excavated in the Caribbean Islands (Rouse and Allaire 1978; Boomert 2000). Following his practice of naming archaeological series for the first site at which diagnostic artifacts were described, Rouse (1992) classified Banwari Trace and similar sites as belonging to the Ortoiroid series. The series is named for three shell middens near the village of Ortoire in southeastern Trinidad, although only one of these contained artifacts (Bullbrook 1953). This name has caused some confusion because the Ortoire sites date to between 1000 and 700 BC, and are thus several millennia younger than Banwari Trace. In contrast, Veloz Maggiolo (1993) named complexes for the site with the most characteristic ("type") artifacts, and therefore called them "Banwaroides."

The Banwari Trace site is located on a hill above the wetlands between the Oropuche and Coora rivers in southwestern Trinidad. Peter O'Brian Harris directed excavations at the site in the late 1960s and early 1970s (Harris 1973, 1976). The United Nations Educational, Scientific, and Cultural Organization (UNESCO) recently recognized the significance of the site, and it has been nominated as a World Heritage Site. Harris and Emily Lundberg conducted additional excavations in 2005 in an effort to better characterize the deposits using new methods of analysis. Unfortunately, in the intervening years, most of the site was removed for use as construction fill.

The site is about 10 kilometers from the coast, and consists of a shell midden about 30 meters in diameter and over 2 meters tall (Boomert 2000). The site has a variety of stone and bone tools. The ground-stone tools are distinctive, and they may have been used for pounding and processing hard or fibrous plants. As Harris (1973:122) notes, these tools typically are shaped by use, such that: "Originally water-rounded flat stones, all share common evidence of coarse grinding round the edge." The deposits also contained large (30 cm) and small pestles, mortars (metates), manos, anvils, and grooved axes. It is worth noting that many of these ground-stone artifacts were created through use, although for the first time there are tools purposely produced by grinding prior to use. There also are small flakes and fragments of bipolar-flaked chert procured from local sources. The bone tools include sharpened tips (2–75 cm in length) for use as spear points, needles, and gorgets for fishing (Boomert 2000:58). In addition, one small potsherd was found on the surface and a second in the upper levels of the most recent excavations (Keegan, personal observation, 2005).

The site shows evidence for changes in subsistence practices over time. The earliest strata exhibit an emphasis on terrestrial animals along with shellfish collecting in nearby freshwater rivers, swamps, estuaries, and the sea. Various land crabs also are common in the site, although there is evidence for a shift from terrestrial to marine resources through time (Harris 1973, 1976). This shift in resource-use at least partly reflected the separation of Trinidad from the mainland with the opening of the Gulf of Paría during the time the site was occupied. In addition, starch grain analysis at the St. John site (Trinidad) revealed evidence for maize as early as 7,700 B.P. (Pagán Jiménez, et al. 2015).

Origins

The question of how ground-stone and shell tool technologies entered the Caribbean is frustratingly complex. The technology is so simple it is possible that grinding techniques developed independently in different places at different times, especially given thousands of years of assemblages containing use-ground tools. The conventional wisdom views these new technologies as arriving with new immigrants (Rouse 1986, 1992). An alternative view is that ground-stone tools were developed independently or were introduced in concert with particular cultigens obtained through exchange. It is more likely that they do not reflect new migrations into the islands.

Independent invention has been dismissed because the earliest sites with these artifacts occur on the circum-Caribbean mainland. Thus the movement of these objects into the Caribbean Islands must reflect population movements (Rouse 1986). The logic is as follows: The Banwari Trace site in Trinidad and the Milford site on Tobago reflect the earliest examples of Archaic Age lifeways that are located closest to the Antilles. Sometime between 5000 and 2000 BC, with the latter date most favored, communities began to migrate north from Trinidad, Tobago, or mainland South America into the Lesser Antilles (Davis 1993). When they arrived in the Greater Antilles, they melded with the existing Lithic Age communities to create a hybrid culture. In fact, Veloz Maggiolo (1991) called this derivative culture the "hybridoide."

There are several problems with this scenario, however. The most significant is that there are no definite Archaic Age sites in the Windward Islands of the southern Lesser Antilles.[3] There are two small and adjacent sites (i.e., Boutbois and Le Godinot) in an unusual interior location on the island of Martinique (Allaire and Mattioni 1983). However, the stone tools in this context were ground through use and do not reflect the purposely made diagnostic tools. By the taxonomic criteria adopted, they cannot be classified as Archaic Age artifacts. The only other possible early site is a rock shelter on St. Vincent that contains flaked stonés in its basal deposits (Hackenberger 1991). Louis Allaire (personal communication, 1993) examined the St. Vincent materials

---

[3] Fitzpatrick (2011) obtained radiocarbon dates of cal. 3280–1750 BC (2-sigma) from conch shell adzes from the Heywoods site on Barbados. However, the site does not have ground-stone artifacts or any other Archaic Age materials. Also, Siegel, et al. (2015) report evidence for fires about 5,000 years ago, which may be evidence of human activity.

and concluded that they are unmodified stones. There also is a wide distribution of unprovenienced ground-stone "axes" in the Windward Islands that may reflect an Archaic Age presence that has not yet been pinpointed (Harris 1983; Sutty 1991). However, the use of ground-stone tools continued throughout later time periods. Without other supporting evidence, they cannot be attributed to the Archaic Age. In addition, many of these objects are so large and heavy that they are unsuited for use as "axes." It is more likely that they were used as hoes to dig in heavy clay soils, which is suggestive of horticultural practices.

Many Archaic Age sites also contain a wide variety of tools manufactured from mollusk shells, especially queen conch. *Lobatus* shell gouges[4] are especially common in sites in western Cuba and northern Venezuela but are absent at this time in other Caribbean sites (Davis 2000; Keegan 1994). This discontinuity does not fit the migration model, so it was suggested that knowledge of *Lobatus* shell gouges must have diffused independently of ground-stone tools. In contrast, their absence at intervening sites in the Caribbean islands has been interpreted as evidence for a direct connection with the Manicuaroid sites of northern Venezuela (see Sanoja Obediente 1987; Veloz Maggiolo 1991); a connection that did not involve the settlement of the Lesser Antilles.

What we know for certain is that ground-stone tools have been found at sites in the Greater Antilles and northern Lesser Antilles beginning around 3000 BC. These tools were present across most of the South and Central American littoral prior to their appearance in the Caribbean (Kozlowski 1974; Rodríguez Ramos 2010, 2013). The shortest geographic distance would involve immigrants carrying this tool-making tradition through the Windward Islands. In addition, the Archaic Age shell tool technology of western Cuba shares its closest affiliations with similar tools found in South America. The two regions could not be further apart, and there are no intermediary sites. Furthermore, the flaked-stone lithics at Jolly Beach, Antigua, are most similar to the technologies of Seborucco, Cuba (Rives and Febles 1988), and Barrera-Mordán, Dominican Republic, although they occur at a much later date (Davis 2000). *The evidence suggests that Archaic Age tools moved from west to east, and not south to north.* In sum, the distributions of specific technologies do not correspond to the closest possible source. The theory of a separate migration of communities from South America making ground-stone tools no longer makes sense.

The alternative is a direct jump from South or Central America into the central Caribbean. Although this may seem to have been a more difficult passage, Richard Callaghan (2013), in a series of voyaging simulations, concluded that movement across the Caribbean Sea is not only feasible, but easier than navigating between the islands of the Lesser Antilles. He concluded that there is no evidence for the distinct Archaic Age migration. Although goods and people

---

[4] These tools were called "gouges" based on the U-shape cutting edge. They more closely resemble "hoes" identified at Ceramic Age sites (Jones O'Day and Keegan 2001).

continued to move into the islands, they did not completely replace indigenous communities.

Climate Change and Anthropogenic Landscapes

The early Archaic Age was a period of environmental instability (Cooper 2013; Higuera Gundy, et al. 1999). Through time, climate continued to adjust toward modern expressions of temperature and rainfall, and marine and terrestrial environments exhibited the final phases of early Holocene adjustments. The humans who occupied the islands at this time not only had to adjust to these changes, their behaviors also significantly transformed island landscapes.

There were significant and localized fluctuations in relative sea levels (Cooper and Boothroyd 2011; Milne and Peros 2013; Nicholson 1976; Scudder 2001; Valdés 1994; Watters 1982), and even minor changes in sea level had significant impacts on coastal marine, estuarine, mangrove, and terrestrial habitats. For example, the rocky intertidal zone in which species such as West Indian topsnail (*Cittarium pica*) and various nerites (e.g., *Nerita versicolor*) were collected occurs on the interface between land and sea. A change of a few centimeters in sea level can drastically affect such ecotonal habitats. Furthermore, changes in coastal habits can occur at a rapid rate. For example, Keegan, et al. (2003) have shown that the ecology of Bluefields Bay, southwestern Jamaica, changed substantially between the ninth and fifteenth centuries AD. There is no reason not to expect similarly dramatic changes during earlier time periods (see Rivera Collazo 2011).

About 3,200 years ago, there was a return to drier conditions, and this trend continued and intensified until about 1,000 years ago (Higuera-Gundy, et al. 1999). In Puerto Rico, there is a marked increase in the amount of charcoal in core samples taken from Laguna Tortuguero, beginning about 5,300 years ago (Burney and Burney 1994). A similar situation is reported for Vega Baja (Siegel, et al. 2005). Because the climate was wetter at this time, the increase in charcoal is attributed to the use of fire by humans.

The lack of a well-rounded suite of subsistence remains in Archaic Age coastal sites previously was related to the expectation that mobile foragers moved between seasonal resource concentrations (Hofman, et al. 2006; Keegan 1994:270; Lundberg 1991:76). Plum Piece on Saba (Chapter 7), although differentiated by its location, material remains, and subsistence strategies, may have belonged to one and the same subsistence/settlement system as these contemporary coastal sites (see also Lundberg 1980, 1991:75), which highlights the diversity of procurement strategies (Boomert 2000:78; Veloz Maggiolo and Vega 1982).

It is also likely that the earliest inhabitants of the islands had a profound effect on the availability of animals in the habitats they occupied. In Tobago, David Steadman and Anne Stokes (2002) observed significant differences in the non-fish species between the Archaic Age Milford 1 site (*c.* 900 BC) and the Ceramic Age Golden Grove site (*c.* AD 800–1100). The older, Milford 1 site contained larger animals, including sea turtles, collared peccary (*Tayassu tajaeu*), paca (*Agouti paca*), and howler monkey (*Alouatta seniculus*). They also identified four species of reptiles and seven mammals, some of which are no longer extant on the island. In contrast, the Golden Grove site exhibited a greater diversity of taxa (numbering 29 species). Species from the Milford 1 site are rare in the Golden Grove site, where there was a shift to small and medium-size vertebrates including toads, lizards, snakes, birds, opossum, armadillo, and eight species of rodents.

The interpretive problem we face is that the presence of ground-stone tools and the absence of pottery are taken to represent what Goodwin (1978) has recognized as a *stage* of cultural development. What is needed is a broader and more encompassing perspective that engages the availability of raw materials and food resources. As previously mentioned, Pantel (1988) concluded that the major differences observed in flaked-stone complexes could be explained by differences in the stone sources used to create these tools. Sebastiaan Knippenberg (2006) has conducted a similar study of the availability, distribution, and quality of the sources for ground-stone tool production. Raw material availability and selection contributed to the diversity recognized in ground-stone tools throughout the islands.

The same is true for differences in subsistence practices. It is not enough to compare different sites on different islands and then develop a generalized portrait of diet for this time period. Every island has its own unique set of resources, and previous inhabitants of the islands affected their availability. For example, green sea turtles are the highest ranked species in terms of the marginal rate of returns in both calories and protein (Keegan 1992). Thus, we would expect this animal to be the favored food whenever it was available. Yet the inhabitants of islands that lack extensive seagrass beds on which the turtles feed and/or adequate nesting beaches had a more limited access to these animals. Furthermore, if this species was targeted, then the availability of turtles would have declined through time in concert with human predation. The bottom line is that faunal remains cannot be used as a characteristic of a particular stage of cultural development without first considering environmental characteristics and prior human occupation (deFrance 2013).

Archaic Age Assemblages in the Greater Antilles

All of the Archaic Age sites[5] in Puerto Rico and the Virgin Islands have been classified as belonging to the Ortoiroid series (Rouse 1992). Within this series, three complexes (local styles) are recognized:

1. The Coroso complex of Vieques Island, which is similar to assemblages in the northern Lesser Antilles, includes pebble tools used as percusors

---

[5] Archaic Age sites in the Lesser Antilles are discussed in Chapter 7.

and grinders, flaked-stone tools, *Lobatus* columella tips, quartz, and red ochre (Lundberg 1991).

2. The Cayo Cofresí complex of eastern Puerto Rico is distinguished by the presence of well-formed ground-stone pestles, which are reminiscent of Banwari Trace.

3. The Krum Bay complex (St. Thomas) has flaked igneous stone and pebble hammer stones and grinders, crude bifacially worked tools resembling celts or wedges, shell beads and discs, *Lobatus* columella tips, coral files, quartz, and red ochre (Lundberg 1991).

The differences between complexes may reflect separate aspects of the same subsistence-settlement system (Lundberg 1991). However, it is not possible to define more specifically the relationships between these complexes. Interpretation has focused on the classification of tool forms in their most general and specific expressions. For this reason, artifacts from this area are classified as Ortoiroid to indicate a Trinidad source; while those from Hispaniola and Cuba are classified as Casimiroid to indicate continuity from the Lithic Age.

Archaic sites in Hispaniola are grouped together in the Courian Casimiroid subseries (Rouse 1992:57). Courian sites date to between 2000 BC and AD 145. They have been identified on the north (Ft. Liberté) and south (Ile à Vache) coasts of Haiti (Moore 1982). The Courian subseries is best known for its macroblade technology. These flaked-stone blades exhibit substantial continuity with Lithic Age technology. The blades resemble spearheads, backed knives, and end scrapers. It is assumed that these tools were used to hunt crocodiles, sloths, manatees, and whales (Rouse 1992:58; Veloz Maggiolo 1991:101). Couri "hunters" may have been responsible for the extirpation of sloths (Veloz Maggiolo 1991; Steadman, et al. 2005). In addition to blades, Courian assemblages are characterized by single- and double-bitted axes, conical pestles, stone and coral balls, mortars, hand grinders, and complex ornaments. The names for these tools have been assigned on the basis of form, not function. For example, the single- and double-bitted axes are made from basalt, a material that does not hold a sharp cutting edge. These tools may have been used for digging in heavy clay soils in the same manner as a hoe (e.g., harvesting roots, planting tubers). Red ochre was used as body paint and as a treatment for the dead.

An alternative classification was developed by Marcio Veloz Maggiolo (1991), who identified three distinct traditions: A flaked-stone tradition along the dry south and west coasts of Hispaniola; a Banwari-looking ground-stone tradition in southeastern Hispaniola; and a hybrid of these traditions represented by the widespread El Porvenir culture (typical Courian Casimiroid).

The Cuban Archaic Age has been classified as the Redondan Casimiroid series and is sequentially divided into Guayabo Blanco (2000 BC to AD 300) and Cayo Redondo (post–AD 300) cultures (see the previous discussion of Kozlowski's classification). Sites are located in the interior and along the coast, and both open-air and rock shelter sites are known. The material culture resembles that of the Manicuaroid series of eastern Venezuela, but it also shares the distinctive ground-shell gouge with similar sites on the St. John's River in Florida. The Cuban Archaic has the most developed shell-tool inventory, including gouges, plates, cups, tips, and hammers (Dacal Moure 1978). The flaked-stone tradition continued, although with less secondary flaking, and blade tools declined in quality and quantity. Ground-stone artifacts include manos, pestles, balls, *corazones* (heart stones), stone discs, bowls, cups, and *gladiolitos* (daggers).

In addition to ground-stone tools and the absence (or more accurately, infrequency) of pottery, Archaic Age communities have been characterized as non-agricultural foragers. Recent paleobotanical studies have challenged this assumption by demonstrating that "wild grain and fruit trees were established food resources prior to the entry of ceramic-manufacturing cultures into the Caribbean islands" (Newsom 1993). Plants identified in Archaic Age deposits include: guáyiga or coontie (*Zamia debilis*) and cupey (*Clusea rosea*) (Veloz Maggiolo and Vega 1982), sapodilla (*Manilkara [zapota] sp.*) (Pearsall 1989), wild avocado (*Persea americana*), yellow sapote (*Pouteria campechiana*) (Rouse and Alegría 1990), primrose (*Oenothera sp.*), mastic-bully (*Mastichodendron foetidissimum*), trianthema (*Trianthema portulaca*), and palms (Palmae) (Newsom 1993). Because some of these plants were introduced from outside the Caribbean (notably Central America), and others represent extensions beyond their present ranges, it is likely that these plants were managed, if not cultivated outright (Newsom 1993; Newsom and Wing 2004). Recently, Jaime Pagán Jiménez (2013; Pagán Jiménez, et al. 2015) has undertaken the analysis of starch grains recovered from Archaic Age grinding tools. He found evidence for virtually all of the cultigens (except manioc) that traditionally are associated with Ceramic Age introductions. In addition to the species noted by Newsom (1993), Pagán Jiménez also found evidence for maize (*Zea mays*). This new evidence is indicative of simple horticulture. The identification of cultigens in Caribbean Archaic Age sites is not surprising, given the fact these cultigens were domesticated in the surrounding mainland centuries before their introduction to the islands.

In the same way that foragers in the eastern woodlands of the United States cultivated a suite of local plants called the "Eastern Agricultural Complex" (Ford 1985; Riley 1987), a similar Caribbean Horticultural Complex may have existed during the Archaic Age (Keegan 1987). Archaic Age tools are used to cut and fell trees, dig heavy soils, and process plants for food. In addition, the increased incidence of charcoal in sediment samples suggests intensive burning of large tracts of land (e.g. Burney and Burney 1994; Siegel, et al. 2005; 2015).

The one clear picture that emerges when Archaic Age sites are compared is that there was enormous variability. The animal component of Archaic Age diets was derived from the collection of a wide variety of marine mollusks, fishes, and turtles (Davis 1988; Narganes Storde 1991b). The dominant resource varies among sites as a reflection of local availabilities. The lack of a well-rounded suite of subsistence remains suggests that sites were occupied seasonally as communities moved between resource concentrations (Alonso 1995; Lundberg 1991). Stable carbon and nitrogen isotope ratios in Archaic Age skeletons indicate a diet dominated by marine species from coral reef and sea-grass habitats (see Keegan and DeNiro 1988) along with a substantial contribution from C_4 grasses (Stokes 1998).

The variability observed in tool forms, tool sources, tool functions, animal use, and plant-use highlights the importance of local landscapes. Although Archaic Age communities often are characterized as highly mobile (Rouse 1992), even following seasonal rounds (Veloz Maggiolo and Vega 1982), the Plum Piece site (Saba) demonstrates such mobility in its recurrent abandonment and reoccupation (Hofman and Hoogland 2003; Hofman, et al. 2006). Mobility is a feature of all human societies, so an important way of restructuring the question regards the degree to which different communities establish long-term ties to particular locations. Recent investigations at the Maruca site and Angostura site in Puerto Rico have demonstrated that at least some Archaic Age communities had a more sedentary existence, and that the organizational requirements of settled life produced more complex organizations (Rivera Collazo 2011; Rodríguez Ramos 2010). These studies are part of a trend focused on explaining specific social and cultural arrangements, rather than on fitting the evidence to particular categories (see Rodríguez Ramos, et al. 2013).

Archaic Age Pottery

The term "Pre-Arawak Pottery Horizon" was introduced to describe the occurrence of small quantities of pottery at archaeological sites that have a predominantly Archaic Age tool kit (Rodríguez Ramos 2005, 2010; Rodríguez Ramos, et al. 2008). This designation made sense because it generally was assumed that pottery was first introduced to the Caribbean by Arawak-speakers from South America beginning about 500 BC (see Chapter 3). The tendency has been to interpret the pottery at Archaic Age sites as intrusive. Yet there is mounting evidence that pottery vessels were made and used by some Archaic Age communities long before the beginning of the Ceramic Age (Rodríguez Ramos, et al. 2008; Ulloa Hung 2005).

Mark Harrington (1921) was the first to mention pottery in Archaic Age sites during his extensive research in Cuba. Within sixty years, twelve sites across Cuba had been assigned to what was called a "proto-agricultural" phase that was dated to between 500 BC and AD 500 (Dacal Moure and Rivero de la Calle 1984:111). The number of these sites has increased dramatically in recent years (e.g., Godo 1997; Rodríguez Ramos 2010; Rodríguez Ramos, et al. 2013), and the earliest date for this phenomenon has been pushed back to 2160 BC (Jouravleva 2002:36). Even Rouse (1942:133), in his research in the Maniabon Hills of eastern Cuba, mentioned the presence of pottery in the El Nispero site, but he concluded that it was "deposited there after the abandonment of that site...."

Similar sites have been identified in Hispaniola, Puerto Rico, the U.S. Virgin Islands, and the northern Lesser Antilles. Rainey (1941:24) and Rouse (1941:50) mention the presence of pottery at the Couri 1 site, and Moore (1998) found "small crude sherds" at the Source Pascade II site, which was dated to 1090 BC. The discovery of pottery in association with seven stone balls and a broken Couri blade at the site of Île à Rat to the west of Cap Haïtien also may reflect this phenomena (see Chapter 6).

The best-documented sites outside of Cuba are in the Dominican Republic. Sites include El Curro in the Puerto Alejandro area of Barahona, which dates to 1450 BC (Ortega and Guerrero 1985). Pottery associated with an Archaic Age tool kit is described from the El Caimito and Musiépedro sites, which date to as early as the first century BC (Veloz Maggiolo, et al. 1974, 1976; Rimoli and Nadal 1980). El Caimito pottery was interpreted as evidence for transcultura-tion between the Archaic Age El Porvenir culture of Hispaniola and the early Ceramic Age Hacienda Grande colonists of Puerto Rico. According to Rouse (1992:92): "It would seem, then, that the makers of El Caimito pottery were El Porvenir people who copied Hacienda Grande-style pottery, thereby creat-ing a dual culture. Because their El Porvenir heritage was dominant and their ceramics was borrowed, I have assigned them to the Courian Casimiroid sub-series." The pottery at these sites is discussed in consideration of the develop-ment of Ceramic Age cultures in the eastern Dominican Republic (Chapter 5).

The first mention of pottery in Archaic Age contexts on Puerto Rico was for the Coroso complex at the Playa Blanca and Jobos sites (Rouse 1952). Numerous other sites have been identified since then, including the Angostura site with a date of 2700-1800 BC (Rivera Collazo 2011). At the Paso del Indio site, a deeply buried stratum, below 2–2.5 meters of sediments, was dated to 2630 BC (García Goyco and Solís Magaña 1999). Other early evidence for pottery in Puerto Rico is reviewed by Rodríguez Ramos (2010; Rodríguez Ramos, et al. 2008). At the Gramobokola site on St. Thomas, Bullen and Sleight (1964) recovered pottery in contexts dating to 870 BC. Potsherds also were found in the vicinity of the Chanel Hill site, which also dates to 870 BC (Lundberg 1989:134).

The presence of pottery in Archaic Age contexts can no longer be denied (Figure 2.6). Still, we need to consider the conventional explanation that the pottery in these sites is intrusive. We can do so by looking closely at the paste, petrographic, and decorative characteristics of Archaic Age pottery. Cuban archaeologists have conducted the majority of research on Archaic Age pottery (Jouravleva 2002; Ulloa Hung 2005; Ulloa Hung and Valcárcel Rojas 2002, 2013). Given the small number of sherds at most sites and their wide distri-bution, it is not surprising that there is significant variability. The following discussion is based on characteristics summarized from the work of Reniel Rodríguez Ramos and colleagues (Rodríguez Ramos 2010; Rodríguez Ramos, et al. 2008).

FIGURE 2.6 Archaic Age pottery from the Corinthia III site, Cuba (*c.* 270 BC) (courtesy of Roberto Valcárcel Rojas).

The main vessels forms are small (4–12 cm orifice) to medium (18–24 cm orifice) globular bowls with round or straight bottoms and boat-shaped (navicular) vessels. They were manufactured by coiling, and tend to have a thickness less than 1 centimeter, but range mostly between 4 and 8 millimeters. There also are clay plates and griddles at some of the sites, and these appear to have been made by flattening slabs of clay on a rigid surface. Some clay griddles have a raised, single coil around the circumference.

Temper tends to consist of sand, crushed rock, and/or quartz grit. In addition, grog temper has been noted in Cuba and the Dominican Republic (Veloz Maggiolo, et al. 1976; Rimoli and Nadal 1983; Ulloa Hung 2005). Some sites also have organic tempers, including calcined shell, charcoal, and/or ash (Zucchi 1985); although in Cuba, these compose less than 30% of the temper categories (Jouravleva 2002:41). Finally, the use of self-tempering clays has been noted in a small number of cases.

Pottery from these sites is usually highly oxidized, which indicates the use of open-air firing techniques. There are, however, some sherds with black cores that may indicate a reducing environment or incomplete firing in an open-air environment. Based on their study of sherds from Cuba, Ulloa Hung, et al. (2001:39) concluded that the pots were fired at relatively low temperatures (600° to 900° F).

The vessels seem to have coarse finishes, although this may be a function of their age and post-deposition deterioration. At most, the vessel surfaces appear to have been smoothed, and in some cases, smoothing seems to have been accomplished with a spatula-like tool. Most of the sherds from this time are plain, although some are decorated with red, pink, white, and black paint; and incised, punctate, and modeled designs. The paints or slips were applied to the exterior, and in some cases the interior, of the vessels. Occasionally they occur in combinations with a red foundation and black or white paint over the red. The combined use of paint and incision is observed in some late Archaic Age sites (Castellanos, et al. 2001).

Incision is the most common technique, and it exhibits a great deal of variability. Rodríguez Ramos, et al. (2008) summarize the decorative treatments as follows:

> [L]ineal incisions were made parallel to the rims (e.g., Dacal Moure 1986; Lundberg 1989), perpendicular to the rims (e.g., Valcárcel Rojas, et al. 2001; Tabio and Guarch 1966), and in angular patterns (e.g., Castellanos, et al. 2001). In other cases curvilinear incision patterns have also been documented (e.g., Paso del Indio; Veloz Maggiolo, et al. 1976; Haviser 1989).

There is also zoned punctation (Ulloa Hung and Valcárcel Rojas 2002), and the filling of incisions with black paint (Veloz Maggiolo, et al. 1976).

From these descriptions, it is clear that there was enormous variability in the manufacture and decoration of pottery vessels. Unlike Saladoid pottery, which has a highly formalized grammar (Roe 1989), these pots seem to represent a period of experimentation in which different pastes and different decorative techniques were explored. The one constant seems to be that the vessel shapes mimic the shapes of containers that were made from gourds. For instance, by cross-cutting a gourd, you obtain a round or globular vessel, while a transverse cut yields an oval (navicular) vessel. The decorations also may reflect designs that were used to decorate perishable containers made of wood or gourds, and they are similar to designs preserved on stone bowls from this time period. The transposition of designs from other media to pottery has been suggested for later ceramic styles, notably Meillacoid pottery from Hispaniola (Rouse 1992).

In an effort to explain why Archaic Age communities adopted pottery making, Reniel Rodríguez Ramos (2010) has argued that we need to adopt the view of pots as tools (see Braun 1983). He notes an initially low frequency of pottery in the sites, the relatively small size of the pots, the absence of evidence for their use in cooking foods, and that their globular and boat shapes mimic the shapes of gourds that were cut for use as serving vessels. He concludes, "they were first made for functions that were earlier performed by other containers, and not for carrying out new tasks." In this regard, they seem to have replaced gourd containers for serving wet foods in ceremonial, ritual, and other social contexts.

Over time, the frequency of pottery in otherwise Archaic Age sites increased. Pottery vessels may have assumed new uses, such as cooking, and as Ceramic Age communities were established, interactions further influenced the Archaic Age communities that already were familiar with pottery. Pottery may have been introduced at an early date from the surrounding mainland, where pottery-making developed centuries earlier, or it may have been invented independently in the islands. Whatever the case, pottery vessels were in use prior to the Ceramic Age expansion, and the technological and decorative aspects of this pottery represent unique traditions, traditions that certainly contributed to later expressions of pottery technology and stylistic development in the Greater Antilles.

European Encounters with Archaic Age Communities

It generally is believed that Archaic Age practices survived in western Cuba until after the arrival of Columbus (Rouse 1992). However, this belief is based on a model of population expansion in which Ceramic Age communities expanded their territory at the expense of indigenous Archaic Age communities (Keegan 1989a; and see Chapter 8).

Like many other questions of Spanish encounters with the indigenous communities, this one begins in confusion. In his 1516 memorial to Cardinal Cisneros, Bartolomé de Las Casas noted that there were four Cuban societies whose souls should be saved (Lovén 1935). These were the Guanahacabibes (Guanahatabey) of the Cape of Cuba; and three others who shared a similar culture: the inhabitants of the small islands along the north and south coast of Cuba (Jardines del Rey); those living in the Bahamas (Las Islas de Los Lucayos); and the Ciboney, who were kept as servants by the other Cuban Indians (see Sauer 1966:185; Rouse 1987). Based on his descriptions, it is clear that all four (including the Ciboney) made pottery and practiced agriculture (see Chapter 1). Although Las Casas and Velázquez lived in Cuba for some time, their reports apparently were not substantiated by first-hand observations. Lovén (1935) concluded that the discoverers and conquerors never visited the western part of the island and lacked direct knowledge of the Guanahatabey.

Present accounts of Cuba all indicate a lack of Ceramic Age materials in western Cuba (e.g., Tabio y Rey 1966). However, Lovén (1935:3) reported that "numerous finds in Pinar del Rio prove that Taínos must once have lived there." Although Narváez described large settlements ruled by chiefs upon his entry into Habana province, these have never been identified. The negative evidence is not sufficiently strong to identify who lived in western Cuba at the time of Spanish contact (Keegan and Rodríguez Ramos 2005).

Conclusions

The earliest evidence of humans in the insular Caribbean has been found in Cuba, Hispaniola, and Puerto Rico (Rodríguez Ramos, et al. 2013). The oldest sites, which date to about 5000 BC, were called Casimiroid by Rouse (1992). The material culture is composed primarily of chert flakes and blades that are similar to contemporaneous stone tools from Belize (Wilson 2007). The majority of the Caribbean sites are quarries and workshops, a situation that suggests that they may have been locations at which high-quality chert was collected by seasonal visitors for export to chert-poor islands and the mainland. We know little else about life in the islands at this time.

It has been proposed that the Lithic Age way of life disappeared around 3000 BC with the introduction of a ground-stone technology by new immigrants from Trinidad. Rouse (1992) proposed that, after the Lithic Age colonists arrived in the islands, they severed all ties with their homeland. The arrival of ground-stone tools therefore required new immigrants. Trinidad, where such tools first appeared around 6000 BC, provided the likeliest source. These tools were associated with a "superior" way of life that was transported as part of a cultural assemblage. It was proposed that Ortoiroid "peoples and cultures" from Trinidad migrated north through the Lesser Antilles to Puerto Rico where they met and assimilated the Casimiroid.

One problem with this scenario is that none of the sites labeled "Ortoiroid" in the Antilles have the same material assemblages as that identified on Trinidad. One could argue that the earliest sites were ephemeral and have not yet been discovered, or that later adaptations masked the initial cultural signal. Lacking a general signature, emphasis has been placed on the "edge grinder" as the diagnostic type artifact. However, this artifact is ubiquitous in Archaic Age sites and it occurs along the north coast of South America as far as Panama (Rodríguez Ramos 2005:4). "Given the broad chronological and geographical distribution, how can edge grinders be viewed as diagnostic or type artifacts of the Ortoiroid series?" (Callaghan 2010:145).

A more pressing problem is the glaring absence of Archaic Age sites (Ortoiroid) south of Guadeloupe. Callaghan (2010) has shown that neither navigational abilities nor post-depositional natural processes (i.e., volcanism) can be held accountable. It is possible, due to previous lack of attention, that such sites await discovery. However, very detailed systematic surveys of the Lesser Antilles from Guadeloupe south have failed to reveal any new sites (Callaghan 2010). The conservative solution is that there was no Ortoiroid colonization of the southern Lesser Antilles. "The current evidence for an Ortoiroid migration beyond Tobago is very lacking. What has been classified as Ortoiroid could at least as easily be Casimiroid" (Callaghan 2010:146). It is far more likely that the Casimiroid evolved through continuous ties with Central America and that new practices (including ground-stone tools and a variety of cultigens) arrived in the islands through exchange. Such exchanges included people, goods, and ideas (Hofman and Hoogland 2011).

The Casimiroid migration is justified because the islands previously were unoccupied. If no one was living on an island, then migration is the only way to explain the sudden appearance of humans. For the next 2,000 years, the non-Arawak Casimiroid expanded through the Greater Antilles and as far south as Antigua and perhaps even Martinique (Callaghan 2010) and developed diverse lifeways (Rodríguez Ramos, et al. 2008). Pottery became at least a minor component of their cultural inventory, beginning as early as 2600 BC (Rodríguez Ramos, et al. 2008), and "the Antillean botanical trinity of manioc, sweet potatoes, and maize ... has all been documented during Archaic Age times in Puerto Rico at least since 1300 BC" (Pagán Jiménez 2013; Rodríguez Ramos 2010:31) (Figure 2.7). Additional cultigens, including yellow sapote and sapodilla, were obtained from Central America. Although the *modo de vida* was characterized as "mobile foragers" (Rouse 1992), there is evidence for sedentary communities. Finally, there is every reason to assume that exchange continued throughout the Archaic Age, beginning as lifelines to parent communities (e.g., Hofman, et al. 2014; Keegan 2004). Subsequent developments indicate that exchange relations with the "Intermediate Area" or Isthmo-Colombian region intensified through time (Rodríguez Ramos 2010, 2013).

Dispersion across the Greater Antilles (except Jamaica) initiated contacts with a plethora of environments. Local accommodations encouraged diverse behavioral repertoires, observed in the variable material expressions observed across the Antilles. These accommodations required differing means of social articulation, reflected in both local and regional expressions of identity. Moreover, the material manifestations and social and political arrangements

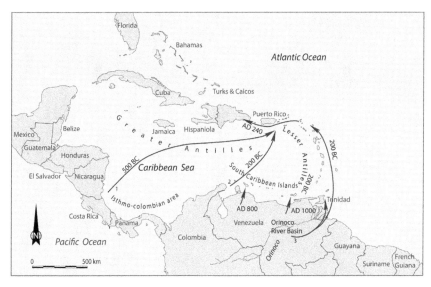

FIGURE 2.7 Map of hypothesized movements of people, goods, and/or ideas into the early Caribbean (courtesy of Menno Hoogland, after Keegan 2010).

changed through time. The result was a multi-dimensional, chaotic mosaic of communities. It remains impossible to address R. Christopher Goodwin's (1978) question of whether the Archaic is an *Age*, a *stage*, or an *economic pattern*. From the perspective of a Realist, it is, in fact, all three. In the chapters that follow, we consistently use the name "Archaic Age" to designate the diverse social and cultural expressions that began with the earliest colonists of the islands and that were transformed over time. These were the first indigenous societies to interact with the Ceramic Age colonists who arrived in the islands between 800 and 200 BC (Hofman, et al. 2011). We recognize that this nomenclature is not ideal, but we needed a consistent means for distinguishing them from later arrivals.

CHAPTER 3 | The Early Ceramic Age

ARAWAK COMMUNITIES FROM CONTINENTAL America began to enter the Caribbean Sea between 800 and 200 BC, and interacted with the indigenous Archaic Age communities (Figure 3.1). The Antilles was the terminus of population expansion that began on the upper Amazon and included most of riverine lowland South America (Boomert 2000; Heckenberger 2002; Hill and Santos Granero 2002; Lathrap 1970). The Antillean branch of colonists is called "Saladoid" because they shared similar ways of making and decorating pottery vessels, and had an economy based on farming. The sudden appearance of Saladoid communities in Puerto Rico and the northern Lesser Antilles marks the beginning of the Ceramic Age. Several models have been proposed to explain early Ceramic Age migration, infiltration, and colonization of the islands of the Lesser Antilles (e.g., Bérard 2013; Fitzpatrick 2013; Giovas and Fitzpatrick 2014; Keegan 2004; Rouse 1992; Siegel 1992; Wilson 2007).

The Early Ceramic Age colonization was a dynamic and chaotic sequence of events. Every island was colonized at a different time; the colonists may have come from different places in coastal South America, Central America, and later from within the Caribbean Islands. Communities adjusted to the diversity of local conditions; individuals negotiated solutions for themselves and their families; notions of social distance constrained their movements; ideas concerning what foods were appropriate influenced their subsistence practices; ideas concerning marriage and social alliance affected their residence patterns; and the role of ancestors in mediating natural forces beyond their control may have influenced the development of iconographic imagery and mythological beliefs. The unique characteristics that define the meanings of Saladoid composed the Saladoid *experience*.[1] We must also recognize that this experience did not occur in isolation. Archaic Age communities continued as independent

---

[1] Terms such as *social formation, culture*, etc., carry with them a great deal of historical baggage. We use the term *experience* to recognize that culture is a lived phenomenon, a shared experience that has boundaries defined by the perspectives of the individuals who chose to affiliate with a self-defined (egocentric) social unit. In this regard, every individual has a somewhat different interpretation, and assigns a somewhat different meaning, to their social network.

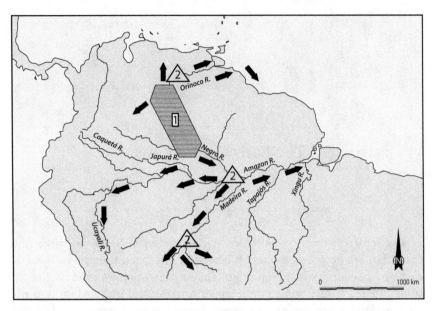

FIGURE 3.1 Proposed locations of Proto-Arawakan languages in northwestern Amazonia (hatched box); secondary centers of dispersal in the Middle Orinoco, Central Amazon, and Upper Madeira (triangles); and major routes of expansion (arrows) (courtesy of Menno Hoogland, after Michael Heckenberger [2002:map 4.2]).

entities, and the problematic Huecoid was juxtaposed (Chanlatte Baik 2013; Oliver 1999). The complex relationships between Archaic Age, Saladoid, and Huecoid will be explored later. For this reason, we begin with the more neutral designation, Early Ceramic Age.

Linguistic evidence suggests that sometime before 1,000 BC, Arawak communities began to move rapidly through the Negro and Orinoco flood-plains, up and down the Amazon, and into the Caribbean and Guiana coasts (Heckenberger 2002, 2013; Zucchi 2002). The center of dispersion is not certain, but appears to be the northwest Amazon between the Upper Amazon in Brazil and the Middle Orinoco in Venezuela (Lathrap 1970; Rouse 1992).

These Arawak colonists, including those who migrated into the Antilles, shared a system of cultural meaning and continuity in the broader cultural pattern. Summarizing Heckenberger (2002), Arawak speakers reproduce a *habitus* predisposed to perpetuate an ethos of settled village life, commonly coupled with large, fixed populations, fairly intensive subsistence economies, and landscape alteration (rather than mobility and low impact); institutional social ranking based on bloodline and birth order; and regional integration (particularly coupled with a social preoccupation with exchange and a cultural aesthetic that places great symbolic value upon foreign things) and a foreign policy commonly characterized by accommodation and acculturation of outsiders.

The impression that widely dispersed Arawak speakers maintained a recognizably similar pattern of culture for more than a millennium suggests that the broad cultural characterizations that are often made by Caribbean archaeologists may provide a reasonable general outline of Saladoid societies. Nevertheless, such optimism must be tempered with the recognition that these general patterns mask enormous variability through time, over space, and between specific socialities. Heckenberger (2002) is quick to point out that the development of the social body depends on other, more localized, contingent, and historical factors: the interplay of multidimensional social, cultural, and ecological factors that interact variably under contingent sociohistorical conditions. Arawak speakers moved along the major river drainages of South America, north to the Caribbean coast, and into the Antilles. They shared a common cultural *habitus*, while at the same time adapting to local social and environmental conditions. During their expansion, they interacted with Archaic Age communities in northern South America through intermarriage, coercion, and warfare (Schmidt 1917; Steward and Faron 1959).

The Saladoid branch is named for a distinctive type of pottery made in South America and the islands. Typically distinguished by white-on-red painted designs, it is widely distributed along the Orinoco River valley and coastal Venezuela (Rouse and Cruxent 1963). Saladoid pottery was not the only, or even the dominant, type in the region. Various other pottery series are recognized, and some probably preceded Saladoid on the lower Orinoco (Barse 2009; Zucchi 1991). The islands appear to reflect a" natural" progression downstream along the Orinoco River until it spilled out onto Trinidad, Tobago, and the rest of the southern Lesser Antilles. The only significant constraint was the distance between Grenada and the "mainland" (Rouse 1992). Archaeological evidence from the Lesser Antilles and Puerto Rico initially supported the interpretation that, about AD 1, Saladoid communities from the lower Orinoco departed from the mainland at Trinidad (Boomert 2013). Early Ceramic Age pottery in the islands was associated with Saladoid pottery, named for the Saladero site on the lower Orinoco. It was distinguished as consistent with pottery found at the Cedros sites on Trinidad, and was given the name "Cedrosan Saladoid" (Boomert 2000, 2013; Rouse 1992). Following the colonization of Trinidad, Saladoid supposedly island-hopped its way to Puerto Rico following the precept of stepping-stone expansion (Keegan and Diamond 1987). This model was so simple and straightforward that it remained unquestioned until the 1980s (Keegan 1985). It is still used by some archaeologists (e.g., Boomert 2013), and often in general histories (Higman 2011), today.

Beginning in the 1980s, sites with earlier radiocarbon dates were discovered in the northern islands (Chanlatte Baik 1981; Haviser 1991; Petersen 1996). The Tecla and Maisabel sites in Puerto Rico, Sorcé/la Hueca on Vieques, Trants on Montserrat, Morel on Guadeloupe, Hope Estate on St. Martin, and Indian Creek and Royals on Antigua all returned dates between 800 BC and AD 100 (at a 2-sigma range). Archaeologists were confronted with explaining why the earliest Saladoid and Huecoid sites were located in the more northern and often smaller islands, and why these permanent villages were centuries older than the villages located on the larger Windward Islands that were closer to the South American mainland. The initial reaction was that early sites in the Windward Islands of the southern Lesser Antilles had not yet been identified, and the beginning of the Antillean Saladoid was simply expanded to incorporate these islands without any specific evidence. Today, it is generally recognized that the earliest Ceramic Age sites are located on the more northern islands, and that the Windward Islands were sparsely inhabited in this initial expansion (Fitzpatrick 2013; Hofman, et al. 2011; Keegan 1985; Wilson 2007).

The initial model in which Saladoid expansion followed the intervisible chain of islands from the Orinoco Delta to Puerto Rico (with Grenada as the only significant water gap) no longer fits the data. Our first issue is explaining why the northern islands were settled centuries before the southern islands. To address this question, we need to examine the goals, options, and constraints of island colonization (Keegan 2004). To do so, we need to jettison some classificatory baggage. For this reason, we begin by calling the initial period of colonization the Early Ceramic Age. We will return to more specific "cultural" designations later.

From Forest to Sea

It has been commonly assumed that the Early Ceramic Age colonists of the Antilles originated in the tropical forest along the banks of the Orinoco River (Rouse 1986; Steward and Faron 1959). Because some of the sites, notably Indian Creek on Antigua, were located upriver and toward the interior of islands, it was suggested that the earliest sites maintained an inland, tropical forest focus based on practices developed along the rivers of lowland South America (Keegan and Diamond 1987), and only later were they established along the coast. This inland/coastal sequence theory was so pervasive at one time that it was used to explain settlement patterns in the Bahama archipelago (Sears and Sullivan 1978), where it is difficult to settle very far from the sea (Keegan 1995). Early Ceramic Age communities did have subsistence practices based on tropical forest horticulture, but the majority of their settlements, early and late, were located close to the coast. These initial coastal site locations may have been based on facilitating communication by canoe trips between widely dispersed communities. Today, the inland/coastal dichotomy is largely ignored because it added nothing to our understanding of the Early Ceramic Age.

Indigenous communities of northeastern South America did live in the tropical forest along rivers; however, they also lived along the coast (Rouse and Cruxent 1963). There is evidence that in both locations, they developed watercraft at an early date. Although there is no archaeological evidence for these boats, the conditions under which they were used provide the basis for speculation (see Wilbert 1976). The most likely vessel was a dugout canoe augmented with sideboards (Callaghan 2013); there is no evidence for sails

(McKusick 1960). The exchange of people, goods, and ideas between islands indicates continuity in relatively long-distance voyaging (Hofman, et al. 2010; Mol 2013). Finally, Archaic Age excursions successfully reached the islands millennia earlier, so the ability to cross water gaps from the mainland to the islands, and within the islands, has never been viewed as a significant constraint to Caribbean Island colonization.

The first crossing from mainland South America to the Antilles is the longest, and vessels had to be able to cross water passages of at least 150 kilometers. Given the winds and currents throughout the Caribbean, rafts were not adequate to reach any of the islands from the surrounding mainland. Potential departures from the North American Gulf Coast may have been constrained by the speed of the Gulf Stream, which flows between Cuba and the Bahama archipelago and the mainland. The Gulf Stream may have been strong enough to prevent travel from North America to the islands on vessels without sails (Seideman 2001; cf. Callaghan 2007). Nevertheless, Cuban archaeologists have noted material culture similarities with the U.S. Gulf Coast (Chapter 6).

Being a sailor, Columbus was greatly impressed by the indigenous dugout canoes with brightly painted bows and sternposts housed in special sheds on a beach in southern Cuba (Dunn and Kelley 1989; Lovén 1935), and others in the Bahamas. He reported that dugout *canoa* could hold up to ninety men and could be paddled almost as fast as a Spanish caravel could sail (about 6 knots/hour) (Dunn and Kelley 1989). When their canoes were swamped by a wave, they would right the vessel, bail it with a calabash, and be back on their way in short order. Their canoes reportedly were hewn from a single log, using fire to char the wood and stone or shells tools to hollow out the log. The silk cotton tree (*Ceiba pentandra*) was favored because it has large, straight trunks that are very light in the water. The wood is very buoyant due to its low specific gravity. Canoes were made in several different sizes, depending upon whether they were to be used in near-shore activities or long-distance voyages. Columbus observed large canoes in the Bahamas and Cuba. Dugout canoes provided rapid passage along the coast and between islands (Figure 3.2). Their importance is apparent in the observation that cultural traditions were more closely related across water gaps than they were at opposite ends of the same island (Watters and Rouse 1989).

The movement of "Lithic" and Archaic Age foragers into the islands appears to represent fluid processes of exploration, extraction, and later settlement accomplished across large stretches of open water. Exploitation zones were identified during exploratory voyages, mobile foragers moved through these zones, temporary settlements (or camps) were established, and only later was a complete contingent of settlers assembled, possibly in a series of stages that took place over time (Hofman, et al. 2011). Although this perspective oversimplifies the processes of island colonization at this time, the later movement of settled Arawak farmers required a different form of social organization (Ensor 2013a).

FIGURE 3.2 Dugout canoe manufacture in the Kalinago territory, Dominica (photo by Menno Hoogland).

Archaeological evidence indicates that Early Ceramic Age settlements reproduced autonomous communities. Island colonization was not based on the free-flow movement of individuals, but instead involved the movement of integrated households and communities. Early Ceramic Age settlements required the movement of entire communities that reproduced economic, social, and political entities. This community pattern is expressed in integrated, autonomous settlements that were occupied for centuries (Siegel 2010). Early Ceramic Age settlement patterns are indicative of a different form of social organization. As a social process, island colonization involved the participation of individuals who shared practices that specified marriage alliances, property rights, social obligations, inheritance, residence patterns, descent reckoning, social status, etc. (Keegan 2010). If a community was to be successful in colonizing any area, it had to replicate the social arrangements necessary for their biological, social, and political survival.

John Moore (2001) has shown that the potential for success is greatly enhanced when a colony maintains strong ties to one other community. An interesting result of his demographic computer simulations is that the success of a colony is not greatly increased by maintaining ties to more than one community. Thus, a colony with a "lifeline" (Kirch 2000) that connects it to one other community has a much greater chance of survival than does one without such ties. Colonies with multiple ties were only marginally more successful than those with only one connection. The question is, at what point do the centripetal forces that tie communities together yield to the centrifugal forces that tend to pull them apart?

In his review of the colonization of the Antilles, Peter Siegel (1991) noted that very little attention had been paid to how humans actually reached the islands. The issue of why new territories were colonized often is addressed in terms of push-or-pull models (Keegan 1985; Roe 1989). In other words, were they forced to leave the mainland (pushed), or were they attracted to the islands (pulled)? Actually, push and pull are two sides of the same coin. Being pushed or pulled reflects a cost/benefit ratio that favored the islands over the mainland. It seems obvious that the islands were attractive locations for settlement, especially for horticulturalists (Keegan, et al. 2008). All of the islands have terrestrial habitats that could easily support tropical horticulture. In addition, despite their depauperate terrestrial fauna, many have abundant marine resources that could have been exploited easily by individuals with knowledge of fishing and collecting in riverine and coastal mainland settings. In the same vein, Archaic Age societies found sufficient resources to support widespread populations for thousands of years (Veloz Maggiolo 1993).

If we accept that the islands were attractive in the resources they offered, then we next need to consider what might have prevented people from moving there at an earlier date. The main factors are transportation technology, knowledge that the islands exist, and social organization (Keegan 2004, 2010). As mentioned above, transportation does not seem to have been a major constraint. Knowledge that the islands were out there might have been influential, because one cannot see Grenada, the first major island of the Lesser Antilles. However, once Grenada was discovered, it was possible to see islands on the horizon all the way to the Virgin Islands (Sleight 1965). In fact, when the islands of the Caribbean are mapped according to viewscapes, the region takes on the appearance of a "continent divided by water" (Torres and Rodríguez Ramos 2008). The Anegada Passage in the Virgin Islands presents the only other water gap in the Antilles across which islands are not visible. Human mobility between islands, following the discovery of Grenada, was not significantly constrained by evidence for other island targets. In other words, the geographic evidence supports the notion that humans expanded northward through the Lesser Antilles to Puerto Rico. The problem is that the archaeological evidence does not fit this scenario. A possible exception is the Pearls site (Grenada), where there is one radiocarbon date of 200 BC and Huecoid pottery has been identified. However, the deposits that were excavated were jumbled during airport construction, the early date is from a level *above* a more recent date, and the only intact context comprises 5 centimeters at a depth of more than 1 meter (Hofman, personal observation, 2013; Keegan, personal observation, 1990).

Another consideration is island size. Biogeographers have proposed that large islands are superior to small islands because they present a larger target, support larger and more diverse populations of terrestrial animals, and can support larger populations over the long run (Keegan and Diamond 1987). There is a similar view in Caribbean archaeology that small islands would not be attractive to communities living on a continental mainland. Thus, the colonization of islands often is characterized as a hardship, and island societies often are portrayed as backward, or less advanced, than their mainland counterparts (Rainbird 1999; Terrell, et al. 2001). In our opinion, the issue of island size has been overstated, especially with regard to the initial colonization of an island (Keegan, et al. 2008). First, although small islands do support smaller populations of terrestrial animals, these animals were never of great importance in Caribbean diets (deFrance 2013). Second, marine animals were of far greater significance, and many small islands (e.g., Anguilla, Saba) are located on marine banks with far greater marine productivity than their larger neighbors (e.g., Hispaniola and Puerto Rico). Finally, most small, traditional villages focus their activities within a 5-kilometer catchment area (Newsom and Wing 2004; Wing and Scudder 1983). Thus any island of at least five square kilometers could meet the terrestrial needs of the initial colonists. This may explain why many Early Ceramic Age settlements are located on some of the smaller islands in the northern Caribbean. Large islands do provide the potential for more substantial long-term growth. However, we can ask whether long-term consequences were a consideration of the first to settle an island, or whether their main focus was on achieving short-term goals (e.g., Giovas and Fitzpatrick 2014).

In sum, the islands of the Caribbean form a relatively unbroken (intervisible) chain that happens to be invisible from the surrounding mainland. Once the islands were discovered, they would have been viewed as attractive places to live. All that was needed was boats to reach an island and to continue ties with the parent or related community on the mainland or another island. There are definite risks involved in establishing a new colony, especially one that is separated from its progenitor by a substantial water crossing. Of primary concern is maintaining an adequate spouse pool, which is difficult for small and isolated populations. In many ways, the major constraint to overcome was "social distance" (Keegan 1995, 2010), because it was necessary to assemble social units that could establish viable colonies.

Biogeographers and archaeologists have argued that the Lesser Antilles are a classic example of a stepping-stone archipelago in which population movement should have progressed northward island by island (Keegan and Diamond 1987). However, the first well-dated Early Ceramic Age sites in the Antilles are all located in the northern islands: Puerto Rico, Vieques, Virgin Islands, Montserrat, Antigua, and St. Martin. Radiocarbon dates from Puerto Rico and the northern Lesser Antilles indicated that these colonies were established somewhere between 800 and 200 BC (Hofman, et al. 2014). It is possible that the discovery of earlier-dated settlements in the northern islands results from the fact that most recent research has been conducted in these islands, and that they are more completely explored and dated. To some degree this once was true, but substantial investigations have been initiated in the Windward Islands over the past ten years, and no sites with comparably early dates have been identified, with the possible exception of Pearls on Grenada, where material culture remains have been found similar to those in the northern islands (Chapter 7).

The stepping-stone model suffers from critical problems. The fatal flaw is that it is contradicted completely by the archaeological evidence. The model does not fit tendencies in human fertility or in the expected patterns of expansion in a linear geography (Keegan 2010). The initial conditions that led communities to leave South America were not alleviated by emigration of a single small group, and most of the Early Ceramic Age settlements known to date are located in the northern islands. In addition, simulation studies have shown that making direct jump from South America to the Greater Antilles may have been far easier than progressing through the Lesser Antilles island by island (Callaghan 2013). Island *colonization* did not proceed solely from south to north, although the Windward Islands may have been explored prior to settlement (Siegel, et al. 2015). So far, it appears that the earliest colonies were on Puerto Rico and neighboring northern Lesser Antillean islands. Our conclusion is that there were numerous waves of migration by communities from South and Central America.

Creating Identities

The dominant culture historical framework is based on Irving Rouse's (1986) concept of island colonization. Rouse devoted his career to promoting the view that the Early Ceramic Age settlement of the Caribbean was accomplished in essentially one migration, called Saladoid, and that all subsequent "peoples and cultures" shared this common ancestry (see Siegel 1997, 2010). Rouse's position is understandable as a reaction, first to those who viewed "Taíno" as having been imported from the "high civilizations" of South America (Steward and Faron 1959, and the notion of Circum-Caribbean Chiefdoms), and second to those who claimed that every new pottery style represented a separate migration from South America (e.g., Rainey 1940; Veloz Maggiolo 1991). The result was that the Caribbean migrations were reduced to an either/or dichotomy (Rouse 1986, 1992). Either a single community settled the islands, or the islands were settled by multiple migrations. We prefer a third alternative (Figure 3.3).

A key issue for physicists is explaining why subatomic particles in some experiments act like waves and in others act like particles. The colonization of the Caribbean offers the same enigma. Migration models often are based on the movement of individual propagules (Carbone 1980; Moore 2001), yet the distributions of material culture appear as waves (Ammerman and Cavalli-Sforza 1984). We need to "vibrate" between what are viewed as two different perspectives but are in fact two expressions of the same phenomenon.

FIGURE 3.3 Faces of the Early Ceramic Age, site of Pearls, Grenada. Not to scale (courtesy of Neil and Colin Willcox, photos by Corinne Hofman and Menno Hoogland).

FIGURE 3.4 David R. Watters and James B. Petersen (on screen) excavating at the Trants site (courtesy of David Watters).

The Early Ceramic Age communities of the Caribbean were the product of unique historical circumstances within the islands and not simply transplants from the surrounding mainland. None of the migrations implanted a unique and fully developed *culture* in the islands. As Heckenberger (2002) pointed out, Saladoid and other Arawak speakers shared general cultural similarities, and the Arawak diaspora was a tsunami that spread in multiple directions and consumed all of the other societies it encountered (Santos-Granero 2002). In this regard, the diversity observed in Early Ceramic Age pottery reflects the diverse historical contributions reflected in its creation.

The general features of pottery decoration that are used to define the Early Ceramic Age occur over a wide area, from the Guiana coast to the Orinoco River floodplain, across the north coast of Venezuela and Colombia and into Central America (especially Panama and Costa Rica). No single location contains all of the characteristics observed in the Antilles. This entire area provided the nursery for island colonization, and it is likely that social units from throughout the entire region were involved in the settlement of the Lesser Antilles and eastern Greater Antilles (Hofman, et al. 2011). We must be prepared to recognize multiple (semi-) independent movements of social units that broadly shared what is defined as Arawak Culture.

During these movements, some probably settled the first island they encountered; others leapfrogged existing settlements, crossing longer water gaps and choosing islands that were more to their liking. In order to counter the risks of isolated settlements in a dispersed pattern, they must have maintained ties with at least one other community, be that the parent community or other villages encountered during their migrations. The continued expression of shared motifs on decorated pots and small personal icons of shell and stone symbolically mediated these sociocultural connections.

The islands of the Lesser Antilles were always linked to developments in South America and later to the larger islands of the Greater Antilles. The identification of Barrancoid influences in the southern Lesser Antilles, beginning about AD 200, is consistent with this view. There was always a flow of information, goods, and people through the islands. And, although some islands seem to have pursued divergent courses, the connections were nonetheless present. Cultural development in the Lesser Antilles involved the continuous flow of ideas and people between the various islands and the mainland (Hofman, et al. 2007). The information and communities that arrived on any island were somewhat different from those arriving on any other island, and the interpretation of information flows on every island reflected local circumstances.

The preceding has followed a somewhat tortuous course of logic, so we will try to summarize our ideas about island colonization during the Early Ceramic Age.

1. Arawak societies (partially represented by Saladoid pottery) dispersed across northern South America during the first millennium BC.
2. Arawak expansion on the mainland reflects a high level of mobility and the possession of watercraft that could be adapted for seagoing voyages.
3. There probably were voyages of exploration into the Greater and Lesser Antilles before permanent settlements were established.
4. Something happened in South America or in the exploration of the Antilles that caused the islands to be viewed as attractive places to live.
5. The earliest known Ceramic Age colonists settled on Puerto Rico and the northern Lesser Antilles sometime between 800 and 200 BC.
6. Given the early dates for the northern islands, it was reproductively impossible for a single propagule of colonists and their offspring to have settled every island in the Lesser Antilles in turn prior to their arrival in Puerto Rico.
7. Early Ceramic Age pottery exhibits diverse influences that cannot be traced to a single source.

The emerging portrait of the Early Ceramic Age is a mélange. The gradual movement of communities into the Antilles was likely to have been the outcome of multiple migrations incorporating multiple communities living along coastal South America by communities that shared Arawak traditions, including making pottery vessels. It is likely that the initial conditions that stimulated migration into the Antilles continued to fuel dispersal from South America, especially if the islands were viewed as attractive locations. Given the large areas of South America over which this general pottery series were shared (Rouse 1992:53; Rouse and Cruxent 1963), it is likely that a number of different autonomous communities entered the Antilles at this time, as is reflected in the diversity of styles at Early Ceramic Age sites (e.g., la Hueca site, Vieques; Hope Estate site, St. Martin; Hacienda Grande site, Puerto Rico) (Bonnissent 2008; Chanlatte Baik and Narganes Storde 1990; Haviser 1997; Hofman, et al. 2011; Rouse and Alegría 1990). These traditions continued for years as isolated communities allied themselves with others to mitigate the risks associated with widely dispersed, low-density settlement. Although these communities shared certain pottery modes, they were all distinctive.

After reaching Puerto Rico, further expansion to the west ceased. There is no conclusive evidence for Early Ceramic Age pottery ("Saladoid") in the eastern or western Dominican Republic (cf. Voss 2015). It has been suggested that further expansion was constrained by the presence of Archaic Age communities (Rouse 1992), but we presently lack an acceptable explanation. After abandoning expansion to the north and west, population growth in eastern Puerto Rico and the northern Lesser Antilles fueled dispersal toward the south into the Windward Islands (Fitzpatrick 2013; Keegan 1985). Jay Haviser (1997) suggested that expansion toward the south could account for the north-coast emphasis in settlement locations on the northern islands; however, more recent studies do not support this (Bradford 2002; Bright 2011). Internal migrations were complemented by repeated interactions with the mainland.

Trants Site, Montserrat (c. 400 BC to AD 500)

The Trants site is located on the eastern, windward shore of Montserrat adjacent to the island's airport. Montserrat is of volcanic origin, and one of its volcanoes is still very active, causing the recent abandonment of a substantial part of the island. The site is situated on the only sizeable stretch of flat terrain near sea level along the windward coast. Precipitous cliffs mark the rest of the coast. The Farm River provides a freshwater source just south of the site. The climate is tropical, with strong easterly trade winds and less than 1000 millimeters of rainfall annually. This windward side of the island supports predominantly low scrub vegetation.

David Watters and James B. Petersen investigated the site in the 1990s in anticipation of new construction at the airport (Figure 3.5). Today it is buried under meters of volcanic ash from the recent eruptions. The site had excellent stratigraphic integrity and superb preservation. The primary historic use of this land as pasture probably contributed to its integrity. There was a substantial surface scatter (prior to the recent volcanic eruptions). Detailed surface collections revealed that Trants was a large village of oval shape, approximately 275 meters (north–south) by 225 meters. Soil analyses confirmed this arrangement and defined a plaza at the center of the community (Petersen 1996).

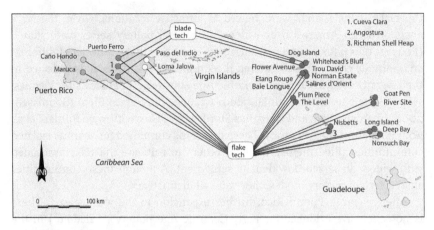

FIGURE 3.5 Dense networks of exchange in the northeastern Caribbean tied together by lithic resources (courtesy of Menno Hoogland, after Hofman et al. 2014).

Trants is one of the earliest Ceramic Age sites in the Antilles. It was settled before 400 BC and was occupied continuously for 800–900 years. As Petersen (1996) notes, it is remarkable that the community plan—an oval village with houses and middens surrounding a central plaza—was maintained for almost a millennium. Pottery was the most abundant artifact, and stylistically it is classified as Saladoid, although some Huecoid elements also were identified (Watters and Petersen 1999). The principle modes are white-on-red, black-on-red, and white-and-black-on-red painting, along with zoned incisions and zoned-incised crosshatching (Petersen 1996). Only 7.5% of the excavated pottery sample was decorated (Watters and Petersen 1999). There is little evidence for a post-Saladoid occupation at the site.

The site provides evidence of a well-developed lapidary industry. Beads and pendants made from non-local rocks and minerals are common. Diorite, carnelian, rock crystal, amethyst, aventurine, turquoise, jade group, and serpentine were recovered during excavations (Watters and Scaglion 1994). The objects made from these materials show evidence of specialized production and exchange. For example, 65% of the bead debitage and 88% of the bead blanks in the site are carnelian, but only 1.1% of the finished beads are carnelian. In contrast, complete amethyst beads are common at Trants, while amethyst debitage is rare. The Pearls site, Grenada, shows exactly the opposite distribution (i.e., amethyst debitage and finished carnelian beads were common at Pearls, while carnelian debitage and finished amethyst beads were common at Trants). In this regard, the site reflects the significance of widespread networks of exchange that served to link widely dispersed settlements (Chapter 7).

Faunal samples indicate that vertebrate remains at Trants were split almost equally between land animals and reef fishes (Reitz 1994). Oryzomyine rodents were the most common land animals. This equal abundance of terrestrial and marine animals is typical of early sites in the region. It appears to document an economy based on farming, with associated garden hunting of rodents (Linares 1976) and the exploitation of marine resources. Trants is characteristic of Early

Ceramic Age sites in the northern Lesser Antilles, including Hope Estate on St. Martin, Indian Creek on Antigua, and Tecla in Puerto Rico (Chanlatte Baik and Narganes Storde 2002; Hofman, et al. 2014; Watters and Petersen 1999).

Hacienda Grande Site, Puerto Rico (c. AD 150–500)

The Hacienda Grande site is the type-site for pottery from this time period. Located on the northeast coast of Puerto Rico about 25 kilometers east of San Juan, the site overlooks an old oxbow lake that once formed the main channel of the Río Grande de Loiza, whose present artificial channel is 1.2 kilometers west of the site. It is 1.6 kilometers from the Atlantic Ocean. The site is nestled between two hills (*mogotes*). It is close to river, beach, mangrove, lagoon, and open-sea habitats in a region of subtropical moist forest habitat (Rouse and Alegría 1990). The area is well watered and has especially fertile soil.

Ricardo Alegría and Irving Rouse were the principal investigators of the site, although other archaeologists have visited the site over the past fifty years. At least eight seasons of systematic fieldwork have been undertaken since 1948 (Bullen and Bullen 1974; Roe 1985; Rouse 1952; Rouse and Alegría 1990). In addition, the site has been extensively looted for more than fifty years. There are also earlier disturbances caused when later occupants of the site dug pits into the older deposits. The site was used in historic times for sugar cane and coconut plantations. The earliest date for the site is AD 150, which is substantially later than the earliest sites from this period, but it is one of the oldest sites in Puerto Rico. There is evidence that the site was in continuous use until AD 1700 (Bullen and Bullen 1974), but the focus here is on the early components of the site, which have been classified as the Hacienda Grande style of Saladoid, but there is again a Huecoid component (Rouse 1992).

Hacienda Grande was a medium-sized village and was the base from which the population spread into the interior along the Loiza River (Rodríguez López 1990). It measures about 200 meters (north–south) by 150 meters, with deposits reaching a depth of 110 cm (Rouse and Alegría 1990). Like most of the early sites, it is a circular to oval central place surrounded by middens (Siegel 2010). With regard to subsistence, deposits reflect an initial abundance of terrestrial animals (especially land crabs) that was replaced by a preponderance of marine species and domestic and captive animals (e.g., dogs and guinea pigs) (LeFebvre and deFrance 2014; Wing in Rouse and Alegría 1990). Human burials exhibit heavy occlusal wear of the molars of both sexes that may have resulted from sand adhering to crabs and mollusks in the diet (Mickleburgh 2013; Walker 1985). In addition, females alone exhibit a second form of dental pathology as interior wear on their incisors. Processing fibrous plant materials in the mouth may produce such wear (Crespo, et al. 2013). Axes, beads, and pendants were made of both conch shell and stone, including greenstone. Flaked-stone tools were produced using both bipolar and direct percussion (Rodríguez Ramos 2010; Walker 1985). There are small three-pointed stones (*cemís*) in the site, which are considered the precursors of larger and more elaborate *trigonoliticos* that are associated with the Late Ceramic Age (Walker 1997).

The artifact that has received the most attention is the pottery (Roe 1985; Rouse 1952, 1992; Rouse and Alegría 1990). Pottery in the Hacienda Grande style is thin, well made by coiling, and well fired. This style comprises complex vessels with straight and sharply angled profiles. Bowls tend to be open and come in hemispherical, boat, kidney, double, and turtle shapes. Flanges were applied to horizontally extend rims. Incense burners are rare but diagnostic. Thirty percent of the pottery is decorated, with a wide variety of techniques employed. These include polychrome painting (red, white, orange, and black), incision (including zoned-incised-crosshatching), modeling (including zoomorphic lugs), and handles. There was a greater freedom of expression in this style than in other styles (Roe 1989). Griddles compose a significant part of the assemblage, reflecting a change in food processing in comparison to Archaic Age communities.

With regard to pottery classification, the Early Ceramic Age has been attributed to the Arawak diaspora on the mainland, and specifically Saladoid series styles and its expansion into the Orinoco Delta and Trinidad (Rouse 1986, 1992; Rouse and Cruxent 1963). All of the modes, including decorative motifs, identified at these early sites and found in association with painted pottery, were classified as Saladoid. Pottery assemblages with a wide range of painting, incision, and other modes were termed "Cedrosan Saladoid" after the Cedros sites in Trinidad where this style was first identified (Boomert 2000; Rouse 1992). Moreover, the Saladoid series had only one subseries (Cedrosan) for decades, and most archaeologists still speak only of Saladoid.

Luis Chanlatte Baik (1981) was the first to challenge the classification of all Early Ceramic Age pottery as Saladoid. Chanlatte Baik and Yvonne Narganes Storde (1990, 2002) have excavated the site of Sorcé/la Hueca almost continuously for the past forty years. The site is located on the southwest coast of Vieques Island in the Caribbean Sea. Vieques measures about 25 kilometers long by 7 kilometers wide and 31.5 kilometers southeast of Puerto Rico. The island is hilly, particularly in its central portion, and there are numerous creeks and streams. Present environmental conditions are semi-arid, and the area of the site was used for sugar cane production and cattle ranching for hundreds of years.

The site lies on a high, flat plain overlooking the east bank of the Río Urbano, which flows into the Caribbean Sea less than 1 kilometer away. Several middens are located along the high riverbank, while others occur along several steplike ascending terraces to the west. Both groups of middens occur in horseshoe arrangements (Chanlatte Baik 1981; Narganes Storde 1995; see also Oliver 1999). Their small size, in comparison to the much larger, contemporaneous Hacienda Grande style sites, argues for a modest occupation (Roe 1989:275), although radiocarbon dates indicate that the site was occupied for a long period of time. The two components at Sorcé/la Hueca date primarily to between 200 BC and AD 200, although dates into the 17th century also have been reported (Chanlatte Baik 2013). The material assemblages of the two midden groups are completely different.

The eastern la Hueca middens are composed of unpainted pottery with the primary mode of decoration being zoned-incised-crosshatched designs (ZIC). Most vessels are small with flat bases, and some have figurative modeled motifs (e.g., a dog figure). These Huecoid vessel shapes are distinctive. Pottery griddles are present and indicate tropical forest practices of food preparation. A remarkable aspect of the site is the production of small zoomorphic pendants, including the famous raptor with a trophy skull, and beads using exotic lithics along with a few gold objects and a jaguar tooth pendant (Chanlatte Baik and Narganes Storde 2005; Boomert 2003). Isotopic analysis indicates that the jaguar lived in northwestern Venezuela (Laffoon, et al. 2014).

The western middens contain painted pottery that is classified as Cedrosan Saladoid. The pottery includes "diagnostic" bell-shaped vessels, among other forms. Decorative motifs are geometric and figurative and are executed with painting alone and with crosshatching and modeling techniques that also are often painted. Pottery griddles are common. Lithics include scrappers, cores and flakes, and shell and stone beads. However, there is no evidence of the stone ornaments that are abundant in the la Hueca middens.

Redefining the Early Ceramic Age

The Early Ceramic Age initially was classified as Saladoid, and scholars assumed that there was a single migration into the Antilles from the lower Orinoco River (Rouse 1986, 1992). The discovery of a unique material assemblage at the site of Sorcé/La Hueca called this classification into question (Chanlatte Baik 2013; Chanlatte Baik and Narganes Storde 2002). Rouse (1982) and others (e.g., Siegel 1991, 2010) argued that the Huecoid simply represented a subseries of Saladoid; although their pottery was different, they still belonged to the same cultural stock. This debate reached a standstill because the evidence from one site was not enough to address this issue fully.

This situation changed when Miguel Rodríguez Lopez (1991) discovered the Punta Candelero site in Humacao, eastern Puerto Rico. The site not only corroborated the presence of a Huecoid horizon but also added the dimension of containing Huecoid materials without any association to Hacienda Grande style deposits. It provided a case in which the Huecoid materials were found in isolation, and indicated that Huecoid represented a unique material culture and not a specialization within the Saladoid.

Reniel Rodríguez Ramos (2001, 2010) sought to clarify this question by conducting a lithic analysis of the materials from the two archaeological sites where the Huecoid manifestation was discovered. The hypothesis was that if these two shared similar cultures, then this should be most readily evident in their lithic repertoires. Diachronic lithic studies have demonstrated that stone-tool production in the Caribbean was the most conservative element of material culture through time (Knippenberg 2006). Rodríguez Ramos (2010) concluded that the lithic assemblages associated to these two cultural manifestations were sufficiently distinct to identify them as culturally independent. In other words, Huecoid and Saladoid reflect separate lithic, and by extension, cultural traditions (Figure 3.5).

A final issue concerns the temporal sequence established for the appearance of this cultural manifestation. The evidence generated, at least in Puerto Rico, shows patterns that do not seem to accord with the supposed directionality for the movement of Huecoid across the island (Rodríguez Ramos 2010). For instance, the earliest assay for this manifestation has been generated from El Convento site in northern Puerto Rico, which has been dated to 270 BC (Miguel Rodriguez López, personal communication 2003), and at Maisabel on the north central coast, there are Huecoid ceramics in a sealed stratum below the Hacienda Grande deposits (Rodríguez Ramos 2010; Siegel 1992). In comparison, the earliest dates from the La Hueca and Punta Candelero sites, both to the east, are around 170 BC. Thus, the limited evidence available thus far seems to contradict the supposed east to west movement of Huecoid along the northern coast of the island.

Furthermore, it is not clear how Rouse's (1992) taxonomic categories correspond to Chanlatte's model, in which Huecoid is identified as a distinct Agroalfarero-I Culture that was a separate, earlier migration than Saladoid, which he calls Agroalfarero-II Culture (Chanlatte Baik 1981, 2013). José Oliver (1999) has noted that a major issue in solving this "Huecoid problem" has been that the opposing models have used scales of analysis and methodological assumptions that are not necessarily comparable.

A possible explanation for La Hueca is that it reflects the continuation of pottery making from an earlier Archaic Age horizon. This explanation is consistent with the proposed movement of ceramic motifs from west to east, the emphasis on modeled and incised decorations and the exclusion of painted motifs, differences in vessel form, and the differences noted in the stone-tool assemblage. The presence of a Saladoid site close to La Hueca and dating from about the same time period would then reflect two different societies that maintained different traditions, yet lived close to each other and interacted. Rouse's (1992) framework is based on a biological classification system in which only one "species" can occupy a niche. Yet there are numerous examples from South America, New Guinea, and elsewhere in which communities with different cultural backgrounds live close to each other (Hill and Santos Granero 2002; Welsch, et al. 1990).

Morel Site, Guadeloupe (c. 400 BC to AD 1400)

The Morel site is located directly on the beach of the Atlantic coast of eastern Grande-Terre, Guadeloupe, locally known as Morel-plage (Figure 3.6). It is situated about 1 kilometer from the actual town of Moule and the Audoin River. The coastal landscape has been severely altered by human and natural

FIGURE 3.6 Excavations at the Morel site, Guadeloupe (photo by Corinne Hofman and Menno Hoogland).

interference since precolonial times. Today, the former beach is eroded, and the dunes have disappeared. The site was discovered in the 19th century but was only the subject of intensive investigations during the 1950s and 1970s (Bullen and Bullen 1973; Clerc 1964, 1968, 1970). Between 1993 and 1999, several investigations were undertaken by the Service Régional de l'Archéologie of the Direction Régionale des Affaires Culturelles (DRAC) and Leiden University under the direction of André Delpuech, Corinne Hofman, and Menno Hoogland (Delpuech, et al. 2001; Hofman, et al. 1999, 2014). The earliest component at Morel is a southern expression of mixed Huecoid and Saladoid material culture.

The context of the earlier excavated material is difficult to trace. The site is composed of settlement and midden areas. Its four components (Morel I–IV), are roughly dated 400–200 BC, and have long been used in Caribbean chronological charts to characterize the ceramic sequence for the northern part of the Lesser Antilles (Rouse 1992). A large number of features have been excavated, and these have been interpreted as post-holes, hearths, and burials. The quantity of dog burials deposited with the human burials is notable (Grouard, et al. 2013; Hoogland and Hofman 2013; Plomp 2012).

Huecoid ceramics include bowls and dishes with unrestricted simple contours, restricted simple contours, and unrestricted composite or inflected contours. The latter vessel type is typical for the Huecoid pottery and represents the body, head, and tail of an animal (creature), with an alter ego on the head. Vessels have mostly flattened rims; otherwise they are rounded or sometimes slightly tapered and thin-walled, between 4 and 7 millimeters. Surface colors are predominantly light reddish brown, yellowish red, and light yellowish brown. Most surfaces are smoothed to lightly burnished. Diagnostic decoration modes are curvilinear-incised zones. These zones may be filled with punctation or crosshatching. Other typical modes are modeled zoomorphic adornos, punctate rims, and small nubbins (Hofman and Jacobs 2000/2001; Hofman, et al. 1999).

The Morel Saladoid pottery includes painted ware and ZIC (zoned-incised crosshatched, although its execution is different from Huecoid ZIC); a variety of jars, bowls, and dishes with unrestricted simple contours; bowls with unrestricted composite contours; jars with independent restricted composite or inflected contours; and bowls with unrestricted inflected contours. The most typical vessel type of the painted ware is the inverted bell-shaped bowl with an unrestricted composite contour and a thickened rim. The inverted bell-shaped bowl is often decorated with white-on-red paint. Besides this type of bowl, boat- or kidney-shaped vessels, bottles, and jars with circular to ovoid shapes and hemispherical bowls do occur. These vessel types have rounded, inwardly thickened, or flaring rims. D-shaped and rounded handles were distinguished for the painted ware, and numerous perforated lugs were also observed.

Most of the vessel surfaces were light reddish brown to reddish brown and yellowish red, and red. In general, the greatest color intensity and contrasts were observed within this category. Some sherds are gray to dark gray or brown to dark brown. Smoothing, burnishing, and polishing were all used to finish the vessel surfaces.

Diagnostic decorative modes include bichrome white-on-red (WOR) or red-and-black painting. The painted motifs are often stylized, geometrical figures. Other modes are linear-incised lines (sometimes used to outline painted designs), simple linear incision (occasionally filled with white paint), modeled-incised animal or human heads applied on tabular lugs, and nubbins. The latter are rather large and often red-slipped. Painted pottery generally bears black soot on the interior vessel surface.

ZIC ware is characterized by hemispherical bowls and dishes with unrestricted simple or composite contours and rounded, flattened, and outflaring rims. Some vessels have perforated lugs attached to the vessel wall. Vessels have brown to grayish brown colors, and surfaces are often burnished to polished. Decorative modes include fine-line incisions and ZIC on rims and inside surfaces of the dishes and bowls. These are similar to the Pearls Inner Rim Incised category from Grenada (Bullen 1964).

The Morel site has provided numerous local and non-local rock types. Semiprecious stones were found in burials and in the midden areas. These include beads and amulets of amethyst, carnelian, serpentine, and jadeite (Knippenberg 2006). The worked shell collection is very rich as well (Lammers-Keysers 2007). Zoomorphic representations of birds and frogs are common. Two wooden amulets were recovered from the site after a hurricane in the late 1980s. These amulets were in the shape of a dog and of a jaguar (Petitjean Roget 1995, 2015). The faunal assemblage indicates a heavy reliance on reef fishes. In addition, land crabs were common in the early Saladoid middens (Grouard 2002).

The archaeological evidence strongly supports the conclusion that there are at least two distinct cultural traditions represented in the Early Ceramic Age. These have been named Saladoid and Huecoid, or AGRO-II and AGRO-I, respectively (Chanlatte Baik 2013; Rouse 1992). The pottery and lithic technologies are distinct, although they often occur in mixed contexts. Thus, these different traditions were seemingly contemporaneous. Moreover, the mixing of contexts makes it difficult to specify other characteristics that might be used to distinguish them.

The relationship between Saladoid and Huecoid assemblages is not entirely clear, although they share a common exchange network expressed through the monopolization of lithic sources and the manufacture of specific objects. Unfortunately, the tendency has been to lump everything together as "Saladoid" because Saladoid "peoples and cultures" were defined first (Rouse 1992). Our contention is that we need to take a step back and rethink the historical contingencies that created the different expressions that are now seen. The multiplicity of traditions and expressions are apparent. Nevertheless, there are recognizable patterns that transcend more localized differences.

Settlement Patterns

Early Ceramic Age sites occur on both volcanic and limestone islands in the Lesser Antilles and Puerto Rico. These islands have a tropical monsoon–type climate. The south and west coasts of the Puerto Rico and most elevations below 400 meters in the Lesser Antilles have a tropical wet and dry climate with annual rainfall over 2000 millimeters. Temperatures are relatively constant most of the year. The climate is distinguished by a dry season of four to six months during the somewhat cooler winter months. These dry periods are never entirely without rain, but they are sufficient to induce seasonal patterns in the vegetation. Paleoecological evidence indicates that up to AD 850, the climate was substantially more arid than today (Beets, et al. 2006; Higuera-Gundy 1991; Malaizé, et al. 2012). All of the islands receive strong easterly trade winds, and there are occasional tropical storms and hurricanes during the summer and fall that at times have devastating consequences.

Sites occur in both coastal and inland locations close to rivers. It was at one time believed that the earliest sites were located inland on river drainages to take advantage of prime agricultural land (Keegan and Diamond 1987). Recent studies have shown that coastal settlements are more common, though both inland and coastal locations were used simultaneously (Curet 1992; Siegel 1992). Jay Haviser (1997) noted a preference for north coast locations during the Early Ceramic Age, but Margaret Bradford (2002) has since shown that there is insufficient evidence to identify specific preferences for particular sectors on an island.

Given the relatively small size of most islands, it is often difficult to justify the designation of a site as "inland." Nevertheless, sites up to 5 kilometers from the coast are known from Grenada (la Fillete site), Antigua

(Indian Creek and Royals sites), and other islands (Bullen 1964; Murphy 1999). In Puerto Rico, there was a tendency for the earliest sites to be located on the coast and for population to expand toward the interior over time (Chapter 4). For example, in the Río Loiza drainage in Puerto Rico, the Hacienda Grande site, which is located near the coast, was the base from which population spread upstream (Rodriguez López 1990; Rouse and Alegría 1990).

Villages were relatively large at this time and were occupied continuously for centuries (Watters and Petersen 1999). They are distributed at regular intervals along the coast in Puerto Rico (Siegel 1995), and there is no evidence of site hierarchy until late in this period. Large houses occupied by extended families were arranged in oval or horseshoe-shaped villages around a central plaza (Curet 1992). In many cases, the plaza served as a cemetery (Keegan 2009; Siegel 1996). The most complete evidence for housing comes from the Golden Rock site, St. Eustatius, where eight large and six small structures dated to between AD 200 and AD 900 were excavated (Versteeg and Schinkel 1992). The large structures were circular to oval, with diameters ranging from 4.5–19 meters. Several of these have alignments of smaller posts extending from one or two sides as windscreens. These structures have been compared to the modern Amazonian *maloca*. The largest could have housed up to sixty individuals.

Golden Rock Site, St. Eustatius (c. AD 200 to AD 850)

The Golden Rock site is located at the President Roosevelt Airport on St. Eustatius. This is a volcanic island with a tropical marine climate that has a mean annual temperature of 27°C and very little daily or seasonal variation. The relative humidity averages 75%. The island receives strong easterly trade winds and abundant sunshine. Although variable, there is a drier season from January to May and a wetter season from June to December. The area of the site receives around 1100 millimeters of rainfall per year. There are presently no streams or rivers, and water must be obtained from the island's groundwater lens. The site is at the center of the island, 4 kilometers from the north and south points of the island and 1.5 kilometers from the east and west coasts. It is in the middle of a 560 hectare plain, called the Cultuurvlakte, which has easily worked, well-drained soils with good water-retention capacity. This is prime agricultural land.

Research at the site was accelerated because the site was threatened by the expansion of the airport (Versteeg and Schinkel 1992). Two middens separated by an open space characterize the site. The archaeological deposit is very shallow. The middens date from AD 200 to the 9th century, which is at the end, actually after the end, of the Saladoid on other islands. In this regard, the site is an excellent example of how pottery styles and series continued for centuries in some locations after traditional time-space systematics would have them end (cf. Rouse 1992). In quantity and weight, pottery is the most common artifact category. About 20% of the pottery is decorated with WOR painting, ZIC, and other typical Early Ceramic Age motifs and techniques. There is striking uniformity in the pottery over a long period of time.

The most remarkable aspect of the site is the well-preserved post-holes. A number of round structures between 7 and 19 meters in diameter were identified. These houses are characterized by their round shape and by strong vertical supporting posts that were deeply set in the ground. Middens were located behind the living areas. A cleared open plaza area was identified north of the houses. Eleven burials were excavated in this area. Several of the burials had grave goods, including a child's burial with eighty-one quartz beads. Also in this central area, one of the smaller structures on the site was encountered. This particular structure is unusual for its rectangular shape. Its shape and location suggest that it may have been used as a men's house.

The faunal remains and stable isotope analysis revealed an overwhelming reliance on fish. Grouper, scad, and tuna compose 75% of the faunal sample. Sea turtles are also important. Two land animals, rice rat (*Oryzomys* sp.) and agouti, are also present, the latter of which was introduced from South America. Mollusks are fairly common, with West Indian topsnail (*Cittarium pica*) the most common and queen conch relatively rare. There are numerous shell artifacts, including trumpet shell scrapers (*Charonia variegata*), conch lip celts, a fishhook, atlatl spurs, and carved pendants and beads. Coral tools and coral three-pointers are common. Lastly, *lignum vitae* and satinwood are the most ubiquitous wood types in archaeobotanical samples.

Subsistence Economy

A mixed economy of horticulture, hunting of land animals, fishing, and mollusk collecting is the characteristic pattern for the Early Ceramic Age (Keegan 1999; Newsom and Wing 2004; Petersen 1997). The presence of clay griddles is used to infer a common form of food preparation. The development of irrigation systems at the end of this period may be tied to the intensification of maize cultivation (Ortiz Aguilú, et al. 1991; Pagán Jiménez 2013). Fruits including guava, cockspur, mastic-bully, *Manilkara*, and palms; and potherbs including trianthema and primrose have been identified in archaeobotanical samples (Newsom 1993; Newsom and Wing 2004). A wide variety of other fruits, tubers/rhizomes/stems (e.g., *Zamia debilis*), and seeds (e.g., Panicum grasses) were available (Veloz Maggiolo and Ortega 1996).

The islands have a depauperate terrestrial fauna, the most important of which were a variety of small rodents (e.g., Oryzomys, hutias), birds, reptiles (iguanas, crocodiles, and turtles), land crabs, and snails (Newsom and Wing 2004; Pregill, et al. 1994; Reitz 1994; Reitz and Dukes 1995; Wing 1996). It is possible that hutias (*Geocapromys* sp.), a cat-size rodent, were domesticated along with guinea pigs (*Cavia porcellus*), and these animals were transported between islands and imported from South America (deFrance 2013; Giovas, et al. 2012; LeFebvre and deFrance 2014; Wing 1993). Other transported mammals include agouti, armadillo, and opossum (deFrance 2013; Newsom and Wing 2004). Domesticated dogs were raised and possibly eaten, although dog burials at this time suggest they were not predominantly raised for food (Plomp 2012; Sauer 1966). Marine resources were of greater importance in the diet than at other Saladoid sites. The sites contain a diversity of fish (especially parrotfish, groupers, and snappers), sea turtles, mollusks (especially queen conch), and occasional marine mammals (Wing and Wing 1995).

Stable-isotope analysis suggests that during the first half of this period, the diet was focused on terrestrial sources of protein (hutia, iguana, land crabs, freshwater fish) but that marine sources of protein became increasingly important over time (deFrance, et al. 1996; Stokes 1998). The contribution of marine foods increased throughout the culture historical sequence (Pestle 2013; Petersen 1997; Pregill, et al. 1994; Reitz 1994; Stokes 1998; Wing and Wing 1995).

Human remains indicate a strong and generally healthy population. At several sites, the skeletal population had numerous dental problems (Budinoff 1991; Coppa, et al. 1995). Caries and extreme wear of the occlusal surfaces of molars was common to men and women, and may reflect a starchy and gritty diet (Crespo, et al. 2013). Second, wear along the interiors of incisors is found only in females and may have resulted from processing vegetable fibers (Mickleburgh 2013).

Material Culture

It has been suggested that Early Ceramic Age technology was relatively simple and apparently available to everyone (Figure 3.7). Every household probably manufactured most of the articles that they used, although some individuals were probably renowned for their craftsmanship (Roe 1980). There is evidence for wood, stone, bone, and shell working, as well as lapidary work, weaving, and pottery making (Olazagasti 1997; Righter 1997). The importation of jadeite, and the sophisticated production of stone and shell beads, amulets, and pendants suggest some specialization in production and exchange (Garcia Gazco, et al. 2013; Harlow et al. 2006; Rodríguez Ramos 2010). Other activities, like canoe building, would have required individuals with a specialized knowledge of construction techniques and associated rituals (Shearn 2014; Wilbert 1976), as well as the cooperative efforts of several individuals.

The most common artifact in archaeological sites is pottery. Early Ceramic Age pottery, as described above, was made predominantly from local clays, and composed of well-made pottery vessels including complex shapes decorated with red, black, WOR, and polychrome painting; ZIC, incision, punctation; modeled and incised zoomorphic adornos; strap and loop handles (Rouse

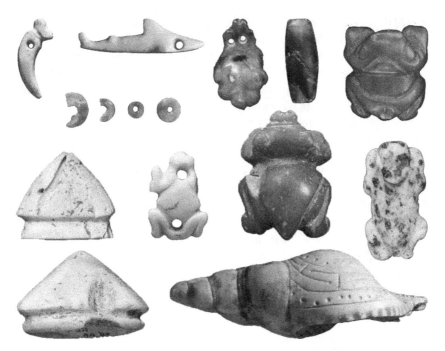

FIGURE 3.7 Shell and lithic paraphernalia from Early Ceramic Age sites in the Lesser Antilles. Not to scale (photos by Corinne Hofman and Menno Hoogland).

1992). Within the islands, there is evidence for the movement and exchange of pottery vessels, especially between volcanic and limestone islands (Fuess, et al. 1991; Gustave, et al. 1991; Hofman, et al. 2007).

Saladoid pottery is among the finest quality and most elaborately decorated pottery in the Americas. There is homogeneity of style in Saladoid pottery that is a sign of intense interaction (Hofman 1993:207); at the same time, individual artisans were free (and perhaps encouraged) to combine elements and motifs in unique ways. There is obvious repetition in complex vessel shapes and in the motifs and designs used to decorate them, yet each vessel is distinctively unique (e.g., Chanlatte Baik and Narganes Storde 2002). Moreover, even though the number of different elements was limited, individuals demonstrated enormous personal creativity and artistry in creating a vessel, while still preserving the modes of the culture (Roe 1989, 1995).

Pottery vessels also were put to secondary uses. In Barbados, the Grenadines, and Grande-Terre (Morel), stacks of Saladoid pots with their bottoms knocked out have been found in coastal swamp settings (Hofman and Hoogland 2015a). These have been interpreted as wellheads that provided access to fresh water. These wellheads may have been used to avoid salt intrusion due to rising sea levels and an increasingly arid climate (Harris and Hinds 1995; Hinds and Harris 1995). Potable water is a critical resource on some of these islands, and extraordinary efforts to maintain a water supply probably characterized particular places at certain times.

There is a wide range of tools made from a wide variety of materials. Axes and adzes were made of *Lobatus* shell and of ground and polished metamorphic rock, often greenstone. There also are flaked-stone tools made from chert, which reflect continuity with those who preceded them (Bartone and Crock 1991; Bérard 2008; Rodríguez Ramos 2010). Most of the stone tools are expedient, meaning that flakes were used after being struck from the cores and were not further shaped or retouched. Some of these chipped stones may have been set in wooden boards for grating cultigens (Berman and Pearsall 2008; Walker 1993). Stingray-spine projectiles and shell atlatl spurs indicate that spears and arrows were used. Bone needles may have been used to sew cloth or make fishing nets. Shell and bone fishhooks are present but not common. Gourd containers and woven baskets were used. Clamshell scrapers, along with hammers, picks, net gauges, and gouges/hoes made from *Lobatus* and other gastropod shells are common (Lammers-Keysers 2007; Serrand 2001a). Canoe paddles, seats, and mortars were made of wood, and wooden amulets were recovered from the Morel site (Petitjean Roget 1995). A wide variety of corals was used as abraders, rasps, and drills (Kelly and van Gijn 2008). In sum, the Early Ceramic Age expresses a sophisticated technology that utilized all of the various materials that were available in their environment. The technological aspects of their lifeways are now being studied in detail.

There was an active and sophisticated lapidary industry utilizing exotic raw materials such as amethyst, carnelian, quartz, aventurine, serpentine, and jadeite in the manufacture of small amulets and beads (Boomert 2000; Holdren 1998; Watters 1997). Beads and other ornaments were also made of *Lobatus* shell and mother of pearl (Chanlatte Baik and Narganes Storde 1990). The lapidary industry is evidence of extensive trade within the islands and between the islands and South America (Serrand 2001b; Watters and Scaglion 1994). Rocks obtained from the mainland were used to make polished petaloid celts, and cherts from a few sources in the Lesser Antilles (e.g., Antigua and St. Martin) were traded over extensive areas (Knippenberg 1999, 2006; Rodríguez Ramos 2013).

The best evidence for extensive trade is the similarities in ceramic assemblages throughout the region during this period. Connections with South America are prominent in the appearance of Barrancoid influences between AD 350 and 500 (Boomert 2000). Barrancoid series pottery supplanted the Saladoid pottery that preceded it in South America, although connections were maintained with the communities that were established in the Caribbean. Toward the end of this period, connections with South America were less pronounced in the northern islands as local styles became more distinctive (Curet 1996, 1997; Hofman 2013).

Sociopolitical Organization

The Saladoid is inferred to reflect a tribal-based organization that has been described as egalitarian (Curet 1992, 1996; Siegel 1992). However, the notion that Saladoid communities were egalitarian has been questioned (Petersen, et al. 2004), and Heckenberger (2002) has suggested that there already was a well-developed social hierarchy before the islands were colonized. Because they lived in relatively large, independent villages, it is likely that one lineage in each village occupied a superior position. At the time of European encounters, there is evidence that the indigenous communities practiced matrilineal descent and matrilocal and avunculocal residence (Keegan, et al. 1998). For these practices to emerge, the Saladoid communities also must have been preferentially matrilineal, even though heritable property and offices were limited (Keegan 1997). This form of social organization is common for other major episodes of population expansion among, for example, the Bantu in Africa and Austronesians in the Pacific (e.g., Divale 1974; Jordan, et al. 2009). Residence patterns probably were matrilocal, but during periods of high residential mobility, they certainly were flexible.

Villages were built around a central plaza where quotidian activities and communal rituals could have taken place. The small size and wide distribution of ritual objects suggests a more personal and less communal character to these ceremonies (Curet 1992). At some sites, the central plazas were carefully planned burial grounds with hundreds of interments and few overlapping burials (Crespo-Torres 2000; Curet and Oliver 1998; Keegan 2009; Siegel 1997). There is no fixed pattern to the orientation of burials, although two-thirds of those at the Punta Candelero site, eastern Puerto Rico, faced east (Rodríguez López 1997). There are few grave goods with any of the burials, and those that occur are not spectacular. The artifacts are mostly personal possessions of the dead that seem highly selective. Grave goods include artifacts for communicating with the spirits, such as manioc beer bottles and nostril bowls for inhaling a narcotic snuff, food for use in the spirit world, and stone necklaces that may reflect personal status (Righter, et al. 1995). At the Maisabel site, one individual was found with a stingray spine projectile point between his ribs, which was interpreted as evidence for raiding or warfare (Siegel 1992).

Saladoid burials in the central plaza in Puerto Rican sites have been explained as evidence for ancestor worship (Siegel 1992, 1997). It is assumed that these individuals lived in the community in which they were buried, and that by burying them in a central place, they could be kept present in spirit, especially during the rituals and ceremonies that were held in this public space. Thus, the living members of the community could look to the ancestors for supernatural intervention and maintain spiritual ties to those who lived before them.

The notion that central-place burials reflect immediate access to revered ancestors as part of a system of ancestor worship seems so logical that it has passed from hypothesis to fact. The image of the central plaza as the *axis mundi* represented as a tree that ties the underworld, where the ancestors are buried, to the land of the living and the sky world of the spirits is a compelling image (Siegel 1997). Yet there remains the issue of why the Puerto Rican Saladoid adopted the practice of central-place burials, and what this practice meant in terms of the social organization of their communities. Although ancestor worship remains a viable hypothesis, there are alternatives.

The social implications of circular villages merit closer scrutiny. Michael Heckenberger (2002) has proposed that circular villages were part of the Arawak mindset, a *habitus*, if you will. He suggests that this community plan developed in South America at an early date and then spread to the Caribbean during the Saladoid colonization of the islands. Bradley Ensor has proposed a more detailed explanation for circular villages. Ensor (2003) notes that this community plan often is associated with societies that used Crow/Omaha kinship terms (also see Ensor 2013b, 2013c). The use of such kinship terminology is consistent with the identification of matrilineal and matrilocal patterns of residence and descent proposed for the Saladoid colonists (Keegan and Maclachlan 1989). Finally, there are no cross-cultural examples of ancestor worship in egalitarian societies.

An alternative to ancestor worship is that individuals who lived their adult lives in other communities were returned to their natal or clan community for burial. In an unpublished paper (n.d., cited with permission of the authors), Paula G. Rubel and Abraham Rosman note that:

> Archaeologists considering the question of the social structure ... have dealt with the relationship between mortuary practices and societal definitions of the social person, as well as the relationship between mortuary practices and the rank system (Saxe 1970). Thus far they have not usually been able to deal with the question of descent. (cf. Hodder 1979)

In societies that practice exogamy, every community is composed of natal residents and in-marrying spouses. One result is that individuals who trace descent to the same apical ancestor are widely scattered among different communities. Rubel and Rosman (n.d.) note that individuals often are returned to their natal or clan village for burial in societies that practice patrilineal, matrilineal, or cognatic descent reckoning. Although the conditions under which an individual would be returned to their natal or clan community for burial have not been formalized, one measure seems to be the degree to which an individual was incorporated into the clan of their postmarital residence. From the examples given by Rubel and Rosman (n.d.), it appears that men are more often returned to their natal village, and that women, especially those who contribute offspring to their new community, are less likely to be returned after death.

An interesting case concerns avunculocal residence, which Keegan and his colleagues have suggested for the precolonial Caribbean (Keegan and Maclachlan 1989; Keegan, et al. 1998). Rubel and Rosman (n.d.) note:

> [A]vunculocal post-marital residence results in a situation in which a woman is usually born in her father's village (among his clansmen), on marriage moves to the village of her husband and his matri-kin, and at death is carried to the cemetery of her own clan. Throughout her life, she never resides in the village of her own clan. Only in death is she surrounded by her own clansmen.

In sum, the main issue is the connection between postmarital residence and where spouses are buried. It cannot be assumed that the individuals buried in a community were lifelong residents of that community. The possibility that individuals who lived elsewhere during their married life were returned to their natal or clan village for burial—"post-mortem mobility"—must be considered (Keegan 2009).

Cosmology

The representation of South American flora and fauna on pottery vessels suggests that a mythological connection was maintained with the mainland at this time (Roe 1995b). At the onset of this period, dogs (*Canis familiaris*) are found buried among the deceased humans (Figure 3.8) (Grouard 2001; Grouard, et al. 2013; Hofman and Hoogland 2004; Hoogland and Hofman 2013; Plomp 2012; Roe 1995a). The dogs, all but two adult specimens, were buried with their legs pulled together as if they were tied with a rope. The crania of some of these dogs had been removed, and one dog was buried with four shell beads around the neck and another had a *Lobatus gigas* shell on the pelvis (Grouard 2001; Hoogland and Hofman 2013; Plomp 2012). Similar mortuary practices for dogs are known from the Huecoid sites of Sorcé/la Hueca on Vieques, and Punta Candelero on Puerto Rico (Roe 1995a; Wing 2008:380). Variation in mortuary practices seems to increase during the later phase of the Saladoid. An important break from earlier times is that dogs seem no longer to be part

FIGURE 3.8 Dog burial from the Morel site, Guadeloupe, circa AD 200–400 (photo by Tom Hamburg, courtesy by Corinne Hofman and Menno Hoogland).

of the burial population. However, skeletal remains of dogs, including parts of the skull and jaw, are documented from the midden at Golden Rock (van der Klift 1992:75, 78). Sites on St. Martin and Guadeloupe also have yielded the skeletal remains of dogs in midden areas, particularly dog teeth, which were sometimes perforated for use as amulets (Grouard 2001; Hoogland and Hofman 2013). Peter Roe (1995a) has suggested that dogs replaced jaguars in the mythology as a form of mythic substitution (i.e., because jaguars did not live in the islands).

The most ubiquitous and widespread ornaments are very small stone and shell amulets and beads. Their size and distribution argue for household versus communal ritual use, while their repetitive character reflects a complex iconographic symbolism (Curet 1996; Roe 1995b). Small three-pointed "stones" (some are made of conch shell) make their appearance at this time. Based on Spanish writings, these commonly are associated with the cult of the *cemí*, and in particular with the deity called *Yocahu* (McGinnis 1997; Oliver 2009; Walker 1997). Although the connection between Spanish observations and objects manufactured 1,500 years earlier is tenuous at best, it has been suggested that these objects originated early in the colonization of the islands and then evolved over time. Bowls with nostril tubes for inhaling narcotics, small biomorphic dishes for inhaling snuff, bottles used as alcohol containers, and incised cylinders used as incense burners are widespread. These reflect the use of narcotics to communicate with the supernatural. The continuing importance of inhaling bowls may be reflected in their curation as heirlooms (Fitzpatrick, et al. 2009).

One also sees the first appearance of petroglyph sites (Figure 3.9), like Trois-Rivières, Guadeloupe (Hofman and Hoogland 2004). The significance of petroglyphs and cult sites at this time may point to a redefinition of public or communal gatherings at fixed locations. It is possible that the shamans as mediators with spiritual beings increased their power by gradually reinforcing their leadership during communal ceremonies (Hofman and Hoogland 2004). The large number of amulets portraying predators and prey as alter egos, and snuffing vessels laden with symbols and imagery of mythical creatures, indicates the importance of ceremonial performances and emphasizes the crucial role of the religious leader within these early horticultural societies (see also Siegel 1996, 2010).

Conclusions

Among the most common artifacts in Saladoid sites are small clay zoomorphic faces that adorned the sides of pottery vessels. These "adornos" are emblematic of the Early Ceramic Age. Looked at one way, different adornos can look remarkably alike, even if they come from different islands. Yet, turn each adorno and take a different perspective, and you see subtle and sometimes

FIGURE 3.9 Petroglyphs from the Trois-Rivières site, Guadeloupe (photos by Corinne Hofman and Menno Hoogland).

striking differences. The Early Ceramic Age is much the same. A great deal depends on one's perspective.

The initial perspective focused on tracing the ancestry of the "Taíno, the people who greeted Columbus" (Rouse 1992). The distribution of pottery with "Saladoid" motifs was plotted from Puerto Rico back to northeastern South America and the Orinoco River, and later pottery styles were all linked to this Saladoid tradition. As new sites that presented different types of data were found, the process resembled the piecing together of a jigsaw puzzle. Research at Maisabel in Puerto Rico indicated that villages were circular, houses at the Golden Rock became the archetype for structures, faunal analysis at Trants came to represent Saladoid diet, and so forth. The general perspective was one of a homogeneous culture stretching from South America to the heart of the Caribbean. We have repeated these generalizations because that is the information available to us, but we anticipate that ongoing research will produce more robust perspectives.

The first assault on that perspective came from Luis Chanlatte Baik. Although it has taken twenty years for the implications of his discoveries at la Hueca to be appreciated, Caribbean archaeologists have finally begun to look at the diversity that is evident in Early Ceramic Age societies. The notion of a single Saladoid migration has been challenged, local interaction spheres have been identified, variations in subsistence remains are now recognized, and a more sophisticated consideration of settlement patterns has been initiated. In sum, the idea that there was only one Saladoid Culture has been discarded, although some archaeologists still cling to the old ways.

As more and more data become available, the general similarities in Saladoid material culture are now far outweighed by the differences between sites and islands. The similarities that remain can be described as a veneer; a thin layer that, when viewed from one perspective, masks the underlying variability (Keegan 2004). It is like the plastic coating on particleboard furniture that makes chips of wood that are glued together look like real oak cabinets. Yet there is a good reason for this veneer. Saladoid communities colonized islands that are aligned across 2,500 kilometers of the southern North Atlantic and Caribbean Sea. The economic, demographic, and social risks inherent in island colonization promoted the need for regional integration. The sharing of pottery decorations and other items of material culture reflects similar ways of adapting to similar island settings, but more importantly, it reflects the expression of shared needs. Communities on widely scattered islands needed each other, and they displayed their allegiance in their iconography. Their highly decorated pots were the "uniform" they wore so that all could see they belonged to an extended social group.

The shift from viewing Saladoid Culture as simply the precursor to a "Taíno" Culture has profound implications; implications that are only now being recognized. Population expansion during the Saladoid does not reflect the migration of one community from South America. The islands were not settled in turn, but instead reflect a complex pattern of settlement and perhaps even abandonment. Diets reflect differences between the resources available on different islands and the waters surrounding them, and probably reflect local concepts of what constituted a proper meal. Exchange networks linked islands and mainland(s) in different ways (Hofman, et al. 2007; Hofman and Hoogland 2011; Laffoon, et al. 2015). Shell tools were not made and used because stone was not available as a raw material for tool manufacture; both shell and stone were used simultaneously. In sum, the Early Ceramic Age communities, the "peoples and cultures" called Saladoid, had a thousand-year history. We are just beginning to write their story.

| Post-Saladoid Puerto Rico

PUERTO RICO MERITS SEPARATE attention for several reasons. First, there is a long history of systematic research by local professionals as part of a national-identity movement that recognizes the indigenous inhabitants as one of the three social, cultural, and biological pillars of modern society (Laguer Díaz 2013). Second, as a U.S. territory, the island has attracted archaeologists from the United States, especially because federal Cultural Resource Management regulations apply to all federally funded projects. The U.S. Navy and the Army Corps of Engineers have sponsored numerous, large-scale federally funded projects. Third, and perhaps most important, Irving Rouse identified Puerto Rico as *the* nexus for cultural development in the islands during the Ceramic Age (Rouse 1992). Therefore, the evolution of the "Taíno" has been written as the history of cultural developments on the island (Siegel 2010). Many of these studies have taken the Spanish sources as their starting point and then tried to fit the archaeological record to the documentary evidence (Curet and Stringer 2010; Oliver 2009; Siegel 2010).

In this chapter, we largely ignore the written history and adopt a more pro-gressive approach. By viewing cultural developments as expressions of local accommodations, we offer interpretations that are free of Spanish tyranny (Maclachlan and Keegan 1990). In this regard, we demonstrate that the archae-ology of Puerto Rico is fascinating in its own right.

Dispersion (c. AD 500–900)

Beginning around AD 500, there were sweeping cultural changes throughout the Caribbean and extending through the rest of the Americas. These changes culminated in more recognizable patterns that stabilized around AD 900. The timing of changes in specific locations varied, because this was a period of transformations at varying scales. Thus it is impossible to assign particular patterns to a single date. For example, the Saladoid veneer began to disap-pear in Puerto Rico around AD 500, although it persisted for several centuries in some locations (e.g., Culebra, a small island off the east coast of Puerto

Rico, see Oliver 1995; eastern Puerto Rico, see Carlson and Torres 2011; Virgin Islands, see Lundberg 1991). What followed is best described as a metamorphosis; a complete transformation emerging from internal contradictions.

Contributing to this transformation were significant changes in climate that occurred between AD 800 and 1000 (Beets, et al. 2006; Cooper 2013; Malaizé, et al. 2011), with the earlier date marking the onset of a significantly drier climate that culminated in a long and severe drought. The island's population also was increasing (Curet 2005), which put growing demands on local resources. The bottom line is that drier conditions beyond human control differentially affected environmental productivity. At the same time, a growing population needed to capture more resources. It is not our contention that climate change or population growth caused cultures to change in particular ways. We are simply establishing initial conditions. We next turn to the archaeological evidence to explore how communities at different times and in different locations acted to ameliorate the effects of climate change and accommodate, and even promote, a growing population.

Crab/Shell Dichotomy

The first significant change has been called the "Crab/Shell dichotomy." It was first proposed by Froelich Rainey (1940) following excavation of the Cañas site in south-central Puerto Rico. The upper levels of the site contained pottery that lacked the elaborate vessel shapes and decorations that characterize Saladoid pottery and were instead primarily undecorated, boat-shaped and hemispherical bowls with red slip. This pottery was associated with substantial quantities of marine mollusks. Beneath levels with this Ostiones-style pottery there was a sterile layer below, beneath which he encountered Saladoid pottery in association with substantial numbers of land crab claws. The differences between these deposits were so dramatic that Rainey (1940) suggested that the Saladoid should be called the "Crab Culture" and the Ostionoid the "Shell Culture."

The association of crabs with Saladoid pottery and marine shells with Ostiones pottery is found throughout Puerto Rico and at Saladoid sites in the Lesser Antilles. However, because the inhabitants of the Lesser Antilles did not adopt Ostiones-style pottery, this issue is largely confined to Puerto Rico. There has since been a great deal of debate concerning what this Crab/Shell dichotomy means in terms of cultural development (see Rodríguez Ramos 2005).

Victor Carbone (1980) proposed an ecological explanation for this phenomenon. He suggested that changes in climate resulted in drier conditions that reduced the habitat for land crabs and limited their availability. In concert with climate change, he also proposed, the archaeologically identified decline in land crabs reflected overexploitation. In short, he concluded that increasing arid conditions limited the spatial distribution of land crab habitat, and continued human predation of smaller, more restricted populations of land crabs resulted in overexploitation that contributed to their extirpation. Carbone (1980) suggested that nature and culture were both contributing factors. However, mollusks were not completely absent from Saladoid sites, and crabs were not completely absent from Ostiones sites. The issue is one of relative abundance. The frequency of mollusks increased at sites dated to the late Saladoid, as represented by Cuevas-style pottery (Rouse 1992), and the shift from crabs to mollusks was not simultaneous across the island. If climate change was the prime mover, then we would expect the shift to happen at the same time everywhere. It does not.

Archaeologists also toyed with the idea that the early Saladoid sites were located inland along river terraces and that their initial diet reflected an orientation toward the land. The shift to marine resources was viewed as the outcome of adaptation to island life, an adaptation that apparently required a millennium. Yet Saladoid sites are strategically located along the coast of Puerto Rico, and the major post-Saladoid shift was a dramatic increase in inland settlements. Even the effort to explain these changes using optimal foraging theory (Keegan 1989b) added little more than obfuscation.

Returning to initial conditions, we know that land crabs and marine mollusks were both available at the same time. There probably were fluctuations in their availability, seasonally and over longer time scales, but access does not appear to be the issue. Furthermore, environmental factors, processes of adaptation, and even diet breadth and patch selection do not provide satisfactory answers to this seemingly spectacular change in diet. The obvious solution is that Saladoid communities preferred land crabs, Ostiones communities preferred marine mollusks, and each disdained the other (Keegan 2006b).

A Plethora of Pottery Styles

Based on the clear stratigraphic separation of the two components at Cañas, Rainey (1940) concluded that they represented two distinct cultures—the implication being that Ostiones represented a new migration into Puerto Rico. The problem with this scenario is that there was no obvious source for such a migration, and Ostiones-style ceramics were found in association with Saladoid ceramics at other sites. Thus it was concluded that Ostiones was the local offspring of Saladoid. This conclusion has been generally accepted, with only a few dissenting voices (Keegan 2006b; Rodríguez Ramos 2010). As will be made clear in the next chapter, we suggest that Ostionoid pottery developed from interactions in the eastern Dominican Republic.

The Saladoid were not the only inhabitants of Puerto Rico. Archaic Age communities preceded their arrival and survived on the island until at least AD 200 (Rodríguez Ramos 2010; Rouse and Alegría 2010). Marine mollusks were a major component of the Archaic Age diet, while land crabs were eaten at a much lower frequency (Goodwin 1979; Newsom and Wing 2004). In addition to diet, Rodríguez Ramos (2005) has demonstrated close affinities between the lithic tools that compose Archaic Age and Ostiones assemblages. Saladoid lithics are dissimilar and based on alternative flaking techniques. The evidence suggests that Rainey's Shell Culture was indeed a distinct Culture. Moreover, this Culture maintained its traditional reliance on marine mollusks and flaked- and ground-stone tools, to which was added an increased reliance on pottery vessels.

This combination of pottery style, emphasis on marine mollusks, and stone tool industry suggests that Archaic Age traditions reflect indigenous transfor- mations that occurred in concert with the arrival of Saladoid colonists. Sites with Ostiones-style pottery appear in Hispaniola, Jamaica, and the Turks & Caicos Islands around AD 600–700 (Keegan 1996b; Hofman, et al. 2008; Ulloa Hung 2013), simultaneously with their appearance in Puerto Rico (Rodríguez Ramos, et al. 2013; Siegel 2010). It is hard to imagine that the Ostiones style originated in Puerto Rico and then spread across the northern Greater Antilles in such a short time. It is more likely that Ostiones in Puerto Rico reflects human mobility and/or the movement of goods and ideas from Hispaniola into Puerto Rico.

Keegan (2004) has described the Saladoid expression as a "veneer." This veneer expressed a shared identity among communities. It is a material mani- festation of a "lifeline," a shared expression of beliefs that fostered coopera- tion during the risky period of island colonization known as the "beachhead bottleneck" (Keegan and Diamond 1987). During the initial phase of island colonization, when populations were small and widely scattered, there were compelling reasons to maintain long-distance relations for access to spouses and other limited resources (e.g., specific lithic raw materials), and to miti- gate the impacts of local disasters. The significance of these needs declined as populations grew and communities settled in and adjusted to the particu- lar conditions on each island. The result was the abandonment of a regional iconography expressed in ceramics, and the emergence of local pottery styles (Hofman 1993). Local styles were always present, but archaeological investi- gations have focused on the relatively narrow range of diagnostic decorative modes used to identify Saladoid (Bérard 2013).

A component of this transformation may have been a change in the ways shared identity was expressed. It is possible that a widely shared world-view continued, with the media of expression changing from pottery to lithics (Roe 2009). After the Saladoid in Puerto Rico, there is much greater empha- sis on petroglyphs, pictographs, and stone sculpture (Hayward, et al. 2009; Hayward, et al. 2013). This change may reflect the influence of Archaic Age communities who had a much stronger reliance on stone objects, includ- ing incised and punctate decorations on stone bowls and axe-shaped objects (Rouse 1992:97–98).

The changes in regional pottery styles and the shift away from Saladoid vessel shapes and motifs reflect a significant transition in Puerto Rico at this time. Whether this transformation was the result of population growth, the influence of new immigrants from Hispaniola, an increasing expression of local identities, an evolved adaptation to island life, a change in the material representation of beliefs, the adoption of a new world-view, and/or other factors remains to be demonstrated. The detailed investigation of these possible explanations has been hampered by a focus on continuity. This emphasis on similarity has blinded us to the reality of diversity (Hofman and Bright 2010; Hofman, et al. 2010; Keegan 2004; Wilson 2007).

In addition to Ostiones, researchers have identified Monserrate and Santa Elena pottery styles for the initial post-Saladoid in Puerto Rico, along with a continuation of earlier Cuevas style and possibly even La Hueca style (Chanlatte Baik 2013; Rodriguez Ramos, et al. 2008; Roe, et al. 1990). The tendency has been to lump these styles into an overarching series called "Ostionoid." This taxonomic device creates an uninterrupted linear trajectory to the culture history that begins as Saladoid and then continues unabated as Ostionoid (Rouse 1992; Siegel 2010). In this view, the transformation becomes simply a natural stage of cultural evolution. However, this is *the* case where we need to "avoid the –oid" (Keegan 2001), and look more closely at local developments to understand the mechanisms, processes, and patterns of culture change. For instance, Lisabeth Carlson and Joshua Torres (2008:333): "What is shown at AR-39 is that Ostiones-style bowls appear early in this location and persist concurrently with Cuevas based forms, which is contrary to typically conceived notions regarding rapid replacement of earlier forms of material culture with newer developments across the Greater Antilles (Rouse 1992)."

The most important styles at this time have the following characteristics:

La Hueca style (*c.* 800–200 BC to AD 400) is named for the site on Vieques Island off the east coast of Puerto Rico, and it has been observed elsewhere in Puerto Rico and the Lesser Antilles. The style was described in the previous chapter. Very late dates have been obtained from the La Hueca site (AD 1540); these are not generally accepted, but if they are correct, then this style has an inordinately long time span (Chanlatte Baik 2013:177–178).

Cuevas style (*c.* AD 400–1000) is named for the Cuevas site located 11 kilometers upriver along the Río de Loíza on the north coast (Rouse 1952). The most common vessel form is open bowls (~60%–80% at these sites), including inverted bell shapes common in Saladoid, constricted bowls with graceful carinations (~20%), and oval shapes similar to Ostiones boat-shaped vessels (Carlson and Torres 2008:289–290). Vessel bases are mostly flat, but round, concave, annular, and pedestal forms also occur. Handles and tabular lugs, including semi-lunate shapes and simple points, rise above the rim on opposite sides of round and oval vessels. Thick and heavy D-shaped strap handles are found on large, round, cooking or storage vessels. Griddles are a small percentage of the assemblage. The vessels have been described as "plain," "graceful," and "drab" (Rouse 1952:336–338). Their thin walls (~5–6 mm), finely tempered paste, gracile execution, and "light brown to ivory with a chocolate tinge" coloration convey a simple elegance. The main form of decoration is red paint, executed in circles, semicircles, horizontal and vertical stripes, and spirals. Cuevas is found at sites across all of Puerto

Rico (Carlson 2008:Fig 2.2). Cuevas pottery is classified as late Saladoid, and elements of Cuevas pottery may have crossed the Mona Passage to the Dominican Republic.

Ostiones style (*c.* AD 600–1200) was first identified at the Cabo Rojo site near Punta Ostiones in southwestern Puerto Rico (Rainey 1940; Rouse 1992:95–96). It is characterized by thin, hard, and smooth vessels that are largely undecorated except for red painting, red slip, and black smudging. Simple modeled lugs and geometric figures on vessel walls are uncommon but increase in frequency and complexity over time. Later, "modified Ostiones" pottery is primarily red with entirely geometric incised designs, most commonly executed as vertical, oblique, and horizontal parallel lines (Rouse 1952:342). Vessel shapes are typically straight-sided open bowls and navicular (boat-shaped) vessels with loop handles that rise above the rim on either end. Christopher Espenshade (2000) has identified ten different vessel types based on size and shape. From the beginning, there is an obvious division between "redware" (finely made vessels) and "crudeware" (Goodwin and Walker 1975), although all of the pottery became thicker and coarser over time. The style is found throughout Puerto Rico after AD 900. It is the predominant style on the western half of the island, and it blends with Santa Elena–style pottery on the south coast near Ponce (Torres 2013).

Monserrate style (*c.* AD 600–1000) is named for the site on the northeast coast near Luquillo Beach. It is considered the equivalent of pure Ostiones for the eastern half of the island. In contrast to Ostiones, Monserrate is characterized by thicker, coarser, and rougher simple vessel shapes with outcurving sides. "Vessel shapes consist of relatively open hemispherical or globular bowls and a high percentage of boat-shaped vessels with strap handles" (Carlson and Cordell 2011:171). Most of the pottery is plain, but red-painted and red-slipped exterior surfaces, as well as black, negative resist, and smudging occur (Curet 2005:20–21). Tabular lugs and strap handles also are common, and incisions are rare or absent. This style has received the least attention to date (but see Gutiérrez and Rodríguez 2009). It was not described in Rouse's (1952) initial description of styles, and it serves mostly as a transitional phase between Saladoid and Santa Elena. Its absence from the initial classification scheme may be due to its greater prominence in the Virgin Islands and its movement westward into Puerto Rico.

Santa Elena style (*c.* AD 900–1200) is eponymously named for a site on the north-central part of the island inland from Toa Baja. It can be characterized as "evolved Monserrate," and it shows the continued practice of making vessels with simple shapes that are thick, coarse, and rough (Curet 2005:21–22). It resembles pottery from the Virgin Islands and is the thickest pottery in Puerto Rico, ranging from 8–16 millimeters (Rouse 1952). The primary shape is the well-rounded, simple hemispherical bowl that is strongly convex and shoulderless. Most of the bases are flat. The surfaces are unpolished, and there is some restricted red painting. Rim points, ovoid and rectangular lugs, and strap handles are present. Decorations are simple and executed in appliqué or molded, with incision and punctation filling spaces. Incision is executed as horizontal and vertical parallel lines.

Population Growth and Settlement Patterns

This period is characterized by rapid population growth and the expansion of the population into the interior (Figure 4.1). There is a continuation of the Saladoid practice of establishing sites along riverbanks near the coast, but upriver sites begin to appear at the base of the limestone foothills (*mogotes*) and in the central valleys (Curet 2005:19). The coastal Saladoid (Maisabel) and Huecoid (Punta Candelero) have Cuevas and early Ostiones components, with these later styles mixed at Punta Ostiones, Monserrate, Collores, Cuevas, Rio Tanamá 2, and others. When they were first discovered, many of these sites had mounded middens as visible components of their topography. These middens reflect the roughly circular arrangement of large villages with central plazas and communal houses (Curet 2005). As Lisabeth Carlson (2008:20) notes: "Cuevas sites present a continuation of Saladoid culture, however that culture appears to be transforming, and this is expressed in the simplification of the material culture style."

An excellent example of early Ostiones sites is the early upriver settlement of Río Tanamá 2. One reason we chose this site for discussion is that its neighbor, Río Tanamá 1, embodies the transformation in community layout that will be addressed later in this chapter. Thanks to this, we are able to control for environmental factors and benefit from Carlson's (2008) wisdom in the excavation of both sites.

Rio Tanamá 2 Site (c. cal. AD 350–890)

The Río Tanamá 2 site (AR-39) is located 11 kilometers from the coast and about 1.5 kilometers upstream from the confluence of the Río Tanamá and the Río Grande de Arecibo, at the foot of the limestone hills known locally as *mogotes*. It is located on a level floodplain that is today subject to periodic flooding. For this reason, the area was targeted for the construction of a levee by the U.S. Army Corps of Engineers (USACE). Lisabeth Carlson (2008) directed a phase III mitigation that was limited to the USACE easement.

The entire area was once planted in sugar cane (Tosteson 2008). Phase II excavations conducted by hand revealed that the plow zone was completely disturbed, so the site was mechanically stripped in 2-centimeter levels to a depth of 25 centimeters during Phase III excavations. Approximately 1,500 square meters were stripped, with diagnostic artifacts recovered during stripping and all features noted during hand cleaning (Carlson 2008:57). Plow scars and canal features at the base of the excavations document the extent of historic disturbance.

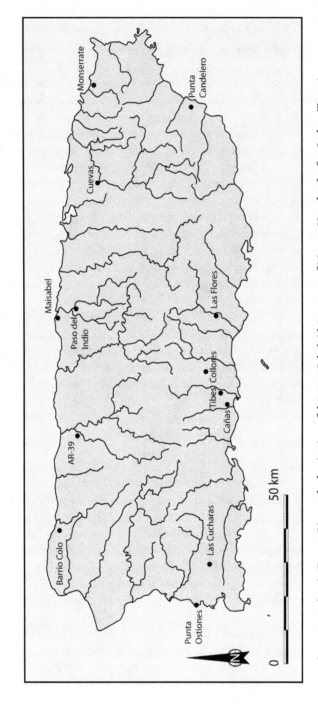

FIGURE 4.1 Important sites in Puerto Rico at the beginning of the post-Saladoid (courtesy of Menno Hoogland, after Joshua Torres).

The excavations revealed a nonlinear configuration of four discrete middens. Post stains were observed, but no patterns were detected. A central plaza was not apparent, but the absence of a plaza and post-stain patterning may be due to the limits of the excavation. The available evidence does suggest that the site layout was similar to others from the same time period.

Of special note is a large borrow pit (feature 13) measuring 11 by 14 meters with an irregular depth and up-sloping edges (Carlson 2008:105–117). It is a conglomeration of several depressions that were dug in at least two phases and then filled with refuse and meta-volcanic cobbles (Figure 4.2). This feature is unique in that the deposits are below ground, unlike the mounded middens more typical of this and other sites. Carlson suggests that the pit was dug to obtain soil for the construction of mounds that were used to raise structures above the level of the floodplain. Although such house mounds have long since disappeared, their construction would have been justified by the very wet conditions at the site. In addition, two very large post stains (50 cm in diameter) were found 50 centimeters northeast of feature 13. In profile, they had a depth of only 25 centimeters, which is far too shallow for a post of this size.

After removal of the soil, the next stage involved depositing river cobbles and trash in the open pit. River cobbles are concentrated at the bottom of the pit, which probably reflects efforts to enhance its drainage. Beyond drainage, Reniel Rodríguez Ramos (2008) found that some of the cobbles had a single flake removed, indicating that they were being tested for their suitability in manufacturing flaked-stone tools. Furthermore, filling the pit with trash and

FIGURE 4.2 Large pit feature at Río Tanamá 2 site, Arecibo, Puerto Rico (courtesy of Lisabeth Carlson).

organic debris most likely involved much more than simple garbage disposal. The pit is very similar to a form of composting to enhance soil fertility that is still practiced on the island (Rodríguez Ramos 2013).

Eight one-by-one–meter units were excavated by hand across the feature. These provided an *in situ* record of pottery, lithics, fauna, botanicals, and two partial human burials. Six radiocarbon dates provide a two-sigma range of cal. AD 350–880. The four dates from feature 13 indicate that it was used throughout the occupation of the site. The uppermost surfaces of the site that once surrounded the borrow pit appear to be missing. Their absence is due to more than just historic plowing. Sediment cores indicate that the river was once much closer to the site and that the surface of the site may have been stripped by major floods (Carlson 2008:336). Floods also may have led to the abandonment of the site in the late 9th century.

The earliest radiocarbon date is an accelerator mass spectrometry (AMS) date from a human femur recovered from the bottom of the southern area of feature 13. It has a two-sigma range of cal. AD 350–530. Carlson (2008:335) suggests that "[h]uman cranial remains and a femur (representing two individuals) were placed at the base of the southern borrow pit ... to mark this location as belonging to a specific group or clan of peoples when the site was initially settled." This association of human remains with origins is a continuing theme in the settlement of Puerto Rico.

The site contains a mixture of Cuevas- and Ostiones-style pottery. Cuevas pottery makes up about 40% of the early contexts and declines over time to about 10%. Cuevas has a much finer paste, and there is evidence that access to the clays used to manufacture this pottery also declined over time. Various raw materials and lithic forms are present. These include chert from Antigua used for the bipolar flaking of microliths that may have been used in grater boards, and shale from Vieques Island. These non-local lithic sources are not present at AR-38. Edge-ground cobbles, edge-battered cobbles, nutting stones, milling stones, and stone balls (*esferolíticos*) are common and reflect the processing of a diverse suite of plants similar to those found in earlier Archaic Age assemblages. These tool forms are less common at the adjacent Río Tanamá 1 site. There also is evidence for the manufacture of stone beads.

Starch-grain analysis of griddles and lithics indicates that the flat clay griddle surfaces were used for a variety of purposes and were not limited to baking cassava bread. Beans, sweet potatoes, panacoid grasses, guayága/marangueys (*Zamia* sp.), and maize were identified (Pagán Jiménez 2008). This suite of plants is associated with house gardens in the Late Ceramic Age (Newsom and Wing 2004). Here they reflect a well-integrated horticultural system based on intercropping in family gardens.

The main component of the faunal assemblage is terrestrial mammals. Hutías and spiny rats were the most common, and there is evidence that dogs were butchered and eaten. In addition, fourteen species of birds were identified, none of which have the plumage that might signal ceremonial use. Finally, marine fish were imported from the coast, which is located about 11 kilometers from the site. The means by which such fish were obtained is unclear, but it does represent the integration of inland and coastal settlements also observed on the south coast of the island (Torres 2012).

Egalitarian, Hierarchical, or Heterarchical?

The history of Puerto Rico has been written to conform to the evolutionary paradigm of band, tribe, chiefdom, and state. The earliest inhabitants are portrayed as simple foragers possessing a band level of organization that may have evolved tribal tendencies (Steward and Faron 1959). According to an often-repeated scenario, these simple folk were displaced and then completely replaced by Saladoid colonists (Rouse 1992).

Peter Siegel (2010) has devoted considerable attention to cultural evolution in the Caribbean. He was one of the first to emphasize the concentric layout of Saladoid sites emerging from his excavations at Maisabel on the north-central coast of Puerto Rico and ethnographic research among the Wai Wai of lowland South America (Figure 4.3) (Siegel 1992). Using ethnographic analogy, he proposed that the Saladoid Culture was characterized by an egalitarian form of organization in which positions of leadership were achieved and not inherited (Siegel 1996). Thus one of the hallmarks of the post-Saladoid in Puerto Rico was the emergence of social hierarchies based on inherited status and rank.

Although Siegel makes a compelling argument for the structure of Saladoid cosmology and the importance of ancestor veneration, his conclusions do not warrant, nor are they dependent, on the Saladoid political economy being egalitarian (Petersen 1996). It is important to correct this misinterpretation because it has long influenced perceptions regarding the development of complexity in the region. Based on the common set of attributes shared by Arawak speakers (Heckenberger 2002, 2005; Santos Granero 2002; Schmidt 1917), we believe that Saladoid communities arrived in the islands with ranked lineages and inherited status. Their institutions were based on both hierarchical ranking and heterarchical association. Current confusion derives from conflating *egalitarian* and *autonomous*. The first relates to social structure, while the second defines the capacity for independent action. The distribution of Saladoid sites confirms their autonomy.

Mortuary practices have been used to mark this transition. Saladoid settlements tend to have circular, oval, or horseshoe shaped community plans, with human remains often buried in the central clearing or plaza (e.g., Maisabel, Tibes, Tutu, and Punta Candelero sites; Curet and Oliver 1998; Righter 2002; Siegel 1992, 1996, 1999). Beginning about AD 500, there was a shift in burials from the central plaza to the interiors of houses (Curet and Oliver 1998). Although burials do occur in a variety of other contexts (including middens, caves, and outside houses), the shift from central plaza to household reflects an important change in the treatment of the dead.

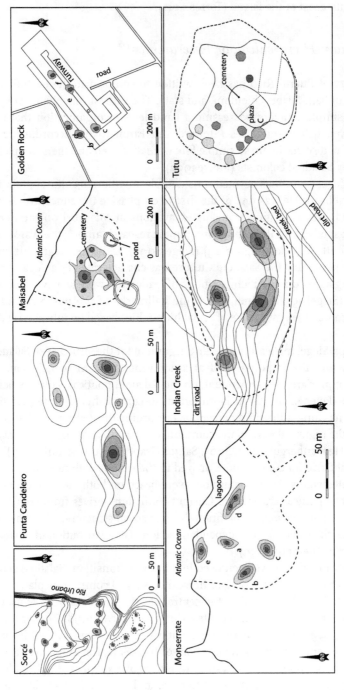

FIGURE 4.3 Maps of settlement layouts at several sites in Puerto Rico (Saladoid Burials paper) (courtesy of Menno Hoogland, after Peter E. Siegel).

Saladoid burials in the central plaza have been interpreted as evidence for ancestor veneration (Siegel 1992, 1996, 1997). It is implied that these individuals lived in the community in which they were buried, and that burying them in a central place ensured that they were present in spirit, especially during the rituals and ceremonies that were held in this public space. Thus, the living members of the community could look to the ancestors for supernatural intervention and maintain spiritual ties to those who had lived before them. Ancestor veneration seems a logical hypothesis. The image of the central plaza as the *axis mundi* that ties the underworld, where the ancestors are buried, to the land of the living and the sky world of the spirits is a compelling image (Siegel 1992, 1996, 1997).

The issue is not whether Saladoid communities practiced ancestor veneration. The issue is whether or not central plaza burials were exclusively an outcome of this practice. Keegan (2009) has argued that central plaza burials represent a social process in which the deceased members of a clan are interred in their clan cemetery. Post-mortem mobility is an important component of this process. It involves the return of individuals who resided in other communities during their adult life. In other words, an individual who moved to live in another community at marriage was returned to the natal community at death. The social glue that bound one community to another was marriage. Alliances between families, clans, and villages were formalized through the exchange of spouses and the exchange of the dead. The return of a deceased spouse to the clan village completed the circuit of birth and death. The abandonment of central-place burials in favor of burials beneath domestic structures is a symptom of the emerging localization of social identity, and a stronger expression of estate, lineage, or "House" (Morsink 2011; Torres 2012; Samson 2010).

Settlement Landscape and Community Structure (AD 900 and Beyond)

The post-Saladoid Culture in Puerto Rico has been divided into two chronological phases. The first is conceived in terms of the disappearance of the Saladoid and the emergence of the Ostionoid; the second is constructed as the transitions toward "Taíno." We do not accept this evolutionary sequence, but its adoption by others merits attention. Our timing for these transformations is approximate and general. We adopt relatively early dates because it is rare to find the earliest example of any phenomenon, and because changes were not simultaneous across the island. New practices did not emerge *sui generis* and sweep across the island. General patterns are apparent only after they become widespread. In this regard, some will find the AD 900 date arbitrary and perhaps too early. Nevertheless, with the possible exception of the drier Medieval Warm Period and wetter climate that began around AD 950, there are no other significant external factors to explain the trajectory of cultural development (Cooper 2013).

The most comprehensive study of the settlement landscape for this time period was conducted by Joshua Torres (2012) in the hill country associated with the Ceremonial Center of Tibes north of the modern city of Ponce in south-central Puerto Rico. While previous studies emphasized regionality in the context of world systems, Torres emphasized "community," which he defined as

> a group of people who live in proximity to one another within a geographically limited area, who have face-to-face interaction on a regular basis and who share access to social and natural resources. Social relations and group membership is based on relations of kinship, marriage, economics and founded upon recogniz-able ideological and symbolic frames of reference. (Torres 2012:415)

A key point is that local communities, while linked together, are also diverse. Their common history and connections to others constitute their unique identities, which are apposed to other, similarly constructed identities composed of kin groups and sodalities.

Despite the fact that Saladoid villages, and this settlement pattern, held sway for between six and ten centuries, the Saladoid pattern of large, relatively autonomous villages, few in number, and located along major river drainages on the coastal plains was transformed. At this time, the number of sites across the island increased dramatically as the population expanded into the interior of the island. The number of sites increased until around AD 1200, after which there was a stasis or decline (Curet 2005; Rodríguez López 1992:13).

Saladoid and Archaic Age communities did venture into the interior, but the radical change in settlement landscape at this time involved the *dispersion* of population into the foothills and mountainous interior along river drainages. New settlements were established on virtually every level surface suitable for agriculture. A few large villages were established on the coastal plain, but these do not replicate the Saladoid organizational pattern. Instead of one village forming the primary social and political community, new settlements were small hamlets and small villages composed of nuclear family houses that were allied with neighbors in "settlement clusters" (Curet 2005; Torres 2012:449). According to Joshua Torres (2012:417–418):

> the post-AD 600 settlement pattern of the Portugués drainage appears to consist of a dispersed pattern of residential settlements spaced approximately .5 kilometers apart. These settlements are relatively small (typically under 3 ha) and situated along river terraces and available flat expanses of land in the topographically diverse foothills. Larger settlements (generally > 3 ha) appear to be confined to coastal settings (e.g., Carmen, Los Indios, Caracoles) although these are generally limited in number and small dispersed settlements predominate throughout the region during this time.

Torres (2012:457–458) makes an important distinction between *fissioning* and *dispersal* in the processes of settlement expansion. Fissioning occurs through the social reproduction of the parent community by the daughter community. It is a replicative process. In contrast, dispersal involves the movement of small sections away from the parent community. Individual sites do not completely replicate the parent community. The parent community is reproduced through the articulation of community clusters. It is possible that dispersion followed the "Garden Plot" model, in which farmers established field houses away from the main settlement, and these transitioned into hamlets and small villages as the farmers begin to live more permanently near their fields (Butt 1977; Heckenberger 2005). Whatever the particular mechanism was, the dispersion of population fostered significant changes in social organization. Anthropologists have long recognized that changes in social organization usually begin with a change in residence (Ensor 2013a, 2013b; Murdock 1949).

A corresponding shift in house size has been argued based on the relatively few structures that have been identified archaeologically. It has been suggested that the large (*c.* 20 m diameter) extended-family *molaca*-style house was replaced by nuclear family–size structures averaging 8 meters in diameter (Curet 2005), and at Rio Tanamá site 1, there is no evidence for mounded middens (Carlson 2008). Based on his survey, Torres (2012:459–460) concludes:

> small residential settlements were composed of less than ten of these domestic structures at any one point of time. Moreover, history is embodied in the persistence of the settlement, more so than in individual "Houses." There is a diversity of community plans, as opposed to the circular, oval, or horseshoe plan of Saladoid sites.

The construction of stone-lined courts and plazas intensified at this time. Before considering these, we offer Rio Tanamá site 1 (AR-38) as an example of a large village from this time. We chose this site because it postdates and is spatially adjacent to our earlier example, and Lisabeth Carlson (2008) directed the excavation of both sites.

Rio Tanamá 1 Site (c. cal. AD 980–1490)

Rio Tanamá site 1 is located on the level floodplain about 100 meters north of Rio Tanamá 2 (AR-39). A one-meter-wide trench was mechanically excavated between the two sites. The trench failed to reveal any connection between them, and the material evidence and radiocarbon dates confirm their independence. Excavation was limited to the USACE easement and was accomplished by mechanical stripping followed by hand cleaning. The plow zone was removed to a depth of 50 centimeters in 2-centimeter intervals, under constant surveillance. Approximately 1,000 square meters were exposed, revealing a distribution of features over a linear distance of 70 meters.

Despite being located in the same environment as AR-39, AR-38 is completely different (Carlson 2008). A significant difference is the absence of midden deposits at the site, which limited the kinds of materials recovered after stripping. Cuevas-style pottery was completely absent, and a few Boca Chica–style sherds were recovered from house posts associated with two structures. Basalts and andesites were the primary materials for stone tools (90%), and chert was rare. Marine fish are absent, having been replaced by river species. As at other sites from this time period, guinea pig bones appear for the first time (deFrance 2013).

What the site lacks in middens, it makes up for in its abundance of features (Carlson 2008). A total of 286 features were identified and selectively excavated. The majority of these were post stains of various sizes, and no hearths were found. Eight burials were identified and excavated. Finally, a rectangular colonial house, measuring 11 by 6 meters and oriented with the long axis east–west, was identified from nine, 60-to-80–centimeter post stains, three containing preserved wood, spaced approximately 2.5 meters apart (Carlson 2008:125–129). This elevated structure dates to the historic sugar cane industry and affected the precolonial deposit.

Carlson (2008:135–138) identified seven houses and additional stains attributed to windbreaks, drying racks, raised barbecue lattices, and other ancillary structures. The seven houses are in five separate areas, with a cluster of three near the center of the excavated area. Two of these three contain Boca Chica–style sherds in two post stains, with radiocarbon dates that indicate the houses were not occupied at the same time. The majority of post stains contain limestone and meta-volcanic anchor stones. In fact, the primary use of limestone at the site is associated with house construction. The houses were round or oval with a diameter of five to eight meters, which is consistent with other, smaller, and presumably "nuclear family" houses identified for this time period (Curet 2005).

Of the nine burials, 66% were adults, with equal numbers of males and females. Four adults were found in houses, and non-adults were buried outside the houses. This small burial population was of good health, with only a limited number of pathologies, primarily dental caries (Antón 2008). Females exhibited significant tooth wear, which at other locales has been attributed to the processing of plants (Crespo-Torres, et al. 2013; Mickleburgh 2013). Burial goods were restricted to small cobbles (one greenstone) in the chests of two males. Of special note is the complete absence of cranial modification. Cranial modification has long been associated with the Ceramic Age inhabitants of the islands based on Spanish descriptions (Rouse 1992). Moreover, tabular-oblique fronto-occipital flattening has been observed in Cuevas and Ostiones burial populations on Puerto Rico (Crespo-Torres 2000). Cranial modification must be initiated shortly after birth; it presumably serves as a permanent marker of identity (Hoogland and Hofman 2013; Ross 2004; van Duijvenbode 2013, 2017).

Stable isotope analysis indicated a diet of terrestrial protein, C_4 plants (maize and panacoid grasses), and marine protein. The absence of marine fauna suggests that this was not a major component of the diet. However, the isotope values are lower than those recorded for populations for which maize was the staple (Antón 2008:184). One possibility is that fish were being processed on the coast and preserved by salting, so that the transported fillets lacked the bones that would document the consumption of marine fish at the site (Keegan 2007). Oxygen isotope analysis suggested that one of the females "lived the majority of the last 5–10 years of her life in an area different from the other two burials" (Antón 2008:189). Lifetime mobility has been recognized through strontium and oxygen isotope analyses (Laffoon 2013) and promises to be an important means of detecting patterns of mobility and social organization and the possibility of post-mortem mobility (Keegan 2009).

Formalization of Exchange

The construction of formal spaces marked by parallel lines of stones began in the 8th century AD (Curet and Stringer 2010; Oliver 2009) and may have been influenced by contacts with the Isthmo-Colombian region of Central and South America (Rodriguez Ramos 2013:166–167), but their use was particular to the island. Because these spaces conform to the layout described by the Spanish for the Antillean ball game (*batey*), they often are assumed to have functioned as ball courts (Alegría 1983). However, their great range in size, and their occurrence in small sites and locations that are not associated with settlements, indicates that they were used for multiple purposes (Garrow 1995; Espenshade 2009; Torres 2012). One of these purposes was ceremonial exchange.

Exchange relations mirror and reinforce social relations. The communal exchange of gifts and food is a component of all levels of social integration. The dispersion of population reflects a change in residence practices that should initiate changes in how social groups interact. The development of ceremonial centers expresses new forms of social integration. One of the most detailed discussions of the organization and evolution of exchange relations in spatial and social contexts is Paula Rubel and Abraham Rosman's (1978) account of highland New Guinea. What follows is a summary of their ethnology, with specific attention to "star formation exchange."

The societies of highland New Guinea are anthropologically famous for their competitive pig feasts (Rappaport 1968). These exchanges occur in a neutral location, with the two opposing parties facing each other in parallel lines separated by an empty space (Brown 1972). Participants who enter the space between the lines may engage in battle, with individuals along the line throwing spears at them. The outcome is often a draw, with only minor injuries to the participants, but on occasion one may defeat the other (Rappaport 1968).

In addition to these large multi-community feasts that occur about every decade, there are smaller-scale ceremonial exchanges that mark puberty, marriage, death, and so on. (Keegan, et al. 1998; Oliver 2009). In Malinowski's (1922) account of the Trobriand Islanders, one gets the impression that they were constantly preparing, especially women, for ceremonial exchanges. These exchanges were not confined to a single day, but could last for up to a year. In addition, the Kula exchange involved travel to other islands and is described as the equivalent of going to war. We emphasize this point because feasting in the Caribbean has been portrayed as a peaceful "event," with the consumption of special foods signifying chiefly status (see deFrance 2013). Ethnographic accounts present a different picture.

Rubel and Rosman (1978) identify four types of ceremonial exchange, of which the star formation is category 3 (pp. 329–332). This category is based on the Maring, Manga, Kuma, and Chimbu, who all have a dual organization and Big Man polities based on patrilineal descent and virilocal residence. Although these practices do not exactly match those proposed for the Caribbean, dual organization has been proposed (Siegel 2010). The sufficient parameter is a leader who can organize inter-community exchange, and viri-avunculocal residence is the matrilineal equivalent of the segmentary conical clan that characterizes patrilineal societies with virilocal residence; and in both, cross-cousin marriage is preferred (Ensor 2013a; Lévi-Strauss 1969; Keegan and Machlachlan 1989). The New Guinea societies developed through an "expansion and scale of density of population with the concomitant loss of many of the features of dual organization" (Rubel and Rosman 1978:329–330). They also share high population densities and dispersed settlements with communities in Puerto Rico.

Marriage is fundamental. It is through the exchange of spouses that alliances are created, with these alliances formalizing relations at multiple scales of the political economy (Ensor 2013a 2013b). These relations are not strictly peaceful; they also contain elements of animosity. Affines commonly are characterized as the "Other" (Helms 1998) or even "enemies" (Brown 1964). If marriage creates enemies, then we need to accept the potential for warfare as a basic element of human organization.

In the New Guinea societies, multi-community pig feasts take place at intervals of seven to fifteen years (Rubel and Rosman 1978:283). Big Men serve as the nodes in these exchanges (Rubel and Rosman 1978:291). Marriage practices dictate that every community must exchange spouses with its neighbors. These neighbors are similar communities that are considered enemies or allies. Star formation exchange occurs when a clan or tribe invites all of the communities with which they have exchanged spouses to a neutral location (Rubel and Rosman 1978:288–289). The host clan or tribe is positioned at the center, with the invited parties surrounding them. The hosts conduct dyadic exchanges with each of their guests, with each guest group related through marriage. However, the guests only exchange with the host on this occasion, and not with each other. This material expression of the relationship of affine and host serves to link a large number of social units in a regional network.

Plaza de Estrella, Tibes Ceremonial Center

The Tibes ceremonial center is the earliest example of "monumental" architecture in Puerto Rico (Rouse 1992). Located on the Río Portugués near the city of Ponce, the site comprises seven courts of parallel stone lines or pavements, a quadrangular plaza at the center, and an adjacent circular "star-shaped" plaza. L. Antonio Curet has directed a long-term systematic investigation of Tibes (Curet and Stringer 2010). His investigations have not found evidence for large-scale permanent habitation at the site, but there may have been a small residential community that maintained the center (Torres et al. 2014). It fits the pattern in which large-scale ceremonial exchange occurs in a neutral location.

The focal point of the site is a large, quadrangular plaza (Figure 4.4). Adjacent to this plaza is a circular plaza demarcated by stones with project-ing triangular pavements (Plaza de Estrella). This plaza is unique and differs significantly from the parallel-sided courts here and elsewhere in Puerto Rico. Because the plaza is unique, the suggestion has been made that it reflects a

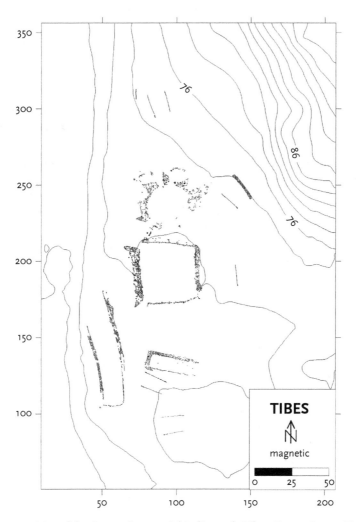

FIGURE 4.4 Map of the Centro Ceremonial Indígena de Tibes, Ponce, Puerto Rico (courtesy of L. Antonio Curet).

fanciful reconstruction created during the initial rehabilitation of the site. It is our contention that the reconstruction is accurate and that the name "Plaza de Estrella" is completely appropriate. In this regard, the shape of the plaza conforms to the formalization of star formation exchange in which the hosts occupied the center of the plaza and were surrounded by exchange partners. The triangular projections provide a physical barrier that could have separated the participants and emphasized that exchange was only with the host and not with each other. Ceremonial exchanges probably occurred on the plaza at long intervals. Moreover, star formation exchange can occur in a non-restricted space, so the plaza itself probably postdates earlier exchanges at the site.

This interpretation raises the question of why there are also parallel-sided courts at Tibes. One possibility is that these courts reflect an earlier time when exchanges only involved two exchange partners. The sequence would commence with hosts having singular exchange partners, with the subsequent development of multi-community exchanges. As population density increased, Rubel and Rosman (1978) observed, a shift occurred from this two-level exchange to the multilevel hierarchy of a segmentary structure. With a multilevel hierarchy, the major exchanges were organized by a smaller number of leaders representing the pinnacle of the pyramid. This configuration is exactly what we observe at the later ceremonial center of Caguana. Here the main plaza is again two-sided, but in this case, the facing stones are embellished with petroglyphs with virtually mirror images of the origin myth (Oliver 2009). The pinnacle of the hierarchy is reduced to two opposing forces.

We suggest that the parallel courts at Tibes were contemporaneous with the plaza. In this scenario, they represent smaller-scale exchanges involving only two groups. Such exchanges would have been more common and reflected situations that only required the participation of the principal actors. Funerals and the exchange of spouses are two examples of ceremonies that require only the participation of agnates and affines.

The validity of our arguments remains to be demonstrated. In this regard, we recommend that the courts be studied as vernacular architecture. Given the formality of the courts, it is likely that each was constructed, maintained, and even reconstructed or abandoned by different social units. Cross-court dimensions may reflect different notions of appropriate social distance. In other words, what constitutes "arm's length?" The length of the court probably reflects the expected number of participants. Formalizing this distance compels the host to fill this distance. A court that is too long or too short materializes on the host's reputation, such that they either are too grandiose or lack support to maintain an adequate facility. In addition, the length of the court will limit participation, with individuals at either end relegated to lower-status locations. The embellishment of courts with stone pavements offers further insights. If our interpretation is correct, the triangular projections at Plaza de Estrella provided formal separation of those engaged in exchange with the host, but not with each other.

Finally, larger-scale spatial arrangements merit further scrutiny. How does the alignment of individual courts relate to the territory of their owner? Which side of the court did the host occupy? Is proximity, in which the court occupies the side of the center closest to the clan village, the primary determinant of location? The location of the quadrangular plaza atop a Saladoid burial ground probably reflects their identification with earlier inhabitants (Curet and Stringer 2010). In addition, beliefs associated with the cardinal directions and astronomical alignments merit further consideration (Robiou-Lemarche 2002; Rodríguez Álvarez 2003).

"Taíno" in Puerto Rico?

The final phase of cultural development on the island is associated with the arrival of influences from Hispaniola. The ability to infiltrate Puerto Rican societies was facilitated by existing social networks. The long-distance mobility and exchange that characterized the Saladoid probably had continued to this point, but it was tempered by an increasing local focus and regionalization. The trend involved a change in kind, but not necessarily in degree. The patterns of mobility and exchange were transformed from linear to multidimensional and chaotic, with the adoption of new modes for expressing social connectedness. This new materialism was no longer expressed in a single pottery style and a limited range of exotic materials. Exchange elevated the status of the prosaic and mundane, as is evident, for example, in the exchange value of yams in Southeast Asia (Morsink 2012).

Pottery has been used as the primary material marker for cultural changes. It is generally accepted that the three styles recognized for this time period— Boca Chica, Capá, and Esperanza—express the elaboration of design elements that first appeared in the earlier styles (Curet and Stringer 2010; Oliver 2009; Siegel 2010). These modes include modeling, incision, and punctation, with the primary motifs viewed as reflecting an emerging Taíno identity (Rouse 1952, 1992). However, it should be noted that these styles tend to be mixed with previous styles, and it is not correct to assume that all other styles ceased to exist when a new style is identified (Rodriguez Ramos, et al. 2013). When viewed solely as modes, they share considerable similarities to Meillacoid designs. In sum, if pottery styles reflect social identities, then Puerto Rico was home to a profusion of social identities at this time.

According to Rouse (1992:111):

> Boca Chica . . . developed farther west along the southern coast of the Dominican Republic. Its potters established a colony in the middle of the southern coast of Puerto Rico, settling at Santa Isabel, on the boundary between the local Ostionan and Elenan potters (Rouse 1986:148–150). They introduced their own form of Chican pottery and influenced the two groups to develop theirs, Capá in Ostionan territory and Esperanza in Elenan territory.

Boca Chica is an intrusive style that has become emblematic of "Taíno" (what could be called "the Chicoid fetish"). It is now well established that these influences extended through Puerto Rico and into the Lesser Antilles (e.g., Crock 2000; Hoogland and Hofman 1999) and westward into Cuba (Guarch Delmonte 1972a, 1972b). The questions that remain are what processes were involved and what shared sets of icons meant to local communities in different areas.

Late Pottery Styles

Boca Chica style (*c.* AD 1200–1500) is named for a site on the southeast coast of the Dominican Republic. In Puerto Rico, it is characterized by thicker and sturdier vessels with fine, hard, smoothed, and occasionally polished surfaces (Rouse 1952:347–350). Various complicated shapes occur, including round and boat-shaped vessels with inturned rims and spherical bottles. In the Dominican Republic, these bottles are associated with both water collection (*potizas*) and the consumption of manioc beer (Harris 1994). Designs are elaborate and complex, often occurring as a continuous band above the shoulder. Incised lines beginning and ending in punctations (line-and-dot) are the classic motif. Appliqué strips and modeling are present. Flat and prismatic lugs adorn the vessels, and modeled anthropomorphic (bat-face) lugs rise facing each other above the rim. There are no strap handles. Boca Chica is most common in western Puerto Rico, but it is found across the island, including the Ceiba 11 site at the eastern extreme of Puerto Rico (Carlson and Torres 2011:403).

Capá style (*c.* AD 1200–1500) is named for a site (also known as *Caguana*) in the interior to the west of Utuado (Rouse 1952:350). This style is found mostly in western Puerto Rico. Rouse (1952:350–352) presents an interesting contrast in describing this pottery. On one hand, Capá sherds are technologically the crudest in the Antilles. Despite being somewhat thinner (about 7 mm) than Boca Chica, most are unusually soft, heavily impregnated with sand, and crumble easily, and the fine clay float or slip on the surface has disintegrated to the point that only small traces are discernable. On the other hand, they are frequently decorated with obvious and complete designs. Vessels are predominantly hemispherical and globular; they are incurving above the shoulder. Lugs are present, with modeled anthropomorphic (bat-face) lugs rise facing each other above the rim. Modeled, incised, and punctate motifs predominate, and the use of appliqué is relatively rare. The designs mimic those of the Boca Chica style, but they are less elaborate and less well executed. Strap handles are absent.

Esperanza style (*c.* AD 1200–1500) is named for a site on Vieques Island. Like Santa Elena, it is similar to styles in the Virgin Islands and is found mostly in eastern Puerto Rico. Vessels are predominantly hemispherical with rounded bases, incurving sides, and a blunt, rounded keel (Rouse 1952:352–354).

Casuela-shaped incurving bowls also are present (Curet 2005:24). The paste is coarse and has an average thickness of about 7 millimeters. Decoration was executed in simple incised designs restricted to shoulders and rarely including line-and-dot. Modeled-incised lugs rise above the rim on opposite sides of the vessel but are rare. These lugs are much cruder than Boca Chica. They appear to represent bats, but they lack the refined appearance of Boca Chica adornos. Painting and strap handles are largely absent.

It generally is accepted that this final stage of development in Puerto Rico was stimulated by changes that originated in eastern Hispaniola with the emergence of Chicoid series pottery. In fact, José Oliver (2009) explicitly links Puerto Rico with southeastern Hispaniola at this time. There is every reason to believe that pan-Caribbean connections existed throughout the post-Saladoid, especially if Ostiones originated in eastern Hispaniola.

In the next chapter, we discuss the emergence of cultural expressions in Hispaniola. Briefly, Ostionoid developed adjacent to the Meillacoid and Chicoid in Hispaniola around AD 600–800. Meillacoid then spread rapidly to Jamaica, Cuba, and the southern Bahama archipelago, while Ostionoid continued to develop in Puerto Rico. There is no reason to assume Meillacoid influences were not also felt in Puerto Rico. Previously it was thought that early Meillacoid was limited to the Cibao Valley in the western Dominican Republic, but new evidence suggests Meillacoid influences were also present in the eastern Dominican Republic. In this regard, Capá and Esperanza styles in Puerto Rico exhibit marked similarities to some Meillacoid styles. The execution and placement of anthropomorphic adornos on vessels and the adoption of linear incision have more in common with Meillacoid than Chicoid, especially during their initial appearance.

The spread of Meillacoid into previously occupied territories implies the introduction of a revolutionary technology. We propose that Meillacoid represents the development and adoption of intensive agriculture. The main form of intensification was the construction of permanent fields by mounding the soil (*montones*) for the monocropping of sweet potato and bitter manioc. This was the production strategy observed by the Spanish (Sauer 1966). The absence of manioc starch grains during the analyses conducted to date (Pagán Jiménez 2013) could be explained by the relatively late introduction of intensive bitter-manioc production. Thus, manioc cultivation did not evolve *in situ*, which we would expect to have left trace evidence. It was instead introduced as a developed agricultural industry that included new forms of manipulation and processing.

We are not saying that Meillacoid colonized Puerto Rico. Our point is that post-Saladoid Puerto Rico was engaged in changes that were occurring at a larger scale, and that the foundations of these changes developed in Hispaniola and then spread to Puerto Rico. Influences from Hispaniola are especially pronounced in the later appearance of Boca Chica on the island. We suggest that these influences arrived long before they became pronounced.

Demography

As previously noted, there was a dramatic increase in the number of sites in post-Saladoid Puerto Rico. This amounted to a five-fold increase (from five to twenty-five sites) in the Loíza River valley of northeast Puerto Rico from Monserrate to Santa Elena (Curet 2005). This trend ends around AD 1200 when the number of sites declines; a trend that also is observed in the northern Lesser Antilles (Hofman and Hoogland 2013). L. Antonio Curet (2005) equates the decrease in site numbers with a decrease in population. He concludes:

> Since to date there is no archaeological evidence for epidemics, institutionalized warfare, famines, or any other major natural catastrophe that might have increased considerably the mortality rates or reduced the fertility rates for this period in Puerto Rico, it is reasonable to suggest that prehistoric cultures either were practicing some kind of population control or were migrating to other areas. (Curet 2005:137)

Curet (2005) recognizes that site numbers may not be an appropriate proxy for population numbers. Moreover, the decline in site numbers seems insignificant in some of the river basins he investigated. For example, the number of sites in the Loíza River valley decreased by only three (from twenty-five to twenty-two). All of the abandoned sites were small in size and were located in low areas along the coast. It is this physiographic region that also saw an increase in site size at this time (Torres 2012). Finally, some sites are not visible when using standard prospecting techniques. Sea level rise, coastal flooding, burial under floodplain sediments (e.g., Paso del Indio; Walker 2005), and historic constructions have all contributed to the invisibility of sites in particular locations. The degree to which natural camouflage has hidden sites from view is undetermined.

With regard to why some sites were abandoned, Curet (2005) examines the possibilities that communities moved from coastal to inland locations; that they were attracted to bigger centers, possibly even centers on Hispaniola; that they fled the island or moved to more defensive locations in response to external attacks; and/or there was localized social and political collapse, as is common in chiefdom-level societies. He suggests that the latter may account for the dramatic abandonment of sites in the Salinas River basin on the south-central coast.

At this point, there is insufficient evidence that total population numbers did decline. First, dating sites solely on the basis of pottery styles may underestimate site numbers, especially when a new style appeared and the occupants of existing sites did not adopt the new style. Second, the restructuring of population distributions may have resulted in some sites' growing in size while others were abandoned. An overall decline in population contingent with the emergence of chiefdoms would be surprising. Keegan and colleagues have argued that *the* major goal of regionally organized economies (e.g., chiefdoms) is growing population by encouraging fertility and attracting followers (Keegan, et al. 1998).

The most significant conclusion of Curet's study is that changes in site number did not reflect a population–resource imbalance (Curet 2005:138). In other words, food scarcity, when measured as a function of agricultural production potentials, was not a cause. Moreover, except for the introduction of guinea pig and an emphasis on interior versus coastal fauna at this time, there is no evidence for substantial changes in the exploitation of animals (deFrance 2013).

Rapid dispersal into the interior began around AD 600. By AD 1200, all of the prime settlement locations in the rugged interior were occupied. This expansion was coincident with a restructuring of spatial organization, reflected in the emergence of "settlement clusters" as well as smaller settlement and structure sizes (Torres 2012:455). Sites also were established for specialized activities such as fishing, cotton production, and salt production (Carlson and Torres 2011), a pattern also observed for the Lesser Antilles, Cuba, and the southern Bahamas (Cooper 2007; Hofman 2013; Sinelli 2013). Special-purpose sites were probably occupied and abandoned at seasonal intervals.

After individual families had laid claim to all of the optimal settlement locations, their farmsteads continued to grow along the lines defined by the "garden plot" model (Torres 2012:457). In this case, the population continued to grow, but the number of sites did not increase. Eventually, the population at some of these sites would have exceeded their production capacities. The reorganization of agricultural production from slash-and-burn family gardens to outfield *conucos* with permanent *monticulos* would have encouraged the consolidation of population in appropriate locations. Small settlements, which did not decline in numbers (Curet 2005), continued because some chose to live away from larger villages, and for the extraction of resources whose distribution was limited. For example, the large interior site of Palo Hincado near the center of the island may have been established to harvest trees for the production of canoes (Ortíz Aguilú, et al. 2001).

Finally, the shift in power relations from coastal to interior locations is evident in the distribution of "chiefly" villages reported by the Spanish. The Spanish reported seventeen chiefs, and only one of their villages was located near the coast (Rouse 1952:Fig. 5). The others were located in the interior along the major river drainages, and seven were located at their headwaters. This distribution was defensive: access to these villages was limited by the surrounding mountains and their positioning above the navigable ranges of the rivers. This pattern is surprising, given that settlement on the coastal plains offered greater access to broader expanses of arable land and marine resources. If Keegan and Machlachlan (1989) are correct in attributing matrilocal residence to Antillean societies, then this pattern may reflect endemic internal warfare. Such warfare is a universal feature of societies at this level of social integration (Ember 1974). It has been proposed as a stage in the consolidation of power among the five paramount chiefs of Hispaniola (Wilson 1990). Chiefly villages in the interior also may reflect efforts to avoid the Spanish invasion by retreating to summer homes in the mountains. Whether or not the Spanish provided a compelling reason to move, it is likely that the facilities already were in place.

Stone-Lined Courts and Plazas

Stone-lined courts became a common feature of the settlement landscape. Although "ceremonial centers" with multiple "monumental" courts have received the most attention, a substantial number of courts occurred in smaller residential contexts. The tendency has been to interpret courts in smaller settlements as simply smaller versions of those found in the larger centers. In this regard, they often are considered places where the ball game was played (*batey*).

Viewed from a perspective of scale, the dichotomy of large and small integrative facilities indicates a two-tier structure. Courts in residential settings do not have the capacity to host large social gatherings. Their construction was local, and their use was related to the needs of the immediate community. Ritual activities related to marriage, puberty, ancestor veneration, and death were likely to have been conducted in these spaces (Oliver 2009; Torres 2012). The formalization of two sides and an empty interior reflects moieties and/or bipartite sodalities based on age, gender, and marriage. Moreover, the close proximity of sites with courts suggests a level of symbolic interdependence and a lack of authoritative controls and administrative hierarchy (Torres 2012:426).

The stone-lined courts in small villages materialized the changing structure of inter-community relations. In Saladoid villages, the central plaza was "public" in the sense that individuals living in the village performed activities in view of other members of the village. The dispersion of population into the interior exploded the enclosed central plaza and required a new means to distinguish public from private. One way that this was accomplished in the tropical lowlands was by constructing roads that connected villages to each other and to their satellite communities. In its most elaborate form, this has been called the "Galactic Polity" (Heckenberger 2005). If we use the community clusters along the Río Portugués as an example, then the regional spatial layout is reminiscent of a galactic cluster (see Torres 2012). Some of the villages are nodes along main routes of travel, others are alongside routes, and still others seem to form endpoints in the network.

The analysis of fauna from La Minerál (PO-42), Los Gongolones (PO-43), and Jácanas (PO-29) revealed substantial quantities of marine mollusks and fish, with fish composing 40% of the vertebrate faunal assemblage (DuChemin 2013). They highlight the integration of coastal and interior settlements (Torres 2012) and may reflect a continuing importance of marine fish in family and clan rituals (cf. Malinowski 1935). In addition, the high incidence of *Turritella* snails and porcupine fish (*Diodon* sp.), both of which produce toxins that can be used to induce trances (Keegan and Carlson 2008:111–116), may indicate the presence of religious specialists (shamans). The other vertebrates are mammals (~22%), including hutía that may have been hunted in gardens, birds (~8%), and reptiles (30%), represented primarily by iguanas and freshwater turtles (DuChemin 2013).

For some of these villages, it may have been advantageous to offer free passage to travelers moving from the coast to the interior along rivers and river terraces that offered a path of least resistance. The stone-lined courts create a formal neutral zone in which visitors could be welcomed and/or interrogated away from private, domestic space. In this way, the space between the stone alignments was transformed and codified as a new form of "public" space that reflected the changing organization of communities. By leaving the two ends open, the stone alignments created a "road" *through* the village. It is dangerous to enter a village where you are not known or where you may be known as an "enemy" (including affinal relatives). This situation became all the more frequent as population dispersed, and they no longer had daily interactions with their neighbors, who now lived in other communities, and even with kin who were not encountered frequently. The "road" served as a physical symbol of hospitality. If the village had stone-alignments, then the community that lived there had made the effort to construct a thoroughfare, and you were free to pass. The traveler (and everyone was probably a traveler at some point) received passage along a domesticated route and the potential for assistance and shelter, while the members of the community gained access to news, non-local goods or raw materials, recruitment of spouses, and other possible benefits.

To the best of our knowledge, stone-lined courts at the smaller interior settlements in Puerto Rico have not previously been interpreted as roads. However, there is a precedent. Las Casas (1992:Ch. 3:299) mentions a similar village layout in the foothills near Higüey in the eastern Dominican Republic. He describes a crossroads where four broad streets, fifty paces wide and a long-bow shot in length, met near the center of this inland settlement. He goes on to say that the streets were used for staging battles. The Spanish described other villages in Hispaniola as being laid out on a grid of streets. While these streets functioned to promote transportation, it is likely that all cleared and maintained open spaces served multiple purposes.

Gary Vescelius is given credit as the first to note that stone-lined courts in Puerto Rico tend to be located in border zones, non-residential, and neutral locations. The occurrence of small courts in neutral locations has been noted by others (Curet 2005; Oliver 2009; Siegel 2010), and this is certainly true of the three main stone-lined court complexes on Puerto Rico. Tibes (Curet and Stringer 2010) and Jácanas (Espenshade 2009) are located on the Portugués River north of the modern city of Ponce, and Caguana (Oliver 1998, 2009) is located in the mountains near Utuado.

The Centro Ceremonial Indígena de Tibes is the oldest of the major ceremonial centers. It is located 10 kilometers from the south coast on a terrace adjacent to the Portugués River, at the edge of the broad coastal plain and limestone foothills. The site began as an average Saladoid village with a semicircular arrangement of mounds around an unmarked plaza that also served as a burial ground (Curet and Stringer 2010). After AD 700, residential activities ceased, and major rearrangement of space began. The most intense period of construction occurred between AD 1000 and 1200. The site covers 16 hectares, and is composed of seven parallel-sided courts, a large and central quadrangular plaza, and the circular "star-shaped" plaza discussed earlier. The courts were constructed by aligning stones mostly collected from the river, but limestone slabs from more distant sources were incorporated. A small number of petroglyphs occurs on the east- and west-facing alignments of the central plaza. The central plaza was constructed over the main Saladoid burial ground, and a second court was built over a second cluster of burials. Joshua Torres (2012) conducted time and energy studies that indicate that, while the site often is promoted as an example of "monumental" architecture, the labor involved in constructing the courts does not approach that scale (Torres et al. 2014). Of additional note is the absence of habitation debris from post-Saladoid contexts and the absence of "elite" foods in the deposits (deFrance 2013).

The site embodies the indigenous development of ceremonial exchange on the island. We already have discussed the characteristics of such exchange in the context of the Plaza de Estrella. What is significant here is the fact that the site was abandoned around AD 1200. Although there is evidence for visitation and limited use after this date, the center ceased to function as such. In this regard, its dematerialization emphasizes a significant reorientation of social practices.

Jácanas is not a multi-court center, but it merits attention because it is located only 4 kilometers north of Tibes on the Portugués River. The site was first occupied between AD 400 and 600, and has deposits containing Cuevas and Monserrate styles that later included pure Ostiones pottery. The site was abandoned from AD 900–1300, after which it was resettled and a large central court was constructed. Capá, Boca Chica, and Esperanza-style pottery mark its resettlement. The court measures 50 by 40 meters and is unusual in that all four sides are enclosed by monoliths. The enclosed sides distinguish it from open-ended courts in other small settlements, which indicates that through-passage was not its primary function. The court is built over a cemetery that may have contained up to 400 burials and dates to the earlier occupation of the site. Seven monoliths in the northern row are decorated with stylistically "Taíno" petroglyphs (Oliver 2009:21). Unlike Caguana and Tibes, where petroglyphs are limited to eastern and western rows, the petroglyphs here are on the north row. The petroglyphs portray individuals as spirits similar to the central images at Caguana, but unlike Caguana, they do not present a legend or story (Oliver 2009). Several of the images have opposing heads, with one part of an above-ground image, and the other inverted below ground. The above-ground head of one of the figures is turned sharply to the side, which may represent decapitation. It is possible that there were additional courts at the site, but it covers an area far smaller than Tibes'. It dates to the abandonment of Tibes and is consistent with other smaller habitation sites with stone-lined courts dating to this time period. It differs from Tibes and those other sites in its clear expression of a non-local iconography.

The most spectacular example of ceremonial architecture is the Caguana site (also known as Capá). The Caguana Ceremonial Center (Figure 4.5) is located in northwest Puerto Rico near the modern city of Utuado, on an old and partially modified terrace of the Tanamá River (Oliver 1998, 2005). It is at the junction of rolling hills and an abrupt Karst landscape. Construction began after AD 1200, and the site was in use until around AD 1500. Irving Rouse (1952) used pottery from the site to define the Capá style.

Fifteen distinct precincts have been identified, two of which were destroyed prior to the site's reconstruction (Oliver 2005:Table 7.2). At the center of the site, there is a large rectangular court with an ovoid court attached. Eight distinct parallel-sided courts surround it. All of the construction involved aligning stones, primarily from the river, and erecting larger monoliths. Floors and large post stains encountered during the original excavations indicate that several large rectangular structures were erected, possibly for use as a chief's house or a temple (Rouse 1992:113). There is no evidence that the site was permanently occupied, no burials, and no evidence that use of the site predates AD 1200.

FIGURE 4.5 Stone-lined courts at the Parque Ceremonial Indígena de Caguana, Utuado, Puerto Rico (photo by William Keegan).

The emergence of Caguana coincident with the demise of Tibes highlights significant and substantial social and political changes on the island (Curet and Stringer 2010; Oliver 2009; Siegel 2010). Oliver (2005:238) notes that the spatial arrangement of the courts at Caguana duplicates those at Tibes, as if the latter served as a blueprint. This replicative quality suggests that Caguana was built on an indigenous social design, but the scale of the monoliths represents a different kind of labor and artistic organization.

The most impressive difference is the twenty-two freestanding monoliths on the east and west sides of the central plaza. Petroglyphs were carved on monoliths facing each other across the plaza. They are attributed iconographically and stylistically to "Taíno" and recount indigenous mythology and legends (Oliver 2009; Robiou-Lemarche 1994).

In our opinion, the petroglyphs served as a "textbook." They expressed beliefs in a concrete way to "others" who were not previously familiar with these beliefs. Moreover, given the substantial number of petroglyphs at numerous locations across the island (Roe 2005), they did so in a manner, if not a language, that already was familiar. In this regard, beliefs were transmitted in a socially (and emotionally) charged space that permanently represented the superiority of these new beliefs. The idea that "Taíno" in Puerto Rico was an evolved social landscape is inaccurate (Oliver 2009).

Cacicazgos

Caribbean archaeologists have long embraced the concept of "chiefdom" because its original formulation was based on the "Taíno" *cacicazgo* constructed from early European accounts (see Redmond and Spencer 1994). Recently, Joshua Torres (2013) has questioned whether the concept has true explanatory power, or whether it is simply a classifying device that encourages "delusion" (Pauketat 2007). He advocates a greater emphasis on local developments as the way to achieve greater understanding (Torres 2012). In doing so, he follows others who recognize the significant role of historical contingency (Curet 2003) and a "mosaic" of cultural diversity (Wilson 2007).

The Spanish chroniclers identified seventeen chiefs (Figure 4.6), each associated with a major river drainage (Coll y Toste 1907). Village headmen within their territories supported these regional chiefs. It is not clear whether or not there was a higher ordering, as was the case in Hispaniola. The continuation of ceremonial centers, each with multiple stone-lined courts, argues for a more heterarchical political organization in Puerto Rico. These centers, with their linear courts, stand in marked contrast to the enormous circular plazas of Hispaniola (Alegría 1983; Wilson 1990).

We are in complete agreement with L. Antonio Curet (2003:19–20), who concluded that Puerto Rican societies had unique ideological foundations, political structure, and organizations that developed from their distinct ancestral societies through different and divergent historical processes. These

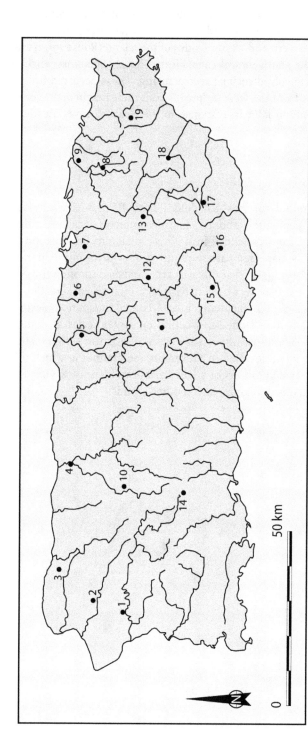

FIGURE 4.6 Locations of the villages of the Porto Rican chiefs: 1) Yagüeca (chief Urayoan); 2) Aymaco (chief Aymamon); 3) Guajataca (chief Mabodamaca); 4) Abacoa (chief Arisibo); 5) Sibuco (chief Guacabo); 6) Toa (chief Aramana); 7) Bayamon (chief Majagua); 8) Cayniabón (chief Canóbana); 9) Jaymanio (chieftainess Yuisa); 10) Otoao (chief Guarionex); 11) Jatibonico (chief Orocobix); 12 Guaynabo (chief Mabo); 13) Turabo (chief Caguax); 14) Guaynia (chiefs Agüeybana 1 and 2); 15) Abey (chief Abey); 16) Guayama (chief Guamani); 17) Guayaney (chief Guaraca); 18) Macao (chief Humacao); 19) Daguao (chief Daguao) (source Coll y Toste 1907:1) (courtesy of Menno Hoogland).

processes involved both internal accommodations and continued communication with communities beyond their borders. The clearest expression is the differences between the eastern and western sides of the island (Rouse 1992) and their comingling on the south-central coast (Torres 2012). The emergence of discrete political units involved societal restructuring. These occurred first in response to incursions from the west (a "push" from their neighbors; Keegan and Maclachlan 1989), and later in response to the Spanish invasion (Sued Badillo 2007).

Conclusions

Working from the ground up, post-Saladoid Puerto Rico is characterized by the dispersion of population and the manifestation of local identities. Communities changed from residence in a single village to the creation of settlement clusters. This dispersed pattern required new forms of integration and accommodation. We suggest that this was accomplished through the creation of stone-lined courts that were used in two ways. First was the creation of liminal space inside villages that facilitated inland/coastal integration. Second was the construction of these stone-lined courts on larger scales at neutral or boundary locations. The most important observation is the simultaneous expression of multiple identities. Before addressing the manner in which this articulates with Spanish suggestions of a pan-Caribbean identity, we need to examine contemporaneous developments on other islands.

CHAPTER 5 | The Meillacoid and Chicoid Worlds

MEILLACOID AND CHICOID POTTERY series have been used to track the emergence of the cultural lifeways described by the Spanish. The main emphasis is on the emergence of Taíno (Curet 2014; Wilson 1997). Taíno Culture has been constructed in four ways (Keegan 2013). First, Taíno presented an exotic culture to the Spanish invaders, and there are several extensive descriptions of their practices recorded by the Spanish. To date, most descriptions of Taíno have relied on documentary evidence. Second, "prehistorians" (Rouse 1972) have employed an evolutionary framework to chart their development and establish culture-area boundaries. Third, archaeologists have documented and excavated Taíno settlements to obtain an understanding of their practices in more specific contexts. Finally, nativist movements currently are redefining Taíno to meet modern political agendas (Laguer Diaz 2013). We no longer consider these frames of reference valid. The name "Taíno" reflects a misuse of the Spanish chronicles by modern historians. We therefore refrain from labeling the indigenous communities Taíno.

Caribbean archaeologists have become increasingly dissatisfied with the "Taíno" concept because it homogenizes what has proved archaeologically to be very diverse indigenous histories (Curet 2014; Oliver 2009; Rodriguez Ramos 2010; Wilson 2007). Embracing this diversity encompasses numerous problems, not the least of which is communication (Keegan 2010).[1] When archaeologists began to investigate the encounter period populations, they started with interpretations based on Spanish documents that portrayed the Indios as all being essentially the same (Ulloa Hung and Valcárcel Rojas 2016; Valcárcel Rojas 2012, 2016; Valcárcel Rojas et al. 2014; Veloz Maggiolo 1997). The primary distinction was between "good and noble" Indios and "fierce cannibals" (Hofman et al. 2008; Keegan 2007). Although most archaeologists today reject this simple dichotomy, they continue to use the initial constructs to structure their research and interpretations. The first attempt to introduce diversity was recognition of other communities identified by the Spanish, including the Caribe, Macorix, and Ciguayo. These have

---

[1] Overcoming such difficulties is an emphasis of the Nexus 1492 project 2013–2019 (www.Nexus1492.eu).

largely served as subordinates ("Other") to the Grand Culture. Diversity within the supraculture is now accepted, but has been addressed primarily through the promotion of an even more nebulous concept called "Taínoness."

When Rouse first introduced his classification scheme, he recognized local styles that were grouped into series that shared different modes and therefore different *traditions*. For the Greater Antilles, the main series were Saladoid, Ostionoid, Meillacoid, and Chicoid. Some researchers interpreted the idea of different traditions to mean different *origins*. The result was that each ceramic series came to be associated with a separate migration into the islands: Saladoid came from the Orinoco River in northeastern Venezuela (Rouse and Cruxent 1963); Ostionoid arrived from an unspecified source (Rainey 1940; Keegan 2006b); Meillacoid came from the Andean area via western Venezuela or Colombia (Veloz Maggiolo 1972; Zucchi 1991); and Huecoid was attributed to a coastal South or Central American source (Chanlatte Baik 1981). Only Chicoid was left as an indigenous development. For Rouse (1992), it was the culmination of an evolutionary sequence that began with Saladoid.

Rouse rejected the notion of multiple migrations (see Siegel 1986b). He completely erased them by introducing the intermediate category of subseries by which he transformed Ostionoid, Meillacoid, and Chicoid into Ostionan, Meillacan, and Chican subseries of a greater Ostionoid taxon. Thus, the pottery styles that he observed to be sufficiently different to warrant separate series denominations lost that status to preserve a single migration and evolutionary sequence. Throughout this book, we avoid using subseries terminology because we reject its utility. Subseries are an artifact of an attempt to fit the evidence to a unilinear sequence of development.

As an aside, we wonder where Rouse would have traced the origins of "Taíno" had he begun his quest from Haiti rather than Puerto Rico. A central premise of our work is that outcomes are strongly dependent on initial conditions. We suspect that if he had begun with the Meillac (Meillacoid) and Carrier (Chicoid) ceramics that he excavated during his dissertation research in Haiti (Rouse 1939), he would have been drawn immediately to the Valdivia ceramics of coastal Ecuador and the early ceramics at Puerto Hormiga and San Jacinto in Colombia (Meggers et al. 1965; Oyuela-Caycedo and Bonzani 2005; Reichel-Dolmatoff 1965). The vessel forms and decorative techniques are remarkably similar to those found in Hispaniola, and both Marcio Veloz Maggiolo (1972:119–120) and Alberta Zucchi (1991) have suggested that Meillacoid and Chicoid motifs were transmitted from this area through Colombia or western Venezuela (also see Steward and Faron 1959).

Given the increasing evidence for continuous relations between the Antilles (especially Puerto Rico and the northern Lesser Antilles) and the Isthmo-Colombian area (Crock 2000; Hofman and Hoogland 2011; Rodríguez Ramos 2011, 2013), one is left to wonder why similar engagements did not include Hispaniola. In fact, it would seem that such contacts were inevitable, given the relatively minor change in voyaging direction required to reach Hispaniola from southwestern margin of the Caribbean Sea or to reach the mainland from Hispaniola (Callaghan 2013).

Foragers and Farmers

Due to the paucity of excavations in Haiti, the most complete evidence comes from research in the Dominican Republic. The earliest occurrence of pottery in substantial amounts occurs in the eastern Dominican Republic at the sites of Punta Bayahibe, El Caimito, Musiépedro, and Honduras del Oeste (Atiles Bido and López Belando 2006; Krieger 1931; Veloz Maggiolo 1993; Veloz Maggiolo et al. 1991). The pottery occurs at sites with the same tools and the same settlement and subsistence patterns as Archaic Age sites. The absence of pottery griddles has been interpreted as evidence that they did not practice agriculture. However, griddles are simply a tool for food processing and do not accurately reflect the presence or absence of agriculture. One radiocarbon date from shell yielded an uncorrected date of 2255 +/– 80 B.P. (305 BC) (Teledyne Isotopes, I-8646) was obtained from the deepest level with pottery at the Musiépedro site (Veloz Maggiolo et al. 1976:271). To account for the marine reservoir effect, the date was calibrated using CALIB ver. 6.0, which yielded a 2-sigma range of cal. 131 BC to AD 279. Unfortunately, these sites are not well documented and in many cases have been destroyed by modern construction.

The early dates for pottery raise issues concerning the origins and development of early farming communities in the Dominican Republic. Previous interpretations have emphasized a Neolithic expansion that began in the Orinoco River drainage and progressed through the Lesser Antilles, Puerto Rico, and then Hispaniola. Early Dominican pottery is mostly undecorated and difficult to attribute to a particular style. The current conclusion is that it reflects local developments that may have been influenced by Saladoid communities in Puerto Rico. In contrast, Marcio Veloz Maggiolo (1993) and Alberta Zucchi have proposed a separate and direct movement of pottery and farming from South America (Zucchi 1991; Zucchi and Tarble 1984).

Rouse (1992:91–92) examined the pottery and concluded that the El Caimito artisans must have copied designs on Hacienda Grande (Saladoid) pottery that they observed through a process of transculturation. Rouse (1992) attributes the origins of linear-incised designs to the Archaic Age communities in the islands. This was a period of dramatic change in the eastern Dominican Republic. Pottery was present prior to this time, but its production and use increased exponentially. A wide variety of cultigens already was available, but their production was intensified. Larger villages with extensive central plazas, large multi-family houses, and earthworks, including *monticulos* and village enclosures, become a recognizable pattern (Veloz Maggiolo 1972; Zucchi 1990:280–281). Some of these features are not common in Puerto Rico (Wilson 1990:24–26). These changes point to a significant restructuring of the indigenous Antillean societies. The reorganization of relations of production, consumption, and social integration all converged to transform incipient practice into new *modos de vida* and social formations.

Pottery Styles in Hispaniola

Ostionoid pottery, which is classified with the Ostiones style of western Puerto Rico, appears in the eastern Dominican Republic around AD 600 (Figure 5.1). The diversity of pottery expressions at this time reflects these emerging social identities (Hofman et al. 2008). The situation was one in which multiple inter-acting communities were experimenting with different economic strategies and social relations. Dominican archaeologists have identified up to eight different styles grouped into phases for this period in the eastern Dominican Republic (Veloz Maggiolo 1993). These styles include the mixing of modes that usually are associated with different series. In this regard, the Ostionoid taxon has been used as a classificatory tool that masks the underlying variability. The logic was that, because Ostionoid followed Saladoid, then all simple post-Saladoid pottery west of Puerto Rico must be Ostionoid. *Ostionoid is not deconstructed Saladoid.*

Haiti is strikingly different. Clark Moore has combined an avocational inter-est in archaeology with voluntary assistance to a local medical mission. Over the past several decades, he has actively sought to document archaeological

FIGURE 5.1 Ostionoid pottery from southeastern Hispaniola. Not to scale (photos by Corinne Hofman and Menno Hoogland).

sites across Haiti, and he even collaborated with Irving Rouse on excavations on the southwestern peninsula (Rouse 1982; Rouse and Moore 1985). The results of Moore's surveys are reported in an unpublished database, which is especially useful because he understands Rouse's pottery classification. Moore (1998) records 898 archaeological sites in Haiti by culture, including 166 Archaic Age sites, two Ostionoid sites, 436 Meillacoid sites (Meillac and Finca styles), and 128 Chicoid sites (Carrier style). The remaining sites include various combinations of these pottery series (see Table 5.1).

One striking feature of this inventory is the nearly complete absence of Ostionoid sites in all of Haiti (n = 4; 0.2% of the total). Of the four sites reported, one is associated with an Archaic Age site, and the other is mixed with Meillacoid and Chicoid pottery. The small number of sites recorded may result from the very limited investigation of Haitian archaeology. Ostionoid sites also have been identified in low frequencies in Jamaica (n = 16), the Turks & Caicos Islands (n = 1), and possibly southeastern Cuba. It has been suggested that Ostionoid represents the breaching of a frontier on the Mona Passage and the rapid expansion of population to the west (Rouse 1986; Wilson 2007). However,

TABLE 5.1 *Archaeological Sites in Haiti by Ages and Pottery Series (Moore 1998).*

	NUMBER OF SITES
Archaic Age	
Lithic	57
Lithic/Ceramic	1
Early Archaic	2
Archaic	166
Archaic/Ceramic	1
Archaic/Ostionoid	1
Archaic/Meillacoid	2
"Preceramic"	17
Ceramic Age	
Ostionoid	2
Ostionoid/Meillacoid/Chicoid	1
Meillacoid ("classic")	1
Meillacoid	321
Meillacoid/Chicoid	14
Meillacoid/Chicoid/Spanish	2
Meillacoid/Lithic	1
Meillacoid (Finca style)	115
Meillacoid (Finca)/Chicoid	12
Chicoid	128
Chicoid/Meillacoid	5
Chicoid/Meillacoid (Finca)	1
"Ceramic"	22

the known distribution of Ostionoid sites is not consistent with a linear expansion of population. It is more likely that Ostionoid pottery was adopted by related communities with a predominantly coastal orientation and then spread among them across Hispaniola, resulting in the colonization of Jamaica and expeditions to southeastern Cuba and the southern Bahamas. Given the technical and decorative characteristics and geographical distribution, it is possible that Ostionoid pottery developed first in the Dominican Republic and then spread east into Puerto Rico and rapidly west to Jamaica, Cuba, and the Turks & Caicos Islands, where beachheads were established but never flourished. It is important to recognize that Ostionoid pottery had a wide distribution across the Greater Antilles, but this phenomenon has not been studied in detail.

The specific characteristics of the two main pottery series were described as follows (Rouse 1939:42–56): The Meillacoid series includes Meillac and Finca styles in Haiti; Baní style in Cuba; and White Marl, Montego Bay, and Port Morant styles in Jamaica. Chicoid styles include Boca Chica in the Dominican Republic; Carrier in Haiti; Pueblo Viejo in Cuba; and Capá and Esperanza styles in Puerto Rico (in our opinion, these could be classified as Meillacoid). Significant variations from the series descriptions are discussed in the text (also see Persons 2013).

Meillacoid pottery has relatively thin walls (3–7 mm) and a hard surface that is smoothed but not highly polished (Figure 5.2) (Rouse 1939:42–56). Vessel shapes include hemispherical bowls and boat-shapes. In the Fort Liberté area (Haiti), the paste has a reddish tint from either the clay itself or some additive; however, pottery to the west of Fort Liberté has grey to black paste, suggesting

FIGURE 5.2 Meillacoid pottery from northern Hispaniola. Not to scale (photos by Corinne Hofman and Menno Hoogland).

a more reducing firing environment. The vessels have rounded rims, with the outward folding of the final coil creating a fillet rim. The vessels typically turn inward at the shoulder (*casuela*), and there occasionally is a ridge of clay along the shoulder. Decorations are limited to the panel between the shoulder and the rim. Decorations include sigmoid and other appliqué (ribbons often with cross-cutting incisions, hand-paw motif, C-shapes, etc.), punctations on the body and lip, and adornos that rise above the rim on opposite sides of the vessel. Some of these lugs or adornos are anthropomorphic and are constructed through the appliqué of facial features. This building of faces is not found in Chicoid adornos. The most distinctive designs are narrow (1–2 mm) incised lines that leave a ridge of clay along the edge of the incision. Crosshatching, oblique parallel lines, alternating inclined units, and straight lines that never end in a dot are common. Strap handles are present.

Chicoid pottery is thicker (7–9 mm), softer, and highly polished (especially Boca Chica style). A wider range of vessel shapes occurs, including effigies and white-slipped bottles. Jars (*potizas*) are common, especially in the eastern Dominican Republic. The paste is grey to brown in color and easily distinguished from Meillacoid sherds. Flaring rims are more common, in some cases with punctations where the vessel flares outward. There is no appliqué. Lugs are large and modeled, giving the appearance of sculpture, and large, decorated strap handles are present. Incisions typically are broad lines (4–5 mm) with smoothed and rounded edges; they are shallower and widely spaced and occur in circular, oval, and rectangular panels (Figure 5.3). Straight and curved lines typically end in a dot.

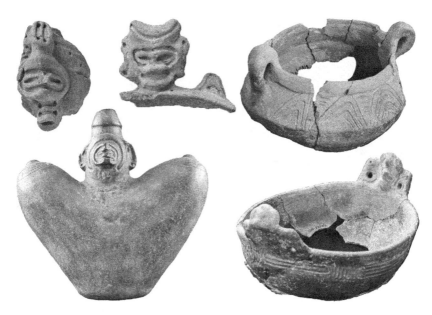

FIGURE 5.3 Chicoid pottery from Hispaniola. Not to scale (photos by Corinne Hofman and Menno Hoogland).

Marcio Veloz Maggiolo (1993) describes a period of transition in the eastern Dominican Republic that he calls the "Atajadizo phase" (AD 840–1300). The transitional character of this period is apparent in the high frequency of Ostionoid pottery at some sites and the appearance of Chicoid pottery at the Juandolio site around AD 850 (Veloz Maggiolo et al. 1974; Ulloa Hung 2013). The sites typically are located one to two kilometers from the sea, often in association with mangroves. An increased emphasis on farming is indicated by the expansion of population along rivers into the interior, the cultivation of river terraces (*várzea*), and the increasing importance of clay griddles (Veloz Maggiolo 1993:73). It has been suggested that farming was based on the slash-and-burn cultivation technique. Maize is present as early as AD 1060 in the interior of the Dominican Republic (Lane et al. 2008), and continued in use until contact (Newsom and Deagan 1994).

An example for this phase is the Juanpedro site (AD 850–1309). The predominant pottery can be classified as Ostionoid. Houses were large and contained thirty to forty individuals, probably members of extended families. There is a cleared central plaza with an irregular, ring-shaped midden (*calzeda*). The site is estimated to have been occupied by around 500 individuals. The animal remains include an abundance of sea turtles, a variety of marine fish (including Scaridae and *Caranx* sp.), an abundance of *Lobatus* sp. and other marine mollusks, land snails, and hutia. Pollen analysis at the site

FIGURE 5.4 El Cabo site, eastern Dominican Republic (photo by Corinne Hofman and Menno Hoogland).

identified guáyiga (*Zamia debilis*), guazuma (West Indian elm), corozo palm (*Acrocomia quisqueyana*), papaya, guayaba (guava), higüero (bottle gourd), and tobacco (Fortuna 1978). Pollen analysis also indicates the presence of maize (Fortuna 1978). The occurrence of clay griddles is taken as evidence for manioc cultivation (Veloz Maggiolo 1993:75); however, recent starch grain analysis of clay griddle surfaces indicates that they were used for multiple purposes (Pagán Jiménez 2011, 2013). In addition to the large villages represented by the Juanpedro site, the settlement pattern included smaller villages, hamlets, homesteads, and activity areas. El Cabo, near Higüey, is a typical village (Samson 2010) (Figure 5.4).

El Cabo Site, Southeastern Dominican Republic (c. AD 600–1500)

The El Cabo site dates between AD 600 and 1504 and is characterized by an Ostionoid and a Chicoid component with several occupation phases (Samson and Hoogland 2007). The archaeological site of El Cabo de San Rafael is located in the southeastern Dominican Republic in La Altagracía province. The site is situated on a stretch of limestone coast overlooking the Mona Passage to Puerto Rico. The site has been excavated by Leiden University under the direction Menno Hoogland and Corinne Hofman. Alice Samson carried out her doctoral research on the houses. One of the remarkable features of the site is that post holes were dug into the underlying limestone bedrock. These post holes provide a permanent record of the indigenous structures. Six house clusters aligned along a promontory above the coast have been identified (Samson 2010). Each cluster had three to five circular houses measuring 6.5–10 meters in diameter. Their construction is similar to that of the South American *maloca*, which is consistent with the houses described by Oviedo y Valdés (1959). It is estimated that each house had the capacity to accommodate thirty to forty individuals. In this regard, the house clusters probably represent clan or lineage compounds. From the 9th to 16th centuries, El Cabo was a town with as many as 250 inhabitants. The houses in each compound show evidence for the replacement, rebuilding, and reorientation of the structures. In addition to houses, possible storerooms, work huts, windbreaks, and fences were identified (Samson 2010).

Samson (2013:368) recognizes houses as the dominant architectural form for expressing the social identity of their occupants. The renewal and rebuilding of houses created a trajectory that linked the inhabitants to those of the past (ancestors). These houses produced historical continuity through "access to origins" in the context of a *Société à Maison* (Helms 1998; Lévi-Strauss 1982). The concept of "House Societies" recognizes that a house is more than a dwelling; it is the primary structure for social integration and interaction. Moreover, it provides a foundation for the development of institutionalized ranking and the differentiation of status.

The ultimate phase of occupation is associated with early colonial European materials (Hofman et al. 2014; Samson 2010; Valcárcel Rojas et al. 2013). Four burials (three adults and an infant) all have local strontium isotope signatures (Laffoon 2012). Three of the individuals are buried inside Chicoid house structures, and the fourth belongs to the Ostionoid occupation of the site and is located under a dense layer of Chicoid midden. The near-absence of burials within houses, as is known from other contemporaneous sites in Puerto Rico and the Lesser Antilles, suggests that the deceased may have been taken to the neighboring caves, cenotes, or other as-yet-unknown locations to be buried.

A study by Hayley Mickleburgh on the teeth and pathologies from the neighboring site of Punta Macao has revealed that the occupants at that site consumed a diet with a medium to high proportion of carbohydrates (mostly starches). In other words, horticultural products were very important in the diet. In addition, the differences in dental pathology between males and females show that the females consumed more root crops than males. The use of teeth as tools has been observed through various micro and macro patterns left by their utilization. The obtained information indicates the manipulation of fibers, particularly by females. Striations on male incisors suggest the tight clamping of a hard object between the opposing incisors, which may have been caused by the use of a bow drill with mouthpiece (Mickleburgh 2013). Analysis of starch grains on teeth and tools revealed that the most-often-identified plant is the guáyiga (*Zamia pumila*). Other plants that were identified in lesser quantities are maize, el lerén or arrowroot (*Maranta* sp.), la gruya or achira (*Canna* sp.), and a domesticated bean (Mickleburgh and Pagán Jiménez 2012).

The indigenous material assemblage consists of locally produced pottery and lithic tools, beads, and pendants, in addition to religious paraphernalia (Samson 2010; Samson and Hoogland 2007; van As et al. 2008). The lithic tools include numerous greenstone adzes, some of which are made of jadeite originating from the Río San Juan region in the northern part of the Dominican Republic (Sebastiaan Knippenberg, personal communication 2012).

The majority of evidence for mobility and interaction is concordant with the expected patterns of a Late Ceramic Age community. However, small numbers of European artifacts, including beads of the Nueva Cadíz type and over 100 fragments of metal, glass, and earthenware (olive jars and Columbia Plain white glazed majolica) were found (Ernst and Hofman 2014). These items were clustered in a tightly circumscribed area, within house structures pertaining to the final phase of the site. These structures evolved during the early colonial period and were associated with elaborate Chicoid paraphernalia.

We may presume that El Cabo was abandoned shortly after 1504, when the region was convulsed by the Higüey wars. It was also one of the last places to come under Spanish control (Oliver 2009; Samson 2010). The situation at El Cabo reflects a very short period during which Spanish materials were incorporated into the local material culture, indigenous repertoires, and practices (Hofman et al. 2014; Valcácel Rojas et al. 2012). However, as the Spanish presence in this region was limited at that time and appears to have been mainly restricted to northern and central Hispaniola, it is unlikely that the community at El Cabo maintained any direct and sustained contacts with the colonizers. It is more probable that the European materials were distributed down the line through preexisting indigenous networks (Hofman et al. 2014). The association with indigenous paraphernalia suggests an integration of these "foreign" items by the local community (Valcárcel Rojas et al. 2013). This may be because their physical appearance and other sensory traits fit within preexisting systems of value (Keehnen 2011).

Northwestern Dominican Republic

The commencement of Meillacoid has been traced to the Cibao Valley near the center of the island. The earliest manifestations are dated to AD 850 at the site of Cutupú (Veloz Maggiolo 1993). Recent investigations by Jorge Ulloa Hung (2014) have documented the extensive presence of Meillacoid sites in the northwestern Dominican Republic in the provinces of Puerto Plata and Monte Cristi, in close proximity to the Meillac type-site near Fort Liberté, Haiti.

In marked contrast to Rouse's (1992) cultural replacement model, Jorge Ulloa Hung (2014) has identified multicomponent sites in the northwestern Dominican Republic that exhibit contemporaneity of series and the mixing of styles (Figure 5.5). Ostionoid pottery at Rio Jobo and Rio Verde is

FIGURE 5.5 View of the estuary from Arismendy, northwestern Dominican Republic (courtesy of Jorge Ulloa Hung).

radiocarbon-dated to between AD 680 and 1020, and to the west at Los Patos it dates to between AD 846 and 1000. It was imported to Grand Turk (Turks & Caicos Islands) from a source in Hispaniola between AD 700 and 1100 (Carlson 1999). Meillacoid pottery is radiocarbon dated to between AD 778 and 1148 at Rio Jobo and Rio Verde, and from AD 894–1452 at Don Julio, Puerto Juanita, and Hatillo Palma. Bois Charitte (Haiti), has yielded a similar date of AD 1050–1413. The range for Chicoid pottery is AD 1000–1531 at Edilio Cruz, La Muchacha, and En Bas Saline (Haiti).

Ulloa Hung (2014) notes a mixing of styles. The mixing of Ostionoid and Meillacoid styles may explain why Meillacoid pottery at the Meillac site near Fort Liberté, Haiti, is described by Rouse (1939) as having red surface finishes. This mixing may reflect intermarriage between communities whose primary reference or social identity was expressed in one or the other pottery style (Ulloa Hung 2014). At the very least, the mixing of styles indicates substantial local interactions. Early linear motifs were coherent for both. Meillacoid eventually became the dominant local tradition, and it exhibits a cultural unity maintained during expansion to the west. Chicoid attributes were later added selectively to the Meillacoid repertoire, but they did not replace the existing motifs, they enriched them (Ulloa Hung 2014). The region cannot be characterized at any time by a single pottery series; *the region was a multicultural mosaic infused with dynamic interactions* (Ulloa Hung 2014:230). In this regard, the classification of pottery according to subseries is not a useful endeavor.

The Meillacoid economy was based on exploiting diverse environments (Veloz Maggiolo et al. 1981). The sites were positioned for access to arable land, proximity to watercourses, a wide viewscape, and ocean access (Ulloa Hung 2013:230, 236, 2014). The latter reflected in an economic link to marine resources. Meillacoid communities were not static or homogeneous. They developed over time, through processes of interaction on multiple scales, while maintaining access to and control of rich spaces of marine resources and diverse social connections (Ulloa Hung 2013:231, 2014).

The first transition involved the syncretism of Archaic Age, Ostionoid, and Meillacoid lifeways that coalesced as the Meillacoid tradition. This tradition is reflected in the effective and efficient exploitation of diverse habitats. Ulloa Hung (2014) concludes that this presented a significant advantage when Chicoid potters began to enter the area, and that Chicoid communities needed peaceful interactions with the indigenous Meillacoid communities to successfully colonize the region. Chicoid colonists also may have succeeded by infiltrating Meillacoid communities, in concert with the large-scale movement of entire villages. In other words, a few individuals established a foothold in an indigenous community through marriage, converted the community to their world view, and opened the opportunity for the larger-scale movement of new villages created through fissioning to establish settlements in new locales. The process of infiltration has been employed to explain one aspect of the Arawak diaspora, and it may have been a basic element of Arawak societies during periods of expansion (Heckenberger 2002; Schmidt 1917).

Meillacoid Revolution

As discussed in the next chapter, the Meillacoid *modo de vida* spread rapidly across Hispaniola to Jamaica, Cuba, and the southern Bahamas (Rouse 1992; Sinelli 2013). The rapid spread of pottery to these places where it was only a minor component of the cultural inventory suggests a significant shift in alimentation. Because faunal assemblages remained relatively unchanged (Colten and Worthington 2013; deFrance 2013), such continued exploitation of the same milieu suggests that the change in diet must have involved a change in the use of plants. This new *modo de vida* is best explained as resulting from the introduction of a suite of tropical forest cultigens and associated cultivation practices. The importance of agriculture in relation to fishing is expressed in the shift of settlement location from the coast to hilltops overlooking the coast (Rouse and Moore 1985:18; and see next chapter) and to more inland locations along rivers. Pottery vessels were introduced as part of the package because they were necessary for the proper preparation of cuisine. The longevity of the design motifs is testimony to the inseparability of the raw and the cooked.

Following Rouse's (1992) framework, every new development completely replaced its predecessor. He dates the demise of the Haitian Meillacoid, except in southwestern Haiti, to the early 13th century when it was replaced by Chicoid pottery. Given the overwhelming number of undated Meillacoid sites ($n = 437$) compared to Chicoid sites ($n = 128$), it is difficult to envision Meillacoid wiped from the face of Hispaniola (Ulloa Hung 2013). Furthermore, Clark Moore (1998) identifies the mixing of six predominantly Chicoid sites with Meillacoid and twenty-eight predominantly Meillacoid sites with Chicoid (Table 5.1). Ulloa Hung (2013) observed a similar situation in the northwestern Dominican Republic, where Meillacoid and Chicoid sites have mixed deposits, including the appearance of Meillacoid motifs on Chicoid vessels, and vice versa. These sites hint at some form of collateral interaction; the explanation for which has a social basis.

During their research at the Bois Neuf site north of Port-au-Prince, Froelich Rainey and J. J. Ortiz Aguilú (1983) identified separate archaeological deposits on either side of the Rivière Seche. The east bank had only Carrier style (Chicoid) pottery, while the west bank had only Meillac style pottery, which suggested contemporaneous segregation. This distribution led Rainey to wonder whether the Diale 1 (Meillac) and Diale 2 (Carrier) sites, separated by only 150 meters along the coast of Baie de Fort Liberté, might represent contemporaneous sites marked by cultural distinctions. This pairing of culturally distinct sites is reminiscent of the much earlier Sorcé/la Hueca sites on Vieques Island (Chanlatte Baik 1981) and the Ostiones and Santa Elena sites in south-central Puerto Rico (Torres 2012). Duality is a fundamental element in social and political organizations, and it has been argued that Caribbean polities were organized by this dialectic (Keegan and Maclachlan 1989). It is our contention that, not only did Meillacoid and Chicoid coexist as distinct cultural manifestations, but that each needed the other.

Meillacoid and Chicoid settlement patterns exhibit a wide range of variability. In addition to large villages, there were specialized production sites (e.g., the Île à Rat site), and numerous villages with *monticulos* and earthworks (e.g., the El Flaco site). The investigation of site variability is crucial to developing a clearer understanding of social dynamics.

El Flaco Site, Northwestern Dominican Republic (c. AD 900–1500)

The El Flaco site is located at the foot of the Paso de Los Hidalgos in the Cordillera Septentrional, which separates the north coast from the Cibao valley (Figure 5.6). El Flaco is approximately 12 kilometers from the coast. The site is situated near the so-called Mirador de Colón along the route that Columbus took when he first entered the interior of Hispaniola. The site is currently being excavated by Leiden University under the direction of Corinne Hofman and Menno Hoogland in the context of the ERC-Synergy project NEXUS1492. The site is characterized by a cultural landscape consisting of a series of platforms encircled by a number of mounds and earthworks. Radiocarbon dates point to an occupation in the 10th to 15th centuries AD (Hofman and Hoogland 2015b).

FIGURE 5.6 Excavations at El Flaco site, Dominican Republic, showing *monticulo* at bottom right (photo by Till Sonnemann, courtesy of Corinne Hofman).

The analysis of the spatial organization of the site indicated the creation of platforms for the construction of the houses on the south flank of the Loma de Guyacanes (Figure 5.7). Soil was removed to flatten these areas and was dumped to the side in the areas where earthen walls and mounds are located. The excavation of several of these platforms revealed the layout of house structures with diameters of about 8.5–9 meters. The larger houses have a double row of posts, a center row with large posts with a diameter of approximately 6 meters, and an outer circle with small posts or alternating large and small posts. The total diameter of these houses is 9 m. The 1.2-meter distance between the two rows is very consistent. In addition to the house structures, there is also evidence of cooking huts: small, round, circular structures with a hearth inside. These cooking huts measure 3–4 meters in diameter.

The stratigraphy of the mounds is complicated and shows evidence of multiple activities over short periods of time. Various lenses represent the deposition of waste, sometimes burned, resulting in thick layers of very fine ash with large quantities of land snails (*Pleurodontes* sp. and *Polidontes* sp.), faunal remains, and pottery. These ash layers are very fertile, and it has been suggested that in certain periods they were used for planting. These lenses are covered with layers of white soil coming from the area of the houses, including unburned garbage deposits. Within these mounds, there is also evidence of cooking activities, represented by hearths with burned ceramics and many pieces of griddle.

Eighteen human burials were encountered in three of the mounds. Burial practices were diverse and complex, and the taphonomy in the majority of the

FIGURE 5.7 Reconstruction of structures on the El Flaco site (courtesy of Menno Hoogland).

cases suggests that the graves were left open until after the desiccation of the body. There is one case of a composite burial with two sub-adult individuals. Both crania had been taken out of the grave, probably after the soft tissues had decomposed.

The pottery encountered at El Flaco is principally Chicoid and Meillacoid, with a little Ostionoid pottery present, especially in the lower layers of the mounds. The intermingling of styles in the northwestern region of the Dominican Republic evidences a landscape of cultural and social diversity and interactions. (Ulloa Hung 2014). Next to large quantities of pottery, the material assemblage consists of lithic artifacts, many of which were manufactured of locally available stones. Beads were made of a variety of materials, including shell, pottery, bone, and stone. All of this material is found in the mounds and in the swept areas around the houses. The area of the houses was left very clean.

Île à Rat Site, Haiti (c. AD 900–1500)

Archaeological excavations at Île à Rat provide a stratigraphic record of changes in pottery series through time (Figure 5.8). Île à Rat is a tiny island (<0.5 ha) located 2 kilometers from the main island off the north coast west of Cap Haïtien. It guards the mouth of the Baie de l'Acul (Keegan 2001). The island is composed of calcareous sand with humic enrichment and shows little evidence

FIGURE 5.8 Aerial view of Île à Rat, Haiti (courtesy of John de Bry).

for modern disturbance. The surrounding marine environments include extensive coral reefs, bare sand, and seagrass shoals. The inner part of the bay is a
large lagoon with a constricted opening. It is a major nursery area for marine
fishes, and the entire area is today heavily fished from nearby coastal villages.
Shovel tests revealed that the entire island is an archaeological site.

In 1995, William Keegan (2001) directed the excavation of a 10-by-2-meter
trench near the center of the island. The unit was excavated by hand and
sieved through fine-mesh screens. The first three units were excavated in
10-centimeter levels and the last two by cultural stratigraphy. The deposit is
about 75 centimeters in depth, and there are five distinct strata. Two of these
strata were radiocarbon dated. The deposit accurately reflects the cultural
sequence of Archaic Age, Ostionoid, Meillacoid, Chicoid, and Spanish that has
been defined for Haiti (Rouse 1992). Their stratigraphic separation confirms
the distinct identities associated with these pottery series.

The uppermost level (0–6 cmbs) is a root zone containing Spanish pottery
and a few other artifacts. Members of Columbus's expedition visited the island
on December 20, 1492 (Dunn and Kelley 1989:275). From 6–24 centimeters
below surface, there is a dense concentration of mostly complete, juvenile,
Lobatus gigas shells and Chicoid pottery. Most of the pottery was small-to-large
hemispherical bowls with outcurving rims and multiple rows of punctations
at the curve. They look as if the curve was marked to facilitate the removal of
the outcurving upper portion of the vessels (e.g., like perforations between
stamps). Next, there is a stratum of mostly sterile sand containing beach-
washed coral and water-worn potsherds (24–38 cmbs). Beneath the sterile
zone, there is a dense concentration of mostly complete, juvenile, *Lobatus gigas*
shells, and most of the pottery is Meillacoid (38–54 cmbs). A radiocarbon date
on an individual chunk of charcoal from 40 centimeters below surface yielded
a date of cal. AD 1295 +/– 70 (two-sigma range of 1225–1410; Beta-108547). The
deepest level (54–72 cmbs) also was radiocarbon dated. A single large piece
of charcoal from 57 centimeters below surface gave a date of cal. AD 905–950
+/– 50 (two-sigma range of 790–1010; Beta-108548). At this depth, the pottery includes both Meillacoid and Ostionoid styles. At the very bottom of the
deposit, there were a few artifacts associated with the Archaic Age, including
a section of a Couri-style chert blade and a cache of seven stone balls (*esfero-
lithicos*). These artifacts may represent a separate Archaic Age occupation of
the island, or, because they are associated with Ostionoid pottery, they may
reflect the close association between Ostionoid and Archaic Age communities
(Chapter 6; and see Rodríguez Ramos 2010).

The island is an ideal location for a small settlement amidst abundant
marine resources (Keegan et al. 2008), it affords a vantage of the entire bay,
and it is breezier and less mosquito-infested than the main island. It is possible that the island supports a small freshwater lens, but if water was not
available on the island, there is a freshwater spring a short canoe trip away.
The 70+ centimeters of deposits contain high percentages of decorated pottery,
bowl fragments with burned food encrustations, and a substantial number of

griddle sherds. These deposits contain the full range of materials expected for a long-term settlement, and they do not look like the product of repeated short-term occupations.

One factor in the occupation of the island concerns the procurement of marine resources. A steady supply of fish and shellfish was needed for the large villages that were upriver and away from the coast. The need for marine protein seems to have been especially pressing, given the report that only a five-to-eight-day supply of food was on hand (Sauer 1966). Given the absence of significant populations of terrestrial fauna, specialized fishermen living on the coast would have been crucial to the survival of inland settlements on Hispaniola. In a related case, some of the coastal villages in southern Cuba, where the land was poor, are reported to have specialized in fishing (Lovén 1935:504). In addition, fresh and preserved meats probably were exported to Hispaniola from fishing villages in the southern Bahamas (e.g., Turks & Caicos Islands) (Morsink 2013).

Test excavations revealed that the entire island is literally carpeted with juvenile conch shells (Figure 5.9). There are far more *Lobatus gigas* shells than one would expect in a settlement of this size. In addition, most of the fish bones in the site are the head parts of small fishes, which may reflect the processing of fishes, prior to their export to villages on the main island.

The island has two distinct cultural components separated by a stratum of sterile sand. One or more storm events probably deposited this sand, because

FIGURE 5.9 William Keegan (left) and Brian Riggs drawing stratigraphic profile of the Île à Rat excavations in 1995 (courtesy of Lisabeth Carlson).

the few potsherds recovered from this stratum have an abraded, water-worn appearance. There is very little mixing of the cultural components. The pottery in the lower strata is predominantly Meillacoid (generally dated to AD 900 and 1300 for this part of Hispaniola; Rouse 1992), although there is also Ostionoid pottery intermingled at the lowest levels. Archaeological surveys conducted along the coast revealed small Meillacoid sites on virtually every sand beach in the Baie de L'Acul. These small sites reflect a dispersed population and more direct access to the sea. For some reason, these low-lying coastal beaches were abandoned. The absence of Chicoid sherds on these sites suggests that they were abandoned before the beginning of the Chicoid period (generally dated to between AD 1300 and 1500 for this part of Hispaniola; Rouse 1992). It is possible that inundation by storms and/or rising sea level made these locations unsuited for habitation sometime after AD 1300.

There were changes in fishing practices as well. Stone and pottery net-sinkers are common in the Chicoid deposits on Île à Rat (Figure 5.10) but are absent from the Meillacoid strata. Virtually identical stone net-sinkers have been found at the contact period sites of En Bas Saline and La Isabela in Hispaniola (Deagan, personal communication 2007; Deagan and Cruxent 2002:Fig. 2.8), and they are reported from Jamaica (Allsworth-Jones 2008) and Cuba (Guarch Delmonte 1974:31; Martínez Arango 1997). Despite the absence of such net weights in the Meillacoid strata, the presence of a shell net-gauge suggests the manufacture and use of nets. Because nets can be used in different ways, the

FIGURE 5.10 Stone and pottery net sinkers from the Île à Rat site, Haiti (photo by William Keegan).

difference may reflect a shift in technology. During Meillacoid times, stationary seine nets may have been used, and the grapefruit-sized stone balls found in the deposit may have been the weights for such nets. In contrast, the small, thin, and flat net weights found in the Chicoid deposit would have been ideal for cast nets. The flat surface of these stones would promote their aerodynamic movement when cast, and their thin profile would facilitate the full weight of the stone dropping and closing the net after contact with the surface of the water. Although Richard Price (1966) has reported that cast nets were not used in the Americas prior to European contact, the remains of small, bait-size, schooling fish in precolonial deposits suggests that some means for netting these fish must have been used. Cast nets are the preferred method today for capturing such fish (Keegan et al. 2011).

Finally, there also were changes in how meals were cooked. Meillacoid pottery is characterized by in-turned, casuela, and boat-shaped vessels. In contrast, Chicoid vessels were larger and flared outward from the shoulder. Vessels with a restricted opening are better suited for the transport of liquids, and they limit contamination from dust and dirt. These features were incorporated in Chicoid vessels, which are constricted at the shoulder, but their outward flaring rim would provide greater access to the contents and facilitate their manipulation during cooking (Espenshade 2000). Thus, the foods cooked during Meillacoid times may have emphasized a more liquid process such as boiling fish, while the more open Chicoid vessels would have been well suited for pepper pot and thicker stews, which may have required periodic stirring to prevent the contents from burning. This change in food processing is consistent with Mickleburgh's (2013) dental studies that indicate the consumption of more refined and highly processed foods in the Late Ceramic Age.

The flow of people, ideas, and objects achieves fluidity when styles are viewed as reflecting personal and social identifiers (Hofman and Carlin 2010; Mol 2013; Roe 1995b). Seeing both at the same time is the classical paradox of quantum mechanics: How can something be both a particle and a wave? In this regard, the notion of interaction spheres (and frontiers) limits our capacity to see the whole. Rouse (1986) was the first to recognize that pottery styles are more similar across water passages than across islands. This perspective encouraged a focus on defining interaction spheres. For example, interactions across the Virgin Passage involved eastern Puerto Rico (Santa Elena), the Virgin Islands, and the northern Lesser Antilles (see articles in Delpuech and Hofman 2004); and the Mona Passage linked western Puerto Rico and eastern Hispaniola (Rouse 1992). However, the distribution of styles across the islands suggests that, while these may denote primary contacts, social engagements were not limited to these spheres (e.g., Ostiones/Capá and Santa Elena/Esperanza [and later Boca Chica] in south-central Puerto Rico).

Our point is that major changes occurred throughout the islands between AD 800 and 1300. Meillac and Carrier (and Boca Chica) styles were contemporaneous. The distribution of Meillacoid styles is testimony to a dramatic dispersion across Hispaniola and on to the already occupied islands of Jamaica, Cuba, and the southern Bahama archipelago. The success of this mobility must have been financed by a significant change in lifeways. Meillacoid was far more than a culture waiting to be replaced by a supposedly superior Chicoid Culture (cf. Rouse 1992; Veloz Maggiolo 1993). It is our contention that the shift from Meillacoid to Chicoid was predicated on internal adjustments involving pan-Caribbean social networks. These adjustments cannot be defined in terms of pottery alone (Figure 5.11). In the end, these networks facilitated the dispersion of a set of common ideas (conceived by others as "Taínoness").

The islands of Hispaniola, Cuba, Jamaica, and the Bahamas offered environments that were ideally suited to tropical forest agriculture. Agriculture and the pots used to prepare meals were key factors in the success of this expansion. Although it has long been assumed that the foundations of this economy were based on manioc as the staple crop, recent paleobotanical studies have questioned this assumption (Pagán Jiménez 2013). In fact, given the ecological diversity of the island, we should not expect that a single staple cultigen was emphasized throughout the islands (see Roosevelt 1980). Instead manioc, sweet potato, maize, and guáyiga were probably employed to varying degrees in different locations. The hallmark of tropical agriculture is a reliance on diverse suites of intercropped cultigens (Keegan 2009).

It is highly unlikely that agriculture and pottery were transported *in toto* from the Venezuelan *llanos* to Hispaniola (Zucchi 1991). If these practices developed from contacts with the western Venezuelan coast, then these contacts were likely to have been initiated *from* Hispaniola. In other words, we do not accept the notion of a separate migration to the islands, but we recognize the possibility that influences from Venezuela, Colombia, and Central America

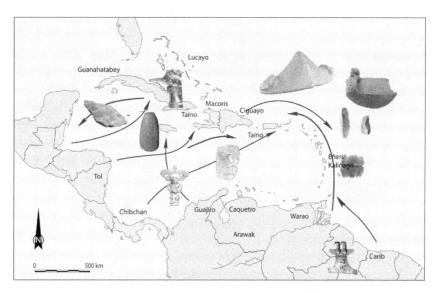

FIGURE 5.11 Hypothesized Caribbean networks of human mobility and exchange of goods and ideas (courtesy of Corinne Hofman and Menno Hoogland).

continued to arrive in the islands through continuing social contacts (Hofman and Bright 2010). The rapid spread of new social and economic relations may be similar to that noted by Michael Heckenberger (2002) for Arawak speakers who reproduce a *habitus* predisposed to perpetuate (a) an ethos of settled village life, commonly coupled with large, fixed populations, fairly intensive subsistence economies, and landscape alteration (rather than mobility and low impact); (b) institutional social ranking based on bloodline and birth order; and (c) regional integration (particularly coupled with a social preoccupation with exchange and a cultural aesthetic that places great symbolic value on foreign things) and a foreign policy commonly characterized by accommodation and acculturation of outsiders.

Social Transformations

Over the past twenty-five years, Keegan and colleagues have emphasized the importance of social organization (Ensor 2011, 2013a; Keegan 2007; Keegan and Maclachlan 1989; Keegan et al. 1998). In creating their model, they were cognizant of potential pitfalls resulting from what they called "ethno-tyranny" (Maclachlan and Keegan 1990). Their efforts were grounded in the archaeological evidence, and their goal was to identify behavioral practices associated with particular forms of social organization and document these in the archaeological record.

The focus on social organization was stimulated by the discovery that over 90% of the Lucayan sites in the Bahama archipelago occur in pairs (Berman et al. 2013; Keegan and Maclachlan 1989). Paired communities (often with distinct pottery styles) have also been recognized in Hispaniola (Rainey and Ortíz Aguilú 1983), Cuba (Persons 2013; Rouse 1942), Puerto Rico (Torres 2012), Vieques (Chanlatte Baik 1981), and possibly Jamaica. Combining settlement-pattern structure, Spanish reports for Hispaniola and Cuba (whence Bahamian colonists), and controlled cross-cultural comparisons, Keegan and Morgan Maclachlan (1989) argued that the Indios of Hispaniola, Cuba, and the Bahamas practiced forms of matrilineal descent with initial matrilocal residence shifting to avunculocal residence with the emergence of a two-tier hierarchy. Their objective was to identify elements of social organization that could be subjected to archaeological scrutiny. This research emphasized that all communities are socially organized, and that aggregate relations structure individual behavior (agency) in meaningful ways (Keegan 2007; Morsink 2013). Michael Heckenberger (2002) has noted commonalities among the Arawak diaspora and the expansion of the Bantu (Africa) and Austronesians (Oceania). Fiona Jordan and colleagues (2009) have used the matrilocal model to explain the distribution of Austronesian mtDNA in the Pacific.

This perspective has been criticized because it is difficult to prove that paired sites were contemporaneous, and because of more general concerns regarding "kinship" studies (Ensor 2011; Samson 2010). Critics instead promote a focus that defines social organization as a form of classification and genealogical (genetic) heritage. This perception reflects their confusion of kinship (i.e., the language of relationships) and social organization, which is reflected in daily and multigenerational practices (e.g., Joyce and Gillespie 2000; Morsink 2013; Samson 2010, 2013). In a Caribbean context, Curet (2002) argues that Spanish descriptions of chiefly succession are too variable to identify a particular form of chiefly succession; a view that is, however, countered by Keegan (2006).

Curet's (2003) argument is based on the lack of conformity between Spanish descriptions from Hispaniola, and on archaeological research in Puerto Rico. Although he argues against the importance of social relations (Curet and Oliver 1998), he concedes: "Hispaniolan and Puerto Rican polities used significantly different ideological foundations, a reflection of differences in the nature of the political structure and organizations" (Curet 2003:19); and "Judging from the striking differences mentioned, they likely developed from distinct types of ancestral societies, and/or through different and divergent historical processes" (Curet 2003:20). The evidence presented here supports Curet's conclusions that Puerto Rican societies developed from Saladoid traditions, and that Hispaniolan societies and their descendants developed from the syncretism of Archaic Age, Ostionoid, and Meillacoid traditions.

With the possible exception of Puerto Rico and the Lesser Antilles, the initial form of social organization was probably matrilineal descent in which a leader was promoted from a specific family (Keegan and Maclachlan 1989; see Heckenberger 2005). Residence was in houses containing large, extended families that originally were based on matrilocal principles. The need for clans to retain both males and females created a viri-avunculocal pattern of residence that maintained the practice of living in large "Houses" (Samson 2010). Marriage was a sufficient organizing principle, but other means of integration were needed to co-opt other communities. These mechanisms included the use and threat of force and religious conversion.

Cacicazgos

Neo-evolutionary studies in archaeology have highlighted "chiefdoms" or Middle-Range Societies since the 1980s. This interest was stimulated by efforts to explain the origins of political hierarchies and social inequality. Perhaps not surprisingly, chiefdoms were found everywhere and quickly became recognized as the most widespread social formation prior to the advent of "states" (Johnson and Earle 1987; Pauketat 2007; Torres 2003). Despite repeated efforts, especially in Puerto Rico (Curet and Stringer 2010; Torres 2012), there is no archaeological evidence for large-scale political hierarchies in the Caribbean, with the possible exception of Hispaniola. In the eastern Dominican Republic, there is a series of huge circular villages surrounding central clearings of up to 12.5 hectares (Wilson 1990).

The "Taíno" *cacicazgo* was the first chiefdom identified in the Americas (Oberg 1955), and it thus attracts attention as a disciplinary legacy (Redmond and Spencer 1994). Caribbean "chiefdoms" have been a major topic of interest (Cassá 1992: Hulme 1998). Keegan and colleagues employ cross-cultural evidence to examine the social transformations that would account for the sociopolitical organization described by the Spanish (Ensor 2013a, 2013b; Keegan 2007). Although they use the term "chiefdom," their concern is with sociality, and not whether the Taíno warrant this label. Second, John Crock (2000), Corinne Hofman (Hofman et al. 2007), and William Keegan (2007) all emphasize mobility, exchange, and control of resources on islands that exhibit organizational complexity but that otherwise would be considered peripheral.

Third, archaeologists working in Puerto Rico have emphasized material correlates of chiefdoms (e.g., Johnson and Earle 1987) to propose an evolutionary sequence for the development of hierarchy and social inequalities attributed to the rise of chiefdoms (Alcina Franch 1983; Alegría 1979; Curet 2002, 2003; Curet and Stringer 2010; Siegel 2010). Puerto Rico is unique in the widespread occurrence of stone-lined plazas beginning around AD 900. They occur in two complexes that are not associated with domestic structures (i.e., Tibes and Caguana), as well as within small habitation sites (Torres 2012). Most of the structures are rectangular in shape, which has led to their association with the soccer-like game *batey* described by the Spanish, although there are some circular stone-lined courts, including the star-shaped court at Tibes. It has been suggested that stone-lined courts reflect contacts with Central America that extend back at least 1,000 years (Rodríguez Ramos 2010, 2013). We addressed this issue in the last chapter, and question whether classifying such structures as evidence for chiefdoms advances our understanding (Pauketat 2007; Torres 2013).

Finally, Kathleen Deagan has approached the issue from a historical perspective by addressing the interactions between the Spanish and Taíno in Hispaniola and Cuba (Deagan 2010; Deagan and Cruxent 2002). Her research was conducted at three of the earliest Spanish colonies: En Bas Saline (Haiti), Puerto Real (Haiti), and La Isabela (Dominican Republic).

En Bas Saline Site, Haiti (c. AD 1492)

Between 1983 and 1987, teams from the Florida Museum of Natural History (then the Florida State Museum) excavated the site of En Bas Saline on the north coast of Haiti, which is named for the Haitian farming community on the site (Figure 5.12). En Bas Saline gained significance just prior to the 500th anniversary of Columbus' first voyage to the Americas. On December 25, 1492, the *Santa María* was wrecked on a reef near Cap Haïtien. Left with only the *Niña* (Martín Alonso Pinzón had departed with the *Pinta* off the coast of Cuba to seek his own fortune), Columbus was forced to leave thirty-nine men in the village of Guacanagarí. They were instructed to build a fort and trade for gold. The

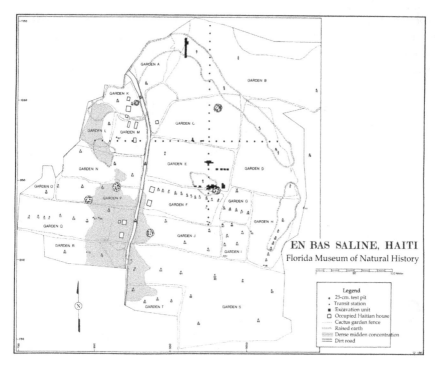

FIGURE 5.12 Map of midden and earthwork distributions at En Bas Saline, Haiti (courtesy of Kathleen Deagan).

location of Guacanagarí's village and the first Spanish settlement of La Navidad is the subject of debate. Tracing Columbus's route, Samuel Eliot Morison concluded that the *Santa María* had sunk just offshore from the Haitian town of Limonade Bord de Mer (Morison 1942). In 1976, Dr. William Hodges, a medical missionary with an insatiable avocational interest in archaeology, discovered a large archaeological site about one kilometer inland from Limonade Bord de Mer, and 10 kilometers east of Cap Haïtien. There are no similar large archaeological sites of the right time period in the area (Deagan 1989).

The excavations were under the direction of Kathleen Deagan (1987, 1988). Her teams produced a detailed topographic map, an electromagnetic conductivity survey, made a complete surface collection, and dug 25-centimeter-square test units at 10-meter intervals across the north–south and east–west axes of the site. In addition, 93 square meters of larger-scale excavations were undertaken to investigate particular features identified by the various types of survey (Deagan 1987:344). During the course of the project, they accumulated a large body of circumstantial evidence to support the identification of this village as the town of Guacanagarí and the site of La Navidad. The evidence included the size and configuration of the site, the highly decorated pottery, a well-like structure not reported for other "Taíno" sites, European objects and animal bones, and evidence for an enormous fire. Sixty-two percent of the excavated artifacts are from post-contact deposits (Deagan 1987:346). All of the pottery is Chicoid, and the later deposits contain "colono-ware" in which Spanish forms were adapted to indigenous manufacturing techniques (Cusick 1989, 1991).

En Bas Saline is located along a now-dry tributary of the Grande Rivière du Nord. It is on the edge of a mangrove swamp and a saline basin, which connect it to the coast. The most visible part of the site is a large, C-shaped earthwork that averages 20 meters wide and 80 centimeters tall. The earthwork was purposely constructed, and is not the result of accretion or midden accumulation, as indicated by borrow pits along its inner side and a very low density of artifacts in the fill of the earthwork itself. It is wrapped halfway around a central plaza and is open to the south. It measures 350 meters north–south and 270 meters east–west (these measurements are for the whole site, including the southern midden, and not just the earth ridge itself; Deagan 2004). This layout is typical of other village sites reported for Hispaniola (Rainey 1941; Rainey and Ortiz Aguilú 1983; Veloz Maggiolo 1991, 1993).

One surprising result of Deagan's research is that maps produced using the electromagnetic survey and surface collections revealed a mirror image to the earthwork. In other words, although the ground was level, soil conductivity and the density of materials on the surface revealed a C-shaped distribution on the south side of the plaza. Because Deagan was primarily interested in the post-contact occupation of the site, the possible meanings of an oval-shaped village with an earthwork along one side and a midden deposit on the other have not been explored.

There is a mound near the center of the plaza in which the remains of a large oval wattle-and-daub structure of at least 15 meters in diameter was discovered. This structure had been burned. Deagan found a cinder-like substance in this area that was identified as christobalite, a phase of quartz formation that occurs at temperatures of around 1400° C (Deagan 1987:346). The burned structure and christobalite are evidence for an intense fire in which the wattle-and-daub structure must have acted like a kiln.

In addition, Hodges located a very deep pit that he thought was a well. He dug out a small area of it in 1977 and found an infant burial, which he removed to his museum in Limbé. Deagan later excavated the rest of the feature, which appeared to have two or three excavation episodes, extending nearly 2 meters in depth. At the lowest levels, she recovered pig and rat bones. There was also evidence for the *cohoba* ritual (the use of narcotics to communicate with the supernatural), including a snuffer tube and vomit spatula fragment. In sum, it appears that the "well" at La Navidad was periodically reused and that it finally served as a burial pit (Deagan 2004).

Two other features in the plaza were enormous, straight-sided, hearthlike trenches that were filled with debris (e.g., ash, pottery, bones, food remains, and shells). These features are radiocarbon dated to AD 1300, and are likely evidence for ceremonial feasting (see Lovén 1935:506). A similar pit feature was found at the Cinnamon Bay site on St. John, U.S. Virgin Islands, which also has been identified as the aftermath of a feast (Quitmyer 2003; Wild 2001). It is clear from Columbus's diary that he entered the bay at Cap Haïtien before the *Santa María* was wrecked. Although numerous expeditions have been launched to find the wreck of the *Santa María*, none has been successful. These failures are often justified with Columbus's statement that all of the ship's timbers were salvaged to build the fort, and everything else that could be recovered was brought ashore. Moreover, Columbus wrote to the sovereigns that the fort was built in the village of *Guacanagarí*. The fort is thought to have included a moat, tower, and palisade (Deagan 1989). Columbus left instructions for the construction of a tower and moat, but on the return voyage, the one eyewitness report described only a "somewhat fortified" large house (Deagan 2004).

If En Bas Saline was the site of La Navidad and the village of Guacanagarí, the Spanish accounts describe a second-tier *cacique* who owed fealty to a paramount *cacique* (*matunherí*) named Caonabó (Keegan 2007). Clark Moore (1998) has identified a series of large villages along the north coast that are evenly spaced at about 28 kilometers and connected by an indigenous road. The road begins in the west at En Bas Saline and runs east to the village sites at Madrasse, then Carrier, then Mapou, and finally to village sites in the Dominican Republic. He also identified side roads that connect the inland villages to coastal settlements. Sections of the proposed road follow documented sections of the Spanish and French colonial road.

Chicoid villages were constructed around a circular, central plaza. One of the earliest, at El Atajadizo (AD 1000–1300), is located in the southeastern Dominican Republic about 20 kilometers from the coast near the Yuma River. This area is considered the Boca Chica (Chicoid) heartland. The central plaza is bounded by standing stones, with portions of the perimeter distinguished by cobbled pavements (Wilson 2007:124–126). A cobbled causeway leads to the river. The plaza is similar in size to the central court at Caguana (1,456 m² versus 1761 m²), but differs in the latter's being rectangular with petroglyph murals on the east and west sides' standing stones.

After AD 1300, the central plazas at three villages grew to enormous size in northwest Dominican Republic (Wilson 2007:126–130). Coral de los Indios at San Juan de la Maguana is associated with Caonabó, whom the Spanish describe as the most powerful *cacique* on the island (Keegan 2007). The circular plaza measures 691 meters in diameter and covers an area of about 43,000 square meters (10 acres). There is a single monolith with an engraved face at the center of the plaza, and causeways leading to the river, at which there is a substantial quantity of petroglyphs (Weeks et al. 1996). The site is located about 80 kilometers south of a similar site near the Río Chacuey.

The Plaza de Chacuey is oval-shaped, measuring 250 meters by 145 meters, and encloses 29,000 square meters (Figure 5.13). The layout of the site has been interpreted as expressing astronomical alignments (Castellanos 1981). Parallel rows of cobbled pavements (3–3.5 m wide) form a 13-meter-wide causeway that leads to the river. The entrance to the plaza is marked by two standing

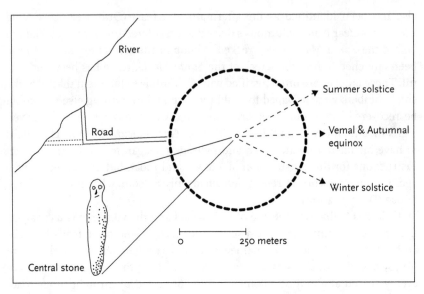

FIGURE 5.13 Map of El Plaza de Chacuey, Dominican Republic (courtesy of Roberto Valcarcel Rojas).

stones, and there are two panels of petroglyphs on rocks in the river. The causeway was constructed using an impressive 4,000 cubic meters of cobbles and earth (Wilson 2007:128). The Plaza La Cacique near the town of Monción in north-central Dominican Republic is also oval and measures 132 by 77 meters (about 10,000 m²). It, too, has parallel pavements defining a causeway that leads west to a stream that drains into the Arroyo Naranjo. Again, petroglyphs were engraved on boulders in the stream (Wilson 2007:130). Smaller circular and oval plazas are characteristic of satellite villages.

It is likely that other large plazas existed on Hispaniola but have not been identified due to historic and modern construction (e.g., the village of the *cacique* Behecchio near Port-au-Prince, Haiti). The plazas that remain are evidence of monumental architecture that required management and control by powerful leaders. They provide the best archaeological evidence for the presence of paramount *caciques* prior to the arrival of the Spanish. With the exception of En Bas Saline, none of these plaza sites has been extensively investigated. In comparison, they dwarf in size the ceremonial centers in Puerto Rico (Wilson 1990). The only comparable earthworks are found in eastern Cuba (Alegría 1983; Guarch Delmonte 1972b).

Finally, the aforementioned plaza sites are all occupied villages. In contrast, the La Aleta site, located 5 kilometers inland in the Parque Nacional del Este, does not appear to have had permanent inhabitants (Beeker et al. 2002; Conrad et al. 2001; Guerro 1981). The site is associated with the *cacicazgo* of Higüey. Access to the site is restricted to helicopter transport and is controlled (and limited) by the Dominican Park Service. More extensive investigations in the future could clarify these issues.

Four ceremonial plazas have been identified there, along with a flooded cavern (Manantial de la Aleta). The flooded cavern contains a remarkable collection of artifacts in a submerged context. Many of the artifacts are unrelated to water collection, and have therefore been interpreted as offerings to the spirits. A small collection of artifacts was recovered and preserved. The twenty wooden artifacts recovered include two *duhos*, a small vessel, four celt handles, a canoe paddle fragment, a *macana* war club, a crocodile figurine, and a vomiting spatula (Conrad et al. 2001). Two gourd fragments, one with incised Boca Chica style designs, were recovered, and many others observed. Baskets are common, but were left *in situ* until recovery and preservation methods are refined. Stone objects included celts, balls, and pestles. The 191 pottery vessels from the cavern included bowls, jars, bottles, platters, and *burenes* (clay griddles), with all of the decorations executed in the Boca Chica style (Beeker et al. 2002). One bowl contained the edible guácima seeds (*Guazuma ultifolia*).

Beeker and colleagues have investigated other caverns and sinkholes in the area. At Cueva de Chicho, the vessels were exclusively bottles used to collect water from the cavern (Beeker et al. 2002). The walls of the cavern are decorated with panels of petroglyphs. Other sinkholes in the area also contain pottery vessels, but these are not yet reported. It is likely that the arid conditions and the limited availability of water promoted a special relationship between the local inhabitants and those sources. The result was a wide variety of offerings that has not been observed elsewhere in the Caribbean. The degree to which such offerings, and possible associated rituals, were controlled by political authority remains to be determined.

Reconstructing indigenous *cacicazgos* and the *caciques* who ruled them is based primarily on Spanish accounts (Vega 1980). Because our primary concern is with the archaeological evidence, we will return to this topic in a separate discussion of colonial encounters.

Sweetness and Power

There is a pan-Antillean distribution of exotic and ritual paraphernalia (Hofman et al. 2008; Oliver 2009; Persons 2013; Siegel 2010). Objects include tiny *Chama sarda* beads, larger conch shell beads with notched edges, shell masks (*guaízas*), *Oliva sayana* tinklers, large quartz and diorite beads, carved greenstone and other exotic stone pendants (including the bound dog, twins, and the crying man), monolithic axes, shell and three-pointed stones (trigonoliticos), Macorix-type stone heads, elbow stones, stone collars, wooden statues, wooden seats (*duhos*), cold-hammered gold sheets, and imported gold-copper alloy *guanín*. In addition, more localized shared expressions include ball courts (*bateys*), stone-lined courts, circular plazas, houses, settlement organization, petroglyphs and pictographs, and burial practices. These lists are not exhaustive.

Because many of these objects have been found in association with Chicoid pottery, it has been assumed that they reflect the materialization of "Taíno" beliefs. Efforts to explain the wide distribution of these objects and their underlying meanings have relied almost exclusively on the account of indigenous beliefs recorded by Friar Ramón Pané in 1497–1498 among the Macorix (Arrom 1974, 1980; Godo 2005; Stevens Arroyo 1988). As a result, many of these objects are simply classified as *cemí*, based on the writings of Pané. *Cemí* has two meanings. In the broadest sense (Oliver 2009:59): "*cemí* is ... a condition of being, not a thing. It is a numinous power, a driving or vital force that compels action; it is the power to cause, to effect, and also denotes a condition or state of being." Oliver (2009:59) translates the word as "sweetness." In a more restricted sense, *cemí* refers to a class of religious portable objects (Arrom 1974; Oliver 2009:3).

Distribution studies have demonstrated that, although many of these objects exhibit a wide distribution, the frequency of their occurrence is quite variable (McGinnis 1997; Ostapkowicz 1998). This is especially true for stone collars, elbow stones, and three-pointed stones, which are found primarily in the southeastern Dominican Republic and Puerto Rico (Walker 1993). Some of the objects found outside the Chicoid core are exact copies (three-pointers have been found at sites as far south as Trinidad), while others appear to be replicas of local manufacture. Others have a long history preceding the Late Ceramic Age. Three-pointers, for example, apparently began as small pointed shell and stone objects with a concave base that evolved into true three-pointers with the addition of lobes on either end that created the appearance of a pointed phallus. In sum, the common assumption that these objects represent the beliefs of a specific culture (called "Taíno") is unwarranted.

Attributing meaning to these objects based solely on the writings of a Catholic friar who recorded his observations among the Macorix (which glosses as "foreign tongue") is even more tenuous. We do not deny that Pané's observations provide insights and context. Oliver (2009) has demonstrated that the petroglyph murals at Caguana and Jacaná (Puerto Rico) are consistent with the mythology Pané described. However, it is not appropriate to generalize those writings to all Late Ceramic Age contexts. In his detailed examination of lowland South American mythology, a second region from which Caribbean archaeologists seek inspiration (Siegel 2010), Peter Roe (1982) documents local variability in mythical stories, reversals in which the meanings are opposite among different and even related communities, mythic substitution in which one animal comes to take the place of another, subtleties such as color (e.g., yellow jaguar versus black jaguar), and the evolution of mythical beliefs and ritual practices over time.

This Pan-Antillean distribution is reminiscent of the Hopewell (100 BC to AD 500) and the later Southeastern Ceremonial Complex, formerly Southern Cult (AD 1200–1650), objects that were widely distributed across the eastern United States (Carr and Case 2006). Hopewell is characterized by a population dispersed in hamlets of one to three households and small clusters of hamlets. Because individual hamlets were neither economically nor demographically

sustainable, they came together at certain key earthworks to exchange people, information, and resources (Carr 2006). These "symbolic communities"
formed a larger, self-identifying social unit united by common purpose. The
boundaries were fluid, decision-making was situational, and leadership was
temporary and achieved. As in certain Caribbean communities, multiple conical to low circular mounds, not associated with single residential communities, were used for a variety of purposes, including the burial of individuals
from different residential communities (Carr 2006:76–78).

The Southeastern Ceremonial Complex is a particular kind of religious worship associated with the Mississippian Culture. Here there is a stronger distinction of hierarchy between a centralized political economy with paramount
chiefs at the major mound centers (e.g., Cahokia, Etowa) and decentralized
kinship or clan-based societies in the hinterlands (Cobb 2000; Galloway 1989).
Caribbean societies never achieved the level of artistry or earthwork construction recorded for the Mississippian.

In both Hopewell and Southeastern Ceremonial Complex cases, the raw
materials were obtained from across the eastern United States, ranging
from the Great Lakes to the Gulf of Mexico and from the Atlantic coast to the
Mississippi River and beyond. Objects made from these raw materials exhibit
an equally broad distribution. Because many of the objects were recovered
from mounds and burials, they are interpreted as reflecting status differences.
These differences were locally constructed. The distribution of exotic objects
far outreaches the effective control of any political center.

Hopewell seems to be the better analog for the Caribbean. Its objects are
associated with the construction of large earthworks that served as meeting
places for autonomous residential communities. The wide distribution of
earthworks and ceremonial objects reflects the breadth of interactions, and
pan-regional ceremonialism that was not associated with hierarchical political
management or control. With regard to Hopewell, Carr (2006:68) notes:

> By associating the ideological, ceremonial, and material-symbolic dimensions of
> Hopewell with its interregional guise but not its local expression, and by focus-
> ing locally on subsistence and settlement patterns Caldwell and Struever inad-
> vertently took Hopewell out of its local context, that is, decontextualized it, and
> removed it from the social actors and social roles who produced it, that is, imper-
> sonalized it.

The same could be written for the Caribbean. Caribbean communities
were never isolated entities. What remains to be demonstrated is their
degree of autonomy on local, regional, and broader scales. This will require
more detailed investigations of individual sites and small regional territories
(e.g., Persons 2013; Ulloa Hung 2013). At present, all we are willing to con-
cede is that these objects circulated through social networks that conditioned
processes of mobility and exchange (Hofman and Bright 2010; Keegan 2015;
Mol 2013, 2014).

Chicoid Expansion

The emergence of an apparently new social formation commenced in the eastern Dominican Republic after AD 950. It took place in an arid and semi-marginal location relative to their neighbors at the interface between Hispaniolan Meillacoid and Puerto Rican Ostionoid. This Late Ceramic Age social formation emerged on the Mona Passage, where these distinct cultures collided. Boca Chica style pottery, especially in the southeastern Dominican Republic, is the most elaborate and refined pottery in the Chicoid series. Around AD 1200, communities in the eastern Dominican Republic began to expand their opportunities by co-opting the territory of their neighbors. This regional transformation did not involve significant changes in technology or economic practices. It was a social and ideological transformation that was accomplished through warfare, exchange, marriage, and religious conversion.

Chicoid pottery is considered emblematic of "Taíno" (Rouse 1992). Diagnostic Chicoid motifs include curvilinear designs, circles with a dot in the center, broad-line incised with polished surfaces, engraved anthropomorphic faces with a characteristic "Chicoid eye," and white-slipped and mammiform bottles. There is also a change in vessel shapes. However, efforts to explain the development and spread of this pottery and associated ritual paraphernalia have all taken Spanish documents as their starting point. As a result, archaeological evidence has been manipulated to conform to Spanish descriptions under the assumption the Chicoid completely replaced other pottery styles in the areas that were colonized (Curet 2005; Keegan 2007, 2013; Oliver 2009; Siegel 2010).

The spread of Chicoid pottery has been associated with the rise of hereditary leaders, the *caciques* who sought to establish economic hegemony over ever-larger regional territories through dominion expressed in the extraction of tribute (Moscoso 1981, 1986). Like all colonizing communities, they adapted their strategy to the indigenous communities they encountered. Their strategy to the west involved infiltration through marriage and possibly the initial establishment of neighboring, segregated, settlement pairs. The survival of Macorix close to the "Taíno" heartland suggests a relatively peaceful transfer of power in which prior beliefs were maintained under a Chicoid umbrella (Keegan 2007:24–27). These relationships may have been based on prior relations established when their ancestors coexisted in the eastern Dominican Republic before AD 900. Alternatively, the capacity of communities, whose identity was expressed in Chicoid pottery, to assemble large armies in the Vega Real in response to the Spanish is evidence of their capacity to use force.

The situation in Cuba reflects infiltration through the establishment of a colony and conversion of local ceramicists to the expression of Chicoid modes. In the Lesser Antilles, Saba is clearly a colony (Hofman and Hoogland 2011;

Hofman et al. 2014; Hoogland and Hofman 1999), while Anguilla appears to reflect local allegiance (Crock 2000). Rouse (1992:111) identifies a Chicoid colony at Santa Isabel on the south coast of Puerto Rico, from which it supposedly influenced the transformation of Ostiones and Santa Elena styles to Capá and Esperanza styles, respectively. However, the colonization of Puerto Rico displays archaeologically a stronger element of religious conversion. Puerto Rican societies maintained their distinctive identities. There is no evidence for the widespread adoption of earthworks (*calzedas*) or mounds (*monticulos*); the settlement pattern remained dispersed, their houses small, and their pottery distinctive (Curet 2005; Siegel 2010). According to Oliver (2009), the major expression of Taínoness was an increasing fascination with *cemí*. But even this maintained a local flair. Petroglyphs are displayed in uniquely Puerto Rican contexts (e.g., Caguana and Jácanas), and the distribution of *cemí* idols encompasses primarily Puerto Rico and the eastern Dominican Republic (Oliver 2009). It is possible that what we assume to be a singular expression expanding from a Chicoid homeland is actually the syncretism of competing ideologies.

Conclusions

Humans first reached the island of Hispaniola around 5000 BC. Their origin has been traced to Belize and coastal Central America (Wilson et al. 1998). It is possible the initial incursion occurred near Port-au-Prince, given the high density of lithic scatters in the area. This location is adjacent to similar early deposits in eastern Cuba (e.g., Levisa sites). The earliest tools are a variety of large lithic blades. Because most of the sites from this period are quarry sites, it is unlikely that these blades reflect the entire tool kit. Blades alone do not provide the necessary range of tools required to successfully extract necessary resources. Unfortunately, we know little else about this initial colonization.

It is likely that the initial colonists maintained close ties with their homeland. Maintaining access to a sustainable spouse pool was the first imperative for overcoming the inherent risks of a beachhead bottleneck (Keegan and Diamond 1987). Continued communication, probably initiated from Hispaniola, led to the import of a variety of cultigens (Newsom and Wing 2004) and the adoption of a ground-stone technology for processing plant foods. There is no solid evidence for a separate Archaic Age migration from Trinidad (*contra* Rouse 1992), which is why we have collapsed Rouse's Lithic and Archaic Ages into a single Archaic Age.

Following colonization, the population continued to grow and disperse across the island, eventually reaching Puerto Rico. This dispersion into diverse biomes would have resulted in a diversity of adaptations and the creation of distinct communities. Some of these practiced incipient forms of horticulture and experimented with the manufacture and use of pottery. The use of pottery was firmly established at Archaic Age communities in the eastern Dominican

Republic by AD 200. The Archaic Age represents over 4,000 years of indigenous development, and we are only beginning to recognize its full ramifications (see Rodríguez Ramos 2010).

Communities characterized by Saladoid pottery appeared in Puerto Rico sometime between 400 and 100 BC. There is no evidence that Saladoid communities were established in Hispaniola, with some possible Cuevas elements pottery in the eastern Dominican Republic. It strikes us as remarkable that there is no solid evidence for exchange between Puerto Rico and the Dominican Republic at this time. The chronology for cultural development in Hispaniola is incompletely known. There is a significant gap between the beginning of the Ceramic Age in Puerto Rico and its commencement in the Dominican Republic. Small quantities of pottery were found at the El Caimito site, including the line-a-and-dot motif that became characteristic of Chicoid pottery. Veloz Maggiolo (1993) describes this period as one of incipient cultivation, perhaps with an emphasis on *Zamia* cultivation.

During the 9th century, the eastern Dominican Republic was a melting pot. Archaic Age pottery, Cuevas style, Ostionoid, Meillacoid, and perhaps early Chicoid potters coexisted on the eastern end of the island. Ostionoid pottery may have developed in this area, and communities making pottery in this series spread rapidly to the east and possibly into Puerto Rico. The rapid spread of Ostionoid pottery may reflect its adoption among Archaic Age communities, rather than the movement of entire communities. Ostionoid sites have a distinctly coastal orientation, and they lack the centuries-long longevity of the sites with other pottery styles.

Veloz Maggiolo (1993) and Zucchi (1990) have suggested that Meillacoid pottery was inspired through contact with coastal Colombia and western Venezuela. If this is true, contacts were probably initiated from Hispaniola. Whatever its origins, simple, unpolished vessels with incised designs become the hallmark of this series, in combination with appliqué and punctation. Meillacoid was the dominant pottery by AD 900, which may reflect synergy and transculturation among societies previously identified by distinct styles. The major transformation appears to have been an intensification of swidden horticulture (slash-and-burn or "casual" cultivation), with the possible introduction of new cultigens from South America. Intensified agricultural production is reflected in a shift from coastal and mangrove settings to hilltops overlooking the coast. These hilltop locations emphasize arable land over access to marine resources, although marine resources continued to make significant contributions to diet.

Chicoid pottery first appears in the southeastern Dominican Republic about this time. Like Meillacoid, the design motifs are incised. However, the series differ in breadth and depth of the incising, the emphasis of curvilinear designs, polished vessel surfaces, engraved anthropomorphic adornos, and the absence of appliqué on Chicoid pots. At least in its earliest manifestations, Chicoid and Meillacoid coexisted, perhaps even in paired communities. Interactions are reflected in the mixing of styles, the addition of elements from one by the other, and the selective adoption of techniques and motifs (Ulloa Hung 2013). In summary, Chicoid did not simply replace Meillacoid through a new wave of population expansion (*contra* Rouse 1992).

Chicoid pottery is predominant in some areas after AD 1300. Mounds are more common, although these also occur at Meillacoid sites (Ulloa Hung 2013). Middens are arranged around central plazas; large earthworks, causeways, and roads were constructed; and the distribution of sites across the landscape has the appearance of a Galactic Polity as described for lowland South America (Heckenberger 2005). Some sites grew to enormous size. There is no evidence for changes in subsistence practices (deFrance 2013; Newsom and Wing 2004), although sites located in the interior have a higher frequency of terrestrial animals and riverine and lacustrine fish. The reorganization and intensification of agriculture is evidence for population growth. Such changes probably reflect management and control exerted by hereditary chiefs. The archaeological evidence is consistent with Spanish descriptions of *caciques* and *cacicazgos* (Keegan 2007). Given the pan-Antillean distribution of ceremonial objects and religious symbols (Oliver 2009), and the creation of ritualized landscapes (Alegría 1983), it is tempting to attribute the spread of Chicoid to a religious conversion or theocratic chiefdom. This is the essence of "Taínoness" (Oliver 2009; Rodriguez Ramos 2010; Wilson 2007). However, we do not yet fully understand the diverse multi-scalar processes that conditioned even generally recognized outcomes. Much more research is needed, especially at the local scale. Moreover, we need to move beyond a reputational system that casts Caribbean culture history as a linear progression.

CHAPTER 6 | Cuba, the Bahama Archipelago, and Jamaica

CUBA, JAMAICA, AND THE Bahama archipelago share the complete transformation of their historical trajectories with the arrival of Meillacoid pottery beginning in the 9th century AD. Cuba has the longest history. Explorers from Central America originally settled on Cuba as early as 5140 +/– 170 B.P. (Pino 1995). What followed were millennia of expansion into, and adaptation to, the island's diverse environments, as reflected in diverse stone and shell tool assemblages, and the eventual adoption of farming and pottery during what we have called the Archaic Age. These indigenous communities and the Meillacoid immigrants interacted in ways that produced Cuba's unique transcultures. Jamaica apparently was not settled until communities making redware pottery (Ostionoid) and practicing a restricted range of farming arrived in the 8th century AD. Although we currently lack sufficient chronological controls, we believe redware pottery quickly disappeared and was rapidly replaced by Meillacoid pottery within a few centuries. Current evidence suggests that the Bahama archipelago was first colonized by Archaic Age communities from Cuba who had recently adopted a greater dependence on pottery vessels (*protoagrícola*). They arrived in the central Bahamas in the 8th century AD and spread rapidly through the archipelago (Berman and Gnivecki 1995). Two distinct later waves of influence are observed. There were Meillacoid and later Chicoid incursions from Hispaniola in the southern islands, beginning in the 13th century AD (Sinelli 2013), and Meillacoid influences from Cuba in the central and northern Bahamas, continuing communications that began earlier (Berman et al. 2013).

This chapter interrogates the processes of immigration, expansion, adaptation, and transculturation expressed on these islands. Our goal is to demonstrate that the changes observed do not represent a single evolutionary trajectory. Moreover, we have noted similarities within the islands and between the islands and surrounding mainland to highlight pan-Caribbean influences expressed in local developments. Whether these represent migrations, mobility, exchange, diffusion, independent invention, borrowing, copying, or spurious correlations need to be considered independently for every specific case.

Cuba

Archaeological investigations in Cuba date back more than a century (Dacal Moure 2004; Dacal Moure and Rivero de la Calle 1984; Ulloa Hung and Valcárcel Rojas 2013). Yet the archaeology of Cuba has not been integrated fully into general Caribbean frameworks. It has been suggested that the island was marginalized by modern political disputes and the lack of access to Cuban scholarship by North American scholars (Curet et al. 2005; Berman et al. 2005; Kepecs et al. 2010). Furthermore, Cuban archaeology adopted a theoretical orientation dominated by the historical materialism of Karl Marx and Friedrich Engels after the Castro revolution (Ensor 2000; Montane M. 1981; Vargas Arenas 1985; Veloz Maggiolo and Pantel 1988, 1989). This theoretical perspective did not coincide with that of mainstream North American archaeologists (Davis 1996; Rouse 1992).

In the following review, we structure our discussion by employing the Cuban emphasis on modes of life (*modo de vida*). This orientation recently has come under internal criticism for being a classification scheme that focuses on economic development and history in which economic stages are fixed and static, and limited attention is given to transitions between stages (Torres Etayo 2010; Ulloa Hung and Valcáracel Rojas 2013). Cuban archaeologists have used a variety of names to describe the history of the island, including *preagrícolas*, *apropiadores ceramistas*, *agroceramistas*, *fase agricultores*, *comunidades neolíticas*, *etapa agroalfarera*, and *comunidades tribales agroceramistas*. For simplicity, we have reduced these to three in order to provide a common framework for addressing the precolonial history: *preagroalferera*, *protoagrícola*, and *agricultores ceramistas*.

Preagroalferera (Archaic Age)

The Archaic Age was discussed in Chapter 2, but a few details concerning Cuba merit further review (Figure 6.1). More than 2,012 sites on the island have been designated *preagroalferera* (Jimenez Santander et al. 2012). The oldest are identified by the presence of lithic macroblades in the zones of Mayarí and Levisa in the east. There are no subsistence remains associated with these sites. Lithic technology is the major focus of research (Febles 1982; Kozlowski 1974, 1980), with hunting identified as the primary activity, based on tool form. The tendency has been to treat these blades as evidence for a single, shared Seboruco-Mordán tradition. However, investigations in Villa Clara Province provide evidence for the diversity in regional tool assemblages that is expected for communities living in diverse environments (Morales 2010). In addition, similarities are recognized between artifacts found in Cuba and the Western Lithic co-tradition of the United States (Davies et al. 1969; Febles 1991). Although connections with the southern United States have been largely ignored by North American archaeologists, this remains an important possibility to explore.

Stage	Chronology	Phase	Type Site	Other Sites	Predominant Aftifacts
				Mejias	Ground stone and pottery without burén (Griddle)
Protoagricola	1500-1000 BP	II	Arroyo del Palo		Ground stone and pottery without burén
				Majibacoa	Ground stone and pottery without burén
				Cayo Jorajuria	Microliths and simple pottery without burén
				Aguas Verdes	Microliths and simple pottery without burén
	2000-1500 BP	I	Caminar		Microliths and simple pottery without burén
Agroalfarera	500 BP	III	Espirito de Banes		Meillacoid pottery with Chicoid influences
				Loma de Cementerio	?
				El Morillo	?
				Los Ciguatos II	Chicoid pottery
	650 BP	II	Laguna de Limones		Chicoid pottery
	800 BP		Portrero del Mango		Meillacoid pottery with ostionoid characteristics
				Los Ciguatos	Ostionoid pottery with Meillacoid influences
				Lom de la Forestal	Ostionoid pottery with Meillacoid influences
				Aguas Gordas	Ostionoid pottery with Meillacoid influences
	1000 BP	I	Damajayabo		Ostionoid pottery

FIGURE 6.1 Schema of Cuban developments (from Keegan 2007).

It is generally accepted that the island was first occupied around 5000 BC by communities that migrated from coastal Central America (specifically Nicaragua, Belize, and Honduras). Currently, there are no reliable radiocarbon dates to support this conclusion. The Caminar Abajo site has registered the earliest radiocarbon dates (4700 +/− 70 and 6460 +/− 140 years B.P.; Ulloa Hung and Valcárcel Rojas 2013:236). However, recent investigations at the site and new radiocarbon dates indicate that the site is several thousand years younger (Roksandic et al. 2013). These more recent dates are more consistent with the archaeological assemblage at the site.

The Caminar Abajo assemblage is characterized by artifacts of the Banwaroid tradition, which generally is dated to around 2500 BC. The rock shelter exhibits evidence of multiple uses by different communities at different times. The deposits include evidence for domestic activities (e.g., hearths and food processing) along with a substantial number of burials. The location of the site suggests an emphasis on mangrove resources, and starch grain analysis identified maize, sweet potatoes, and legumes. "The various uses indicate a complexity and diversity in the use of space that is far from the idea of hunter camps with only superficial evidence of lithic artifacts" (Ulloa Hung and Valcárcel Rojas 2013:236).

Caminar Abajo is more typical of the Archaic Age. Most archaeologists in the region maintain a distinction between a Lithic Age (i.e., flaked macrolithic blades) and an Archaic Age (i.e., ground-stone tools). In our opinion, there is not enough evidence to make such a hard-and-fast distinction, especially with regard to separate migrations. It is true that the use of ground-stone tools increased through time, that (potential) cultigens arrived from the mainland, that incipient agriculture emerged, that plants and animals were transported within the islands, and that socially constructed communities expanded into new territories where they encountered unfamiliar environments. It is impossible to construct an accurate portrait of ethnogenesis until more comprehensive studies of settlement patterns, subsistence practices, tool use, iconography, mobility, exchange, and chronology are completed.

Protoagrícola (Incipient Agriculture)

The protoagrícola stage is considered transitional between the Archaic Age and the Ceramic Age. As discussed previously, it is observed throughout the Greater Antilles (Jamaica excepted), where it is recognized by the occurrence of pottery in association with Archaic Age artifact assemblages (Rodriguez Ramos et al. 2008). The sites of Arroyo del Palo and Mejias, for example, contain simple pottery in association with fishing and gathering implements (Tabio and Guarch 1966). These implements include a variety of expedient and formal tools made from marine shells, alongside various stone artifacts. The assemblages found at different sites contain diverse combinations. While some archaeologists attribute this diversity to seasonal activities and adaptation to distinct environments (Ulloa Hung and Valcárcel Rojas 2013:238; Veloz Maggiolo and Vega 1982), others have sought their origins outside the Caribbean islands. For example, lithic assemblages from Aguas Verdes, Caminar, and Playitas have been likened to those at Jaketown in the Mississippi Valley and Momil I in Colombia (Febles 1991).

José M. Guarch Delmonte (1990) emphasized the complexity of cultural expressions in Cuba. He recognized that these could not be pigeonholed in a time-space framework or static *modo de vida*. Diverse environments were exploited, and sites ranging from camps to more stable settlements indicate differences in the organization of economic activities and in technological complexes. He attributed diversity to local indigenous developments, expressed first in plant management and incipient agriculture, combined with increasing interactions with Ceramic Age communities resulting from migrations. The next stage emerged through processes of transculturation (in the original sense of Ortiz 1983). Transculturation is not simply the exchange of people, goods, and knowledge between two distinct cultures. It involves complete transformations through the dialectics of individual and group, adoption and rejection, acceptance and disdain, force and supplication, synergy and syncretism.

Agricultores Ceramistas (Ceramic Age)

It should come as no surprise that Guarch Delmonte (1990) described the *agricultores ceramistas* stage as *"variantes culturales,"* in recognition of local diversity at regional scales expressed in pottery styles and adaptations to these spaces, diverse interactions, and forms of development. The Ceramic Age in Cuba emerged through the arrival of new populations and the interaction of communities with unique identities expressed in their material culture. It is impossible to fit these developments into a single frame of reference. As described for Hispaniola and Puerto Rico, the Greater Antilles was multicultural from the beginning, and multidimensional in its material manifestations.

The earliest pottery phase in Cuba has been dated to the 9th century AD, based on uncalibrated radiocarbon dates from the El Paraíso and Damajayabo sites of AD 820 and 830. When these dates were calibrated, they shifted to AD 1084–1146 at 1-sigma (Persons 2013:98). However, other calibrations suggest that Meillacoid pottery in this area could date to the 7th century AD (Cooper 2007). The importance of these early dates for the Cuban Meillacoid, independent of that suggested by the calibrations, is that they indicate that this occupation was initiated or arrived in eastern Cuba at the same time as Meillacoid on Hispaniola.

Meillacoid pottery coexists with red-painted pottery in the area. If this red-painted pottery is Ostionoid, then southeastern Cuba is the only area with Ostionoid pottery. Rouse (1992) classified red-painted pottery from the Arroyo del Palo site as Ostionoid; however, Cuban archaeologists have refused to adopt this terminology because it is part of a unilinear model for the development of pottery series. In their words, "The convergence of Ostionoid and

Meillacoid decorative elements seem to be evident in an Archaic Age context on the eastern portion of the island, Arroyo del Palo (cal. AD 895–1223)." The significance of this case is that there is a local ceramic (non-Saladoid) that incorporates new traits and perhaps influences the new style (Godo 1997:27; Jouravleva and González 2000; Ulloa and Valcárcel 2002:165). "The site is included in the Ostionan Ostionoid subseries (Rouse 1992:95) because this detail has been ignored or denied" (Ulloa Hung and Valcárcel Rojas 2013:241). As mentioned for Haiti and Jamaica, the coexistence of these styles suggests that they represent distinct identities, not a unilinear evolutionary sequence (Ulloa Hung 2013).

Southeastern Cuba was an important zone for Meillacoid on the island (Trincado Fontán and Ulloa Hung 1996:76). Martínez Arango (1997) has suggested that the first Meillacoid settlements were located between Guantánamo Bay and Santiago de Cuba, and Trincado Fontán and Ulloa Hung (1996:75) have proposed that this style represents a separate migration from the Guyana coast that followed the ocean current that runs along the south coast of Cuba. However, in the opinion of Roberto Valcárcel Rojas (2008), there could be other zones, like the Banes Archaeological Zone, where Meillacoid occurs very early in time in relation to sites in the southeast and originated from a different migratory movement. Nevertheless, if Cuban Meillacoid originated elsewhere, then Haiti remains the most likely source of the Ceramic Age colonists (Rouse 1992; Ulloa Hung and Valcárcel Rojas 2013).

There is also an ecological border in the southeast that appears to have influenced the distribution of population in this province. This ecological frontier bisects the bay at Santiago. To the east, there is the desert of Imias in the rain shadow of the Sierra Maestra mountains. This area has the lowest rainfall in the country (only 600–800 millimeters per year), and the land is characterized by vegetation adapted to semi-arid and xerophytic conditions. It is unsuited for traditional agriculture except along the rivers (Sara and Keegan 2004). From the western half of Santiago Bay, rainfall increases to between 1,200 and 1,400 millimeters per annum, and the vegetation is semi-deciduous and small gallery forests. Periodic flooding of rivers in the area renews soil fertility each year, and the combination of rainfall and soil fertility provide excellent conditions for agriculture (Martínez Arango 1997:288; Trincado Fontán and Ulloa Hung 1996:76).

Trincado Fontán and Ulloa Hung (1996) have recognized significant differences between the archaeological sites to the west and east of this environmental divide. They conclude that the semi-arid environment precluded permanent settlement along the coast in the eastern zone and that only temporary settlements were possible. They identified three types of land use: *conchales, paraderos,* and *sitios de habitación.*

Conchales range in size from 500 meters to 1.5 kilometers in length and are composed of large conchs (*Lobatus gigas, Cassis madagascarensis, Melongena melongena*) and other species. They are essentially shell heaps, and the only artifacts are shell picks, which may have been used in the process of extracting the animal from its shell. Because they are located close to sites with Meillacoid pottery, they have been interpreted as Meillacoid procurement sites (Trincado Fontán and Ulloa Hung 1996:76).

Paraderos are small sites that were used for a short period of time. Deposits typically range from 4–6 centimeters deep. They correspond to small and rustic farmsteads (*viviendas*) where a few individuals lived to conduct fishing and/or farming for a brief period of time (Trincado Fontán and Ulloa Hung 1996:77). Only a few fragmentary artifacts are found in these sites.

Sitios de habitación have a range of sizes. The largest measure about 100 by 180 meters, but most are in the thirty-to-forty-meter size range. Sixteen early sites have been identified between Punta de Maisi and Santiago Bay. They typically are only a few meters from the sea, close to one or two rivers, have small topographic features that allow for a defensive posture, are close to mangroves and a barrier coral reef, and have land that is suited for agriculture in the vicinity (Trincado Fontán and Ulloa Hung 1996:76). In the drier eastern zone, agriculture probably focused on bitter manioc and/or guayiga because this plant is more amenable to the semi-arid climate. This interpretation is supported by the high frequency of *burenes* (clay griddles), although recent studies indicate that *burenes* were used for more than baking cassava bread (Pagán Jiménez and Rodríguez Ramos 2008).

Trincado Fontán and Ulloa Hung (1996:78) identified other differences between the eastern and western zones. To the east, the sites were smaller, and there was a lower density of site materials. They suggest that these sites represent small villages composed of four to six families. Most of the vessels in these sites were hemispherical bowls (~70%), which may reflect a preference for pepper pot cooking. Decorations are infrequent, and there is a limited range of decoration, numbering only three to eight motifs. The most common motif is incised parallel lines. Moreover, these motifs were not combined to form new design motifs. To the west, where climatic conditions are better suited to agriculture, there is a wider range of vessel shapes and decorations, and larger villages are found (Matrinez Arango 1997).

In summary, the earliest Meillacoid settlements in Cuba probably occurred in the area the Spanish registered as the indigenous province of Bayaquitirí. From the beginning, they may have coexisted with Ostionoid communities that were established somewhat earlier.[1] These cultures can be distinguished by the preference for red-painted decorations on the vessels manufactured by the latter, and by the preference for incised decorations by the former. Red-painted decorations disappeared soon after Meillacoid pottery arrived in the area. The significant differences between Meillacoid communities to the east

---

[1] The status of Ostionoid in Cuba is a subject of contention. Many Cuban archaeologists do not agree that redware pottery can be classified as Ostionoid (Roberto Valcárcel Rojas, personal communication 2014). Whether or not they represent typological categories, they do reflect distinct material expressions.

of Santiago Bay and those living to the west correspond to differences in the ecologies of these zones.

Meillacoid sites in the province show a remarkable degree of continuity from the time of initial settlement through the arrival of the Spanish (Trincado Fontán and Ulloa Hung 1996). Faunal remains in middens indicate a stable diet for depths of 50–70 centimeters, based largely on the capture of fish and mollusks. *Burenes* are abundant throughout this period. There was little change in lithic artifacts, with manos and mortars, net weights, some raw material, flaked-stone tools, and polished petaloid celts present. Shell tools exhibit little change in variety or frequency, shell ornaments remain largely the same, and coral abraders are common during the entire period. This continuity in material culture occurs despite continuous changes in the population dynamics of the region. An increase in the density of potsherds per level suggests that the population of the area increased through time, and there is evidence for the continuation of peaceful relations in the province. Finally, there are distinct patterns of habitation and diverse forms of resource exploitation among the Meillacoid sites in Cuba. The presence of marine resources at inland sites points to exchange between inland and coastal settlements on the island. This practice also is observed in Hispaniola and Puerto Rico at this time (DuChemin 2013; Ulloa Hung 2013).

Irving Rouse's (1942) research in the Maniabon Hills is one of the few Cuban studies that explicitly conform to his methodology. For this reason, it provides an important contribution for understanding general patterns of settlement in the western Caribbean. His report describes 190 sites or zones where archaeological materials are reported. For some of these, there was too little information for detailed analysis. Therefore, he used a total of ninety-seven sites to define three types of settlement.

Thirteen sites were identified as Archaic Age (called "Ciboney" by Rouse), although he noted that some might be sub-Taíno (Meillacoid) resource-procurement sites that simply lack pottery (Rouse 1942:133; cf. Lundberg 1985). These sites are all located on the coast and in coastal swamps close to a source of freshwater. They are composed primarily of shells, and a variety of conch shell tools is present (e.g., gouges, blades, lips, plates, and tips). Working from the assumption that the presence of pottery in sites reflects the arrival of a new, distinct "sub-Taíno" culture, he distinguished between two types of village sites. One type has ordinary refuse middens, and the other has shell heaps. The former reflects patterns associated with Meillacoid occupations throughout their range.

The ten sites with shell heaps were located near the shore in locations favorable for fishing. They are similar in location to *Preagroalfarera* sites (Archaic Age), although they are usually on points of land instead of inlets. More recent investigations have determined that these are Meillacoid sites (Roberto Valcárcel Rojas, personal communication 2014). The sites are mostly smaller than the hilltop sites and are composed of two to ten middens. Rouse (1942) suggests that these were fishing villages that complemented the agricultural villages located on the neighboring hills. Indeed, Christopher Columbus described small fishing communities with houses shaped like Moorish campaign tents (also described for the Bahamas) on the north coast of eastern Cuba during his first voyage (Dunn and Kelley 1989:117, 119, 121).

The 74 village sites with ordinary refuse middens and little shell were all located on hilltops typically about 4 kilometers inland and overlooking the coast with a view of the sea (Rouse 1942:135). None of them was on the coastal plains. They were all located adjacent to good agricultural land and close to a freshwater source. Like their counterparts in Jamaica (Allsworth-Jones et al. 2006; Wesler 2013), Haiti (Rouse and Moore 1985:18), and the northwest Dominican Republic (Ulloa Hung 2013), the Cuban sites line the edge of the hill region. They were all much larger than the coastal shell heap sites, with an average size of 2,500 square meters and five to ten mounds. The sites are longer than they are wide because they hug the hilltops. Rouse (1942:134) concludes that they were villages because they all have deep midden deposits, in some cases up to 3 meters. The mounds were widely spaced and irregular in shape and arrangement. The number of mounds was not a good index of village size. For example, El Mango with three mounds was apparently as large as La Campana with sixty (Rouse 1942:135). The variability noted for mounds (*monticulos*) probably reflects a variety of uses and functions (Ulloa Hung 2013).

The Yayel site has a possible plaza, and the La Macagua site has circular areas between the mounds that have been interpreted as the locations for houses similar to the platforms that have been documented at the Late Ceramic Age El Flaco site in the northwestern Dominican Republic (Hofman et al. 2013). The larger sites occur in pairs on adjacent hilltops. A similar pairing of settlements has been identified for sites in the Bahamas (Keegan 1992; Keegan and Maclachlan 1989). Another similarity to the Bahamas is the use of caves for burials (Winter 1991). Burials were found in twenty-nine caves in this area, and some individuals were interred in karst sinkholes. Caves, sinkholes, and flooded caverns were used for burials and ceremonial offerings in the Bahamas and the eastern Dominican Republic as well (Beeker et al. 2002; Conrad et al. 2001; Keegan 2007).

The pottery in this area has predominantly Meillacoid motifs, although the line-and-dot motif is noted for Aguas Gordas. Jorge Ulloa Hung and Roberto Valcárcel Rojas (2013) note similarities to Meillacoid designs executed in the Montego Bay style on Jamaica. A "figurine" from the Aguas Gordas site is very similar to handles found on a canteen form of vessel known only from western Jamaica (cf. Rouse 1952:Plate 4k; Rodney-Harrack 2006:Fig. 10.7). Rouse (1942:37) reports that most of the animal bones in the sites are hutia, although fish are also common. Marine mollusks are common at many of the sites (Valcárcel Rojas 2002:124, 2012), and clamshells predominate at Baní. The use of clamshells for scrapers at this site mirrors a practice that is common throughout the Caribbean at this time (Dacal Moure 1979; Lammers-Keijsers 2008; Jones O'Day and Keegan 2001; Serrand 2001).

Regional Integration

The seventy-six agricultural communities in the vicinity of Banes provide evidence for the development of regional centers (Ulloa Hung and Valcárcel Rojas 2013). Banes is located in the Maniabon Hills area investigated by Rouse (1942) and discussed above. The sites have Meillacoid pottery and are located on hilltops overlooking the sea. The area is socially isolated, separated from other populations by a large open space, with no neighboring sites of any importance (Valcárcel Rojas 2002:91). Calibrated radiocarbon dates indicate that the Ceramic Age in the Banes region began around AD 1100 and continued up to and beyond the Spanish occupation (Persons 2013:63).

The earliest site is Aguas Gordas, with a date of AD 950 +/− 105 (Pino 1995; Valcárcel Rojas 2002). The site is located on an almost perfectly round hill about 50 meters in height and 50 meters in diameter, with about fourteen mounds varying in height from 0.5–3 meters distributed around the rim (Rouse 1942:81–82). Pottery decoration was based on Meillacoid themes and exhibits a strong degree of continuity and conservatism. With the arrival of Chicoid influences in the 13th century AD, there was a limited adoption of new elements, and these were restricted to the modification of features that already were present. There is a recognizable addition of curvilinear designs at this time, but linear, rectilinear, appliqué, and punctate designs continue from earlier times (Figure 6.2). Conch tools are abundant,

FIGURE 6.2 Pottery vessel from Banes, Cuba (courtesy of Roberto Valcárcel Rojas).

much more so than stone, and clamshell scrapers also are present. A variety of ceremonial objects made from shell and stone were recovered, and Rouse (1942: 82) comments on the high incidence of *adornos* (lugs with anthropomorphic faces). There is a high degree of continuity in all aspects of culture (Valcárcel Rojas 2002:95).

The settlement pattern reflects the specific selection of fertile land near the sea, hilltop locations, and access to potable water. Site locations follow a pattern established during the initial occupations, and the sites are continuously occupied for long periods of time. The regional pattern of settlement is that of a larger center (e.g., Aguas Gordas, El Chorro de Maíta, Potrero de El Mango) surrounded by smaller satellite communities (Valcárcel Rojas 2002:91). Several distinct clusters of sites are recognized (Valcárcel Rojas and Rodríguez Arce 2005). There is an integration of the agricultural communities expressed through community-based craft specialization and a shared development process (Valcárcel Rojas 2002:94).

Valcárcel Rojas (2002) concludes that Banes was a tightly integrated and strongly conservative region composed of interacting social units. These were physically isolated from their neighbors, and materially manifested their distinct identity. He demonstrates that regional organization was not something imposed by the arrival of Chicoid pottery. Regional integration was organic and reflected a long sequence of internal development. These regional configurations expressed their distinct, internalized identities and maintained their independence in interactions with other similarly constructed social, cultural, and political organizations. Lourdez Domínguez (1991) has noted similar developments at Meillacoid sites in south-central Cuba.

Brooke Persons (2013) recently completed a study of the Banes archeological area. She conducted a seriation of pottery attributes to identify historical modes in order to establish tighter chronological controls for dating sites. A GIS (Geographic Information Systems) based analysis of the temporal distribution of sites revealed that the earliest Ceramic Age sites occurred in pairs. The two main sites at this time were Aguas Gordas and El Mango. The second phase involved a substantial growth in population and the founding of numerous other settlements. Among these new settlements, Loma de Baní and El Chorro de Maíta developed into primate villages. Persons found that the distribution of these four sites demonstrates their position as the centers for local polities. These four sites, along with the Esterito site just south of the Banes archaeological area, are evenly spaced at around 10 kilometers, and are surrounded by numerous satellite communities that are mostly located within 5 kilometers of their respective center. This density of settlements surrounding evenly spaced centers that were separated by buffer zones reflects an initial two-tier social and political hierarchy. A striking characteristic of these political centers is the high frequency of ritual objects relative to satellite communities (Persons 2013). These stone and shell beads, pendants, amulets, wooden statues, wooden seats (*duhos*), and pottery effigies are typically associated with "Taíno." However, and as discussed in the previous chapter, it is not clear what this pan-Antillean distribution represents. It is not explained by labeling it "Taíno" and then attributing it to Spanish accounts of Macorix religion.

Persons (2013) concluded that these centers reflect the emerging hierarchy expected for simple chiefdoms. Of note is the decline of Aguas Gordas from its early preeminence. After AD 1350 (El Mango III phase), the site decreased in size and relative importance in relation to the four other regional centers, while El Chorro d Maíta increased in importance. This importance is reflected in the Spanish *encomienda* established at the site and a burial ground that includes Spanish and exotic objects interred with the bodies, Christian burial, and individuals of African and Mayan ancestry (Valcárcel Rojas 2012, 2016).

El Chorro de Maíta, Banes (c. AD 1200 to post–AD 1550)

El Chorro de Maíta is located 4 kilometers from the coast at an elevation of 160 meters in the Banes region (Figure 6.3). The site (also called Yaguajay) and the surrounding area were visited by Irving Rouse in 1941 (Rouse 1942:90–107); mapped and evaluated in 1979 and excavated by José Guarch Delmonte in 1986 and 1987; and re-studied by Roberto Valcárcel Rojas (Valcárcel Rojas and Rodríguez Arce 2005; Valcárcel Rojas 2012, 2016). It is a large settlement covering about 22,000 square meters, with a central burial area of about 2,000 square meters. The burial area is the only known open space on the site (there could be others), and it has been inferred that it served as a plaza. Middens surround the open space. The site is especially noteworthy for its size, unique cemetery,

FIGURE 6.3 Recreated cemetery at El Chorro de Maíta, Cuba (photo by Menno Hoogland).

and high incidence of ceremonial objects (especially quartzite beads and metal objects). Roberto Valcárcel Rojas (2016) recently has argued that, in its final period of occupation, the site was a Spanish *encomienda*.

El Chorro de Maíta is part of the Yaguajay cluster. The site is paired with the smaller and less spectacular El Bonaito site; three other village sites, a ceremonial cave, funerary cave, and two campsites complete the cluster (Valcárcel Rojas and Rodríguez Arce 2005:132–133). All of these sites share cultural features. This cluster, and others in the Banes region, is reminiscent of community integration in Ostionoid Puerto Rico (Torres 2012). El Chorro de Maíta has the highest concentration of highly valued quartzite beads, and there is evidence that these were being manufactured at the site. Bead-making points to craft specialization and the control over access to and distribution of exotic goods expected for a regional center (see Costin 1991). Midden contexts with European ceramics dated to between AD 1490 and 1550 show that the site was occupied until well after the arrival of the Spanish.

The burial area at the center of the site has recently attracted considerable attention. The detailed re-examination of the unique characteristics of the burial ground, physical attributes of the dead, and associated burial goods indicates that it might be the product of Spanish domination (Valcárcel Rojas 2016; Weston and Valcárcel Rojas 2016). At least 111 burials have been reported from the site, with the majority excavated by Guarch Delmonte ($n = 108$). In relation to precolonial practices, most burials in the Banes area typically are in caves. There are no other cemeteries. The skeletons often were interred in a flexed position accompanied by pottery vessels, some with food residue, but other grave goods are uncommon. In contrast, the burials at El Chorro de Maíta are located in a central location, and twenty-four (22.2%) have burial goods, including stone bead necklaces and metal objects, but no pots. At least thirteen of the burials are in a prone position with the arms across the chest or by their sides (Valcárcel Rojas 2012). A high frequency of metal objects is associated with a small portion of the burial community ($n = 18$; 16.6% of the total). The most common metal artifact is a hollow brass tube that is 29 millimeters long and 2 millimeters in diameter. These aglets (*agujetas*) or lacetags were made and used by Europeans to fasten clothing. Lacetags sheathe the ends of cords to prevent the lace or cord from unraveling (a modern example is the plastic tip of a shoelace).

It is not clear whether this was an indigenous burial ground that was converted to a cemetery under Spanish rule, or was solely a product of imposed burial practices. Extended burials are a common Christian practice. The association of lacetags with six of the extended burials confirms that this practice postdates the arrival of the Spanish and might indicate that these individuals were buried in European clothing. Strontium-isotope analysis identified twenty-two of the individuals as non-local (25%) (Laffoon 2013; Laffoon et al. 2013; Laffoon 2016). At least one was probably African, and another, with cranial modification not observed in the Antilles, probably was Mesoamerican. The movement of individuals from different areas to a central location was a common practice in the *encomienda* system imposed by the Spanish (Valcárcel Rojas 2012, 2016).

There are essentially equal numbers of males (n = 39) and females (n = 44). The important factor seems to be access to the burial area, with no evidence for restrictions on specific location, nor for the marking of graves, because older burials often were disturbed by more recent interments. Other than dental pathologies (Mickleburgh 2013), the individuals appear to have been of generally good health (Valcárcel Rojas et al. 2011). The most decorated burial is a female age twenty-six to thirty-five (individual 57A) who was interred with beads of gold, quartzite, coral, vegetal resin, *guanín* pendants, and a non-Antillean *guanín* bell and bird's head pendant (Valcárcel Rojas et al. 2010). The latter is identical to Tairona pectorals from Colombia. This burial documents the high status attributed to some women (see Sued-Badillo 1989).

The presence of secondary burials and evidence for cranial modification and the conservation of crania in the cemetery (Valcárcel Rojas 2012; Valcárcel Rojas et al. 2011) suggest indigenous practices linked with a cult of the ancestors. The inclusion of burial objects with children suggests the hereditary transmission of status. This interpretation fits ethnographic examples of this practice and is consistent with a *habitus* based on lineage and class (Heckenberger 2005; Helms 1998; Keegan 2009).

The largest systematic collection of metal objects comes from El Chorro de Maíta. Roberto Valcárcel Rojas and Marcos Martinón Torres (2013) have reviewed the evidence for the use of metals before and after the arrival of the Spanish. Very few gold objects have been recovered during systematic excavations. Gold can be found in riverine alluvial sand ("placer") deposits in several locations in the Greater Antilles. The recovery of gold and *guanín* objects from Saladoid and Huecoid contexts in Puerto Rico (Siegel and Severin 1993; Chanlatte Baik 1981) document its early use. This early date coincides with the expansion of Colombian gold work, and Colombian gold was imported as part of the Isthmo-Colombian engagement (Rodríguez Ramos 2010, 2013). The virtual absence of gold objects at these and later sites is taken as evidence that gold was of limited interest to the indigenous communities of the islands. Although gold probably never was abundant, Valcárcel Rojas and Martinón Torres (2013) suggest that its significance is masked by its restricted use. In addition, the interest in gold was intensified by Spanish demands.

The Spanish recognized that the indigenous societies were far more interested in a gold-copper alloy, called *guanín* in the islands. *Guanín* is more iridescent than pure gold and has a very particular smell. Because smelting was unknown, *guanín* had to be obtained from South America through exchange (Boomert 1987). The best examples are the *guanín* figurines from Santana Sarmiento and El Chorro de Maíta that match objects produced by the Zenú and Tairona in Colombia (Valcárcel Rojas and Martinón Torres 2013:Fig. 34.1). *Guanín* in the islands was associated with the male gender, and it reportedly was used to pay for wives (Valcárcel Rojas and Martinón Torres 2013:505). Because brass has the appearance and smell of *guanín*, it was greatly appreciated by the indigenous individuals who eagerly traded pure gold for brass (e.g., hawk's bells and *agujetas*) (Vega 1979). The non-Antillean sources of *guanín* reference other spaces, and contributed to its association with the ancestors and the mythical world (Valcárcel Rojas and Martinón Torres 2008; 2013:505; see Keegan 2007; Oliver 2000).

In contrast, pure gold was collected from placer deposits and cold-hammered into sheets. These sheets were used as inlays in wooden statues and seats (*duhos*), and as nose ornaments and pendants. Gold was associated with the female gender. Given the significance of gold in the late Ceramic Age, it is possible that continental metals were being replaced by Antillean sources (Valcárcel Rojas and Martinón Torres 2013:517–518).

> Their different technological and geographic origins give these metals specific places in both real and symbolic value systems. From this perspective, gold is a means of qualifying individuals whereas *guanín* is, in addition to this, a foremost emblem of the dynamic and interconnected character of the insular universe and of the latent link with continental spaces and ancestors. (Valcárcel Rojas and Martinón Torres 2013:519)

Chicoid Influences

The manifestation of Chicoid in Cuba is very different from its expressions in Hispaniola and Puerto Rico. Chicoid influences are most apparent in north-eastern Cuba, where the motifs are mixed with Meillacoid expressions. More than ninety sites have been identified in the area, including twenty-nine habitations and twenty-two funerary sites (Torres Etayo 2010). Chicoid motifs dominate the pottery assemblages in this area (Guarch Delmonte 1972a, 1972b). Chicoid decorative elements reflect local interpretations, and the pottery is of poor quality. For example, Guarch Delmonte (1972b) illustrates a wide variety of "Taína" pottery from eastern Cuba that shows curvilinear Chicoid motifs executed with a pointed stylus. The execution is more typical of Meillacoid, and it lacks the smooth, broad-line characteristics of Chicoid pottery from the eastern Dominican Republic (Hofman et al. 2013).

Chicoid influences may have begun to arrive as early as the 11th or 12th centuries AD, but these may reflect the mixing of Meillacoid and Chicoid that occurred earlier in Hispaniola (Ulloa Hung 2013, 2014). Chicoid manifestations are most apparent after the 13th century and occur in low frequency across Cuba, including the site of Los Buchillones near the center of the island. In keeping with efforts to acknowledge similarities with cultures outside Cuba, Cuban archaeologists recognize commonalities with Weeden Island pottery from Florida (Ulloa Hung and Valcárcel Rojas 2013:242–243). There are, however, significant differences between them, including the centuries-earlier dates for Weeden Island (AD 200–900), and the absence of the elaborate effigy vessels recovered from Weeden Island sites (Milanich 1984).

Four sites in eastern Cuba with plazas bounded by earthworks merit description. These were first reported by Mark Harrington (1921), and their construction is similar to that described for large plaza sites in the eastern Dominican Republic (Wilson 2007:130–132), Haiti (En Bas Saline), and the southern Bahamas (MC-6). However, there is no use of the freestanding stone alignments, pavements, or the formalization of ceremonial space observed in Puerto Rico at Tibes, Jacanás, and Caguana (Alegría 1983; Guarch Delmonte 1972a; Oliver 2009).

The Laguna de Limones site is 3 kilometers southwest of Punta de Maisí and is named for a small freshwater pond located about 100 meters east of a large, rectangular earthen enclosure (Guarch Delmonte 1972a:30–36; Harrington 1921:304–308). The walls of the enclosure are about 45 centimeters high and 5 meters wide at the base. The north wall is about 69 meters long, the east is about 169 meters long, the west is about 156 meters long, and the 87-meter south wall is angled to the south, creating an opening at the southeast corner (it looks as if someone has left a door slightly ajar) (Torres Etayo 2010). The floor of the plaza is sloped slightly toward the east to facilitate runoff from rainfall. To the south of the enclosure, there are at least nine mounds (four to the east and five to the west) in two parallel rows measuring 182 meters by 22 meters (west side) and 200 meters by 100 meters (south side) separated by a 30–40 meter open space. The open space of this "Asiento de Aldea" has very few artifacts, and a cream-colored stratum that suggests it was purposely made (Torres Etayo 2010). The mounds are constructed of local rocks and soils mixed with household refuse and denote the residential area of the village. This arrangement of mounds on opposite sides of a constructed open space is similar to that observed at MC-6 in the southern Bahamas (Keegan 2007:Fig. 7.2).

The Pueblo Viejo site has a rectangular earthen enclosure with rounded corners constructed of mounded gravel and cobbles (Guarch Delmonte 1972a:36–39). It is about 3 meters high and 4–5 meters wide at its base, and measures about 250 meters on the east and west sides, 85 meters on the north, and 135 meters on the south sides. It is located on a mesa top overlooking the Windward Passage. The Monte Cristo site has a parallelogram-shaped enclosure with rounded corners. Harrington (1921) observed the enclosure and estimated it to be about 42 meters wide. Two large mounds were associated with the enclosure, with one located inside the enclosure (Guarch Delmonte 1972a:23; Wilson 2007:132). Other mounds were observed, but the vegetation was too dense for more detailed investigation.

There is also a fourth site with a linear earthwork in the area, although it is not an enclosed space. The Big Wall site has a linear mound about 1.8 meters high that runs in a northwesterly direction for about 85 meters and is 10–15 meters wide. The mound is constructed entirely of village refuse (Harrington 1921:297–298). Two low mounds about 80 centimeters high and 7 meters in diameter are adjacent to the linear mound at either end, and may have served as the foundations for structures. A shorter mound (about 25 meters long and 8 meters wide) is located about 20 meters west of the "Gran Muro de San Lucas" (Guarch Delmonte 1972a:Fig. 2). This configuration of a linear earthwork and associated mounds is similar to that described for the Chicoid site of En Bas Saline, Haiti (Deagan 1989). A large, roughly circular mesa, with refuse deposited around its margins, encompasses the site to the west. The majority of the pottery is described as Chicoid, and a vomit spatula was recovered during excavations (Harrington 1921).

In addition to sites with linear earthworks, Harrington (1921) discovered natural (but often augmented) and human-constructed mounds at many of the sites he visited in eastern Cuba (Guarch Delmonte 1972a). As previously discussed, *monticulos* are common in Chicoid and Meillacoid sites in the Dominican Republic. These features are a development of the Late Ceramic Age. Although there is a tendency to associate these with a particular type of agriculture described by the Spanish, excavations indicate that they were used for multiple purposes, including residential foundations, refuse deposits, landscape modifications, and burials, in addition to farming (Ulloa Hung 2013; Guarch Delmonte 1972a; Harrington 1921; Hofman et al. 2013).

Los Buchillones Site (*c.* AD 1220–1640)

An excellent example of cultural diversity in the Late Ceramic Age is the Los Buchillones site (Figure 6.4). The site is located on the north-central coast in the province of Ciego de Avila. Dry-land excavations were conducted in the 1980s, and underwater excavations between 1996 and 2001. Twenty-three AMS dates on archaeological materials and preserved wood and thatch date the site to sometime prior to AD 1220, with continuous occupation to AD 1640

FIGURE 6.4 Excavations within the cofferdam at the underwater site of Los Buchillones, Cuba (courtesy of David Prendergast).

or later (Peros et al. 2006). The pottery is described as "Chican Ostionoid," but given the variability known for this subseries, it is not exactly clear what this means. The site is at least 50 meters wide and 500 meters long, trending to the northeast, although surveys along the coast indicated that it may have extended over 2.2 kilometers and had as many as eighty structures (Cooper et al. 2010:94). Presently, the site is partially bisected by a narrow sand berm (chernier), with most of the site underwater in the Bahia de Buena Vista and the Punta Alegre Lagoon. Offshore house locations have been identified by groups of post butts made from mahogany (Swietenia mahogani) and lignum vitae (Guaiacum sp.) (Valcárcel Rojas et al. 2006). The area contains the remains of 40 structures whose wooden elements are preserved in submerged deposits. The house structures are round (between 9 and 12 meters in diameter), rectangular, and oval (8.5 meters by 6.2 meters) (Cooper et al. 2010; Jardines Macías and Calvera Roses 1999; Pendergast et al. 2002); other wooden constructions may be weirs and non-residential structures.

Los Buchillones is unlike any other site discovered in the Caribbean. The preservation of organics, including hundreds of wooden artifacts (duhos, effigies, and vessels) and wooden posts, resulted from their deposition in calm, shallow, marine and lagoon sediments. The nearest example of precolonial structures built over water is on Lake Maracaibo, Venezuela. Geoarchaeological studies indicate that the site was originally constructed in the Punta Alegre Lagoon. Changes in the coastal geomorphology resulted in the landward migration of the chernier and its reduction in width, which resulted in the site now residing mostly in the Bahia de Buena Vista (Peros et al. 2006:Fig. 8). However, despite the preservation of posts, rafters, stringers, and thatch, there is no evidence for the house floors required to live in structures built on pilings.

The faunal assemblage shows a strong marine focus (Cooper et al. 2010). Terrestrial animals account for only 13% of the Minimum Number of Individuals (MNI). Marine fish (58%), marine mammals (18%), and sea turtles (4%) dominate the deposits. Los Buchillones was probably associated with the smaller sites located on the offshore cays in Jardines del Rey archipelago (Cooper 2007). These sites have entirely marine faunas. The high frequency of Lobatus gigas debitage is evidence for the manufacture of shell tools, and possibly for specialization in their production. These sites also contain clay griddle sherds that evidence some form of plant processing. In addition, sherds with wickerware basket impressions suggest communication with the Bahama Islands, where matt-impressed sherds are far more common (Berman and Hutcheson 2000).

Conclusions

The archaeology of Cuba provides a much clearer picture of the emergence of Archaic Age societies in the Caribbean. We concur with archaeologists on the island that these developments manifested a variety of expressions reflecting differences in the organization of economic activities, in technological complexes, and in social arrangements (Guarch Delmonte 1990). Cuban archaeologists also have been more willing to consider pan-Caribbean interaction networks. They recognize that such engagements do not imply migration or whole-scale borrowing. In this regard, if the starch grain identification of maize in Cuba at an early date is correct (Pajón et al. 2007), then Cuba may be the source for the earliest introduction of maize in the southeastern United States (*c.* 100 BC to AD 200). The flint variety of early maize in the southeastern United States is significantly different from varieties that were transported from Mexico into the southwestern United States, and there are significant differences in the ways these different varieties were cultivated (Riley 1987; Riley et al. 1990). The route of transmission currently is unknown, but Cuba provides the nearest possible source.

Archaic Age communities in Cuba began using pottery in small quantities as early as 2600 BC (Jouravleva 2002; Ulloa Hung and Valcárcel Rojas 2002), and they initiated plant management and incipient agriculture. These practices also are observed in Hispaniola and Puerto Rico (Rodríguez Ramos et al. 2008). Red-painted pottery appears on the southeastern coast of Cuba in the early 9th century AD, where it may be a continuation and reformulation of indigenous pottery, or may reflect Ostionoid influences from Hispaniola and/ or Jamaica. Its timing relative to the appearance of Meillacoid pottery suggests that both arrived at about the same time and may thus reflect prior mixing of these series in Hispaniola. The rapid spread and adoption of Meillacoid pottery suggests that this reflects the introduction of new forms of social and economic organization. The location of sites on hilltops overlooking the coast indicate a stronger reliance on agricultural production, and the continuation of coastal fishing villages argues for the integration of activities through the exchange of inland and coastal resources. The construction of villages with earthworks surrounding a central plaza mirrors the community plan observed in the Dominican Republic (Alegría 1983; Veloz Maggiolo 1993).

The picture that emerges is one of numerous communities with local identities distributed across the island. These identities are expressed in the diversity of pottery styles through the differential selection of specific motifs from a general Meillacoid grammar (see Roe 1989; Ulloa Hung 2013). These communities did not exist in isolation; they were involved in interactions and exchanges at various social and geographical scales. Cultural developments were not the singular progression toward "Taíno" (*sensu* Rouse 1992). Chicoid influences are apparent in eastern Cuba, and to a lesser degree across the island, but they reflect local interpretations and not the imposition of an external force. As expressed by José Guarch Delmonte (1990), Cuban archaeology must be addressed as "*variantes culturales.*" Because their emphasis was on the agricultural *modo de vida*, there were few attempts to define particular pottery styles comparable to those developed by Rouse (1992).

The founding of agricultural communities, marked by the arrival of Meillacoid pottery in the 10th century AD, established recurring patterns of settlement specifically adapted to the region in which they were located. The continuity and conservatism observed in the Banes region highlight the distinctive character of regional integration, while Los Buchillones reflects its diverse expressions. Cultural developments in Cuba represent multidimensional manifestations.

Bahama Archipelago

The Bahama archipelago is a chain of small limestone islands that stretches over 1,000 kilometers, from 100 kilometers east of West Palm Beach, Florida, to within about 120 kilometers of Haiti and Cuba (Figure 6.5). A British survey conducted in 1868 counted twenty-five islands and almost 3,000 cays. The archipelago today is divided between the independent Commonwealth of the Bahamas and the British Crown Colony Turks & Caicos Islands. Interest in the archaeology of the Bahamas received a substantial boost in the decade prior to the Columbus Quincentenary.

Mary Jane Berman and colleagues (Berman et al. 2013) recently divided the Bahamas into Non-Lucayan (AD 700–1300), Early Lucayan (AD 700/800–1100), and Late Lucayan (AD 1100–1530+) periods. The main distinguishing feature is sites at which only non-local pottery is found, and Lucayan sites at which locally made Palmetto ware predominates. There are no Archaic Age sites in all of the Bahamas. The culture history falls entirely in the Ceramic Age, and commences about AD 700 (Keegan 1992; cf. Granberry 1956; Sears and Sullivan 1978). For reasons explained in Chapter 1, we are here avoiding use of the name "Lucayan."

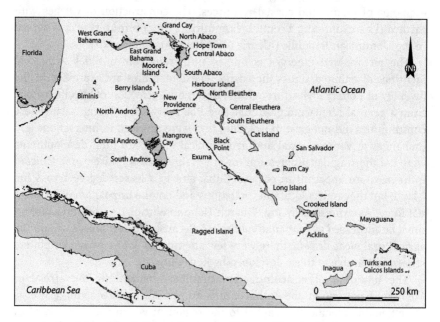

FIGURE 6.5 Map of the Bahamas (courtesy of Menno Hoogland, after Joshua Torres).

It is worth emphasizing that there is no evidence for human settlement anywhere in the Bahamas prior to AD 700, and that no typical Archaic Age sites have been found. The earliest sites are represented by temporary activity areas, seasonal camps, and short-lived villages whose deposits contain a preponderance of pottery of non-local origin. Because pastes tempered with igneous and metamorphic sands could not have originated in the calcareous Bahamas, they must have been imported from the Greater Antilles. The same is true for most lithic tools (Berman et al. 1999). The best examples of temporary and seasonal procurement sites have been excavated in the Turks & Caicos Islands, while the best example of an initial settlement is the Three Dog site on San Salvador.

Coralie Site, Grand Turk, Turks & Caicos Islands
(c. AD 700–1100)

The oldest site in the southern Bahamas is located on Grand Turk, Turks & Caicos Islands. The Coralie site (GT-3) was established on the western margin of North Creek at the north end of Grand Turk around cal. AD 705 (Figure 6.6) (Carlson 1999). It was excavated by William Keegan and Lisabeth Carlson between 1995 and 1997. The site is located about 1 kilometer from "north wells," one of only two freshwater sources on the island. The archaeological deposit is composed of a thin stratum spread over a large area. Toward the creek, the site is overlain by up to 60 centimeters of sand, which probably accumulated during a period of higher sea level that commenced after AD 800 (Scudder 2001). Radiocarbon dates indicate that the site was repeatedly reoccupied over four centuries, and that different centuries can be attributed to different areas of the site. In addition, a canoe paddle was recovered underwater from a peat deposit in North Creek adjacent to the site. The paddle was radiocarbon dated to AD 1100, the final occupation phase. All of the pottery in the site is Ostionoid, and the paste contains quartz-sand tempers that indicate it was manufactured in the Greater Antilles. Petrographic analysis indicates a source in Hispaniola (Cordell 1998).

FIGURE 6.6 Excavations at the Coralie Site, Grand Turk (photo by William Keegan).

The Coralie site contains a unique assemblage of fauna. The bones of green sea turtles (*Chelonia mydas*), iguanas (*Cyclura carinata*), and large fish (5–20 kg) dominate the faunal remains. There are virtually no invertebrates in the site except *Lobatus gigas* shells that were used to line basin-shaped cooking hearths. The method of cooking is also unique in the Caribbean. Turtle meat, iguanas, fish, hermit crabs (*Pagurus* sp.), and spiny lobster (*Panulirus argus*) were cooked together in the carapace of a green turtle.

The site documents what happened to the indigenous fauna after humans first reached an island (Carlson 1999). Within 200 years, mature breeding turtles apparently had been extirpated, and fishing focused on juvenile turtles that were feeding in North Creek. Giant iguanas were taken during the initial occupation, but their size diminished in later deposits. There is a shift in birds through time, as ground-nesting boobies (*Sula sula*) and flightless Key West quail doves (*Geotrygon chrysia*) were consumed first, and open grassland thick-knees (*Burhinus bistriatus*) were taken later. Finally, a native tortoise (*Geochelone* sp.) that was similar in appearance to the Galapagos tortoise, and previously unknown for the island, was targeted during the final phase of occupation.

The Coralie site shows that communities in Hispaniola knew about the Turks & Caicos Islands by AD 700 and that they found it economically reward-ing to travel 120 kilometers by canoe to exploit the abundant marine resources in the waters surrounding Grand Turk. Nowhere else in the Caribbean are sea turtle remains found in such abundance. It is possible that turtles, processed meats, and other marine and terrestrial animals were exported to Hispaniola. The thin strata, the dating of different areas of the site to different centuries, and the superposition of turtle carapace hearths, reflect slightly shifting, mul-tiple reoccupations of an area of only 240 square meters (Carlson 1999). This sequence of seasonal or short-term occupations at a very specific location over a 400-year period suggests ownership of fishing territories.

It is not clear why the Coralie site was abandoned. One factor may be that returns to production fell below an acceptable rate. A separate factor was the changing cultural geography. Rouse (1992) dates the complete replacement of Ostionoid pottery by Meillacoid pottery in northern Hispaniola to about AD 800 (cf. Ulloa Hung 2013). The fact that the dates for this site extend centuries later indicates that it is not likely that the individuals who visited the site were displaced from their homeland during the time they were traveling to Grand Turk. In addition, communities making Palmetto ware pottery had begun to arrive from the north and settle in the Turks & Caicos by AD 1100, while those from Hispaniola using Meillacoid pottery began to visit the island at this time (Carlson 1993; Sinelli 2010).

The value of resources on Grand Turk is evident in respect to Hispaniola. A comparison of the faunal remains at the Coralie site with those recovered from excavations at the contemporaneous fishing village on Île à Rat is reveal-ing. All of the fish at Île à Rat were in the 1–2 kilogram size range, and there was a major focus on invertebrates, including both mollusks and echinoids. Moreover, the conchs (*Lobatus gigas*) in the site were all subadult in the one- to two-year age classes. The differences between these contemporaneous sites are stunning. They show that by AD 1000, the near-shore coastal environment of northern Haiti was already severely depleted. The same process of resource depletion commenced on Grand Turk with the Coralie site (Carlson and Keegan 2004).

The Coralie site illustrates the role of small islands in detecting evidence for broader processes of environmental change. Archaeologists have noted the inundation of Ostionoid deposits throughout the Caribbean, including Jamaica (Keegan et al. 2003), Puerto Rico (Vega 1981), and San Salvador (The Bahamas) (Berman and Gnivecki 1995). Explaining the causes of inundation is complicated by coastal erosion and tectonic activity, especially at sites located on dynamic shorelines where site sediments are identical to beach sediments. In contrast, the Coralie site is located on an inland lagoon, and the sediments deposited on the initial Ostionoid occupation exhibit a slow accumulation in calm, shallow water (Scudder 2001). Tiny land snails in the deposit indicate that, when the site was founded, there were sea grapes growing along the shore (Carlson 1999). At around AD 800, this habitat was flooded by a significant rise in the level of North Creek. It is therefore likely that whatever other local processes were at work along Caribbean shores, there was also a pan-Caribbean rise in eustatic sea level. This rise in sea level had important implications for the ecology of coastal zones.

Small Islands

Island archaeologists exhibit a strong bias toward large islands, and the Caribbean is no exception. Large islands support a greater diversity of terrestrial habitats, and have the capacity to support larger human populations and the consequent development of social complexity (Keegan and Diamond 1987). However, one can ask whether any human society settled an island with the long-term intention of social evolution. Small islands provided attractive procurement and settlement locations with regard to their potential to satisfy short-term goals.

Small island settlements throughout the Caribbean played key roles in resource procurement, colonization, access to already occupied larger islands, defense, viewscape, and ritual activities (Bright 2011; Keegan et al. 2008). An island with as little as 14 square kilometers of arable land could support a minimum viable population of 400 people (Keegan et al. 2008). Also significant is the distribution of abundant marine resources on shallow banks associated with small islands. The most productive fishing grounds in the Caribbean are the Grenadines (between Grenada and St. Vincent), Saba Bank, Anguilla Bank, Pedro Banks (Jamaica), Turks & Caicos Banks, and Bahama Banks. Small islands provided far greater access to marine fish than their larger neighbors did. The Coralie site illustrates that, at an early date, they were already willing to travel long distances to exploit locations of high marine productivity.

Peter Sinelli (2010, 2013) has conducted the most intensive investigation of small islands with early sites. His research focused on thirteen sites on small cays and Middle Caicos on the east side of the Caicos Bank and the Turks Bank. The sites date to between AD 1160 and 1300, and contain mostly imported pottery with Meillacoid designs. At this time, Lucayans had established permanent settlements on at least Middle Caicos (Keegan 2007), so the Meillacoid visitors were encroaching upon an occupied territory. Most of these predominantly Meillacoid sites were seasonal camps, but at least one exhibits evidence for year-round, long-term occupation. Numerous floors surrounding a cleared oval central plaza evidence the permanence of the site on Middleton Cay (Sinelli 2010). Radiocarbon dates indicate the site was first settled around AD 1160, and there is evidence for Chicoid influences between AD 1300 and the late 15th century.

Some of the sites in Sinelli's study have evidence for small-scale bead making, and one appears to have been used solely for ritual activities (e.g., Pelican Cay, which is little more than a rock off the north coast of Middle Caicos; cal. AD 1050, 2-sigma 980–1180). Even when evidence for other activities is present, the main reason these sites were established was to exploit the abundant marine resources of the 2,800-square-kilometer Caicos Bank. The use of small islands is common throughout the Caribbean. They were used exclusively by men for ritual activities by the Carib in the Lesser Antilles (Honeychurch 1995) and the small islands off the coast of Venezuela (Antczak and Antczak 2006).

Governors Beach Site, Grand Turk, Turks & Caicos Islands
(c. AD 1100–1300)

The Governors Beach site (GT-2) is located on a west-facing beach on the southern end of Grand Turk near "south wells," the other freshwater source on the island (Figure 6.7). William Keegan and Lisabeth Carlson excavated the site between 1989 and 1993. A very similar site, called Corktree (GT-4), recently was identified near the Coralie site, but only limited excavations have been completed (Carlson 2010). It is noteworthy that faunal remains at the Corktree site are similar to those at Coralie, suggesting that the different diet at Governors Beach reflects cultural rather than environmental factors. Both sites were seasonal camps established by Haitian communities to facilitate specialized craft production.

The Governors Beach site was first occupied around AD 1100. Non-carbonate tempers and petrographic analysis indicate that all of the pottery was imported from the Greater Antilles (Carlson 1993; Cordell 1998; Keegan 1997). All of the pottery is Meillacoid, except for one tiny red-painted Ostionoid sherd recovered from the deepest deposit. The sherd may reflect contact with the Coralie community (12 kilometers to the north), but the characteristics of the two sites are completely different.

The site was a shell bead workshop at which disc-shaped beads were manufactured from the thorny jewelbox shell (*Chama sarda*). This shell is

FIGURE 6.7 Barbara and Reed Toomey excavating a structure and area of fire-cracked rocks with round concrete polishing platforms inside at the Gouvernor Beach site, Grand Turk (photo by William Keegan).

noteworthy because it is one of the few that retains its color for centuries. While the bright pink of the *Lobatus gigas* shell's periostracum will fade to white in a decade, *Chama* shell beads retained a brilliant scarlet color after 800 years in the ground. Excavations yielded more than 1,500 complete beads, and more than 4,400 blanks, partially drilled beads, and beads broken during production. In addition, there were thousands of pieces of broken shell and other scrap from bead making. The tools used in the manufacturing process including *Lobatus gigas* nippers used to break the *Chama* shells into a rough bead-like shape, manufactured concrete platforms made for the polishing of bead blanks, *Lobatus gigas* anvils for the bipolar flaking of imported chert used for drill bits, and over 550 pieces of chert, of which about fifty were spent drill bits (Carlson 1993).

An analysis of tiger lucine shells (*Codakia orbicularis*) from the area of the site dated to the early 13th century indicates that they were all collected during the same season (Irvy Quitmeyer, personal communication 1992). The shells indicate that the site reflects a dry-season occupation during which people came to Grand Turk when they were not otherwise involved in agricultural activities. The shallow deposits indicate that the site was seasonally occupied, after which they returned to Haiti. At the Coralie site, the emphasis was on high-ranked foods, while at the Governors Beach site, the emphasis was on bead making (Carlson 1993, 1999).

The faunal remains in the site are significantly different from those identified at Coralie, despite the fact that these sites may have been contemporaneous toward the middle of the 12th century. Where the Coralie site contained mostly sea turtles, iguanas, and large fish, the Governors Beach site had mostly the head elements of grunts (*Haemulon* sp.). It is possible that the inhabitants of the Coralie site had extirpated sea turtles, iguanas, and tortoises on the island before the Governors Beach site was established. Alternatively, because the focus of activities at the site was bead making, the people may have limited their efforts in food procurement to fish, for practical or religious reasons. Grunts school in the shallow reefs near the site and are among the most common fish captured in basket traps (Keegan 1986b). A reliable supply of fish could be obtained by setting traps on the reef. Thus food procurement could be accomplished without substantially interfering with the primary activity at the site. In addition, the high incidence of fire-cracked rock at the site is also common at fishing camps at other sites (Keegan and de Bry 2013; Vernon 2007). It is possible that these rocks reflect the practice of preserving fish by smoking them on a barbecue (*barbacoa*); a practice also noted at the Kelbey's Ridge site on Saba (Hofman and Hoogland 2011). The high frequency of fish-head elements suggests that the heads were eaten at the site and smoked fillets were carried back to Haiti. Today, fish heads are considered to have the tastiest flesh and often are reserved for special guests. A similar practice may have occurred at the site, reflecting higher status consumption, and not just break-of-bulk for shipping. In other words, the fish heads were selected for consumption and not just the discard from a heavy and relatively meatless part of the fish.

Cathy Costin (1991) has proposed four factors in the organization of production that can be used to distinguish different types of craft production. The evidence at Governor's Beach points to the presence of craft specialization. With regard to "context," a group of bead makers had to be assembled, outfitted, and transported to the bead-making site. All of the pottery, chert, and a quartzite pestle were brought from the Greater Antilles. Twenty-five-centimeter round polishing platforms (identified as concrete by elemental analysis) were constructed and sheltered in 3-square-meter structure. Production required the participation of individuals intimately familiar with the collection, breakage, drilling, and polishing of the shell. This expedition was an expensive proposition and probably was not undertaken by novices. The "intensity" of the activity is reflected in the site's being established for a single purpose. This activity was conducted at a great distance from the mundane, and even quotidian activities such as food preparation appear minimized. Bead making was the focus of intense "concentration."

Finally, the "constitution" of the product can be characterized as an elite good. Beads were not utilitarian. Moreover, these beads were imbued with a value beyond the labor invested in making them. They were red, the color of life and male potency (Roe 1982), and they came from a place far away, across the sea. They were exotic and thus of greater value than objects that could be fashioned locally on Hispaniola.

The making of beads was accomplished in a spiritual setting. The pottery was of fine quality, and included two effigy vessels and an enigmatic object. The enigmatic object is a broken ceramic manatee flipper. It is possible that this was a lug attached to a vessel, but it is equally likely that it was used as a vomiting spatula. One of the effigy vessels is in the shape of a porcupine fish, and the other has a life-sized bat executed in realistic detail on the side of the vessel. Porcupine fish are interesting because they contain a potentially deadly neurotoxin. Because their bones are found at sites throughout the islands, it is apparent that they learned how to avoid the effects of this toxin. It is also possible that the toxin was used in appropriate doses to produce trances that mimic death. Porcupine fish is the main ingredient in the powder used by practitioners of voodoo to turn someone into a zombie (Davis 1985; Keegan and Carlson 2008:114–116). The vessel has the same shape as other bowls with nostril tubes used for inhaling narcotic snuff (see Fitzpatrick et al. 2009). It was intentionally smashed, with its sherds scattered over a wide area, and the side of the bowl that would have had inhaling tubes is missing. Finally, the faunal remains provide evidence for a restricted diet. The absence of evidence for cooking pots and plant processing suggests that the site was occupied entirely by men.

There is evidence that the site was abruptly abandoned around AD 1280. A variety of valued objects were abandoned or destroyed, including the almost 400 complete shell beads that were thrown into a fire (Carlson 1993). Several effigy vessels (including the porcupine fish vessel), and exotic tools and other objects were discarded. For example, a Triton's trumpet shell (*Charonia variegata*) trumpet, which was so worn that one could detect where the person who blew the trumpet had held the instrument in their hands, was abandoned. There is no reason that an object of such long use should have been left behind. The evidence suggests that the occupants of the site were forcibly ejected and forced to leave the island for good. They may have had a hostile encounter with the itinerant bead makers at the Corktree site; or, more likely, local communities that had been established in the Caicos Islands for almost two centuries began to exert their authority. The fact that the indigenous communities of Middle Caicos controlled the production and distribution of salt and salt fish, including trade with Haiti, beginning around AD 1400, is telling (Keegan 2007; Morsink 2012).

The early sites in the Turks & Caicos Islands document a high degree of mobility, the willingness to exploit resources at distant locations from the home village, the use of hallucinogens, craft specialization, and the ritualized production of high-value goods by communities who lived in Hispaniola and traveled to these islands around AD 1200.

Permanent Settlement

The early sites in the Turks & Caicos Islands have been interpreted as evidence that Hispaniola was the homeland for the colonists of the Bahamas (Keegan

FIGURE 6.8 Palmetto Ware pottery with linear incisions (photo by William Keegan).

1992). It now seems that these sites reflect exploration and extraction activities originating from Hispaniola that did not result in permanent colonies (although the very small site on Middleton Cay appears to be a permanent outpost; Sinelli 2010). The more likely scenario is that communities in northern Cuba established the first permanent settlements in the central Bahamas (Berman et al. 2005; Berman et al. 2013). The transformation from Cuban to Bahamian is expressed in the manipulation of local materials for the production of pottery. This process was complicated by poor plastic qualities of the soil and the absence of igneous and metamorphic sands for tempering. The distinguishing characteristic of archaeological sites in the Bahama archipelago is large quantities of locally made Palmetto ware. This type of pottery is ubiquitous and composes at least 90% of most pottery assemblages.

Palmetto ware is coiled, low-fired earthenware made from local clays that settled in inland ponds and mangrove habitats (Figure 6.8). The high natural saline content of the clays enhances their binding with the shell temper. It is commonly reported that the pottery was made from Bahama red loam, which is made up of fine dust particles that were wind-transported from Africa (Mann 1986). However, a recent study by Donald Gerace and John Winter (2015) has demonstrated that these soils are not well suited for pottery making, and that the pottery was made with clays collected from pond and mangrove sediments. The red color, caused by firing rather than original coloration, seems to be the source for this confusion. It also has been reported that the temper was crushed clamshells (Sears and Sullivan 1978). However, unburned shell will explode during firing, and more recent studies have determined that calcined conch shell was the principle temper (Mann 1986).

Palmetto ware originally was described from pottery recovered at the Palmetto Grove site on the island of San Salvador (Hoffman 1967). It was called a "ware" because there was only one "type." It was fired in an oxidizing environment and is mostly unslipped. Vessel shapes are hemispheric, carinated, and boat-shaped, along with flat, mass-molded griddles (Berman et al. 2013). The vessels break easily, sherds are friable, roots often penetrate incompletely fired cores, and surfaces exfoliate and erode, all of which limits the study of the mostly plain body sherds recovered during excavations.

Several local "wares" have since been identified (Bate 2011; Granberry and Winter 1995; Winter and Gilstrap 1991). These wares denote variability in pottery production, but the meaning and general adoption of these categories have not been established. Abaco red ware is partially oxidized with a buff slip and is found primarily in the northern Bahamas. Crooked Island ware is reduce-fired with a red slip applied and occurs primarily in the central Bahamas. Because these differences can be subtle and their identification is as yet incompletely internalized, the tendency has been to call all of the pottery "Palmetto ware." Plastic decorations occur in low frequency (less than 10%). They include incised parallel lines and crosshatch designs, rim points, and sigmoid and incised sigmoid appliqué (Sears and Sullivan 1978). These decorations show a marked affiliation with Meillacoid designs. The most common form of decoration is basket impressions on the base of griddles and occasionally on the lower portion of hemispherical vessels. These "matt" impressions were transferred during the molding of griddles. They include intricate weaves and complex forms that were purposely executed (Berman and Hutcheson 2000; Hutcheson 2015). Basket-impressed sherds have been recovered from sites on small islands in the Jardine del Rey archipelago off the north coast of Cuba. The meaning attached to these designs is under study (Hutcheson 2015).

The oldest dated Lucayan site is Preacher's Cave on the north coast of Eleuthera, with a calibrated date on triton shell of AD 560–720 and a burial dated to AD 810–1010. The Three Dog site and Pigeon Creek site on San Salvador, and the Pink Wall site on New Providence (Nassau) have yielded dates in the 8th and early 9th centuries (Berman et al. 2013:266–267). Small, shallow middens and low artifact densities characterize the sites. The sites appear to reflect a high degree of mobility involving village movement every few years (Berman et al. 2013).

Imported pottery at the Three Dog site (San Salvador, Bahamas) has affinities to the Arroyo del Palo style of northern Cuba (Berman and Gnivecki 1995; Tabio and Guarch 1966), which is considered *protoagrícola* during this time period). A rapid reconnaissance of the Jumentos Cays, located 100 kilometers west of the main islands of the central Bahamas and 150 kilometers from the north coast of Cuba, identified several small precolonial sites with Palmetto ware and imports. Although the dates for these sites have not been established, petrographic analysis of pottery recovered from these fishing camps or way stations reveals connections between Cuba and the central Bahamas (Keegan and de Bry 2013). In addition, Jago Cooper (2007) has reported Cuban pottery that looks very similar to Palmetto ware on the small islands off the north coast. It is possible that permanent colonies were established in the Bahamas through the extension of lifeways developed on the islands off the north coast of Cuba. As with Meillacoid sites to the south, bead making was an important activity. The available evidence suggests that the first permanent colonists came from Cuba and settled in the central Bahamas (Berman and Gnivecki 1995). Concurrently, Meillacoid visitors from Haiti were exploiting resources in the southern Bahamas.

Previous efforts to explain the colonization of the Bahamas have relied on Rouse's (1986, 1992) model of different Ceramic Age cultures progressively expanding from Puerto Rico to the west and north. Thus, the first permanent settlements typically have been attributed to an Ostionoid expansion (Berman and Gnivecki 1995; Keegan 1992; Sears and Sullivan 1978). Investigations in Cuba have revealed the virtually complete absence of Ostionoid pottery on the island, with the possible exception of southeastern Cuba. As various Meillacoid influences from Hispaniola began to infiltrate Cuba around AD 1000, pottery became a far more important component of the Archaic Age tool kit. It was communities with this *protoagrícola* economy who initiated the settlement of the Bahamas (cf. Ulloa Hung and Valcárcel Rojas 2013:239).

This Archaic Age Cuban presence in the Bahamas is justified by several historical contingencies:

(1) The simultaneous expansion of ceramic use in Cuba and the earliest sites in the Bahamas;
(2) Striking similarities between pottery from the Arroyo del Palo site and the Three Dog site;
(3) The development of a new kind of pottery made from local clays and calcined shell that probably was invented in one location and then spread throughout the Bahamas;
(4) The rapid adoption of shell tools in the Bahamas (a long-standing tradition in Cuba) in the absence of appropriate lithic raw materials;
(5) A high degree of mobility in the Bahamas where sites were occupied for relatively short periods of time;
(6) A continuing emphasis on the extraction of marine resources.

Furthermore, the calibration of radiocarbon dates has shifted the arrival of recognized pottery series (Ostionoid and Meillacoid) a full two centuries later in time. These revised dates indicate that the Ceramic Age in Cuba began around AD 1000, three centuries after the Bahamas were colonized, and that Meillacoid pottery did not arrive in the Banes region until AD 1100 (Persons 2013). Banes is considered the most likely source of Bahamian colonists (Berman and Gnivecki 1995, 2013). In summary, the Bahamas were colonized centuries prior to the beginning of the Ceramic Age in Cuba.

The identification of Archaic Age influences in the colonization of the Bahamas provides the opportunity to compare cultural developments throughout the Caribbean from a common perspective. We no longer accept that pottery and agriculture were introduced by a wave of migrants from the South American mainland that displaced the indigenous Archaic Age inhabitants. We can now examine complementary cultural trajectories in contrasting environments and different islands.

Late Ceramic Age

Archaeological surveys conducted throughout the archipelago identified Palmetto ware sites on all of the major islands and many of the smaller cays (Bahamas Archaeology Team 1984; de Booy 1912, 1913a; Sullivan 1974, 1976, 1980; Keegan 1985). More than 110 cave and 390 open-air sites were reported for the Bahama archipelago when Anthony Aarons did an inventory in 1990 (Craton and Saunders 1992:Table 1; Keegan 1997:Table 3.1). Because the distribution of sites was weighted to the south, Keegan (1992) concluded that the southern islands were colonized first. Subsequent research has indicated that this distribution was misleading due to factors such as inadequate survey coverage, previously unrecognized windward settlements, and the criteria used to define a "site." It is no exaggeration to claim that, if you look closely enough, you will find a site on every beach in the archipelago. In fact, the longer beaches often have several discrete sites (Keegan 1992).

The high degree of residential mobility observed continued during the Late Ceramic Age. For example, subsurface deposits at the Clifton site extend over 400 meters along the western shore of New Providence (Vernon 2007). Based on its length, location, and six overlapping radiocarbon dates that cluster in the mid-12th century, the initial investigators concluded that the site was two large villages separated by an open plaza. Subsequent excavations revealed four activity zones composed of shallow deposits (less than 25 centimeters), little midden accumulation, minuscule amounts of pottery, few other artifacts, and an abundance of fire-cracked rock. This evidence points to repeated short-term occupations along the shore. The Bahamas are highly susceptible to hurricanes, so limiting investments in permanent facilities may account for the ephemeral character of most sites (see Cooper 2013). The relatively rapid turnover in settlements provided opportunities to reshuffle individuals and initiate new forms of social engagements.

The indigenous communities made extensive use of the coastal zones. There were permanent villages, but short-term occupations and activity zones vastly overshadow their number. The settlement patterns and land/sea activity zones are more reminiscent of the mobility attributed to the Archaic Age than that associated with sedentary farmers on Hispaniola. Moreover, the sites are exclusively coastal; there is no evidence that sites were ever established in the interior of the islands, despite repeated surveys in the interior (Keegan 1992;

contra Sears and Sullivan 1978). The number of sites appears to increase over time, which may reflect a growing population, the practice of occupying sites for short periods of time, and/or the dispersion of activities across the landscape. This dispersed pattern of landscape use also has been noted for the Lesser Antilles at this time (Hofman and Hoogland 2004).

Following a walkover survey of about 1,500 kilometers of Bahamian shoreline, Keegan (1985) classified the sites he discovered based on the linear distance of surface scatters. Different site types were identified to avoid comparing villages and special-purpose sites. The distribution of "village" sites revealed that more than 90% of such sites across the archipelago were paired, a practice also observed in the Maniabon Hills of Cuba (Rouse 1942). "Settlement pairs" were defined as habitation sites that occur within each other's 5-kilometer diameter terrestrial catchment. The pattern of two sites in close proximity separated by a much longer distance from the next pair was clearly visible on maps for each island, and the pattern was confirmed using nearest-neighbor analysis. Excavations at MC-12 and MC-32 on Middle Caicos provided radiocarbon confirmation that these villages were occupied contemporaneously in the 13th century (Keegan 2007). The pairing was interpreted as reflecting social relations between communities. A careful reading of the Spanish chroniclers suggested that the pattern was produced by matrilocal/avunculocal residence in a society organized by matrilineal descent (Keegan and Maclachlan 1989).

Very few sites have been systematically excavated, so it is only possible to offer general observations. Most of the sites can be characterized as an alignment of structures atop a lee-shore dune facing a sand beach and backed by a swale. The contours of the shoreline limited community organization to a linear plan. Sites have less frequently been found behind rocky shorelines, points of land, on the margins of tidal creeks, and on the windward coasts (Keegan 1997). On the windward coasts, they usually are associated with a tidal creek that provided access to the sea. A tidal creek in the Bahamas is a shallow embayment with a narrow opening to the sea (Sealey 1985). These "creeks" are often of substantial size. Columbus mentions a peninsula on Guanahaní (the first island he visited; today identified as San Salvador) that had six houses, which he described as looking like Moorish campaign tents (Dunn and Kelley 1989:93). This description matches the Hispaniolan *caneye* described by Gonzalo Fernández de Oviedo y Valdéz (1959; Keegan 1997). The only partially excavated structure in the archipelago was at MC-12 on Middle Caicos. Five dark post stains at 3-meter intervals enclosed a circular area of hard-packed sand of approximately 6 meters in diameter.

Their diet exhibits a strong reliance on marine resources (Newsom and Wing 2004; Wing and Scudder 1981). A wide variety of reef and seagrass habitat fish taxa are abundantly represented in faunal samples. The types of fish indicate diverse capture techniques, including hook-and-line, spears, nets, and basket traps (Keegan 1986b). Birds, hutía, iguanas, sea turtles, freshwater turtles, and crocodiles are infrequently recovered. Marine mollusk shells are substantial components of midden deposits, especially tiger lucine, tellins, other clams, and conchs from sand and seagrass substrates; and nerites, chitons, and West Indian topsnails from rocky intertidal habitats. The most important mollusk was the queen conch (*Lobatus gigas*) due to its abundance (Doran 1958), large meat package, and the shell's suitability for making a wide variety of tools (Jones O'Day and Keegan 2001).

The sites are typically associated with hardwood coppice vegetation. These woodlands provide good agricultural land in comparison to Whitelands Formation soils, which are sterile sand on which few sites of any size are located. Starch grain and phytolith evidence on chert microliths found evidence for chili peppers, maize, manioc, squash, and several kinds of wild and domesticated roots and tubers (Berman and Pearsall 2008; Berman et al. 1999). The presence of maize in early sites, and its description by Columbus, indicates that it was an integral component of their gardens (Figueredo 2015). The large size, thick walls, and shell temper of hemispherical pots suggests that one type of cooking was "pepper pot" stews.

Indigenous boats carved from a single log visited Columbus' ships. These *canoa* ranged in size from the largest, which could carry "forty to forty-five men," to very small dugouts paddled by one man (Dunn and Kelley 1989:69). A miniature canoe, possibly part of a burial offering, was recovered from a blue hole on Andros Island, and canoe paddles have been recovered from More's Island (Abaco) and Grand Turk. The Islanders offered parrots and balls of cotton thread (and small cloth "cloaks") in exchange for anything the Spanish would give them (Keegan 2015). Columbus describes one exchange in which sixteen balls of thread, weighing about 10 kg., were exchanged for three Portuguese copper coins (Dunn and Kelley 1989:71, 73). Joost Morsink (2012, 2013) has explored the significance of cotton and salt in shaping taskscapes and exchange. Working at the site of MC-6 on Middle Caicos, he found that fish, salt, and cotton were exploited during their seasonal availabilities to create a complete annual cycle of activities. These resources were produced for export to the Greater Antilles as salt fish, raw salt, and balls of cotton thread. The importance of this export industry is reflected in the unique arrangement of the site with an enclosing raised earthwork midden, stone-lined pit structures in the midden ridge, a central court with stones aligned to mark the transit of the sun and stars, and a road connecting the site to salt-producing Armstrong Pond. The site reflects the materialization of social relations and the significance of seasons, especially as marked by the transit of the Orion constellation (Keegan 2007). In this regard, the site documents the importance of social relations between the southern Bahamas and Hispaniola.

Large canoes and massive balls of cotton thread provide evidence for long-distance voyages of exchange. The villagers at the north end of Long Island directed Columbus to round the north end of the island and head south to find the "king with much gold." These directions to Cuba suggest continuing interactions with that island, as do small sites on the Jumentos Cays. It is likely that the very small islands in the Jumentos Cays were used as way stations and water sources during long-distance voyages to and from Cuba (Keegan and de Bry 2013). Finally, Columbus observed scars on the bodies of the men. His inquiry about this was met with gestures he took to mean that they fought with men who came from other islands. Trading and raiding often are two sides of the same coin (Keegan 2015). As was the case in Melanesia, trading expeditions may have ended in battles (see Macintyre 1983).

MC-6 Site, Middle Caicos, Turks & Caicos Islands
(c. AD 1400–1600)

MC-6 is truly unique (Figure 6.9). Despite being extremely difficult to reach and excavate, it attracted repeated expeditions between 1977 and 2010. The history of research and excavation results have been described elsewhere in great detail (Keegan 2007; Morsink 2012; Sullivan 1981). The main point here is that MC-6 was a locally controlled *entrepôt* (Sullivan 1981). Ninety percent of the pottery is Palmetto ware, and the other 10% is decorated Chicoid vessels and (manioc beer) bottles imported from Hispaniola (Troumans 1986). It was not a "Taíno" outpost or colonial settlement (*contra* Keegan 1992).

The site is located on the first permanently dry land above a 6-kilometer-wide *salina*. The *salina* is a seasonally flooded marl flat that today is only 25 centimeters above mean sea level. Given the raised midden at the edge of the *salina*, slightly lower sea level and sedimentation of the *salina*, it is likely that canoes could have been paddled right up to the site when it was occupied.

FIGURE 6.9 Excavations at MC-6, Middle Caicos (courtesy of Shaun D. Sullivan; from Sullivan and Freimuth 2015).

MC-6 was measured during topographic mapping at 270 by 70 meters, with the margins defined by midden ridges. Sullivan (1981) identified two plazas. The western plaza (170 meters long east–west), called Plaza I, was larger, and the midden ridges were punctuated by eight stone-lined pit features around a central court. There are four pit features on the north side, three on the south side, and one (possibly double) on the east side at the juncture of the two plazas. He interpreted these features as semi-pit houses, but repeated excavations have failed to determine how these features were used (Keegan 2007; Morsink 2012). Clearing the plaza revealed a stone-lined court defined by a double row of undressed limestone rocks. In addition, an indigenous road originated between structures III and VI and connected the north side of Plaza I to Armstrong Pond.

The stone-lined court at the center of Plaza I is a remarkable piece of engineering. It is virtually flat, exhibiting only 10 centimeters of grade despite 500 years of weathering. The northern and southern margins of the court are flanked by double rows of undressed limestone that are incorporated into earthen ridges. Soil analysis revealed that the court was leveled with marl soils transported from the *salina* (Roth 2002). The long east–west axis measures about 31 meters. Where the stones stop at the eastern and western ends, the court is about 15 meters wide. Those edge markers, combined with the discovery of a stone at the center of the court with a ball-size depression, led Sullivan to propose initially that this was a ball court (*batey*). When it was first discovered, researchers assumed that the rows of stones were parallel, but the detailed topographic map showed that the double rows of stones bow proportionately along their course. At its widest, the court measures 19 meters. Sullivan (1981) noted astronomical alignments marking the summer solstice and the transit of Orion. Keegan (2007) has suggested that the entire site is an on-the-ground representation of the constellation based on the alignments and close association of Orion's transit with the four seasons.

The site's defining feature is its proximity to Armstrong Pond. Today, the pond produces vast quantities of solar-distilled salt along its margins during the summer. Joost Morsink (2012) studied the sediments in Armstrong Pond and demonstrated that it began to produce quantities of salt in the early 15th century, just prior to the founding of MC-6. Sullivan (1981) had his sixteen-member team collect salt for 15 minutes during the height of the dry season in July 1977. Their labors produced 480 liters of salt, weighing more than 542 kilograms. The historic importance of salt (at times called "white gold") as a nutritional need and for the preservation of meats is well documented. The availability of terrestrial and possibly even marine sources of meat was limited on Hispaniola. Although fish provided a significant source (Newsom and Wing 2004), fishing has unpredictable returns, and the flesh will spoil within a week. The large populations of Hispaniola required a stable and reliable source of meat, and this need could only be met by salting fish. The Lucayans at MC-6 combined unprecedented access to salt and the marine productivity of the Caicos Bank to produce salt fish for export to Hispaniola (Morsink 2012).

Sullivan (1981) also defined an eastern plaza, Plaza II, measuring 100 meters east–west based on its raised earthwork perimeter and a low frequency of artifacts. He suggested that this was the commoner's plaza, but subsequent excavations failed to reveal any evidence of habitation (Keegan 2007). Plaza II was probably a permanent agricultural field constructed for the production of cotton and maintained through organic enrichment (i.e., composting) and the addition of Bahama red loam from an area near Armstrong Pond (Morsink 2012; Roth 2002). Morsink (2012) has argued that cotton production was a significant component of the taskscape at MC-6, given its expressed value and the timing of seasonal labor requirements. The Spanish also reported that the *cacica* Anacaona controlled workshops on Hispaniola where a wide variety of cotton goods was produced (Keegan 2007). Based on modern production yields, this three-hectare garden could have produced up to 2,500 kilograms of cotton per year (Yafa 2005).

In sum, a variety of high-value goods was produced at MC-6 for export to Hispaniola. Indigenous Bahamians controlled both production and exchange; their status was expressed in the construction of a unique port of trade charged with symbolic capital. It is possible that the site continued in use well after the arrival of the Spanish. Sharyn Jones O'Day (2002) obtained two AMS dates from bird bones as part of her study of the faunal assemblage. The conventional radiocarbon ages are reported as 400 +/– 40 B.P. (AD 1550; Beta-155021) and 320 +/– 40 B.P. (AD 1630; Beta-155020), with 2-delta ranges of AD 1430–1630 and 1460–1660, respectively. Combined with the radiocarbon dates obtained by Morsink (2012) and a brass nose ornament recovered by Sullivan, it is possible that activities at the site continued unmolested well into the early colonial period (see also Berman et al. 2013; Sinelli 2010). Common sense suggests that it was advantageous for the Spanish to allow indigenous production of useful goods (e.g., salt, salt fish, cotton), especially if these activities were conducted at a distance from the Spanish colony.

The (Not So) Empty Islands

As the indigenous societies of Hispaniola collapsed under Spanish oppression, the Spanish turned to neighboring islands as a source of slave labor. Peter Martyr reported that 40,000 individuals from the Bahamas were imported, and this number is consistent with population estimates for Hispaniola, which show a brief increase in the Indio population in the early 1500s (Keegan 1997). The indigenous inhabitants of Las Islas de Los Lucayos were especially prized for their abilities as divers, and they were sold at a premium to the managers of the pearl-fishing industry headquartered at Nueva Cádiz on Cubagua Island off the north coast of Venezuela (Granberry 1979–1981). Juan Ponce de León encountered only one old man when he traversed the Bahamas in 1513 on his way to discover Florida. Some have suggested that the islands were completely depopulated by this date (Sauer 1966). This conclusion is challenged by a spate of radiocarbon dates that document a continuation of indigenous lifeways at some locations as late as the early 17th century (Berman et al. 2013:275; Jones O'Day 2002; Sinelli 2010). Whether these refugees survived through isolation like the Maroons in Jamaica and elsewhere (Agorsah 2013), or were incorporated into the Spanish economy through their semi-independent production of particular goods (e.g., cotton, salt) remain open questions (Morsink 2012).

Jamaica

Jamaica has a rich history of archaeological investigations (Figure 6.10) (Keegan and Atkinson 2006). Local, "avocational" archaeologists have been the driving force behind most of the archaeological research. Their primary interest has always been in the history of *their* island and the British Commonwealth. As a result, investigations were published primarily in local venues such as the *Journal of the Institute of Jamaica* and the newsletters of the *Archaeology Society of Jamaica*. This local emphasis has resulted in Jamaican archaeology's being characterized as a "black hole," the least studied of the major islands in the Caribbean, and as absent any prior systematic archaeological research. However, this characterization of Jamaican archaeology is false (Atkinson 2006). Unfortunately, general reviews of Caribbean archaeology have failed to give appropriate recognition to investigations conducted in Jamaica (e.g., Rouse 1992; Sued Badillo 2003; Wilson 2007).

Steeped in years of antiquarian interest and early 19th and 20th century prospecting (e.g., de Booy 1913b; Duerden 1897; Longley 1914; Reichard 1904; Sherlock 1939), the primary emphasis in Jamaica was the description of artifacts that were unique and exotic; in many cases these were works of art and objects that had never been described before. The Yale Caribbean Program introduced a more systematic approach to Jamaican archaeology when Robert Howard conducted dissertation research in 1947–1948. Howard was specifically interested in how Jamaica fit into Irving Rouse's developing taxonomy for the Caribbean. In contrast to the previous interest in objects of art, the culture-historical approach focused on the mundane and everyday artifacts of life. This approach asked when and where were particular forms of pottery decoration and other artifacts found. In essence, the change reflected a shift from searching for the exotic to determining where the everyday could be found.

Howard's (1950) dissertation describes in detail archaeological investigations that had been conducted prior to 1950. In this regard, it was an important starting point that provided an initial inventory of archaeological sites and descriptions for material remains. He recorded seventy-five midden sites, twenty-seven cave sites, and nine rock art sites (Keegan and Atkinson 2006:Table 1). In his later publications, Howard (1956, 1965) fitted Jamaican archaeology into the dominant classification scheme of the time.

Howard's research inspired Dr. James Lee, a geologist, who organized surveys, site visits, and made collections across the island (Lee 1991). His collections and extensive field notes were donated to the University of the West

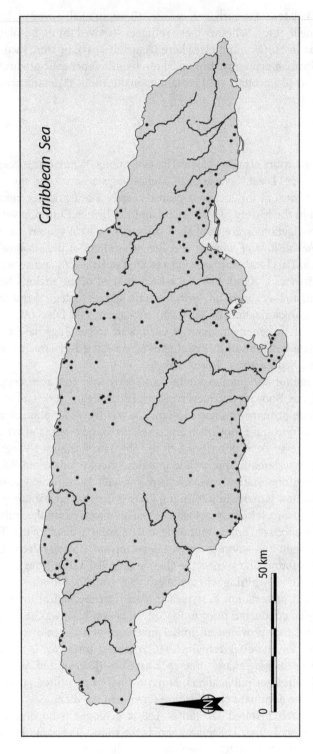

FIGURE 6.10 Archaeological sites in Jamaica (after Atkinson 2006: Figure A1).

Caribbean Sea

50 km

N

Indies after his death. These materials were curated and published by Phillip Allsworth-Jones (2008); they figure prominently in this discussion. That publication also reprinted the earliest comprehensive account of Jamaican antiquities, written by J. E. Duerden (1897). To the present, most of the research has focused on identifying site locations, classifying them according to Rousean systematics, and the analysis of faunal remains recovered from test excavations (Allsworth-Jones 2008; Scudder 2006). In recent years, some Cultural Resource Management (Richards 2006) and larger-scale excavations have been initiated (Allworth-Jones and Wesler 2012; Keegan et al. 2003), but this phase of research is still in its infancy (Wesler 2013).

The most surprising aspect of Jamaican archaeology is the complete lack of any evidence that Archaic Age explorers ever visited the island (Callaghan 2003). This is especially surprising because Jamaica has a long history of avocational interest alongside well-trained archaeologists in the Jamaica National Heritage Trust. If there were Archaic Age artifacts on the island, then it is likely that someone would have recognized them, especially because both professionals and avocationalists are well aware of this issue. It should be noted that Sven Lovén (1932) reported the discovery of stone "dart points" from Old Harbour, Jamaica. However, projectile points are not common in Caribbean archaeological sites, and there is some question as to what these mean in terms of Jamaican archaeology (Harris 1991).

Pottery Series as Distinct Cultures

The first permanent settlers arrived in Jamaica sometime around AD 700. The earliest dates are associated with the Little River pottery style. The Little River site was excavated by Marion DeWolf in 1933, and is the first at which redware pottery was identified (De Wolf 1953). The Alligator Pond site is a good example of this style (Silverberg et al. 1972; Vanderwal 1968). Howard (1956, 1965) classified the Little River style as part of Rouse's original Ostionoid series.

Sixteen open-air and three cave sites with redware pottery have been reported (Allsworth-Jones 2008). Only three have been excavated; none have been reported in detail; only two radiocarbon dates have been obtained (Wesler 2013:256). Redware sites were established in coastal settings and exhibit a strong reliance on marine fish and mollusks. As with the Ostionoid site on Grand Turk (Carlson 1999), marine turtles formed a large part of the diet. It is possible that these sites reflect an extension of Archaic Age practices (*protoagrícola* in Cuba), partly reflected by the use of expedient chert tools and an emphasis on sea turtles. Moreover, all of the investigated sites have very shallow deposits, suggesting they were short-term base camps occupied to facilitate logistic foraging. At present, there are far too few data to engage in anything beyond speculation.

The dominant pottery styles on Jamaica are consistent with the Meillacoid series. It is noteworthy that there is no evidence for a transition from redware to Meillacoid. All of the known archaeological sites are single component with no co-occurrence of the two, nor the mixing of modes as observed in the Dominican Republic (Ulloa Hung 2013; Wallace 1992). There are no stratified deposits that demonstrate the priority of one over the other. The two redware dates are older, but they overlap at the 2-sigma range with early Meillacoid dates from the Cinnamon Hill and White Marl sites (Wesler 2013). To date, there is no evidence for any relations between the communities making these two kinds of pottery.

Three local Meillacoid styles have been identified: Montego Bay style in the west, Port Morant style in the east, and White Marl style across the island (Allsworth-Jones 2008). Meillacoid vessels, including the White Marl style, typically are boat-shaped or hemispherical and turn inward at the shoulder so that the opening (aperture) is smaller than the greatest diameter of the vessel (*casuela*). Filleted rims are common, and incised and appliqué decorations are located between the shoulder and the rim. Meillacoid pottery from Jamaica is distinctive in that the distance between the shoulder and the rim is shorter than that observed on *casuela* vessels in Haiti. The Montego Bay style is also distinctive in that a wider fillet or separate band of clay (in addition to a filleted rim) is affixed at the rim and is decorated with deeply incised parallel lines on this band (Allsworth-Jones 2008).

The culture history of Jamaica involves two separate colonizations in rapid succession. The first appearance of communities using redware pottery (Ostionoid) is associated with a focus on a particular set of resources (e.g., sea turtles) and short-lived settlements. Their lack of longevity stands in marked contrast to Meillacoid communities', many of which were occupied for hundreds of years. It is not clear whether they stopped making their distinctive Ostionoid pottery and assimilated with White Marl, or whether they abandoned the enterprise.

The White Marl site exhibits a more sedentary way of life that is more focused on agricultural production than fishing. Sites are more commonly found on hilltops above the coast, although the Sweetwater site sits between a mangrove swamp and a morass (freshwater swamp). New settlements were established across the island, with a total of 186 open-air (midden) sites, sixty-one cave sites, and numerous rock art sites attributed to the Meillacoid (Allsworth-Jones 2008; Atkinson 2009). Thirty radiocarbon dates range from the mid–eighth century to the European encounter. Meillacoid sites are common in more inland locations, especially on hillsides overlooking the coast (Wesler 2013), similar to settlement patterns in Cuba, Haiti, and the northwestern Dominican Republic. The sites have deep deposits indicative of permanent settlement, and the locations are better suited for agriculture.

Although village layouts have not been investigated, Theodoor de Booy (1913b) excavated a midden on the Retreat property in St. Ann on the north coast. The site is 10 kilometers from the sea on a 400-meter-elevation hill. The hilltop is level with a series of middens positioned around the edge of the hilltop. This location and arrangement of middens is common at Meillacoid sites throughout the Greater Antilles. The pottery in the site was executed in the White Marl style, and there is a large number of handles that are typical of the unique Jamaican canteen. As de Booy noted, despite the similar use of incision and appliqué decorations, the pottery in Jamaica is considerably different from that found on neighboring islands. Land snails (*Pleurodonte acuta*) were the dominant mollusk in the deposits, but marine taxa also were observed (e.g., *Arca* sp., *Lobatus* sp., *Fasciolaria tulipa*).

Archaeological sites near Kingston follow the Meillacoid pattern of settlements on hilltops overlooking the coast (Allsworth-Jones et al. 2007). The city of Kingston is located on the broad, alluvial Liguanea Plain and is surrounded by an arc of hills on the south coast of Jamaica. Meillacoid sites are aligned on this arc of hills at elevations ranging between 610 meters ($n = 1$), below 305 meters ($n = 8$), and between 305 meters and 610 meters ($n = 9$). The locations provide access to agricultural land and defensive positions with a wide view of the surrounding area. Neutron activation analysis of twelve sherds from six sites indicates that pottery was locally made. As at other sites on the island, the Pleurodonte land snail is abundant in the deposits. A similar abundance of Pleurodonte is noted for the inland El Flaco site in the northwestern Dominican Republic (Hofman and Hoogland 2015a, b; Hofman et al. 2013). The sites contain a variety of marine mollusks, and those that typically inhabit mangrove habitats are the most common (see Veloz Maggiolo et al. 1981). Of note is the absence of *Lobatus* shell. Although the meat may have been extracted near the coast and the shells abandoned there, the absence of this shell in the site suggests that it was not an important tool source.

Most of these sites have been severely disrupted by modern construction activities (Allsworth-Jones et al. 2007), and systematic excavations have been too few to provide detailed comparisons. Nevertheless, Sylvia Scudder (2006) was able to compare faunal remains from Rodney's House, White Marl, and Bellevue sites. The Rodney's House site was identified as the earliest of the three, based on a shift from round to fillet rims on pottery vessels. At Rodney's House, there was a significant shift from the early use of land crabs to a later abundance of marine mollusks. The Rodney's House deposits also exhibited a much stronger reliance on marine environments (65% of MNI versus 35% terrestrial). Marine fish from seagrass, mangrove, and reef habitats were common at Rodney's House, and sea turtles, sharks, and saltwater crocodiles also were present.

In comparison, the White Marl site was 62%, and Bellevue 89%, terrestrial (Scudder 2006:Table 8.2). Jamaican hutia or coney (*Geocapromys brownii*), iguana (*Cyclura collei*), Jamaican rice rat (*Oryzomys antillarium*), and land crabs (*Cardisoma* sp.) were the dominant terrestrial taxa, along with a small contribution from birds. Rodney's House is the closest site to the coast, which may account for the higher incidence of marine fauna. Alternatively, the site may represent an earlier practice of marine exploitation that was replaced over time by a more terrestrial focus. Finally, the lower incidence of marine animals at the White Marl and Bellevue sites may reflect the costs of moving marine foods processed on the coast to inland settlements. Specialized coastal fishing communities at which shells and bones were discarded prior to supplying inland villages with meat are common throughout the Caribbean.

FIGURE 6.11 Excavations at the Sweetwater site (photo by William Keegan).

Paradise Park Sites, Westmoreland (*c.* AD 850 and AD 1430)

Between 1998 and 2002, William Keegan excavated two sites at Paradise Park (Figure 6.11), Westmoreland Parish, in southwestern Jamaica at the behest of Tony Clarke (Keegan et al. 2003).[2] The property is on a low-lying coastal plain with the deeply dissected Chebucktoo karst hills to the east. The seaward margin is a series of arcuate, sub-parallel former beach ridges aligned to the present shore. The two sites are situated on the second beach ridge from the coast at an elevation of 1–1.5 meters above mean sea level. A freshwater swamp (morass) forms the landward margin of the dune, and a mangrove swamp and modern dune separate the sites from the sea. The sites were limited to the dry surface of the dune, which had a maximum width of 100 meters. The vegetation is coastal dry tropical forest dominated by large trees that limited the extent of the excavations. The edible Pleurodonte land snail is common in both sites and currently lives on the surrounding vegetation. Their modern abundance suggests there was a similar forested environment when the sites were occupied.

---

[2] To date, only the report on mollusks as environmental indicators has been published (Keegan et al. 2003). A more complete report is being prepared as part of a dissertation. Additional information can be obtained online at http://www.flmnh.ufl.edu/Caribarch/jamaica.htm.

The sites are located to the east of the Dean's Valley River on an abandoned road that connected Cave Settlement and Savanna-la-Mar. Originally identified as one site by Roderick Ebanks in 1991, its investigation began with a shovel-test survey along the road to better define the site boundaries. The result was the identification of two distinct sites separated by a 240-meter vacant space. The two sites reflect separate and independent occupations. The site farther to the east contained only redware pottery (Paradise site), and the one closest to the river had only Meillacoid pottery (Sweetwater site). The excavations afforded the opportunity to investigate these distinct occupations.

The Paradise site, located in a royal palm grove (*Roystonea* sp.), measures about 400 meters long (east–west) by 60–100 meters wide, as constrained by the width of the dune. A total of 29 square meters were excavated to a maximum depth of 60 centimeters, where it extended a short distance below the water table. The site contained only Ostionoid pottery, including redware, red-paint above the shoulder, tabular lugs, loop handles, and black smudging. Only one radiocarbon date was obtained, and yielded cal. AD 850 +/– 60. A single large post stain, interpret to be a center post, was observed and is associated with a dense midden, suggesting that there was at least one large structure at the site. However, extending the excavations failed to encounter additional stains.

A variety of stone objects was present in the deposit. Expedient flaked chert was especially common, with several repetitive tool forms apparent. Fire-cracked limestone also was abundant, and in the Bahamas this may be associated with smoking fish (Keegan 2007). Shell tools were common, including a *Lobatus* celt and *Lobatus* columella picks and nippers. However, no bivalve scrapers were found, which contrasts sharply with the Sweetwater site. The co-occurrence of stone and shell tools indicates their complementary use (Lammers-Keijsers 2008).

The site also contains a substantial number of olive shells, several of which were made into beads and pendants. In addition, the number of broken olive shells suggests that beads and pendants were manufactured at the site. A unique find was an agate ear spool recovered above the post stain. It is 12 millimeters in diameter and has a lateral groove. There is also a hole through the middle that was probably used to insert colorful feathers. A 7-centimeter greenstone pendant sculpted in the shape of the dog spirit also was recovered *in situ*. The beads, ear spool, and pendant illustrate the wide distribution of these types of adornment across the Caribbean region.

The site contained substantial quantities of animal bones, including fish (grunt, jack, and parrotfish), hutia, iguana, and sea turtle. Sea turtle bones dominated the deposit. A surprising variety of marine mollusks was recovered, especially *Lobatus* and Veneridae clams. The mollusk assemblage indicates that foraging focused on the closest marine habitats, and that Bluefields Bay supported an extensive seagrass habitat. The mangrove swamp was either less developed at this time, or those living at the site chose to ignore its animal resources.

The Sweetwater site is located 900 meters east of the Dean's Valley River in a hardwood forest. This location on a dune in the middle of a swamp is unusual when compared to other Meillacoid sites on the island. It measures about 220 meters long (east–west) by about 60 meters wide, constrained by the width of the dune. A total of 82 square meters were excavated primarily in two large blocks, with deposits ranging from 20 centimeters to a maximum depth of 100 centimeters. The site contained only Meillacoid pottery, most of which was undecorated. The few decorated sherds are consistent with the Montego Bay style. Only one radiocarbon date was obtained, and yielded cal. AD 1430 +/– 60.

The materials recovered during excavation were unremarkable. We did not find any evidence for structures; the pottery was mostly plain bowl fragments; and flaked-stone tools and debitage were far less common. The flaked chert that was observed had a noticeably different appearance from that recovered at the Paradise site, although the lithics specialist on the project concluded that the chert in both sites was collected from the river, and that similar flaking techniques were employed. A greenstone or jadeite wedge and a *Lobatus* shell axe were recovered, but there was a paucity of conch shell tools. In marked contrast to the Paradise site, bivalves (*Lucina pectinata* and *Codakia orbicularis*) dominate the deposit (Keegan et al. 2003). The most common tool was bivalve scrapers. This dramatic increase in the use of shell scrapers suggests a significant change in food processing, possibly related to a more intensive use of root crops. In addition, Strombidae were largely replaced by mud conchs (*Melongena melongena*). The mollusks evidence greater exploitation of mangrove habitats. The animal remains include small fish, birds, saltwater crocodiles (which today live near the site), hutia, and one dog tooth. A laterally drilled human incisor was the only ornament other than shell beads.

The positioning of two sites on the same dune offers a unique opportunity for comparisons. The sites express distinct material cultures that date to different time periods. The high incidence of sea turtles and strombids at the Paradise site may reflect the initial occupation of the bay at a time when these highly valued resources were more abundant. Their use, and possible overexploitation, may have resulted in their being less available when the Sweetwater inhabitants arrived. The mollusks in the sites also suggest that the marine environment was changing. Wetter conditions and increased land clearance after AD 900 may have increased the sediment loads transported by the river into the bay. The result was more turbid conditions that reduced the availability of the Veneridae and Cardiidae bivalves that dominate the Paradise deposits, while enhancing the habitats for the Lucinidae bivalves and mangrove-associated *Melongena* that dominate Sweetwater (Keegan et al. 2003). Differences in the use of chert, other shell tools, and especially the higher frequency of shell scrapers, all point to significant changes in lifeways over time.

Conclusions

Despite sharing numerous characteristics with communities on neighboring islands, the archaeology of Jamaica is unique (Allsworth-Jones 2008; Atkinson 2006; Stokes 2002; Wesler 2013). The indigenous Jamaicans decorated their pottery vessels using the same techniques as others, yet the shapes of their vessels and the specific motifs are unique to Jamaica. In terms of diet, there was an emphasis on land animals, especially the hutia, which may have been domesticated on the island (Scudder 2006). Hilltop sites near Kingston and along the north coast are identical to settlement patterns in Cuba and Hispaniola, and the Sweetwater site has the mangrove association attributed to Meillacoid in Hispaniola (Veloz Maggiolo et al. 1981). In addition, the study of wooden artifacts, and the petroglyphs and pictographs that decorated cave walls, provide information about their belief systems and worldview that exhibit similarities that transcend the region (Allsworth-Jones 2008; Atkinson 2009; Saunders and Gray 1996; Watson 1988). The pan-Caribbean production and use of stone and shell beads, pendants, other personal adornments, wooden sculptures, and so on, too often are explained by simply adding the adjective "Taíno." However, at least in Jamaica, there is no evidence for the Chicoid influences that mark the arrival of "Taíno" elsewhere in the region. Detailed studies of "ceremonial" objects are needed to better define their origins, distributions, associations, exchanges, and especially their meanings (e.g., McGinnis 1997; Mol 2014; Oliver 2009; Ostapkowicz 1997, 2015).

Modern interpretations typically begin with the arrival of the Spanish and the accounts of the chroniclers. Unfortunately, very little was written specifically about Jamaica. Despite spending a year shipwrecked off the north coast between June 1503 and June 1504, Columbus wrote very little about his interactions with the Indios. He does mention *caciques*, which has been interpreted as evidence for a chiefdom form of political organization (Wesler 2013:252), but the Spanish reported encounters with *caciques* everywhere they went (even the Bahamas), so the meaning of the term is open to diverse interpretations. "Las Casas says that the islands abound with inhabitants as an ant-hill with ants" (Cundall 1915:1); and Michele de Cuneo's letter of October 28, 1495, reported "an excellent and well-populated harbor ... during that time some 60,000 people came from the mountains, merely to look at us" (Morison 1963:222). These brief comments have been used to portray Jamaica as a typical, albeit less complex, expression of the indigenous societies of Hispaniola (Rouse 1992; Watson 1988; Wilson 2007).

CHAPTER 7

Lesser Antillean Networks

THE LESSER ANTILLES INCLUDE fifteen major islands and countless smaller ones (Figure 7.1). They are characterized by islands of volcanic and limestone origins (Knippenberg 2006; Van Soest 2000). The diverse geological makeup of the Lesser Antilles created a discontinuous distribution of natural resources, which may have stimulated craft specialization by these communities. Such diversity is also reflected in adjustments to variations in rainfall, climate, vegetation, and fauna (Chapter 1).

The continental islands of Trinidad and Tobago are more related to mainland South America, as are the various offshore islands along the Venezuelan coast (Antczak and Antczak 2006). Their terrestrial flora and fauna reflect this mainland allegiance (Carlson 2007; Steadman and Stokes 2002). While the other islands of the Lesser Antilles would certainly have had an exotic aspect to people from mainland communities, there is every indication that their adaptation to and domestication of these unfamiliar island-scapes took place relatively quickly. The islands certainly stood out for their very rich marine resources in contrast to their depauperate endemic terrestrial fauna. Because there were no major predatory species in the islands prior to human colonization, the endemic terrestrial and marine fauna were relatively easy to harvest from forest, estuary, mangrove, littoral, and coral reef environments (Wilson 2007).

Islands are fragile and vulnerable environments (Fosberg 1963). Island populations, in global perspective, actively altered island environments and domesticated the landscape (Fitzpatrick and Keegan 2007; Kirch 1997, 2000; Terrell et al. 2003; Watlington 2003). These transformations began upon their arrival in the Caribbean about 7,500 years ago and cascaded through the islands (Siegel et al. 2014). The earliest colonists intentionally (i.e., transported landscapes) or accidentally (i.e., portmanteau biotas) introduced new plant and faunal species from the mainland and moved endemic species between islands (Hofman et al. 2011).

Exotic flora and fauna were brought in from different parts of the South American mainland. Among such exotic animal species were hutia, monkeys,

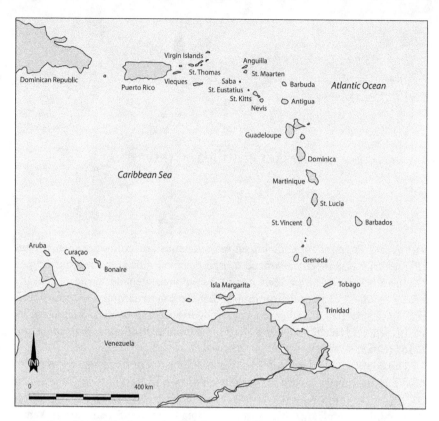

FIGURE 7.1 Map of the Lesser Antilles (courtesy of Menno Hoogland).

guinea pigs, agouti, armadillos, opossums, several birds, and dogs (Newsom and Wing 2004; Giovas et al. 2012; Grouard 2001; Kimura et al. 2016). Imported plants included manioc, maize, sweet potato, papaya, peanut, chili pepper, yellow sapote, avocado, and tobacco (Newsom and Wing 2004; Pagán Jiménez 2011). Environmental alterations, deforestation, and intensive activities such as slash-and-burn and slope agriculture changed the islands' original biotopes (Hofman and Hoogland in press) These impacts, in conjunction with climate fluctuations and the settlers' increasing familiarity with island environments, transformed the cultural landscape. Initial practices were eliminated through the local extirpation of certain endemic species (e.g., sloths, manatees, sea turtles), and new opportunities were recognized and pursued. For example, the Crab/Shell dichotomy was initially proposed to represent different adaptive strategies employed by different Cultures that arrived in the islands via distinct and independent migrations (Rainey 1940; see Chapter 4). However, the Crab/Shell dichotomy is now viewed as reflecting opportunistic, flexible behavior towards terrestrial and marine resource exploitation (deFrance et al. 1996; Keegan 1989b; Siegel 1993). In other words, the emphasis on particular resources shifted through time, and these changes do not reflect separate and distinct migrations into the Antilles.

Some notable climatic changes in the region with alternating wet and dry periods occurred during the Holocene (e.g., Curtis and Hodell 1993; Curtis et al. 2001; Higuera-Gundy et al. 1999; Malaizé et al. 2011; Siegel et al. 2005). Over the course of time, the insular inhabitants had to adapt to these climatological fluctuations and other major natural events such as hurricanes, tsunamis, volcanic eruptions, sea-level changes and others (Cooper 2010; Delpuech 2004; Hofman and Hoogland 2015a). These had an impact on agricultural potentials and the availability of resources, resulting in considerable population stress that influenced lifeways on all levels and led to major changes in socio-cultural behavior (Petitjean Roget 2005; Blancaneaux 2009; Fitzpatrick and Keegan 2007).

Archipelagic resources and mobility yearly cycle

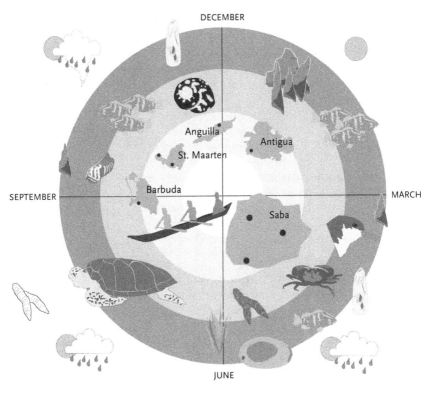

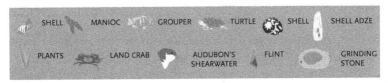

FIGURE 7.2 Distribution of archipelagic mobility and resource exploitation (Hofman et al. 2006).

Paleoenvironmental data from St. Martin and Guadeloupe provide general insights into historical climatic conditions in the Lesser Antilles. A period of drought with hurricanes characterizes the whole of the Archaic Age (from 4300 BC onwards). This period was followed by a less dry period and a diminution of hurricanes during the Ceramic Age (c. 500 BC to AD 800). A major era of drought was again recorded for the period between AD 800 and 1000, the period between the Early and Late Ceramic Age. Snail shell carbon isotope values changed significantly around the time that the Late Saladoid occupation started. This indicates a vegetational response to either wetter conditions (after AD 950), or the replacement of an existing carbon-4 (C_4) plant vegetation by introduced carbon-3 (C_3) crops (Beets et al. 2006; Bonnissent et al. 2001: Malaizé et al. 2011).

Although we have discussed the Archaic Age (Chapter 2) and Early Ceramic Age (Chapter 3), this chapter adopts a more focused perspective on cultural developments in the Lesser Antilles. By focusing on long-term transformations in these relatively small islands, it is possible to more completely specify historical contingencies (Figure 7.2). Therefore, we adopt a chronological perspective that examines cultural developments that began in the Archaic Age, continued through the Ceramic Age, and ended with the imposition of European influences.

The First Islanders

The earliest date for Archaic Age habitation comes from the sites of St. John and Banwari Trace on Trinidad, dated between 7700 and 6100 B.P. (Boomert 2000:57; Pagán Jiménez et al. 2015). The material culture found in sites from this period consists of stone and bone artifacts, some of which are associated with hunting and fishing (e.g., projectile points and peccary-tooth fishhooks). There is a wide variety of ground-stone tools used for plant processing (Harris 1973). Twenty-nine Archaic Age sites are known for Trinidad and Tobago, including eleven midden sites (Boomert 2000:49, 54–55). These sites are considered a part of the Ortoiroid series, which includes the Banwarian (5000–2500 BC) and Ortoiran (1500–300 BC) subseries (Rouse 1992). During the Late Archaic Age, wild vegetable foods became a more significant part of the subsistence pattern (Boomert 2000:75). The earliest evidence of plant management was found at the site of St. John where maize, sweet potatoes, achira, and chili peppers, among others, had been imported from the continent and were grown on a regular basis (Pagán Jiménez et al. 2015).

The rest of the southern Lesser Antilles still presents a blank slate with regard to Archaic Age occupations (but see Siegel et al. 2015). Presently, only Tobago, Barbados, and Martinique have yielded remains potentially attributable to the Archaic Age. The site of Heywoods on Barbados has provided a date of 3980 ± 100 B.P., and it contains artifacts that are not found in other island settings (Drewett 1991; Fitzpatrick 2011). The reliability of sites like Le Godinot and Boutbois (Martinique), reported by Louis Allaire and Mario Mattioni (1983) as potential Archaic Age sites, is questioned because the radiocarbon dates are inconsistent (Benoit Bérard, personal communication 2010).

A range of factors may have distorted the archaeological record for this time period. Chief among these are problems related to site preservation and visibility as a result of local tectonic activity (e.g., subduction and uplift), and hurricanes or other storms that may have affected shorelines by submerging, covering, or erasing coastal sites (e.g., Crock and Petersen 2001; Davis 1982; Delpuech 2004; Littman 2001; Watters et al. 1992; 2001). It is possible that entire islands may now be submerged (Delpuech et al. 2001:103; Hofman and Hoogland 2015a). In more inland areas, sedimentation may have conserved, but also obscured, sites. Severe erosion, landslides, and volcanic eruptions are fairly common on volcanic Caribbean islands (Delpuech 2004), and their potential impact on archaeological site preservation is well documented.

As the data now stand, there are at least three possible scenarios. First, Archaic Age communities in Trinidad, Tobago, and Barbados arrived from South America. Second, the Archaic Age occupants of these islands bypassed the southern Lesser Antilles (Windward Islands) and headed directly to the northern Lesser Antilles, where there is ample evidence for their presence during this period. However, there is no logical explanation for why these islands would have been bypassed. Third, the westward expansion of Lithic Age communities from Central America to Cuba and Hispaniola, then Puerto Rico, and finally the northern Lesser Antilles expressed Archaic Age characteristics (e.g., ground-stone tools) obtained through the diffusion of technology and not the movement of people. In other words, there was not a separate migration into the Antilles of Archaic Age communities from northeastern South America.

Chronometric data show that the Archaic Age in the northern Lesser Antilles can be divided into three phases: An Early Archaic Age dating to between 3300 and 2600 BC, a Middle Archaic Age between 2600 and 800 BC, and a Late Archaic Age between 800 BC and AD 100 (Hofman et al. 2014; Hofman et al. in press). Paleoenvironmental data from St. Martin identified a wetter period during the latter Age (between 800–520 BC). This period partly overlaps with the earliest dates for Ceramic Age sites in the northern Lesser Antilles and Puerto Rico. The oldest phase comprises Jolly Beach, Antigua (Davis 1982, 2000; Nodine 1990; Olsen 1976), and Etang Rouge, St. Martin (Bonnissent 2003, 2008). Middle Archaic Age sites are Norman Estate, Bay Longue 2, Pont de Sandy Ground 1 and 2, Saline d'Orient, Trou David 1 and 2, Pointe du Bluff, and Baie Orientale (St. Martin) (Bonnissent 2008; Bonnissent et al. 2001; Knippenberg 1999; Nokkert et al. 1995; Serrand 2001c), followed by Plum Piece and Fort Bay, Saba (Hofman and Hoogland 2003), River Site, Barbuda (Watters et al. 1992), and Whitehead's Bluff, Anguilla (Crock et al. 1995). Fort Bay, Saba, also has a component dating to the late Archaic Age (Hofman, personal observation 2015) and contemporary with the Corre Corre

Bay and Smith Gut sites on St. Eustatius (Versteeg 2000). These sites date to approximately 800–400 BC. The Sugar Factory Pier site (St. Kitts) produced two dates, one pointing to the earliest phase and one to the latest phase (Armstrong 1978, 1980; Goodwin 1978). The same is true for the Krum Bay site (St. Thomas, U.S. Virgin Islands), which produced only one very early date of 3580 ± 270 B.P., but all dates fall in the late Archaic Age (Figueredo 1974; Gross 1975; Lundberg 1989:84). The latest phase of the Baie Orientale site on St. Martin also belongs to the Late Archaic Age, with a date up to AD 100 (Bonnissent 2008, 2013). Potential Archaic Age remains also have been discovered at the Morel and Pointe des Pies sites (Grande-Terre), Capesterre (Basse-Terre), Guadeloupe, and on Marie-Galante (Fouéré et al. 2011, 2015; Richard 1994; Stouvenot and Casagrande 2015).

Early Archaic Age sites, with some rare exceptions, are typically found in coastal settings. The material remains document a heavy reliance on fish and mollusk exploitation (Newsom and Wing 2004:80; Nokkert et al. 1995; Reitz 1989). Of course, special activity sites will always be encountered less frequently than residential sites, due to the greater impact of post-depositional processes on more ephemeral remains (i.e., limited surface area and low artifact diversity; see also Lundberg 1980:134).

Antigua and St. Martin seem to have been the most densely occupied islands during the Archaic Age. More than forty Archaic Age sites have been identified on Antigua (Nodine 1990; Stokes 1991). Antiguan settlements are generally situated on the low-lying limestone plain along the northeastern coast of the island (Davis 2000). Marine food resources from various environments (e.g., mangroves, shallow muddy and sandy bottoms, and shallow rocky areas) and easy access to flint quarries situated along the northeast shore and on Long Island at Flinty Bay probably influenced settlement location (Knippenberg and Zijlstra 2008; Verpoorte 1993). The northeast coast is relatively uninviting to farmers because airborne salts transported by persistent trade winds hamper plant cultivation. Annual rainfall is also lower here than anywhere else on the island (Davis 2000:91, 101). The Antigua sites have a plethora of flint artifacts and debitage, and this flint is found at all other early Archaic Age sites in the northern Lesser Antilles (Knippenberg 2011). The lithic technology at these sites can be considered expedient and is often based on flake instead of blade production (Crock et al. 1995; Knippenberg 1999).

The site of Jolly Beach, located on Antigua's west coast, is one of the exceptions in terms of location and the production of flint blades (Davis 2000; Gijn 1993; Knippenberg 2001). The west coast overlooks an extensive offshore marine zone with accompanying reefs and readily accessible fauna. At Jolly Beach, mollusk exploitation was focused on eight major species, augmented with smaller quantities of other species. In addition to fish from shallow marine waters and some turtles and manatees, Jolly Beach also provides evidence of a higher reliance on terrestrial fauna compared to other sites along Antigua's shore (Davis 2000). According to Davis (2000:93), the presence of marine flint nodules on the hill at the western edge of the site provided an added incentive for settlement there. Other sites in which similar flint blades have been found are Upper Blake's on Montserrat (Cherry et al. 2012) and The Level, Saba (Hofman and Hoogland 2003). Both sites are located inland at a few hundred meters above mean sea level.

Many other sites on Antigua and neighboring islands belong to the second phase of the Archaic Age occupation. The nearest island to Antigua with an Archaic Age occupation of this phase is Barbuda. The River Site on Barbuda is located on the south coast, 2 meters above mean sea level and close to the shoreline. Sandy beaches are nearby, and the site covers an area of approximately 3,800 square meters. Mollusk remains, especially *Cittarium pica*, were observed at the site (Watters et al. 1992:29). Whitehead's Bluff is located on the northeastern tip of Anguilla at an elevation of 11– 14 meters above mean sea level, exposed to the northeastern trade winds. The area is characterized by karst topography that is sparsely covered by low, wind-stunted vegetation. The site lies approximately 80 meters inland from the rock-bound shore to the west and an estimated 300 meters from Windward Point Bay to the east (Crock et al. 1995:288). There is evidence of a heavy emphasis on mollusks and only a limited set of readily accessible resources that were exploitable at the site. Numerous celts and celt preforms manufactured from *Lobatus gigas* shells characterize the Whitehead's Bluff site. Ground-stone tools include hammer stones, abraders, and a fragment of a mortar.

The Norman Estate site is located in the northeastern part of St. Martin in a relatively flat valley approximately 9 meters above mean sea level and is enclosed by hills to the south and north. A small stream passes by the site to the west, and the northwestern and eastern shores are about 1.5 kilometers away. Subsistence was primarily oriented towards reef fish and mollusks, the most common species of which was *Arca zebra*. At Norman Estate, celts made from *Lobatus gigas* were found, and both sites yielded columella tools. Volcanic rock flakes and water-worn pebbles occurred as well (Crock et al. 1995; Nokkert et al. 1995). Particularly noticeable is the absence of volcanic cores or core fragments at the site.

The Etang Rouge site is in the western part of St. Martin on the peninsula of Terres Basses. It shows multiple occupations and provides very early dates of around 3000 BC from a layer of *Lobatus* shells and stone implements that date to around 1800 BC (Bonnissent 2003, 2013; Martias 2005). Several hearths, cooking, and consuming areas were identified, suggesting the repeated use of the area as a temporary campsite. Several phases of occupation have been discerned: 3300–2600 BC, 2600–2150 BC, 2150–1550 BC, and 1550–800 BC. The most prevalent bivalve species of the earliest component are *Arca zebra* and *Codakia orbicularis; Lobatus* sp. composes the majority of the gastropods, followed by small quantities of *Cittarium pica*. A few shell and stone tools were recovered in association with flint implements.

Plum Piece Site, Saba (c. 1875–1520 BC)

The Plum Piece site is located on the leeward side in the northwestern part of Saba, and situated at about 400 meters above sea level in a mountainous tropical forest (Figure 7.3). Saba is approximately 50 kilometers south of St. Martin and 30 kilometers northwest of St. Eustatius, and the island of St. Croix lies 80 kilometers in a westerly direction. Saba is one of the smallest islands of the Lesser Antilles and has a surface area of only 13 square kilometers. Its small surface area; its pronounced relief, which leads to a slightly higher level of precipitation than the surrounding islands; and its difficult access give Saba an exceptional and unique character. The island is the upper part of an extinct Pleistocene volcano, which rises steeply from the seabed from a depth of 600 meters. The summit, Mount Scenery, stands 870 meters above mean sea level and is often cloaked in fog. One of the most attractive features of the island is that it is situated on the Saba Bank, which is one of the largest and most productive fishing grounds in the region (Keegan et al. 2008).

Carl Zagers and Will Johnson discovered the site at the end of the 1990s. This part of the island is densely vegetated today, which hampers the view and restricts the discovery of sites during field surveys. The plot of land on which the site is situated was cultivated during colonial times, as is evidenced by the presence of terraces, and is today under cultivation of root crops. A survey during the summer of 2001 and excavations in 2002 and 2006 by Corinne Hofman and Menno Hoogland confirmed the presence of an Archaic Age occupation at Plum Piece through the recovery of numerous pieces of flint,

FIGURE 7.3 Archaeological excavations at the Plum Piece site, Saba (photo by Corinne Hofman and Menno Hoogland).

ground-stone, and shell tools from a midden context. Based on the toolkit, the layout of the site, and the analysis of the associated post hole features, Plum Piece is interpreted as a campsite with seasonal indicators and a forest-oriented activity spectrum (Hofman et al. 2006).

The surface area of the site is around 200 square meters and has been preserved, in part, due to slope wash covering the archaeological deposits. A set of archaeological features and a dense midden deposit indicate intensive use of the Plum Piece area at least by 3,300 years ago. The cultivation of plants is suggested by the toolkit, which is composed of many grinding stones. The presence of *guáyiga* or zamia has been suggested by recent starch grain analysis. This plant was probably imported from Puerto Rico or the Dominican Republic (Pagán Jiménez 2011; Hofman et al. in press; Veloz Maggiolo 1993). Other domestic plants, such as maize, sweet potato, and probably annatto (*Bixa orellana*) were identified, together with evidence for the processing and use of wild ginger (Zingiberaceae), arrowroot and calathea (Marantaceae), and mountain cabbage (*Prestoea montana*) (Hofman et al. in press). The conchs from which adzes were fashioned may have had their meat extracted at the beach in order to supplement the diet.

Three radiocarbon dates of land crab samples from undisturbed midden contexts have provided dates of 3430 ± 30 B.P. (GrN-27562), 3300 ± 30 B.P. (GrN-27563), and 3320 ± 30 B.P. (GrN-27564). Calibrated at a 2-sigma interval, the dates fall between 1875 and 1520 cal. BC. The site is of special significance because it shows that at least some Archaic Age communities were seasonally exploiting resource concentrations to pursue specific activities in the "interior" of the relatively small islands of the northern Lesser Antilles (Hofman et al. 2006). Because such sites are difficult to locate due to the density of vegetation and limited access, the site points to the need for more intensive surveys in these locations.

The midden deposits suggest a heavy reliance on terrestrial faunal sources. Mountain or black crab (*Gecarcinus ruricola*) remains, bird bones (particularly Audubon's shearwater [*Puffinus lherminieri lherminierii*]), and pelagic and reef fish (chiefly *Epinephelus* sp., *Acanthurus* sp., *Lutjanus* sp., *Sparisoma* sp., and *Haemulon* sp.) are abundant species in the midden; mollusks are virtually absent. Fish and shellfish remains were well preserved in the deposits, but scarce, which suggests that they were less important for the Archaic Age occupants. The faunal assemblage clearly reflects the exploitation of seasonally abundant resources (Hofman et al. 2006; Hofman and Hoogland 2011).

The crab remains at Plum Piece highlight an unusual situation. Very few crab remains are found at coastal Archaic Age sites (Davis 2000), yet the *Cardisoma* sp. and *Gecarcinus* sp. are common components of early Ceramic Age sites (Chapter 4). There has been a tendency to assume that modern terrestrial and coastal environments accurately represent the habitats of the past. This situation is especially true for coastal habitats because it has long been believed that relatively small groups of humans could not have had a significant impact on the vast oceans (Baisre 2010). This assumption is wrong

(Carlson and Keegan 2004; Fitzpatrick et al. 2008). More recent studies have documented both natural and human-induced landscape modifications.

Plum Piece also has great quantities of ground-stone tools for grinding and rubbing and *Lobatus gigas* shell adzes. The latter may have been used in building canoes. Volcanic core and core fragments are abundant at Plum Piece, which is also the case at Norman's Estate. Flint was imported from Long Island, Antigua, located at a distance of 150 kilometers from Saba. The nearly total lack of cortex on the flint material suggests that cores arrived at the site in a pre-worked condition. However, the scarcity of cores suggests that they were transported further to enable the manufacture of tools at other locations (Hofman et al. 2006; Hofman and Hoogland 2011).

Use-wear analysis showed that most of the flint pieces were used for cutting soft plant materials (Nieuwenhuis 2008). The presence of conch-lip adzes suggest that the inhabitants of Plum Piece captured and ate conch, although they probably extracted the meat at the beach and did not take the heavy, whole shells up to the site. The presence of a large grinding boulder near the midden is evidence that the adzes were polished *in situ*. Several caches of shell adzes in the site suggest a purposeful deposition related to the recurrent abandonment and reoccupation of the campsite.

Late Archaic Age

Many of the sites represent multiple stages of occupation, abandonment, and reoccupation over long periods of time (Delpuech and Hofman 2004). Specific activities would have been performed at particular sites, and it is suggested that such places functioned alternately and complementarily with each other. In this context, the theory has been put forward that the occupants of the northeastern Caribbean islands maintained an annual mobility cycle that took advantage of the seasonal availability of biotic resources and at the same time also targeted non-subsistence activities (i.e., practiced a form of archipelagic resource mobility in its broadest sense) (Hofman 2013; Hofman et al. 2006; Hofman and Hoogland 2011).

An example of the latest phase of the Archaic Age in the Virgin Islands is the Krum Bay site on St. Thomas. According to Emily Lundberg (1991:74), the location of the Krum Bay site in a small sheltered bay within good reach of fishing grounds and pearl oyster beds can be related to a focused collection strategy toward certain mollusk species and reef fish, and the exploitation of pearls during successive reoccupations of the site spanning more than a thousand years. At Krum Bay, no flint was found, but locally available fine-grained rock was used to produce flakes in a non-systematic manner. In addition, pebble hammer stones and grinders, bifacial celts or wedges, shell beads and disks, coral files, and *Lobatus* columella tips were also recorded (Lundberg 1989). Similarly, the site of Sugar Factory Pier on St. Kitts has two distinct layers of Archaic Age material, shell tools, and stone tools showing an older and a younger date of 4100 ± 60 and 2175 ± 60 B.P., respectively (Armstrong 1978, 1980; Goodwin 1978; Walker 1980).

A layer of lithic material and shell remains at the Pointe des Pies site (Guadeloupe) has been radiocarbon-dated to 2830 ± 50 B.P. (Richard 1994). The layer was found beneath Ceramic Age deposits at the site and represents the earliest human habitation of the island.

On St. Martin, the Baie Orientale site has been dated between 800 and 400 BC, with a latest component dating to AD 100 (Bonnissent 2008, 2013). This Archaic Age site covers approximately 500 square meters. It has several structures that represent camp areas. These are associated with different activities: shellfish cooking and consumption, and the manufacture of shell and stone tools (Bonnissent et al. 2001:79–80, 2008, 2013). Corre Corre Bay and Smith's Ghut are the location of the earliest habitation sites on St. Eustatius. Versteeg (2000) found shell deposits containing shell, coral, and stone tools that included Long Island flint at Corre Corre Bay. Mollusk shells from two locations in the deposit were dated to 410–208 cal. BC and 98 cal. BC to 120 cal. AD, after calibration and correction for the marine reservoir effect. These dates concur with those from one of the components of the currently excavated site at Fort Bay, Saba.

A survey of the island of Nevis has generated evidence for two Archaic Age settlements: Hichman's Shell Heap and Nisbett. Both sites comprise shells, fish bones, and shell and stone tools. The sites are located near a freshwater source and large coastal reefs. A shell from the Hichman's Shell Heap site was radiocarbon-dated to 605–290 BC. Neither site produced the ground-stone artifacts commonly found in material assemblages from this period on neighboring islands (Wilson 1989:435; Wilson and Kozuch 2006).

Archaic Age Summary

In Chapter 2, we described the general characteristics attributed to the Lithic Age and Archaic Age (Rouse 1992). Here we provide greater detail to highlight the diversity of Archaic Age manifestations in the Lesser Antilles. All of the known Archaic Age sites in the Lesser Antilles are located in the northern islands. There are no known Archaic Age sites in the Windward Islands south of Guadeloupe. This absence of evidence, despite repeated surveys, suggests that the Archaic Age in the Antilles did not originate in northeastern Venezuela (contra Rouse 1992). The exceptions to this distribution of sites are Trinidad, Tobago, and Barbados, and the recently identified, possibly anthropogenic fires on the islands of Grenada and Martinique (Siegel et al. 2015). Trinidad was connected to the mainland when it was first colonized, and the island supports a continental biota. Therefore, it is not a true example of island colonization (Boomert 2000). Reaching Tobago and Barbados did require the crossing of water gaps. It is likely that these three islands were colonized in a separate migration from South America, although it is difficult to envision these as the product of a single migration, because Barbados has such distinctive artifacts (Bullen and Bullen 1968; Drewett 1991; Fitzpatrick 2011). Recurrent expeditions from the mainland may explain this pattern.

The sites express a number of commonalities. They were all established on relatively small islands and primarily in coastal settings. Most were small and temporary habitations that were abandoned and reoccupied over hundreds of years. This pattern suggests that there was an annual mobility cycle that focused on the procurement of seasonally available resources, combined with specific activities. Nevertheless, the continued capture of fish and mollusks reflects the exploitation of resources that were less seasonally variable. Each site exhibits differences in the marine species that were consumed, which probably reflects local variations in the availability of these species. A variety of shell and coral tools is recognized, but different sites have different tool kits. The wide distribution of flint from Antigua indicates the breadth of social networks (Hofman et al. 2014), but the majority of stone tools at the sites were made from locally available materials. In sum, while it is possible to highlight commonalities, all of the sites express diverse adaptations that may be related to specific resource exploitation and/or activity patterns.

Late Archaic Age northern Lesser Antillean assemblages comprise a combination of flaked and ground-stone tools and worked shell. The lithic technology has been considered simple in comparison to the preceding flaked-stone complexes, and it often was based on the production of flakes instead of blades. For example, flint flakes are present at the Whitehead's Bluff site (Anguilla) and Norman Estate site (St. Martin), but at both sites there is a total absence of blade production (Crock et al. 1995). In contrast, blade production predominates at the Jolly Beach site (Antigua). The frequency of blade production at this site is explained by easy access to the flint sources and the abundance of raw material on Long Island (Knippenberg 1995). The dominance of flake technology, rather than blade technology, on islands distant from Long Island has been related to distance from the source (Crock et al. 1995; Knippenberg 1995). Finally, at the Krum Bay site (St. Thomas), no flint was found, but other fine-grained rocks were used to produce flakes in a non-systematic manner (Lundberg 1989).

Dave D. Davis's (1993) comprehensive study of flaked-stone from the Jolly Beach site (Antigua) revealed that the debitage came overwhelmingly from the manufacture of blades. Yet blades composed less than 15% of the collection. His study reveals the importance of studying, not only what is present, but also what is absent from sites. He also provided a classification scheme that can be used to evaluate similarities and differences between Archaic Age flaked-stone assemblages (cf. Febles 1982; Pantel 1988). A similar perspective has been proposed for the study of Lobatus shell tools, because the shell fragments in the site provide a specific indication of which parts of the shell were removed. The expectation is that the tools were discarded in use areas and not always in the site deposits (Dacal Moure 1978; Jones O'Day and Keegan 2001).

Neolithization of the Lesser Antilles

The initial appearance of Saladoid pottery in Puerto Rico and the northern Lesser Antilles can be viewed as the result of exploratory expeditions, exchange of ideas and information, and the gradual migration of local communities from the mainland that began during the Archaic Age. These local communities were tied together through a vast web of dynamic social relationships in which people, perishable and nonperishable goods, and specific ideas, as well as cultural and social practices originating from the homeland(s), were linked with those of already established insular communities, amalgamating over time (Hofman et al. 2007). The exploitation of flint sources on Long Island, Antigua, may have been an important impetus in forming this northeastern interaction sphere (Hofman et al. 2014; Hofman et al. in press).

Recent research and radiocarbon dates for the Early Ceramic Age indicate that an initial sphere of interaction with coastal South America was established in the area between Puerto Rico and Lesser Antilles sometime between 400 and 200 BC. The Hope Estate site (St. Martin) and Trants (Monserrat) have provided very early dates in the northern Lesser Antilles, ranging between 400 and 200 BC, although even earlier dates of 800–400 BC have been reported (Bonnissent 2008; Haviser 1987; Watters and Petersen 1999). Huecoid and Saladoid pottery characterize the assemblages on these islands. The pottery is accompanied by well-developed lithic and shell industries that incorporated both exotic and locally available raw materials (Rodríguez Ramos 2013; Serrand 2001b). Conflicting stratigraphic data and radiocarbon dates from Early Ceramic Age sites, together with stylistic differences between the Huecoid and Saladoid pottery, has led to many debates and controversies among Caribbean archaeologists over the past thirty years (Bullen and Mattioni 1972; for the "La Hueca problem," see Oliver 1999; and Chapter 3, this volume).

Huecoid pottery has been found predominantly on the more northern islands of the Lesser Antilles up to Puerto Rico. Archaeological sites with Huecoid pottery include: Cathédrale and Gare Martime de Basse Terre, Morel, Anse Ste. Marguerite and Anse Patate sites (Guadeloupe) (Arts 1999; Bonnissent et al. 2001; Clerc 1964, 1968, 1970; Hofman et al. 1999, 2004); Talliseronde and Folle Anse sites (Marie-Galante) (Barbotin 1987, Hofman et al. 1999); Trants site (Montserrat) (Watters and Petersen 1999); Hope Estate site (St. Martin) (Haviser 1989, Hofman 1999); Main Street KPG site (St. Thomas) (Hayes 2013); La Hueca site (Vieques Island) (Chanlatte Baik 1981); and the Punta Candelero, El Convento, Maisabel, and Hacienda Grande sites (Puerto Rico) (Rodríguez López 1989, 1991; Rodríguez Ramos 1999, 2010). Scarce occurrences of Huecoid pottery also have been noted on St. Kitts, Martinique, Dominica; and the southernmost occurrence is at the Pearls site on Grenada (Bullen 1964; Petitjean Roget 1981; Hofman 1993; Hofman, personal observation 2013–2016).

The characteristics of decorated Huecoid pottery were described in greater detail in Chapter 3. The main element is curvilinear-incised zones, sometimes filled with punctation or crosshatching. The latter is predominant in Puerto Rico, Vieques, and St. Thomas (Chanlatte 1981, 1983; Hofman 1999). Vessels in the shape of aquatic animals (fish, crab, turtle) with a zoomorphic adorno as the head and the tail decorated with curvilinear incisions are common (Hofman and Jacobs 2000/2001). Similar vessels occur throughout the north-eastern Caribbean sites and at the Pearls site in Grenada.

Early Saladoid pottery in South America is distributed along the Orinoco River and in coastal areas of the Guyanas (Wonotobo Falls, Western Suriname) along the eastern coast of Venezuela and Margarita Island, as well as in the northern Lesser Antilles and Puerto Rico (Boomert 1983; Rouse et al. 1985; Rouse 1989, 1992). Early Saladoid assemblages are known from Puerto Rico, Vieques, St. Martin, Antigua, Guadeloupe, Martinique, St. Vincent, and Grenada (Bérard 2004; Boomert et al. 2015; Hofman et al. 2004). Early Saladoid pottery in the islands is characterized by the combination of plain, painted (white-on-red; WOR), and zoned-incised crosshatched (ZIC) pottery (Rouse 1989; Rouse and Alegría 1990; Rouse and Morse 1999). Painted and ZIC pottery differ in material and shape as well as in decoration. A possible explanation for the co-occurrence of both decorated wares is that they were used in different, possibly ritual, contexts (Rouse and Alegría 1990).

The earliest pottery-making communities in the Lesser Antilles were first believed to have lived predominantly on the north and east quadrants of vol-canic islands (cf. Haviser 1997), away from the coast, and near rivers or sur-rounded by forest. The reasoning was that the initial colonists recreated their mainland tropical forest adaptation (Keegan and Diamond 1987). However, it is increasingly clear that a variety of different locations were settled, including beaches, mangrove areas, and areas in close proximity to coral reefs. Settlement patterns reflect a balance between access to arable land required by an econ-omy based on horticulture, and coastal access to facilitate inter-community communications and the exploitation of marine resources.

Subsistence practices entailed the cultivation of root, seed, and tree crops, complemented by fishing, mollusk collecting, and the hunting of reptiles and small mammals (Allaire 2003; Keegan 2000b; Petersen 1997). A wide range of local terrestrial and marine resources was exploited. These were augmented by plants and animals imported from the mainland. It commonly is assumed that manioc (*Manihot esculenta*) was the staple cultigen, which was processed and transformed into cassava bread and evidenced by the numerous fragments of clay griddles from this period. However, starch grain analysis has found little evidence for manioc (Pagán Jiménez 2013), and instead evidenced the presence of maize and *Zamia* in some of the sites. It is indeed more likely that gardens included a wide diversity of crops, as is typical of the multi-cropping that char-acterizes tropical horticultural economies (Keegan 2001).

Thick middens with pottery, bone, mollusk, and crab remains characterize the settlements. The expanding exploitation of natural resources, horticultural practices, and landscape modifications altered the island habitats and initiated the disruption of their ecological balance (Fitzpatrick and Keegan 2007). Evidence from the earliest settlements on an island indicates that some animals were extirpated locally (Steadman and Jones 2006; Steadman and Stokes 2002) and that land clearance resulted in significant changes to terrestrial and marine landscapes (Keegan et al. 2003; Siegel et al. 2001).

Dog burials, often alongside human burials, are common in sites of this period until AD 600. At the Punta Candelero and Hacienda Grande sites (Puerto Rico), and the Sorcé site (Vieques), Seaview site (Barbuda), Morel site (Guadeloupe), and Silver Sands sites (Barbados), numerous dogs were found buried in association with human burials. The dogs were buried with shell and stone paraphernalia and other grave goods (Grouard et al. 2013; Hoogland and Hofman 2013; Laffoon et al. 2013; Plomp 2012; Wing 2008). There is evidence that dogs were eaten in later times (Carlson 2008), but these burials indicate that dogs were treated with reverence during early Saladoid times. Peter Roe (1995a) has suggested that dogs replaced jaguars, which have never inhabited the islands, through a process of mythic substitution. If Roe is correct, then dogs occupied the highest tier of the mythology transported from lowland South America (Roe 1982).

At the onset of this period, there was a pan-Antillean exchange network circulating semiprecious stone artifacts, animal tooth pendants, and other exotic raw materials throughout the archipelago (Hofman and Hoogland 2011; Hofman et al. 2007, 2014; Laffoon et al. 2014). Reniel Rodríguez Ramos (2013:159) notes that these personal adornments are all things that "shine." For that reason he called this "the Iridescent Period" (Rodríguez Ramos 2010b).

Some communities specialized in specific raw materials and exchanged finished goods for objects manufactured at other locales. For example, the Trants site (Montserrat) specialized in the production of carnelian beads, with the raw material obtained from Antigua (Watters and Scaglion 1994). Celts made from St. Martin greenstone reflect specialized production at the Hope Estate site (St. Martin). The Sorcé/la Hueca site is known particularly for the manufacture of nephrite and jadeite (possibly from Guatemala or the Dominican Republic) and serpentinite (from Puerto Rico) beads and amulets (Chanlatte Baik 1981; Rodríguez Ramos 2011, 2013). At the Pearls site (Grenada), amethyst was used to manufacture beads (Cody 1991a, 1991b). Quantities of production debris specific to their specialized production were found at each of these sites, while only finished objects were encountered at other sites the region (Waters and Scaglion 1994). Gold from local sources, and *guanín* (gold-copper alloy) from Isthmo-Colombian sources, are found in low frequency (Siegel and Severin 1994; Valcárcel Rojas and Martinón Torres 2013).

Arie Boomert (2000) has interpreted the wealth of material culture associated with these Early Ceramic Age sites as comparable to the materialization of the "Big Man" societies of Melanesia (Johnson and Earle 1987; Rubel and Rosman 1978; Sahlins 1976). According to Boomert (2000), public ceremonies of competitive emulation formed the social process through which tremendous numbers of social valuables were buried in the middens of Huecoid and Saladoid settlement and workshop sites (see Siegel 1992). That interest in specific resources (e.g., flint and carnelian from Antigua, greenstone from St. Martin, serpentinite from Puerto Rico, and amethyst from Grenada) that were known and exploited for many centuries materialized the social dynamics at play in the Early Ceramic Age. The monopoly over resources, the specialized production of personal adornments, and their burial in middens in early Saladoid and Huecoid settlements attest to the competitive and emu-lative behavior of autonomous local communities (Hofman et al. 2014). The exchange of objects that were unique to their source established the identity of particular settlements and at the same time reinforced the social connections between widely scattered communities (Keegan 2004).

The Saladoid habitation on Trinidad and Tobago has been divided into the Cedros and Palo Seco complexes. Pottery belonging to the first has only been found at two sites on Trinidad (Boomert 2000:129). In contrast, Palo Seco pot-tery, which is Saladoid pottery with Barrancoid influences, is far more com-mon, with twenty-nine single-component sites known from Trinidad. The Barrancoid complex of the lower Orinoco, characterized by thick-walled ves-sels with red or black designs and modelled-incised adornos, began to influ-ence the Saladoid inhabitants of Trinidad around the time of Christ (Boomert 2006:160). A gradual adoption of Barrancoid pottery modes is mainly notice-able in the early developments of the Palo Seco complex.

At the San 1 site, located near Manzanilla on the east coast of Trinidad (Dorst 2006), two distinct habitation phases have been found at the site—one Saladoid and the other Arauquinoid. The Saladoid settlement is considered late Palo Seco and has been dated between AD 350 and 650. The excavations revealed the lower levels of a midden deposit, with nine burials within and sur-rounding the midden. These deposits have been interpreted as the outer ring of a circular Saladoid village (Dorst 2008:5). Around 300 BC, the Erin Complex emerged in Saladoid settlements. Boomert attributes this new development to Barrancoid immigrants who settled within existing communities (see Schmidt 1917). Interaction and trade in the region increased during this period (Boomert 2006:160–161). The Arauquinoid complex, which developed in the middle Orinoco around AD 500, apparently influenced only the south coast of Trinidad. The result was a mixing of Barrancoid and Arauquinoid motifs that is called "the St. Catherine's complex" (Boomert 2006:162). Barrancoid influ-ences did reach the northern Lesser Antilles, albeit in a very attenuated form.

Most of the Windward Islands first exhibit evidence for permanent habita-tion beginning around AD 200–400, on the basis of the available data to date. The Ceramic Age colonization of Barbados (i.e., Hillcrest and Chancery Lane sites) also occurs at this time (Boomert 1987:15; Drewett 1991:13). The distribu-tion of the Barbados Palo Seco pottery is limited to the south coast, suggest-ing that settlement came from, and interactions were focused on, the south. Other Windward Islands also were settled for the first time: Carriacou (Grand Bay site), Union Island (Chatham Bay site), St. Vincent (Arnos Vale Field and

Brighton sites), St. Lucia (Grande Anse site), Martinique (Diamant II site), and Dominica (Vieille Case site) (Fitzpatrick 2006, 2015; Fitzpatrick et al. 2009; Hofman et al. 2004). In the northern Lesser Antilles, Anguilla, Barbuda, Saba (Spring Bay 1, Kelbey's Ridge 1, Windwardside sites), and St. Eustatius (Golden Rock site) had their initial Ceramic Age occupations. Despite the heterogeneity observed in Saladoid pottery assemblages in terms of stylistic features, the series has always been described as fairly homogeneous (Hofman and Hoogland 2004). Keegan (2004) referred to this as the Saladoid "veneer."

The social landscape in the Lesser Antilles about this time (c. AD 400–600/800) offers a far more dynamic picture than that of the previous periods (Figure 7.4). Settlements were established in more diverse locations, previously uninhabited islands were settled, and cult sites first appeared, many of which had petroglyphs. The latter are situated along creeks or rivers near the coast; in river valleys or ravines and on top of low, wooded hills; and in rock shelters; only a small proportion was in caves (Dubelaar 1992:27; Hayward et al. 2009).

Several large villages of undifferentiated nature were aligned along the coasts or interior of islands. In contrast to the later post-Saladoid period, which exhibits a more dispersed use of the landscape, it seems that most activities

FIGURE 7.4 Diverse expressions of Saladoid and Huecoid pottery, examples from the sites of Morel, Guadeloupe and Pearls, Grenada (Willcox collection) circa 400 BC to AD 850. Not to scale (photos by Corinne Hofman and Menno Hoogland).

during the late Saladoid took place at the village level and that there was no overarching sociopolitical organization. A similar pattern has been noted for south-central Puerto Rico (Torres 2010).

Burials in Saladoid villages took place outside of the houses, and mortuary treatment seems less complex than during post-Saladoid times. The deposition of grave goods in Saladoid burials could be an indication of some kind of social differentiation. In contrast, grave goods are not substantial at sites from this time period in Puerto Rico, where Siegel (1992, 2010) has suggested that burial paraphernalia were separately deposited in middens. Manipulating the human body after death is common in post-Saladoid burial treatments and points to ancestor veneration and lineage ideology (Hofman et al. 1999; Hofman et al. 2010, 2012; Hoogland and Hofman 2013). Post-burial manipulation of body parts is similar to that described for Puerto Rico (Curet and Oliver 1998). The burial of dogs, sometimes together with humans, was an early Saladoid trait. This practice is not known from late Saladoid or post-Saladoid contexts, although the Heywoods site on the northwest coast of Barbados might be an exception (Drewett 2004:221).

Saladoid middens evidence a broad-spectrum economy. The Golden Rock site indicates that the majority of vertebrate remains belongs to fish (van der Klift 1992:77). Most of the fish species encountered came from coral reef and rocky banks environments. Among the mammals found in the assemblage are the rice rat and agouti, and the main reptiles are sea turtles and iguanid lizards (van der Klift 1992:77–79). Over fifty different mollusk species were encountered, with the most common being the West Indian topsnail (*Cittarium pica*). Dietary reconstructions incorporating dental anthropology and isotopic analyses suggest that most of the diet was based on marine resources (Mickleburgh 2013; Pestle 2013; Stokes 1998; Taverne and Versteeg 1992:91–92).

Saladoid society has been characterized as tribal and egalitarian (Siegel 1992, 2010). However, James Petersen (1996) postulated the existence of lineage-based hierarchical societies (see Heckenberger 2002, 2005). In such societies, the hereditary leaders ("chiefs" or *caciques*) based their authority on origins and descent (Helms 1998) and served as mediators with spiritual beings. They increased their power by reinforcing their leadership during communal ceremonies on the level of the local group or community (Hofman and Hoogland 2004). On a more prosaic level, the construction of canoes and the organization of colonizing and trading expeditions required leaders who could assemble human and material capital.

The recovery of a large round *maloca* structure with a diameter of 19 meters at the Golden Rock site (Versteeg and Schinkel 1992) may well be related to the presence of a successful shaman/leader and the increased importance of such a figure in late Saladoid society (Hofman and Hoogland 2004). An uncommon aspect of the site is that it was abandoned after the Saladoid occupation and never reoccupied. Such permanent abandonment stands in contrast with many other habitation sites of this size in the region that either were continuously occupied or abandoned and reoccupied (Bright 2011).

During the late Saladoid, the production and exchange of semiprecious materials as seen in Huecoid and early Saladoid deposits slowly faded away, and more emphasis was placed on the procurement of local materials and the exploitation of local environments (Hofman et al. 2007). An intensive interaction network continued between Lesser Antillean communities in which local products were produced, traded, and exchanged, but the "veneer" that homogenized interpretations of early Saladoid sites disappeared (Keegan 2004).

Post-Saladoid Developments

Settlement patterns shifted after the Saladoid period, and there was an increase in the number and size of sites beginning around AD 400 (Allaire 2003). A clear site hierarchy arises during the early post-Saladoid period after AD 600–850 (Crock 1995; Crock and Petersen 1999; Hofman 2013; Hofman et al. 1999, Hoogland 1996; Petersen 1996; Versteeg et al. 1993), and the Lesser Antilles was densely populated at this time. The largest post-Saladoid sites are documented for the limestone islands of Anegada, Anguilla (Davis and Oldfield 2003), Antigua (Hoffman 1979; Olsen 1974), Barbuda, and Grande-Terre (Guadeloupe). Petroglyph sites such as Fountain Cavern (Anguilla) (Crock 2000), the Morne Rita Cave (Marie-Galante), and numerous petroglyph sites on Basse-Terre (Guadeloupe), St. Lucia (Johnson 2002; Keegan et al. 2002), St. Vincent, and Grenada (Johnson 2002), fill the social landscape.

Troumassoid series pottery replaced the Saladoid series beginning around AD 600, although Saladoid pottery persisted in the northern Lesser Antilles until AD 850–900. The latest dates were obtained from the Lower Camp site (Culebra), Golden Rock site (St. Eustatius), and the Anse des Pères site (St. Martin) (Hamburg 1999; Oliver 1995; Versteeg and Schinkel 1992). Beginning as early as the 5th century AD, the pottery became thicker, heavier, and softer. Saladoid features like painting (WOR) and ZIC were enriched by areal painting and heavy modelling, and deep, broad-line incisions disappeared (Rouse 1992; Wilson 2007:66). Rims were often thickened, triangular, or flanged, sometimes painted red, and surfaces were frequently polished and of a buff-pink color (Drewett 1991). In the Windward Islands, this phase is also known as "modified Saladoid" (Mattioni and Bullen 1970) or "Troumassée A" (McKusick 1959).

In Rouse's (1992) taxonomy, the pottery styles are classified as the Troumassoid series, with a Mamoran subseries for the northern Lesser Antilles, and Troumassan and Suazan subseries for the southern Lesser Antilles. Not surprisingly, the northern islands show stronger affiliations with the Greater Antilles, while the southern islands are more closely associated with South America. However, the emergence of more localized or microstyles is noticeable and reflects a general decrease in the number and quality of decorated wares and symbolic representations (Figure 7.5). Detailed analyses of the pottery assemblages from Sandy Hill (Anguilla), The Bottom (Saba),

FIGURE 7.5 Diverse expressions of early post-Saladoid ceramics from the Lesser Antilles, circa AD 600/800 to 1250. Not to scale (photos by Corinne Hofman and Menno Hoogland).

Anse à la Gourde (Guadeloupe), and Petite Rivière (La Désirade) document the existence of these micro-style areas (Hofman 2013). These micro-styles reflect increasing autonomy and self-identification at particular sites and islands.

Lithic analysis shows the development of tighter networks for the exchange of lithic materials (Knippenberg 2004). Although there is a decrease in micro-lapidary work of semiprecious stones in these site assemblages, there is an increase of the number and size of ideology-linked artifacts connected with the emergence of Greater Antillean complex societies, suggesting that ceremonial exchange took place over longer distances. Such exchanges were increasingly associated with particular locales (Crock 2000).

Anse à la Gourde Site, Guadeloupe (c. AD 450–1350)

Site structure and burial practices during this time period are best documented at the Anse à la Gourde site (Guadeloupe). The site has been excavated by Hofman and Hoogland from Leiden University, and André Delpuech, then responsible for the Service Régionale d'Archéologie de la Guadeloupe (Figure 7.6).

The Anse à la Gourde site is situated at the northeast end of the limestone island of Grande-Terre, Guadeloupe. This flat island is fully covered by

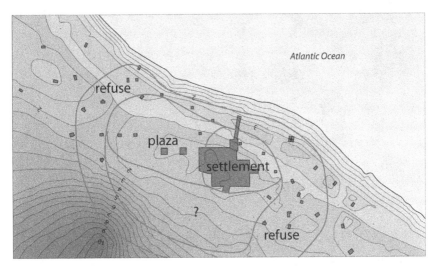

FIGURE 7.6 Layout of the Anse à la Gourde site, Guadeloupe; dark shapes indicate excavation units (courtesy of Menno Hoogland).

limestone of the Plio-Pleistocene Age. The role played by tectonics is funda-mental. A general tipping of the island, caused by subsidence of the western coast, elevated the eastern shore. Large-scale excavations took place at the site between 1995 and 2000 (Hofman 2013; Hofman et al. 2001). A total sur-face area of 1,424 square meters was excavated. The site has an area of 590 square kilometers and rises up to 135 meters above mean sea level. A mid-den in the shape of a doughnut encircles a habitation area and a plaza reflect-ing a Troumassoid reoccupation of the original Saladoid residential space (Figure 7.7). The site is exposed to the Atlantic Ocean.

Four successive occupation phases were radiocarbon-dated to between AD 450 and 1350. The major occupation took place between AD 1000 and 1350. Material remains associated with the latter occupation phases belong to the post-Saladoid or Troumassoid series. The pottery is characterized by vessels with simple shapes, rarely decorated, but often covered by a red slip. Incisions are large and shallow; modelled zoomorphic and anthropomorphic representa-tions occur on the vessel rims. Legged griddles are present. Affiliations to both the northern (Mamoran Troumassoid) and the southern (Suazan Troumassoid) Lesser Antillean pottery complexes are evident.

During the first Saladoid occupation at Anse à la Gourde, the habitation area was located on the coastal dunes. This shifted toward the calcareous pla-teau situated more inland and behind the dunes during the post-Saladoid occupation. It is probable that the dune area was abandoned as a habitation area during this later period because it was considered less appropriate for the construction of houses; sea level continued to rise, and the coast was threat-ened by winds and waves. Palimpsests of habitation are restricted to a relatively

FIGURE 7.7 Excavations at the Anse à la Gourde site, Guadeloupe (photo by Corinne Hofman and Menno Hoogland).

small perimeter, which is suggestive of successive construction phases at the same spot over many decades (Hofman et al. 1999, 2001).

A reconstruction of the post-Saladoid or Troumassoid habitation history and the type of occupations exhibit the following characteristics. First, the large, doughnut-shaped midden area is characterized by the formation of anthropogenic soils that were colored gray by the continuous deposition of organic refuse, charcoal, and ashes. The midden has a surface area of about 1.1 hectares that has an oval shape measuring 200 meters from east to west and 130 meters from north to south. The diameter of this belt is approximately 20–25 meters. The midden is composed of tons of refuse, including faunal remains, shells, and potsherds, which indicates that it functioned as a dump area.

Second, the midden area encircles a habitation area. Only the northern part of this area was excavated. Excavation of the southern part was impossible due to recent construction in this area. The northern part can be divided in two loci. The one in the northeast covers 1,650 square meters and constitutes the area where most of the features were recorded, including post holes, burials, hearths, and refuse pits. Like the midden area, it is composed of grey anthropogenic soils with artifacts scattered around. The intensity of post holes and burials in this relatively restricted area clearly indicates that it was the most intensively used residential space. This restricted space for the construction of the houses may be associated with a symbolic value for this part of the settlement. The large number of burials may refer to a ritual connotation, and it is suggested that this phenomenon contributed to the structuring of the village plan. Third, to the west of the residential area, there is a cleared or empty space that measures 70 by 35 meters. Very few artifacts or features were present in this area.

Within the residential space, the floor plans of small-sized round houses approximately 5–8 meters in diameter occur in conjunction with a larger structure of approximately 12 meters in diameter (Hofman and Hoogland 2011). These houses had single or double rows of posts. The attention devoted to the construction of the houses is manifested by the size of the posts, which in many cases were dug into the bedrock or reinforced with slab stones. Their solidity seems to have been adapted to bad weather conditions such as the tropical storms and hurricanes to which the Atlantic coast is often subjected. There are lighter constructions around the houses. These are interpreted as sheds and racks. A special activity zone is located to the south of the main structures. Large refuse pits, hearths, and food preparation areas were identified in this zone. All of these features and facilities reflect the complex organization of the village, and its changes through time.

Most of the burials are situated within the habitation area, inside or just outside the houses, with only a few located in the midden areas (Hoogland et al. 1999). This seems to be a common practice during the post-Saladoid occupation phases at Anse à la Gourde, and elsewhere in the Lesser Antilles. At Grande Anse, Trois-Rivières on Basse-Terre, the deceased individuals appeared to be of a later date than the houses, suggesting that in this case the deceased were taken back to the village to be interred in their ancestral homes (van den Bel and Romon 2010). At Anse à la Gourde, most of the buried individuals face between east and south, although a minority is clearly orientated toward the opposite directions. The dead were buried within the residential space and under the house floors, indicating a shift from previous Saladoid practices. In all, eighty-three burials were excavated, comprising 101 individuals.

Mortuary practices indicate internal differentiation and personalized treatment of the dead. Complex mortuary practices with a variety of single primary, secondary, partially secondary, and composite burials occur (Hofman et al. 2001; Hoogland et al. 1999; Hoogland and Hofman 2013). The deceased were prepared, wrapped in a basket container or hammock, and then dried above or near a fire (Figure 7.8). They were then buried in a small pit located inside or just outside the house. In certain cases, the burial pit was left open. After some time, presumably after complete decomposition of the body, the cranium or one of the long bones was removed from the grave. Small pits with only human skulls were documented at the site.

Treatment at death and manipulation of the skeletal remains seems to be related to gender. Removal of the skull or long bones, for example, occurs most often within the male population. Children were represented by eleven individuals (13.2%), which is a rather low percentage compared to a model life table distribution of 49% children (Paine 1989; Weiss 1973). The children are between a few months to approximately 14–18 years of age. Only some children received a similar treatment at death as the adults. A few child burials have

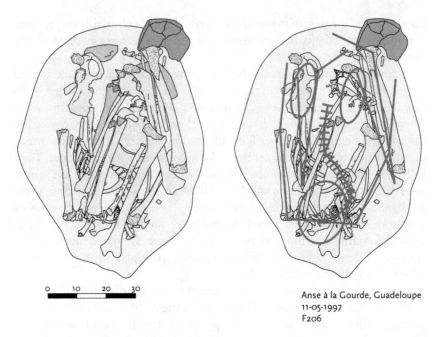

Anse à la Gourde, Guadeloupe
11-05-1997
F206

FIGURE 7.8 Mortuary practices (courtesy of Menno Hoogland).

been found in a refuse context, which may suggest that children could have been buried in the middens or outside the village core.

Grave inventories consist of whole *Lobatus gigas* shells, pottery vessels, quartz, diorite and shell beads, perforated shark teeth, stone axes, and flint cores. Pottery vessels either were used to cover the grave pit or were placed in front of the face of the deceased. Whether the stone and shell beads were meant as grave gifts or were just body or garment ornaments of the deceased is unclear. There is an example of an interred female individual buried with more than 1,100 *Lobatus gigas* shell beads on her pelvis. These beads were probably part of a garment. The total absence of production debris suggests that the shell beads were not produced at the settlement but were an exchange item (Lammers-Keysers 2007). Non-local females, identified through strontium-isotope analysis (Booden et al. 2008; Laffoon 2012), were more often interred with non-local objects than were males (Hoogland et al. 2010). Pottery vessels were placed over two adults (one female and one male) and one child, suggesting that this practice was not related particularly to gender or age (Hofman et al. 2001; Hofman and Hoogland 2003; Hoogland and Hofman 2013).

The site has yielded a wealth of shell tools and ornaments, as well as coral implements and exotic worked bone. Lithic material is both local and non-local, with provenances in Long Island (Antigua) for the flint, St. Martin for the greenstone axes, and Anguilla for the calcirudite or *cemí* stone (Knippenberg

2006). The lithic repertoire further includes a number of beads of diorite and quartz and jadeite adzes.

Faunal samples indicate a heavy reliance on reef fish during all the occupation phases. Oryzomine rodents, agouti (*Dasyprocta* sp.), and land crabs were present in all phases as well, although mammals and land crabs are more common in the Saladoid assemblage. Land crabs also occur in the latest post-Saladoid assemblage (Grouard 2001, 2002). Subsistence during the post-Saladoid shows an increase in exploitation of *Cittarium pica* and *Lobatus gigas* compared to the earlier Saladoid occupation of the site. A clear difference in consumption of *Cittarium pica* between the early and Late Ceramic Age is evidenced by a change from a destructive to a non-destructive method of animal extraction. The former involved making a hole in the shell to extract the animal, and the latter assumes cooking or grilling the whole shell (Nieweg 2000:112). *Acanthopleura granulata* is another species that is present in large quantities next to a great variety of other species occurring in smaller numbers. Vertebrate remains consist of fifty-four taxa of fish (surgeonfish, jacks, triggerfish, and parrotfish), which are present in large quantities, but also abundant are crabs and sea urchins. Mammals are quite rare, compared to the Saladoid occupation where the rice rat and agouti were abundant. This points to a specialized capture strategy during the post-Saladoid period, with a predominant exploitation of fish, crabs, and sea urchins. Exploitation was focused in the vicinity of the settlement and predominantly oriented toward the lagoon, its coral reef, and the estuary zone. This is in contrast with the earlier occupation phases that were more focused on a generalized exploitation, and in which all major ecozones were exploited, including deepwater reefs, river mouths, lagoons and mangroves, sandy sea bottoms and reefs, terrestrial zones covered with vegetation, and estuary zones (Grouard 2001:246–247; Hofman 2013).

Windward Islands (Southern Lesser Antilles)

The southern Lesser Antilles occupies a favorable stepping-stone position on the route from the Greater Antilles to the South American mainland. These islands are crucial for understanding the mechanisms that linked these two main centers of cultural development. The distribution of materials with strong symbolic meanings moved between the islands in both directions. The pottery and other elements of material culture reflect a blending of northern and southern affiliations.

The Troumassan Troumassoid subseries was named after the type-site on the banks of the Troumassée River on the east coast of St. Lucia. It is divided into a Troumassée A (around AD 350) and a Troumassée B (around AD 750). The pottery is distinguished by its thickness and coarseness. Decorations of red-and-black paint, inwardly thickened lips, and pedestal bases on vessels are diagnostic. Vessel shapes are varied, with forms including boat shapes, kidney shapes, and hemispherical and inverted-bell shapes. Over time, painted decorations disappeared, as did fine-line crosshatching. Tripod griddles were introduced, and modelled-incised decorations became more elaborate (Allaire 1977; Boomert 2000; McKusick 1959; Rouse 1992).

The Suazoid series (or Suazan Troumassoid subseries) is named for the type-site of Savanne Suazey (Grenada) (Bullen 1964; Rouse 1992). It is characterized by a very crude, non-ceremonial pottery with scratched surfaces and finger-indented rims and legged vessels and griddles. Alongside this utilitarian ware, there is a finer ware with polished surfaces. The latter are often decorated with red paint, linear or areal painting, or simple incisions of parallel lines, circles, or scrolls on the rims or walls (known as Caliviny polychrome). Modelled-incised lugs with human faces, figurines, and clay pestles are typical (Allaire 1977; Bullen 1964; Hofman 1993; McKusick 1959). In southern Martinique, the sites of Anse Trabaud and Macabou are characteristic of this period (Allaire 1977; Bérard 2013; Hofman 2012; Hoogland et al. 2015). Allaire (1991) notes a shift in settlement to the drier southern parts of the islands accompanied by an increase in griddles for manioc production and spindle whorls for the manufacture of cotton goods.

On St. Lucia, this period was originally classified as the Micoid series (named for the type-site in the town of Micoud). This series included two successive styles called "Choc" and "Fannis" (McKusick 1959). The site of Lavoutte in northern St. Lucia is characteristic of this period and styles. Fifty-two burials were excavated at the site in 2008 and 2009 during a rescue intervention by a team from Leiden University. The burials evidenced very complex and varied mortuary practices dating between the 12th and 15th centuries (Hofman et al. 2012).

Giraudy Site, St. Lucia (c. AD 900–1500)

St. Lucia is one of the Windward Islands. It is leaf-shaped, narrow in the north and fanning out towards the south. A peninsula juts out in the extreme south. It measures 43 kilometers from north to south and 22 kilometers at its widest point from west to east, encompassing a total area of some 600 square kilometers. Martinique lies to the north, and St. Vincent to the south. The Giraudy site is situated in the southern part of the island, in the Beane Field area of Vieux Fort (Figure 7.9). A dense vegetation of trees and bushes characterizes the site area today. The site lies on a flat piece of land, situated between a coastal sand beach to the east and a hill approximately 300 meters to the west. This hill is composed of andesitic agglomerate tuff.

Ripley and Adelaide Bullen first investigated the Giraudy site in collaboration with Eric Branford during the early 1970s (Bullen et. al 1973). They found two occupations at the site, representing separate modified Saladoid and Suazoid components. They excavated several test units and obtained numerous potsherds in association with artifacts of shell, bone, and stone.

A team from Leiden University and the Florida Museum of Natural History continued investigations at the site in 2004 (Hofman et al. 2004). A series of

FIGURE 7.9 Menno Hoogland in a backhoe trench at the Giraudy site, Saint Lucia (photo by William Keegan).

machine-made test units were dug in the site area. The stratigraphy consists of three layers approximately 80 centimeters deep. From top to bottom, the three layers consist of a clay layer (layer 1) and two layers of sand (layers 2 and 3). The clay layer is a disturbed plow zone that covers the two layers of sand. The three strata were removed separately and deposited in separate locations. Each stratum was then screened through quarter-inch-mesh hardware sieves.

Pottery from two time periods belonging to the modified or late Saladoid and Suazoid series was collected. The late Saladoid pottery exhibits a large variety of vessel shapes. Rims are often thickened, triangular, or flanged, sometimes painted red, and surfaces are mostly polished. Decorations consist of areal painting of white-on-red, white-on-black, or black-on-red; curvilinear incisions; and a large range of modeled-incised anthropomorphic and zoomorphic adornos. Only a few fragments bear ZIC.

Simple vessel shapes, scratched surfaces, and legged vessels and griddles characterize the Suazoid pottery. Vessels are thick and poorly constructed but occur in association with finer wares with polished surfaces. The latter are often decorated with red paint, linear or areal painting, and painted scrolls (Caliviny buff-on-plain), simple incisions of parallel lines, circles or scrolls on the rims or walls. Other typical decorations are finger-indentations on the rims, anthropomorphic adornos, figurines, and clay pestles.

The toolkit was composed of various pottery, lithic, shell, coral, and bone tools. These tools include adzes and axes, scoops, clamshell scrapers, and a shell fishhook. A fair amount of paraphernalia was recovered, including beads, pendants, and a *cemí*. Ornaments include a diorite bead, small round beads of greenstone and shell, and shell pendants. A small stone three-pointer and a fragment of human bone decorated with incisions are part of the assemblage as well.

Enormous quantities of subsistence remains were collected from all layers. The Giraudy site is only 500 meters from the beach at Point Sable, so it is not surprising that fishing and mollusk collecting were the main subsistence activities. There are significant differences in the animals that were eaten during the two time periods. There appears to be much greater use of sea turtle (*Chelonia mydas*) during the earlier period, and Guinea pig was identified in a late Saladoid layer. The Suazoid layer exhibits an increase in the number of small fish, and thousands of Carib Pointed-Venus shells (*Anomalocardia brasiliana*) dominate the mollusk assemblage. The observed changes in subsistence practices probably relate to changes in the local marine environment and cultural food preferences.

Social and Political Networks

It has been suggested that the level of sociopolitical integration of the early post-Saladoid societies in the Lesser Antilles probably oscillated between extremes (Hofman and Hoogland 2003, 2011; Hoogland and Hofman 1999). Large social units and settlement systems, formed under successful leadership, may have contrasted with small-sized units and briefly occupied settlements originating from the fissioning of local communities after the collapse of successful leadership. Localized interaction spheres were created through monopolizing and manipulating the manufacture and/or exchange of goods and marriage partners (Crock 2000; Haviser 1991b; Hoogland 1996) out of the need to establish elaborate alliance networks among neighbors and the need to form larger local sociopolitical units (Figure 7.10). This may have resulted in the establishment of several political authorities or peer-polities, each encompassing a number of settlements or even a number of islands (see Renfrew and Cherry 1986). The changing settlement pattern and the appearance of clearly delineated style zones might point to this phenomenon. John Crock's (2000) data from Anguilla fits this pattern; and the data on site location, site size and internal structure, spatial organization, and mortuary practices, as well as artifact composition obtained from the Anse à la Gourde site, suggest that this was a major site dominating a wider region (Delpuech et al. 1999b; de Waal 2006; Hofman and Hoogland 2011).

FIGURE 7.10   Diverse expressions of Late Ceramic Age material culture, after AD 1200. Not to scale (photos by Corinne Hofman and Menno Hoogland).

The complex mortuary practices at Anse à la Gourde evidence social differentiation that may suggest social hierarchies and/or stratification within the society (Hoogland 1996; 1999, Hofman et al. 2001). Mortuary practices reflect the processes of humanization of spiritual beings and the incipience of a monopolization of the society's social and cosmological ideology. Although mortuary treatment is often regarded as a representation of the social personae of an individual at death, rules are fluid, and mortuary treatment is open to manipulation. Manipulation of the identity of a deceased person symbolized by mortuary treatment is an important mechanism for claiming lineage primogeniture (Hofman et al. 1999; Hoogland and Hofman 2013; Hoogland et al. 2010).

Kelbey's Ridge 2 Site, Saba (c. AD 1350)

The Kelbey's Ridge 2 site, radiocarbon-dated to AD 1350, contains evidence for the local manufacture of the pottery that have stylistic affiliations to the Chicoid series (Boca Chica style) of the Greater Antilles. The site also produced ceremonial paraphernalia that is clearly influenced by the Greater Antillean cultures, including a snuff-inhaler made from manatee bone (Hofman and Hoogland 2011, 2013: Hoogland and Hofman 1999). Similar influences and artifacts have been encountered on neighboring islands, including Anguilla, St. Martin, St. Eustatius, Antigua, Guadeloupe, La Désirade, Marie-Galante; and copies of such artifacts are reported as far south as Martinique and St. Lucia (Allaire 1990; Crock 2000; de Waal 2006; Douglas 1991:578, 585, Fig. 5 and 588, Fig. 8; Hofman 1993,

1995b:167; Henocq and Petit 1995; Hoogland 1996:156, Fig. 6.24; Knippenberg 2013; Mol 2007; Nicholson 1983; Rouse 1992:117, Fig. 119 and jacket illustration).

Saba is the smallest island of the Lesser Antilles, with a surface area of only 13 square kilometers. It is situated approximately 50 kilometers south of St. Martin and 30 kilometers northwest of St. Eustatius. The island of St. Croix (U.S. Virgin Islands) lies 150 kilometers in a westerly direction and has long been considered to be the eastern outpost of the "Classic Taíno" interaction sphere during Late Ceramic Age times (Rouse 1992). The finds from the Kelbey's Ridge 2 site document that developments on Saba paralleled those in the Virgin Islands and the Greater Antilles. The eastern boundary of the Greater Antillean influence sphere can be redrawn to include Saba and probably even more southward.

The site is located in the northeastern part of the island on a levelled terrain of triangular form situated at 140 meters above mean sea level and measuring 0.9 hectares. In the west it is bounded by a volcanic dome, which extends toward the south as a ridge. The lava flow of Flat Point forms the northwestern boundary. Kelbey's Ridge 2 consists of a 2000-square-meter elongated and curved surface scatter that stretches along the ridge. Corinne Hofman and Menno Hoogland directed excavations at the site between 1988 and 1991. In all, 382 square meters were excavated, which is about 19% of the total site area. The stratigraphy is simple. The lowest level consists of a very thin (5–10-centimeter) stratum that yielded dispersed precolonial artifacts, including potsherds and low quantities of subsistence debris on top of the sterile subsoil. This layer seems to represent the only undisturbed remnant of the original occupation layer. It is capped by a 30–40-centimeter-thick plow zone containing precolonial artifacts, almost exclusively potsherds, mixed with colonial artifacts. Part of the original occupation surface was incorporated into the plow zone by colonial and recent agricultural activities.

Settlement layout, house sizes and shapes, and burial locations and mortuary practices for this period are best documented at the Kelbey's Ridge 2 site. The investigations revealed large numbers of post holes (180), burials (7), round and oval shaped pits (180), and hearths (4). Five houses were reconstructed as oval and round shapes with diameters between 6 and 8 meters. These houses had a surface area of approximately 57–80 square meters and may have been inhabited by extended families of eleven to fifteen people (Figure 7.11).

Seven burials including ten individuals reveal the complex burial ritual at the site. All seven burials were inside the houses under the house floors. The deceased were all buried in a strongly flexed position, with the knees bent towards the chest. The burials include two composite burials—one cremated— and some parts of the skeletons were absent (skull and long bones). Among the seven individuals, four were children (62% of the burial population). In two cases, children were buried in the same grave as an adult. In one instance, a newborn infant was placed in the grave of an adult female, and in another, the cremated bones of a five-year-old child were placed in the abdominal cavity

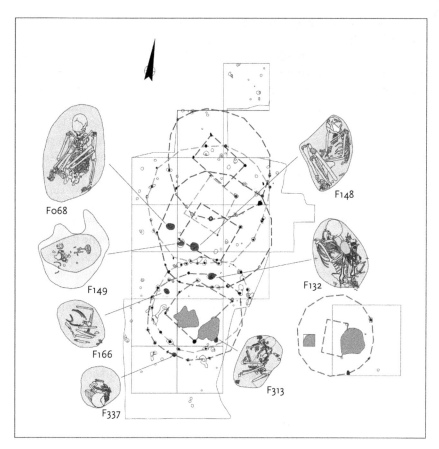

FIGURE 7.11 Houses and burials at the Kelbey's Ridge site, Saba (courtesy of Menno Hoogland).

of an adult male that was made accessible by removing of some of the ribs. The ribs were then redeposited on top of the cremated child. In both cases, the children and the adults were separated by a considerable age gap of two generations. Stone artifacts positioned under the cranium accompanied one child burial, and the composite adult-cremated child burial was associated in a similar fashion with a single hollow bird bone that was probably part of the snuff inhaler found near the grave. Burial treatment and grave manipulation occurred for both adults and children. One child burial was recovered from a contemporary midden deposit at the Spring Bay site, which is located just below Kelbey's Ridge 2 on the waterfront overlooking the Atlantic Ocean (Hoogland 1996). Large quantities of pottery, shell, bone, and stone tools were recovered. Notable is a manatee bone carved in the shape of a fish that probably was used as an inhaler for hallucinogens. Other paraphernalia consist of diorite beads and bone and coral *cemís*.

The pottery assemblage shows strong affiliations to the Chicoid (Boca Chic style) of the Greater Antilles, which is dated to ca. AD 1200–1500 (Rouse 1992). More than 33,000 potsherds were analyzed. The most common vessel shapes are bowls with simple contours. Dishes and bowls with composite contours are uncommon, and necked globular vessels occur in small quantities. Diameters range from 25–35 centimeters. Very few vessels exceed 40 centimeters in diameter. Wall thickness varies between 5 and 8 millimeters. Decoration consists primarily of incision and modelling and, to a lesser extent, punctation. Painted decoration is completely lacking. Incision is predominant and occurs on 63.9% of the potsherds. Incision consists of deep, narrow lines, and incisions ending in punctations (line-and-dot) or arches are fairly common. The incised decoration was most often applied on the upper part of the body directly under the rim and is only very rarely on a red slipped surface. Motifs are diverse and include linear lines, V-shaped motifs, and scrolls. Pairs of parallel lines, either semicircular or straight, are dominant, and a fine horizontal line is found above these designs, bordering the rim. Modelling is second in importance. These are mostly modelled appliqués with geometric, anthropomorphic, and zoomorphic designs. Geometric appliqué consists of notched fillets. Punctation is applied on beveled or double thickened lips and on vessels with red slipped surfaces.

The faunal assemblage is characterized by a large number of fish species. Mammals, birds, and reptiles are far less common. Two species of mammals, rice rats and a single individual fruit bat, account for 23.2% of the vertebrates. Bird species make up only 3.8%, and the reptiles, iguanas, and sea turtles, account for 4.3% of the total number of vertebrates. Fifteen different fish species were identified. The most numerous are surgeonfish (19.9%), groupers (9.9%), triggerfish (9.5%), parrotfish (7.6%), and sharks (4.7%). The invertebrates include fourteen species of mollusks, with chitons and nerites the most numerous. Carbon and nitrogen isotope analysis points to a slight increase in terrestrial food sources in the diet compared to earlier sites on Saba. One explanation for the higher $\delta^{13}C$ values is the increased consumption of C_4 plant crops, such as maize or tropical grasses, in the late period (Pestle 2013; Stokes 1998).

The site has been interpreted as an outpost of one of the Greater Antillean polities driven by a combination of socio-ideological and economic incentives. The outpost may have evolved from a need to obtain specific resources through the exploitation of the substantial fishing grounds of the Saba Bank (Hofman and Hoogland 2011). The presence of black durgon (*Melichtys niger*) in the faunal remains supports this hypothesis (Wing in Hoogland 1996). Lundberg et al. (1992) made a similar suggestion regarding the Late Ceramic Age settlements in the Virgin Islands. It has been proposed that these could have functioned as resource-extraction camps in order to exploit the resource potentials of the small islands and their shallow waters (Keegan et al. 2008). The site also reflects the establishment of support bases or gateway communities to control the movement of goods along the main trade route between the Greater Antilles, the southern Lesser Antilles, and the South American mainland (Hofman and Hoogland 2011; Hofman et al. 2014; Mol et al. 2015). Prestige goods (e.g., *guanín*, black wood, greenstone, feathers, shell ornaments) were channeled in both directions along this route (Boomert 1987; Hofman et al. 2007; Hofman et al. 2014).

Demographic Collapse after AD 1300

The number and size of settlements decreased drastically after AD 1300. Settlements became located in more strategic, defensive locations that are considered non-optimal settings (Petersen and Crock 1999). Remote geographical settings were favored, as evidenced by the Kelbey's Ridge 2 site (Saba) located on top of a 120-meter elevated ridge, and the Morne Cybèle and Morne Souffleur sites located on the 200-meter elevated plateau of La Désirade. All three sites exhibit evidence for connections with the Greater Antilles in either material expression or site structure and burial practices. The two Désirade sites are radiocarbon-dated to around AD 1460–1480. They produced pottery with some affiliations to the Cayo and Suazoid pottery of the southern Lesser Antilles and potentially also with mainland Venezuela. The La Désirade pottery is thin, and vessel shapes are simple. Decorations are characterized by zoomorphic and anthropomorphic modelled-incised figures and punctations. Both sites produced a shell mask, or *guaíza*, that is reminiscent of similar masks from the Greater Antilles (de Waal 2006; Hofman 1995b; Hoogland and Hofman 1993, 1999). Similar masks were found at other Late Ceramic Age sites in neighboring islands and in the Greater Antilles (Crock 2000:14; Crock and Petersen 1999:75–77; Douglas 1991, Fig. 5; Mol 2007, 2014; Rouse 1992:Fig. 29c, and jacket illustration).

The apparent decrease in the number and size of sites on the northern Lesser Antilles mirrors that observed in Puerto Rico (Curet 2005). Combined with the preference for remote site locations, there appears to be discontinuity in social structure from earlier post-Saladoid times. Material culture remains indicate various contacts with the Greater Antilles existed, which in some cases may be explained as the reflection of "esoteric interaction" as postulated by Louis Allaire (1990). Local Lesser Antillean communities were integrated into the larger sociopolitical, economic, and ideological sphere of the Greater Antillean polities; a process that disrupted the independent development of the local communities and marked the beginning of sociopolitical changes in the region.

Morne Cybèle and Morne Souffleur Sites, La Désirade (c. AD 1440–1460)

The sites of Morne Cybèle and Morne Souffleur are both located on the plateau of the island of La Désirade in the Guadeloupian archipelago. The island of La Désirade is an 11-kilometer long and 2-kilometer wide calcareous table mountain, characterized by steep slopes (Hofman et al. 2004). It has a well-exposed volcanic base, consisting of lava with green schist, interbedded chert and radiolarite, and covered by an impressive uninhabited limestone plateau, La Montagne, which reaches up to 275 meters. The extremely steep cliffs and the strong and unpredictable sea currents hamper the accessibility of the north coast of the island from the sea. The entire southern coastline is characterized by a slight slope of the plateau and a coastal plain. This coastal plain is sheltered from the wind, and the reefs that border the coastline protect it from strong sea-currents.

The Morne Cybèle site was discovered and excavated by Pierre Bodu in the 1980s. Corinne Hofman and Menno Hoogland revisited the site in 1994 and dug some additional test pits. The core of the site is estimated to have a surface area of 200–300 square meters. In addition, the material excavated by Bodu was restudied. During a systematic survey of the island of La Désirade by Maaike de Waal in 1999, a second site, Morne Souffleur, was discovered on the plateau, revealing traits similar to Morne Cybèle's (de Waal 2006). A radiocarbon date on a *Cittarium pica* shell (GrN-20090) of 470 ± 30 B.P. from Morne Cybèle corresponds to a calibrated date of AD 1440–1460, which makes Morne Cybèle and possibly also Morne Souffleur the latest sites in the northern Lesser Antilles prior to the European encounters (Hofman 2013).

The two sites are situated along the southeastern ridge of the plateau at an elevation of 205 meters above sea level and extend approximately 20 meters inland. The sites are located on heavily eroded limestone bedrock. The indigenous artifacts are deposited in the cavities of the bedrock, which are produced by erosion. In clear weather, one can perfectly view the islands of Marie-Galante, Petite Terre, and the Pointe de Chateaux of Grande-Terre. A wide horizon is surveyed, and there is a good view over sea (Hofman 1995).

The fragmentation rate of the pottery is relatively high, probably due to erosion and cultivation processes during colonial times. Vessels are characterized by simplicity of shape. More than 50% of the vessels consists of jars or bowls with unrestricted or restricted simple contours, with an average of 23.7 centimeters in diameter and rounded or flat rims and relatively thin walls. Most vessel surfaces are burnished but rarely polished. Their colors vary from brown to reddish-brown. Some, however, are more grayish. Firing colors show incomplete, relatively well-oxidizing conditions. Vessels have flat or concave bases. Griddles have unthickened rims. Only 3.5% of the pottery is decorated by geometric, anthropomorphic, or zoomorphic modelling, often in combination with punctations. Zoomorphic modelling represents a snake, a pelican, and a bat. Anthropomorphic figures are attached to the vessel rims and clearly represent male or female figures with pierced ears, punctations around the eyes, and pronounced eyebrows, similar to some Cayoid vessels from St. Vincent and Grenada. Others are reminiscent of Suazoid motifs. Some anthropomorphic figures have beards and/or head ornaments. More than 35.5% of the vessel rims are decorated with punctations pierced into the wet clay, and over 15% bear fine-line linear designs. Besides ceramics, some flakes represent the limited lithic material. These flakes are of local rocks (tephrite and andesite), which naturally occur on the east part of the island, and there are some polishing pebbles of volcanic origin.

The partly disturbed Morne Souffleur site is situated at the southern border of the central plateau of La Désirade. Surface material consists of an even distribution of moderately fragmented Morne Cybèle–style ceramics and shell fragments, including *Cittarium pica*, *Lobatus gigas*, *Codakia orbicularis* and *Chiton* sp. A beautifully carved and polished *Lobatus costatus* shell mask was found, in addition to two other shell artifacts. Stylistically, the Morne Souffleur pottery assemblage is identical to that of Morne Cybèle (de Waal 2006; Hofman et al. 2004).

Kalinago Archaeology

The final phase of culture history in the southern Lesser Antilles is defined by the emergence of the Carib (Sued-Badillo 1978). Although their modern descendants on Dominica today call themselves Kalinago, we use the name "Carib" to maintain continuity with previous reports. Most discussions of Carib history are based on observations and interpretations recorded by European invaders (Allaire 2013). However, a substantial number of Carib archaeological sites recently have been identified (Figure 7.12). We begin with

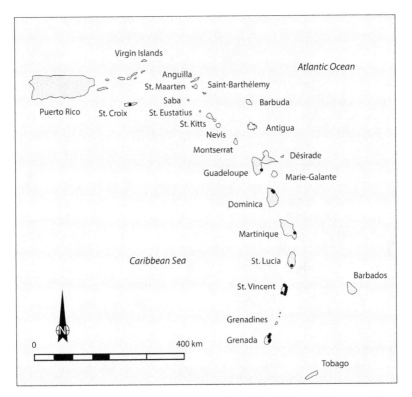

FIGURE 7.12 Distribution of Kalinago sites; indicated as dark areas (courtesy of Corinne Hofman and Menno Hoogland).

a brief discussion of how the documentary evidence has been used to characterize the Carib.

Questions regarding the identity of the Carib continue to dominate the debates. Earlier discussions addressed whether or not the Carib were cannibals (Pekka Helminen 1988; Myers 1984; Whitehead 1988). More recently, the debate has centered on the question of ethnic identity and cultural survival (Dreyfus 1992; González 1988; Hulme and Whitehead 1992; Sued-Badillo 1978). The cultural and societal transformations that occurred between the Late Ceramic Age and the early colonial period in the Lesser Antilles still present an archaeologically under-studied and turbulent era during which the inhabitants of the small islands came under increasing influence from South America and the Greater Antilles, and participated in the last phase of indigenous resistance to colonial powers.

Dave D. Davis and R. Christopher Goodwin (1990) recognized that "the Island Carib problem ... owed its persistence ... as much to the unhesitating acceptance of [aboriginal oral] tradition, and to naïve interpretations of linguistic and ethnohistoric evidence, as it has to the paucity of relevant archaeological data." They called for additional research and for the evaluation of alternative hypotheses: for example, the possibility that Carib culture developed in the Lesser Antilles and did not reflect a late migration into the islands.

Approximately 150 years passed before permanent European settlements were established in the 17th century. These were established despite fierce indigenous resistance from the Carib or Kalinago, a society that claimed origin from the South American mainland and asserted themselves aggressively—particularly between Tobago and St. Kitts. Currently, our views on the colonial encounters in the Lesser Antilles are dominated by the descriptions of the early Spanish, Dutch, French, and English chroniclers. Despite significant scholarly advances by Caribbean researchers in deconstructing documentary bias and European and colonial preconceptions (e.g., Honychurch 2000; Hulme 1986; Hulme and Whitehead 1992; Whitehead 1995), the indigenous past of the Lesser Antilles remains marginalized in the discourse on the archaeology and history of colonial encounters in general. Archaeology spanning the historical divide is virtually nonexistent (but see Hofman and Hoogland 2012; Hofman et al. 2015; Lenik 2012).

Contributing to the problem of determining which historical descriptions are relevant is the question of Carib origins. Two broad models have been proposed (Wilson 1993). One model identifies the Carib as invaders from the South American mainland who entered the Antilles just prior to European contact (Allaire 1987, 1996; Boucher 1992). The other proposes that the Carib were descended from the indigenous communities of the Greater and Lesser Antilles (Davis and Goodwin 1990; Sued-Badillo 1978).

Selecting between these alternatives is complicated by the fact that the Carib have long been archaeologically invisible. As remarkable as it may sound, there were no confirmed Carib sites prior to the 1990s (Rouse 1992:22). Although Cayo-style pottery from St. Vincent was first attributed to the Carib

FIGURE 7.13 Collection of Cayoid pots from Grenada. Not to scale (Willcox collection, photos by Corinne Hofman and Menno Hoogland).

a decade ago (Boomert 1986, 2004, 2011), all of the sherds came from surface collections (Figure 7.13). Other Guiana-related styles developed in the southern Windward Islands of Tobago, St. Vincent (Boomert 1986, 1995, 2003; Kirby 1974), the Grenadines, Dominica, and Guadeloupe (e.g., Morne Cybèle complex) (de Waal 2006; Hofman 1995b; Hofman et al. 2004). Boomert insisted on the similarities between the Cayo pottery and that of the Koriabo complex (ancestral to the contemporary mainland Carib or Kari'na pottery tradition) of coastal Guyana. Cayo pottery was previously documented by Earle Kirby and Henri Petitjean Roget in the 1970s, and extensively published by Arie Boomert since the 1980s (Boomert 1986, 2009, 2011). The Cayo complex was thought to predate Suazoid pottery on these islands (Allaire 1977), but it was later suggested that Cayo gradually infiltrated and replaced Suazoid pottery in the Windward Islands (Boomert 1986, 1995). Boomert (1986) associated this pottery with the Carib occupation of the Windward Islands and argued that the Cayo pottery exhibits strong similarities in decoration and shape to the Koriabo complex of the Guianas. On the basis of this affiliation, Boomert dates the Cayo style to sometime between AD 1000 and 1500, and more precisely to c. AD 1250.

The uncertain context of these finds precluded their definite assignment to the period of European encounters. In the mid-1990s, Allaire (1994) initiated excavations at the Cayo site of Argyle on the southeast coast of St. Vincent, at which early colonial materials were recovered in direct association with the indigenous pottery. The most spectacular find was a small rim sherd inlaid with European glass beads (Allaire 1994). Recent surveys, excavations, and collections studies by Leiden University on Dominica, St. Lucia, St. Vincent, Grenada, and St. Kitts provided preliminary insight into late precolonial and early colonial period settlement patterns and for the first time uncovered Cayo pottery in context with Carib or Kalinago settlement remains at the sites of Argyle, St. Vincent, and La Potterie, Grenada, dating to the 16th to early 17th centuries (Allaire 2013; Boomert 2010; Hofman and Hoogland 2012; Hofman et al. 2015; Petitjean Roget 2015). These discoveries offered a unique opportunity to study the Carib social landscape on regional and local scales and allowed inferences about the transformations of indigenous settlement patterns and organization across the historical divide. The continuity of Suazoid pottery in the Windward Islands alongside the emergence of the Cayo phenomenon is, however, not excluded, but needs to be confirmed by radiocarbon dating.

Currently, more than twenty archaeological sites with Cayo pottery have been found in the Lesser Antilles (Bright 2011; Hofman and Hoogland 2012). These sites occur in the north and south ends of Grenada (Sauteurs Bay, Galby Bay, and more recently at La Potterie and Telescope Point on the northeastern coast) (Holdren 1998; Hofman and Hoogland 2012, personal observation 2013–2016; Petitjean Roget 2015; Henry Petitjean Roget 2015); one site on the Grenadines (Ile de Ronde) (Roget, personal communication 2012); twelve sites on St. Vincent (Mount Pleasant/Rawacou, New Sandy Bay, Owia 2, Spring, Friendly, Fancy, Camden Park, Lot 14, Argyle 1, Brighton, Sans Souci, and Grand Sable) (Bullen and Bullen 1972; Kirby 1974; Boomert 1986; Allaire 1994); and five sites on Dominica (Woodford Hill, Melville Hall, Eden, Sophia Bay, and Walker's Rest) (Boomert 2009:660; Honychurch 2000). Isolated Cayo sherds are reported from Anse à la Gourde (Guadeloupe), the Black Bay site (St. Lucia), and the Macabou site (Martinique) amidst an otherwise-Suazoid assemblage (Bright 2011). The northernmost occurrence of Cayo pottery is on Basse Terre (Guadeloupe) at the sites of Plage de Roseaux (Richard 1994; Serrand 2014), and possibly St. Kitts. Cayo sites on St. Vincent and Grenada are located in strategic positions on top of ridges overlooking the Atlantic Ocean and near rivers on the windward side of the islands, much like the Kalinago territory on Dominica today. Seventeenth-century chroniclers mention that these locations were chosen because of the steep cliffs and rough seas that aided in defending the settlements. Radiocarbon dates and the presence of early European material culture confirm their dates in the 16th to early 17th centuries.

Characteristic features of Cayo pottery include incisions on a flat rim, cone-shaped collars and bodies, and typical appliqué decoration consisting of small adornos made from clay balls that were perforated with a hollow straw, often in combination with hands. Multi-convex vessels with anthropomorphic faces in appliqué, and *caraipe* temper (tree bark, called *cariápe* or *kwep* in Amazonia and coastal Guianas) are common. Cayo pottery reflects a mosaic-like cultural aggregate with mainland Koriabo and Greater Antillean Meillacoid and Chicoid affiliations illustrative of the wide-ranging and diverse composition of Kalinago society in early colonial times (Boomert 1986, 2004, 2009, 2011; Hofman and Hoogland 2012).

Affiliations with the Greater Antilles emphasize the possible role that "Taíno" refugees and/or Carib raids on "Taíno" settlements may have played in the transmission of Greater Antillean stylistic traits to Lesser Antillean pottery assemblages. The presence of early European materials in Cayo assemblages evidences trade relationships between the indigenous inhabitants and the Europeans. Artifacts and paraphernalia in Cayo sites represent an amalgam of South American (Koriabo style pottery), Greater Antillean, and European exchange relationships (Hofman et al. 2014). Diverse influences include bone flutes (deer), teeth pendants (e.g., tapir, European pig, and bear) and a snuffing bowl (manatee).

Argyle Site, St. Vincent

The early colonial Argyle site is located at a strategic position on top of a ridge overlooking the Atlantic Ocean and next to the mouth of the Yambou River in the southeastern part of St. Vincent (Figure 7.14). The Yambou River drains the

FIGURE 7.14 House excavation at the Argyle site, St. Vincent (photo by Corinne Hofman and Menno Hoogland).

Mesopotamia Valley, an area known for its petroglyph sites. The extremely rich agricultural soils in the valley are suited for the cultivation of root crops such as manioc, sweet potatoes, yams, and taller.

In 2009 and 2010, rescue excavations were urgently required due to the construction of a runway for a new international airport at Argyle's location (Hoogland et al. 2011). At the instigation of Henry Petitjean Roget (Guadeloupe) and Kathy Martin (St. Vincent and Grenadines National Trust), a team from Leiden University in collaboration with the St. Vincent and Grenadines National Trust and the International Airport Development Company Ltd. excavated a surface area of 2,800 square meters at the site. The excavations revealed the first complete early colonial Carib settlement in the Lesser Antilles. The site structure completely matches historical accounts. The great majority of the material remains were locally produced Cayo pottery and European trade wares. These were recovered from the eroding slope of the Argyle ridge. The European trade wares consisted of pieces of iron, lead, earthenware (an admixture of late 16th- to early 17th-century Spanish olive jars, and Spanish as well as Portuguese majolica), glass bottles, numerous seed and chevron beads, and tin-glazed earthenware or faïence produced in France (Hofman and Hoogland 2012; Hofman et al. 2015).

Two plazas representing two building phases of the village were documented. The plaza of the first phase measured approximately 10 by 15 meters; that of the second phase, 15 by 25 meters. The post holes of eleven structures were found, including nine round and two oval-shaped houses surrounding the plazas. The latter two have floor plans of 11.8 by 4 meters (consisting of 14 post holes with a depth between 35 and 50 centimeters deep) and 7.7 by 3.5 meters, respectively (consisting of 12 postholes). The round houses have surface areas ranging between 4.5 by 5 meters and 6 by 8 meters and consisting of 10–14 posts are dispersed around the plaza. Three larger features in two of the round houses were interpreted as grave pits because they contained human teeth. Other skeletal material has not preserved due to the high acidity of the soil. These grave pits confirm the practice of burying the dead under the house floors, as described by the chroniclers. The teeth belong to two (sub-) adult individuals aged between 14 and 25 years, of which one is local and the other non-local to the site according to the strontium-isotope values provided by Jason Laffoon (Hofman and Hoogland 2012). As a collaboration between the different stakeholders involved, the Kalinago village is being rebuilt on the location of the original 16th- to early 17th-century settlement.

Conclusions

The Lesser Antilles offers a picture of a very dynamic social and cultural landscape with continuous migrations, colonizations, mobility, exchange, and settlement in diverse habitats over the course of time. The unilinear view of migration and the stepping-stone mode of island settlement proposed during the early years of Caribbean archaeology has recently seen a shift of paradigm. The interface of the Archaic and Ceramic Age is deemed much more intense than previously thought. On some islands, like St. Martin, there is clear evidence of co-occupation of both shell-fishing and plant-gathering communities next to ceramic horticulturalists. The process of neolithization obviously commenced much earlier than previously thought, with plant-management practices among otherwise so-called Archaic Age communities. It is also obvious that communities producing Huecoid and Saladoid pottery co-inhabited several of the northern Lesser Antillean islands and Puerto Rico and that they competed over resources during large feast gatherings.

Large Saladoid villages were aligned along the coasts or interiors of islands, and most activities took place at the village level. A similar pattern has been noted for Saladoid south-central Puerto Rico (Curet and Oliver 1998; Torres 2010). Large habitation sites with continuous occupations or reoccupations of older settlements strengthen the idea of "social memory," whereby individuals rebuild their villages and houses and bury their dead in the same location for many centuries (Morsink 2006; van den Bel and Romon 2009; Hofman and Branford 2009; see also Siegel 1992, 2010) within a framework of a shared worldview and the exchange of goods and ideas. The emergence of cult sites with petroglyphs at the end of the Saladoid may be linked to public or communal ceremonial gatherings at fixed locations (Hofman and Hoogland 2004) and to active engagement with a highly interactive and multicultural social landscape of the post-Saladoid Lesser Antilles. These ideas are consistent with post-Saladoid Puerto Rico, whereby sites like Tibes and El Bronce developed into ceremonial centers that probably served as places where community gatherings were held and where power and identity were negotiated (Curet and Torres 2010).

The highly heterogeneous post-Saladoid material culture in the Lesser Antilles reflects a combination of local developments and inter-community relations on local and regional scales. Long-distance trade decreased, and the northern Lesser Antilles seemed to follow the shifts that occurred in Puerto Rico in respect to sociopolitics and ideology. For Puerto Rico, a change from central plaza burials during the Saladoid to house floors during Elenan Ostionoid times has been related to a shift from community-based identities to individual or familial relationships. This shift would have taken place congruently with a diminution in house size (from communal houses to nuclear family residences) (Curet and Oliver 1998; Siegel 1996a, 1999, 2010). Concomitant changes in burial locations and mortuary treatments show a shift from communal to household group legitimation. Modifications in mortuary practices, burial locations, and house sizes in the Lesser Antilles also coincide with what has been noted for Puerto Rico, and it has been suggested that these changes reflect similar processes in these islands (Hoogland 1996; Hofman et al. 2001).

There is also a shift from uniform pottery style features toward more individualized and humanized representations of spiritual beings and ritual paraphernalia. Rare but eye-catching individual artifacts are telling indicators of the appropriation of Greater Antillean ideas and/or goods throughout the Lesser Antilles in Ostionoid, Troumassoid, and Suazoid contexts. The period after AD 800 may be seen as a period of transition in which status differentiation and hierarchically ranked society evolved, bringing about a shift from achieved to ascribed leadership. Echoing Curet's (1996) ideas on pristine development of complex society, we would also argue that ideology formed one of the bases that the shaman leaders of the northern Lesser Antillean communities relied on to maintain and consolidate their power through time, establishing more restricted social contact networks through which independent local peer-polities interacted in a supra-village context. Kinship ties were possibly the basis for such multi-island communities (Keegan 2000a). Such a network would have been imperative for the continued existence of individual communities, and the collapse of such a system or part of it could have had vital implications in the wider region.

After c. AD 1200, this process was eventually interrupted by the slow absorption or incorporation into the sociopolitical structure of Greater Antillean society, which by then had reached its apogee and was expanding eastward and westward. This process disrupted more-or-less independent lines of development of local communities on the regional scale and marked the beginnings of sociopolitical changes on a large and more dependent level. The northern Lesser Antilles were no longer occupied by permanent villages during this time but were used as ports of trade and lookout posts, and these were established in strategic locations at certain intervals.

In the southern portion of the Antilles, many islands remained densely occupied, and intensive contacts and exchange relations were established with diverse mainland communities into the early colonial period. A pluriform set of mutually influencing and interactive traits and languages (e.g., the Carib pidgin) shared to varying degrees in multiple configurations across a mosaic of communities throughout the Caribbean were the result of these continuous contacts. Historic dichotomies such as "noble Taíno" versus "barbaric and savage Carib" were gradually downplayed and replaced with a more complex and diverse view of Caribbean societies on the eve of European encounter (Hofman 2013; Hofman et al. 2008; Hofman and Carlin 2010).

CHAPTER 8 | Caribbean Encounters

ON OCTOBER 12, 1492,[1] Christopher Columbus went ashore on Guanahaní, the easternmost island in the Bahamas. Columbus renamed the island San Salvador ("Holy Savior"), and it is known by that name today. A substantial number of European artifacts, including pottery, metals, and glass beads, were recovered during archaeological excavations at the Long Bay site (Brill et al. 1987; Hoffman 1987). These artifacts are indicative of a Spanish visit to San Salvador that may date to the probable encounter between Columbus and the island's indigenous communities.[2] Twelve other islands, and even Florida, have been suggested as the location for Columbus's first landfall. However, the sailing directions and descriptions of the islands recorded in the Columbus diary (*diario*) do not strongly support any of these other candidates (Keegan 1992; cf. Fuson 1987).

It generally is accepted that Columbus kept a running journal (*diario*) of his first voyage, that the original was lost, and that a copy of the *diario* was transcribed by Bartolomé de las Casas in 1530 (Fuson 1983, 1987). "The [Las Casas] manuscript consists of seventy-six large-sized paper folios written on both sides in a small, cursive [short]hand, forty to fifty lines to the page" (Dunn and Kelley 1989:5). The most complete modern version is the exact transcription and translation of *The* Diario *of Christopher Columbus's First Voyage to America, 1492–1493*, prepared by Oliver Dunn and James E. Kelley, Jr. (1989).

Columbus's *diario* is unique for its time because ships' logs typically did not include descriptions of the local inhabitants and environments (Henige 1991). As the only written descriptions of the first encounters in the Americas, the *diario* has served as the starting point for most modern interpretations of the

---

[1] October 23rd in the Gregorian calendar.
[2] A clandestine expedition attributed to Amerigo Vespucci, who may have been sent by the Spanish Crown, with financing from wealthy interests (the Medici family of Milan, Italy), to evaluate the claims made by Columbus, reportedly spent three months in the Bahamas in the winter of 1499 (Keegan 1992). Hundreds of enslaved Lucayans were transported to Spain. There are no detailed accounts of their activities in the Bahamas (Keegan 1992). It is possible, but unlikely, that European objects were transmitted to indigenous communities at this time.

precolonial Caribbean. Aside from its use in efforts to identify Columbus's first landfall (e.g., Judge 1986; Keegan 1992; Mitchell and Keegan 1987; Morison 1942; Mitchell 1984), historians and anthropologists have used the *diario* to identify the cultural characteristics of Lucayan, and especially Carib, cultures (e.g., Allaire 2013; Berman et al. 2013; Hulme and Whitehead 1992). Numerous publications on the Carib begin with Columbus (e.g., Allaire 1996, 2013; Hulme and Whitehead 1992; Myers 1984; Petitjean Roget 2013; Whitehead 1984). However, it is our contention that Columbus's observations had absolutely nothing to do with the indigenous Carib (see Chapter 1).

Columbus and Cannibals

The name *Carib*, and several derivations, appears ten times in the *diario* in four separate contexts (Keegan 1996a). First, it was used by Columbus as the name for the subjects (*gente*) of the Grand Khan (*Caniba*). Second, its recording suggests that it was the indigenous name for mythical beings that came from the otherworld to consume the dead and bring them to their final rest (*Caribes*). Third, it was the name of a mythical island inhabited only by men (Carib Island). Carib Island was part of the insular cosmological triad of men:sexual union:women (i.e., Carib:Guanín:Matininó). Fourth, it was Columbus's name for the enemy of the communities he encountered in the Bahamas, Cuba, and Hispaniola (*Cannibales*). Finally, Carib became a general Spanish term for fierce and hostile natives. When Columbus was attacked at the Golfo de las Flechas (Samaná, Dominican Republic) at the end of his first voyage, and then attacked at Guadeloupe and St. Croix during his second voyage, the aggressors were identified as "Carib." Between 1815 and 1820, an area on the coast of northeastern Luzon, Philippines, was labeled "Negros Caribes Bravos" (González, 1987:11). This indicates that the name Caribe also was used by the Spanish to indicate fierce people half way across the globe.

The name Carib was later applied to certain indigenous communities in coastal South America. Caribbean archaeologists have used the name Carib to identify the indigenous inhabitants of the Windward Islands at the time of the European encounter (Allaire 2013; Rouse 1948, 1992; Chapter 7, this book). Today, conventional and popular histories frequently characterize the Caribbean islands as populated by peaceful Arawak and fierce (cannibal) Carib (Amodio 1999; Craton and Saunders 1992; Davis 1992; Michener 1988; cf. Rouse 1948b, 1992:21–23; Sued-Badillo 1978). This dichotomy finds its origin in the *diario*.

In his initial encounters with the indigenous inhabitants of the Bahamas, Cuba, and Hispaniola, Columbus repeatedly sought directions to "the city of the Grand Khan." Not only was he convinced that Cuba was *tierra firme*, he also believed that he was only a short distance from the province of this Asiatic ruler. Columbus expected that such a powerful ruler had a standing army that he used to subjugate the simple peoples encountered in the Bahamas. Columbus associated weapons (e.g., metal swords and guns) and warfare (e.g., raiding to capture slaves) with civilization. In his opinion, the people he encountered in the Bahamas were not "civilized," but he states that they could be converted easily to the Christian faith and put to work in the service of the Lord and the Spanish Crown (October 12, 1492; Dunn and Kelley 1989:65, 67, 69).

Columbus attributed all possible indications of hostile encounters to the *Caniba*, the people of the Grand Khan (Dunn and Kelley 1989:217):

> And they appear to mean that here behind this Hispaniola, which they call Caribata, there is a landmass of exceedingly large size. And perhaps they are right, for they may be oppressed by cunning people, because the people of all these islands live in great fear of those from Caniba. And thus I say again how other times I said, he says, that Caniba is nothing else but the people of the Grand Khan, who must be here very close to this place. And they have ships and come to capture the islanders, and since they do not return the other islanders think that they have been eaten.

The ten passages in the *diario* that mention *"Caribes," "Caniba," "Canima,"* and/or *"Cannibales"* are all abstractions made by Las Casas that indicate the original text was altered, and in places includes anachronisms (Henige 1991; Keegan 2007:35). The characteristics repeatedly attributed to these *Caribes* describe mythical beings: "He [Columbus] understood also that, far from there, there were one-eyed men, and others, with snouts of dogs, who ate men, and that as soon as one was taken they cut his throat and drank his blood and cut off his genitals" (Dunn and Kelley 1989:133). Accompanying this passage, Las Casas noted in the margin, *"todo esto devian de dezir dlos caribes"* ("all this must be said of the Caribes").

The most compelling evidence that Columbus imposed his expectations on the situations he observed comes from his admission that the Lucayans originally identified him as a *Caribe*. Had the native peoples truly known *Caribes* they would not have confused them with the Spanish (Dunn and Kelley 1989:167):

> And when they saw that he [Columbus] was taking this route [east toward the land of the *Caribe*], he says that they could not talk, because the cannibals eat them, and that they are people very well armed. The Admiral says that well he believes there is something in what they say, but since they were armed they must be people of intelligence; and he believed that they must have captured some of them and because they did not return to their own lands they would say that they ate them. They believed the same thing about the Christians and about the Admiral when some Indians first saw them.

At this point in the voyage, Columbus was off the north coast of Cuba. He had changed direction and was sailing toward the east. Columbus does not seem to appreciate the geographical contradictions. He believed that the islands he reached were off the east coast of Asia and that the *Caniba* lived farther to the west. In contrast, the indigenous captives on board his ship were frightened because Columbus was sailing east toward the land of the *Caribes*.

When Columbus departed for Spain from the east coast of the Dominican Republic (January 16, 1493; Dunn and Kelley 1989:353), he was "told" that the (mythical) Carib Island was to be found to the east (Keegan 2007:41–42).

In his account of Macorix beliefs recorded in the Magdalena community in the Cibao valley on the north coast of Hispaniola circa 1494, the Jeronomite friar Ramón Pané confirmed Columbus's assertion that the Spanish were identified as *Caribes* and *Cannibales* (Arrom 1974; Keegan 1996a, 2007; Oliver 2009; Stevens-Arroyo 1988). Pané wrote (Bourne 1906:334):

> And they say that this cacique had affirmed that he had spoken with Giocauuaghama [Yocahuguamá, or Yocahu in the vernacular] who told him that whoever remained alive after his death should enjoy the rule over them only a short time, because they would see in their country a people clothed which was to rule them and to slay them and they would die of hunger. At first they thought these would be the Cannibales; but reflecting that they only plundered and fled they believed that it must be another people that the cemi spoke of. Wherefore they now believe that it was the Admiral and the people he brought with him.

A further complication in interpreting the *diario* is that Columbus did not understand what the native peoples were trying to communicate: "Also I do not know the language, and the people of these islands do not understand me nor do I, nor anyone else I have with me, them. And many time I understand one thing said by these Indians that I bring for another, its contrary; nor do I trust them much, because many times they have tried to flee" (Dunn and Kelley 1989:183, 217). This situation leaves Columbus's interpretations of events in question. It is only by deconstructing the *diario* that insights are gained. Deconstruction involves discounting his *interpretations* and emphasizing his *observations*. In other words, more weight should be given to passages where Columbus described what he saw, and less credence should be given to passages where he interprets what he was told. The same is true of other chroniclers.

Cannibal Raids or Indigenous Trade?

One example concerns whether native Bahamians ("Lucayans") with wounds are evidence for Carib raids (as Columbus reported, and modern scholars have accepted), or whether they reflect one outcome of indigenous exchange.

Specific passages in the *diario* are open to multiple interpretations. An excellent example is the first description of the individuals who met Columbus on the beach at Guanahaní (Dunn and Kelley 1989: 67):

> Their javelins are shafts without iron and some of them have at the end a fish tooth and others of other things. All of them alike are of good-sized stature and carry themselves well. I saw some who had marks of wounds on their bodies and I made signs to them asking what they were; and they showed me how people

from other islands nearby came there and tried to take them, and how they defended themselves; and I believed and believe that they come from tierra firme to take them captive.

These types of interactions were repeated on every island that Columbus visited in the Bahamas. The native peoples made presentations of valued commodities (e.g., cotton thread, parrots, and javelins) and received objects of European origin in return. Although the Spanish placed little value on the objects they offered (e.g., broken crockery, coins of small denomination), the relevant comparison is the value attributed to these exotic objects by the islanders (Keegan 2015).

Columbus's first encounters with the indigenous Lucayans reflect native exchange practices that were triggered upon the arrival of dugouts from other islands. Vessels arrived unannounced, and their attentions were unclear. Face-to-face encounters were necessary to evaluate intentions. Men carrying spears met the arriving party on the beach. Social identities were confirmed, and the tenor for interactions established. Each party then offered various goods, and these were either accepted or rejected in whole. The exchange could end peacefully with both parties satisfied, but unsatisfactory exchanges (as so valued by either party) could result in an immediate fight or delayed retaliation.

Our contention is that the wounds observed by Columbus reflect episodes of exchange within the islands that ended badly. Marauding Carib did not inflict the wounds (cf. Craton and Saunders 1992). The wounds were not inflicted by emissaries of the Grand Khan. In fact, no one would accept the ludicrous notion that Mongols sailing from China were raiding the Bahama Islands. Yet scholars have reached equally fanciful conclusions by trying to reconfigure Columbus's confused sense of political geography. We offer this example as a caveat with regard to all of the written accounts from this time.

Colonial Emergence

Beginning with Columbus's *diario*, a few Spaniards wrote reports that described interactions with indigenous individuals and communities. All of these reports derive from specific contexts; what Braudel (1997) would call *événements*. They offered their interpretations of indigenous practices, and provide accounts of colonial policies dictated by the Spanish Crown. The tendency has been to accept these descriptions as ethnography (Bourne 1906) or ethnohistory (Charlevoix and deFrancisco 1977; Cook and Borah 1971; Sauer 1966). Yet the chroniclers had no training in anthropology or history. They wrote to support political and religious goals, and their interpretations were based solely on their knowledge of medieval European culture. Whatever their motives, the chroniclers distilled indigenous practices into two distinct societies. This dichotomy was based on the relatively amicable interactions with Indios in the Greater Antilles and Bahamas, and hostile relations with the fierce Indios of the Lesser Antilles. Archaeologists have spent years trying to make this dichotomy work, but with little success (Keegan 1996a; Hofman et al. 2008).

The earliest modern use of the Spanish documents accepted their veracity (e.g., Oberg 1955; Lovén 1935; Rouse 1948a, 1948b). Even today, some scholars seek language hegemony by asserting that only native speakers can accurately interpret the documents. Yet the lexicon, spellings, and grammar of 16th-century Spanish and other European languages (including English) are substantially different from their modern counterparts. The documents may be historic accounts,[3] but they are *not* ethnohistory. Ethnohistory requires translation in terms of language, mindset, and context. Moreover, historic reports only become history through continued reinterpretation and the processes of deconstruction (Derrida 1967; Sued-Badillo 1992; Wilson 1993).

Beginning around the time of the Columbus Quincentenary, historians and archaeologists began to question seriously the motives and veracity of the Spanish chroniclers. Christopher Columbus is now viewed as greatly exaggerating his claims, especially the presence of gold and the use of indigenous people as slaves, to promote the importance of his discoveries. "To the Spanish humanist, Ramón Iglesia, Columbus seemed to be writing the promotion literature of a tourist board, which he did with Italian exuberance" (Sauer 1966:29). His son Ferdinand further promoted Columbus's discoveries to maintain the family's legacy and concessions from the Spanish Crown (Keen 1959). The Spanish sovereigns had named Columbus "Admiral of the Ocean Sea."[4] He was entitled to 10% of the profits from all voyages to the Americas and 25% of the profits from expeditions that he directed. He was also awarded the Duchy of Veragua (Panama) and the Marquesas of Jamaica. The Spanish Crown later largely ignored these concessions, however, and stripped the family of its titles and entitlements. Columbus reportedly died in poverty on May 20, 1506.

Gonzalo Fernández de Oviedo y Valdés (1959; MacNutt 1912) arrived in the islands well after the decimation of the Indios. His major contribution is an accounting of the natural history of the islands, which provides some insights into economic activities and the resources that were exploited at the time (Keegan and Carlson 2008). Bartolomé de las Casas, his contemporary, disputes some of Oviedo's observations and interpretations (Keegan 2007). Caution must also be used when using Oviedo y Valdés because he does not always distinguish observations from rumors. He also gives the impression that bananas were native to the islands, when in fact they were introduced by Europeans just prior to his arrival (Keegan and Carlson 208).

Pedro Mártir de Anglería (a.k.a. Pedro Martyr D'Anghiera, or Peter Martyr) never visited the Caribbean, but he collected stories from returning sailors with the goal of defending the Crown's interests. Martyr's personal

---

[3] We use the term "historic" to mean only "recorded at the time."

[4] At this time, "Admiral" meant only "to command," and was not used to describe someone who commanded a fleet of ships.

motives aside (i.e., defender of the Crown), what is missing from historical interpretations of his *De Orbo Nova* is any consideration of its multicultural influences. Spanish expeditions to the Americas were crewed by individuals from across Europe (e.g., Spaniards, Portuguese, Italians, Irish, Englishmen, Frenchmen, and even Africans). Furthermore, feudal kingdoms in Spain had only recently been united under the banners of Castile and León. The stories recorded by Martyr were influenced by the diverse experiences and perspectives of the sailors he interviewed and that he selectively included in his reports.

Sometime around 1496 or 1497, Columbus charged the Jeronomite friar Ramón Pané with recording indigenous beliefs in a village located close to his colony at La Isabela. Pané accomplished this in Macorix territory, where the indigenous community spoke a distinct language (Arrom 1974; Granberry 2013; Keegan 2007; Stevens-Arroyo 1988; Oliver 2009). Following his initial report, Columbus asked Pané "to go and live with another leading cacique, named Guarionex, the lord of many people, since the language of these folks [Taíno] was understood throughout the land." Pané replied: "Lord [Christopher Columbus], how is it that your Lordship wishes that I go live with Guarionex without knowing any language other than that of Macoris?" (Stevens-Arroyo 1988:76). It is not certain that the beliefs Pané recorded can be generalized beyond the relatively small Macorix territory. Furthermore, most scholars have failed to recognize the strong Catholic influences in his account. For example, the Macorix origin myth mirrors the story of Jesus. The father (without a name) sacrifices his son (Yayael), and the son's bones are then transformed into fish, which became the food that nourishes the body and soul (cf. Transubstantiation of the Eucharist). He also recorded only twelve deities (like the twelve Apostles?), with twelve one of the magical numbers of Catholic numerology (Keegan 2007).

Finally, Bartolomé de las Casas arrived in the islands in 1502. He originally was part of the conquest of Cuba, for which he was rewarded with an *encomienda* called La Loma del Convento on the south coast of Cuba (Knight 2010). Las Casas wrote extensively about indigenous practices, but these accounts were not committed to paper until five decades later (Las Casas 1951, 1997; Tyler 1988). Las Casas had long since abandoned his *encomienda*, and proclaimed himself "Defender of the Indians." He opposed the cruel treatment of the Indios that he observed at the hands of his compatriots. His writings depict what would later be called the "noble savage."

Those authors provide the earliest written records of the encounter. The documents are fraught with potential pitfalls, and they cannot be understood without vetting, cross-referencing, transcription, translation, and other methods of deconstruction (Varela 1984). The descriptions of particular behaviors (e.g., farming, hunting, food preparation, fishing practices, tools, burial practices, etc.) appear to be innocuous (Lovén [1935] provides the most complete review in English), but even these were recorded at specific times and in particular locations. Discussions of social and political organization and religious beliefs are colored by interpretations offered from a late-medieval Spanish frame of reference.

The indigenous inhabitants of the Greater Antilles referred to themselves by local place names (e.g., Borinquen or Boriken in western Puerto Rico). They did not have a name that encompassed the entire region. Based on the assertion that they all spoke one language (Las Casas 1951), anthropologists initially called them "Island Arawak" because they lived on islands and spoke an Arawak language (Brinton 1871; Granberry 2013). The name "Taíno" was first suggested in the mid–nineteenth century (Rafinesque 1836). It continued to be used by European and Hispanic scholars, but it did not achieve widespread use by American anthropologists until the 1980s (Rouse 1992). "Taíno" glosses as " 'The Good Ones' or 'The Good People' (*taí*– 'good' + *no* a pluralizing suffix)" (Granberry 2013:63).

Rouse (1986, 1992) recognized three different but related geographical territories. He classified the inhabitants of Hispaniola, Puerto Rico, and eastern Cuba as "Classic Taíno"; those of Jamaica and central Cuba as "Western Taíno"; and those living in the Virgin Islands and northern Lesser Antilles as "Eastern Taíno." A related effort to include the Bahamas in this "ethnic geography" promoted the name "Lucayan Taíno" for the inhabitants of the Bahama archipelago (Keegan and Maclachlan 1989:613). Having achieved official recognition through christening, the next step was to define the characteristics that could be associated with the name. The concept of *Taíno Culture* was crafted in four ways. First, there are the above-mentioned descriptions of indigenous practices, which emphasize similarities with and differences from the European homeland. These accounts have been used to characterize practices throughout the islands, based on the assertion by Las Casas (1951) that all indigenous communities throughout the Greater Antilles and Bahamas were essentially the same.

Second, "prehistorians" (Rouse 1972) employed an evolutionary framework to chart culture history and establish culture-area boundaries (Siegel 2013). Taíno Culture was the highest level of sociopolitical development; the subtext being that this was the goal that all of the inhabitants of the Caribbean sought to attain (e.g., Siegel 2010). Third, archaeologists have documented and excavated early colonial settlements to obtain a better understanding of practices in specific contexts, but with a particular focus on "Spanish" colonial practices (e.g., Deagan 1987, 1989, 1995; Deagan and Cruxent 2002).[5] The indigenous

---

[5] We are uncomfortable with the conventional practice of calling these initial encounters and written records "Spanish." The marriage of Ferdinand II and Isabella I united the feudal kingdoms of Aragon and Castile in 1474 and created a confederacy that did not, however, achieve widespread political hegemony until Charles V in 1519 with the creation of the Holy Roman Empire. When Columbus departed from Cadíz on his first voyage, the Muslim Moors had just been expelled from Granada, and heretics (particularly Jews) may have been on other vessels in the harbor awaiting deportation (Sale 1990). This was a period of turmoil on the Iberian peninsula. It is highly unlikely that anyone at this time considered themselves "Spanish."

perspective is a focus of the Nexus 1492 project, especially the intercultural dynamics (Hofman et al. 2014).

Finally, nativist revivals are redefining "Taíno" to meet modern political agendas (Laguer Diaz 2013). A major objective is to gain U.S. federal recognition of indigenous status. The driving force behind "Nuevo Taíno" comes from Puerto Ricans who currently live in the New York metropolitan area. Individuals still living in Puerto Rico, along with displaced Puerto Ricans (e.g., Castanha 2011), support the modern embellishment of indigenous origins. Yet we have shown that the indigenous population of Puerto Rico was never "Taíno" (Chapter 4). Precolonial Puerto Rican societies developed along unique historical trajectories that were truncated by incursions from indigenous communities represented by the Boca Chica style pottery and other ritual artifacts, which originated in the Dominican Republic (Curet 2003; Oliver 2009). Puerto Rico is better described as a Dominican colony at the time the first voyages arrived from Spain. As with all colonies, "Taíno" influences were restricted to a few isolated pockets.

Archaeologists today recognize that the name "Taíno" is a classification device that has multiple meanings at multiple scales (Curet 2014). Some have gone as far as to suggest that it be replaced with the notion of "Taínoness." We no longer consider this name an appropriate moniker. Nevertheless, it is currently impossible to erase the name "Classic Taíno" because it is so ingrained in the literature.

What follows are some of the details gleaned from the old documents (also see Bercht et al. 1997; Keegan 2013; Kerchache 1994; Lovén 1935; Rouse 1948a, 1992; Sauer 1966; Wilson 1990, 2007). These general descriptions have been used to construct a "generic Taíno," in which observed practices reported for one location are generalized to stereotype indigenous practices throughout the islands. We offer these general observations as points of departure, rather than points of arrival. In other words, the documents provide a basis for interpretation, but only when they are seen in the context of historical contingencies.

Language

Language may be the one common element shared by societies in the Greater Antilles (Granberry 2013). Although Las Casas reported that there were three mutually unintelligible languages on Hispaniola (a common language, Macorix, and Ciguayo), he also indicated that what we call "Taíno" was a *lingua franca* that was understood by all (Granberry and Vescelius 2004). Several dictionaries have been compiled by extracting indigenous terms from the documents (Granberry and Vescelius 2004; Hernández Aquino 1977; Miner Solá 2002). These words have been used to interpret indigenous toponyms (Granberry 1991) and to reconstruct precolonial natural history (Keegan and Carlson 2008). Unfortunately, there are too few words for more comprehensive linguistic studies such as glottochronology (cf. Noble 1965).

Archaeological Research

Most the Spanish accounts are from Hispaniola and Cuba. Yet surprisingly few large-scale, systematic, archaeological excavations have been undertaken at early colonial sites on these islands (Figure 8.1). The most comprehensive are Kathleen Deagan's long-term projects at En Bas Saline, Haiti (Deagan 1987, 1989, 2004); Puerto Real, Haiti (Deagan 1995; Reitz 1990); and La Isabela, Dominican Republic (Deagan and Cruxent 2002); and, more recently, Hofman and Hoogland's research at El Cabo in the eastern Dominican Republic (Hofman et al. 2014; Samson 2010, 2013), and at El Flaco in the northwestern Dominican Republic (Hofman and Hoogland 2015b). In addition, Dominican archaeologists have identified, mapped, and test-excavated a substantial number of sites from this time period (Veloz Maggiolo 1993); and research by Cuban archaeologists at El Chorro de Maíta is documenting early colonial practices (Hofman et al. 2014; Valcárcel Rojas 2012, 2016; Valcárcel Rojas et al. 2012).

Written accounts contributed to a mindscape that suggested we knew everything we needed to know about the precolonial societies. There was no real interest in their archaeology (to be fair, this was complicated by the politics of Cuba, Haiti, and the Dominican Republic). Even the most intensive and systematic excavation offered limited interpretation of the indigenous component (Deagan 1987). Deagan's research focused almost entirely on the "Spanish"

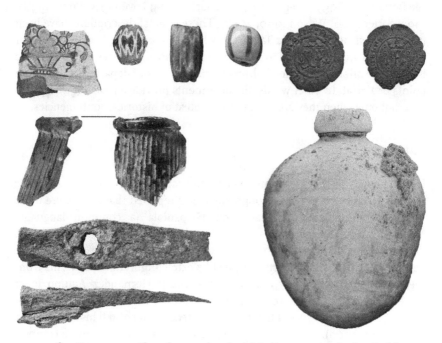

FIGURE 8.1 European artifacts from early colonial indigenous sites in the Caribbean. Not to scale (photos by Corinne Hofman and Menno Hoogland).

component (also see Cusick 1991, 1998, 2000). The result is that we know very little about the archaeology in the places where the majority of the Spanish observations were recorded (Guarch Delmonte 1972a, 1972b; Keegan 2007; Persons 2013).

It is widely accepted that the "Classic Taíno" manufactured Chicoid series pottery (Chapter 4). This distinctive series originated in the eastern Dominican Republic about AD 1000, and then spread east to Puerto Rico and west through Hispaniola and into eastern Cuba (Rouse 1992; see Guarch Delmonte 1972a, 1972b; Persons 2013) (see Figure 8.2).

Descriptions of artifacts and their uses have been instrumental in archaeological interpretations, and many of these are discussed in other chapters. A significant aspect of material culture studies has involved museum curation, exhibits, and public outreach. Catalogs from recent major exhibitions provide outstanding photographs, descriptions, and accompanying texts (Bercht et al. 1997; Kerchache 1994; Milanich and Milbrath 1989). However, archaeological interpretations are complicated by the significant number of local industries producing modern interpretations. These modern objects are sometimes sold as reproductions, but more often they are marketed as authentic ("faux Taíno").

FIGURE 8.2 Ritual artifacts from the Dominican Republic associated with "Taíno". Not to scale (photos by Corinne Hofman and Menno Hoogland)

Indigenous Settlements

According to surviving documents, the indigenous communities were predominantly living in large villages with houses arranged around a central plaza, although some villages were described as having a grid system of streets. It was reported that the *cacique's* house was located in the center of the plaza, or at the entrance to the village adjacent to the main road. Las Casas (1951) describes a village near the modern city of Higüey (Dominican Republic) with a crossroads that was used to stage mock battles. Early European roads followed the precolonial routes that connected large villages in Hispaniola (Moore 1998). Some of these villages reportedly had as many as 3,000 inhabitants and were located at some distance from the coast. The houses reportedly were large, circular constructions of pole and thatch with high-pitched roofs (*caneye*), although there also were octagonal and rectangular structures (*bohío*) (Oviedo y Valdés 1959; Rouse 1992; Sauer 1966). Columbus also described small fishing communities along the coast of Cuba (Dunn and Kelley 1989). The documents indicate that there were special-purpose sites in addition to large villages.

Subsistence

The primary subsistence activity was agriculture. Farmers cultivated "house gardens" (adjacent to their houses), in which they planted as many as eighty different herbs, spices (e.g., chili peppers), medicinal plants (e.g., tobacco), fish poison, thatch, and many other crops that were used in small quantities (Keegan 2000; Newsom 1993; Newsom and Wing 2004; Petersen 1997). More intensive cultivations were made at some distance from the village in large fields (*conucos*) that included permanent mounds (*montones*) on which varieties of manioc (*casabi*), sweet potato (*aje*), maize (*maíz*), zamia (*guáyiga*), fruit trees (e.g., *guayaba, mamey, papaya*), and other plants were cultivated. There is some suggestion that terracing and irrigation were practiced in particular locations (Ortiz Aguilú et al. 1991). The documents largely ignore the cultivation of maize (Figueredo 2015; Keegan 1987), but recent archaeobotanical analysis of phytoliths and starch grains suggests that it was an important cultigen (Berman and Pearsall 2008; Berman et al. 2012; Pagán-Jiménez 2013).

Fish were the main source of animal protein. At least twenty different fish species were named in the documents. A wide variety of marine and freshwater species were captured using several different techniques, including bow-and-arrow, hook-and-line, spears, poison, nets, weirs, traps, and even remora (*pez reverso*)[6] (deFrance 2013; Keegan 1986b; Keegan and Carlson 2008; Price

---

[6] Remora belong to the Echeneidae Family. They have a sucker plate on their head that is used to attach themselves to large fishes, sharks, and sea turtles. Oviedo y Valdés reported that a line was attached to the tail of a remora, and when the fish attached itself to a larger animal, they would reel it in (Keegan and Carlson 2008).

1966; Wing and Reitz 1982). Sea turtles, manatees, cetaceans (porpoises and whales), and sharks (whose teeth were used as tools and vertebrae in necklaces) also were captured. An astonishing number of marine invertebrates were exploited. The most important was the queen conch (*cobo*). Conchs and other marine invertebrates also were used for the manufacture of a wide variety of tools and jewelry (Jones O'Day and Keegan 2001). The islands have a depauperate terrestrial fauna. Nevertheless, a cat-sized rodent (*hutía*) and guinea pigs were consumed (and possibly domesticated), and iguanas were a favored food. Oviedo y Valdés (1959) reported that these terrestrial animals were reserved for the chiefs (*caciques*). Columbus encountered a hunting party in Guantánamo Bay (Cuba) that was capturing and smoking iguanas and fish in preparation for a feast that was going to be hosted by their *cacique* (Morison 1942; Sara and Keegan 2004). One interpretation is that only the *caciques* consumed hutía and iguana (Jones O'Day 2002), but it is more likely that *caciques* only controlled the distribution of these animals during feasts (Keegan 2007).

Meats were preserved for later consumption by smoking (a lattice of green branches over a fire, *barbacoa*), and salting (Keegan 2007; Morsink 2012). An important method of cooking may have been the pepper pot (*casiripe*), in which meats and vegetables were cooked in large pots over a low fire and then eaten with cassava bread. The grating, squeezing, drying, and baking of cassava flour on a flat clay griddle (*burén*) was considered the major food production activity, and cassava bread replaced hardtack in the islands as sustenance for Spanish voyages.

Social Organization

The importance of social organization has been emphasized (Curet 2002, 2003; Ensor 2003, 2013; Keegan 2007; Keegan and Maclachlan 1989; Keegan et al. 1998). This focus was stimulated by the discovery that over 90% of the village and hamlet site types in the Bahama archipelago occur in pairs (Berman et al. 2013; Keegan and Maclachlan 1989; and see Rouse 1942 for paired sites in Cuba). Combining settlement-pattern structure, Spanish reports for Hispaniola and Cuba (whence the inhabitants of the Bahamas originated), and controlled cross-cultural comparisons, Keegan and Maclachlan (1989) argued that the "Taíno" of Hispaniola practiced forms of matrilineal descent, with initial matrilocal residence shifting to avunculocal residence, at least among the elites (*Nitaíno*). Their objective was to identify elements of social organization that could be subjected to archaeological scrutiny. This research emphasized that all communities are socially organized, and that group relations structure individual behavior (agency) in meaningful ways.

This perspective has been criticized because it is difficult to prove that paired sites were contemporaneous (Keegan 2007), and more general concerns regarding "kinship" studies (Ensor 2013). Critics instead promote a focus that defines social organization as a form of classification and genealogical (genetic) heritage. This perception reflects their confusion of kinship (i.e., the language of relationships) and social organization, which is reflected in daily and multigenerational practices (e.g., Joyce and Gillespie 2000; Morsink 2013; Samson 2013). In a Caribbean context, Curet (2002) argues that Spanish descriptions of chiefly succession are too variable to identify a particular form of chiefly succession; a view that is countered by Keegan (2006).

Curet's (2003) argument is based on the lack of conformity between Spanish descriptions from Hispaniola and archaeological research in Puerto Rico. Although he argues against the importance of social relations (Curet and Oliver 1998), he concedes: "Hispaniolan and Puerto Rican polities used significantly different ideological foundations, a reflection of differences in the nature of the political structure and organizations" (Curet 2003:19); and "Judging from the striking differences mentioned, they likely developed from distinct types of ancestral societies, and/or through different and divergent historical processes" (Curet 2003:20). In sum, there probably was not one expression, but rather diverse expressions. Nevertheless, the identification of matrilineal descent and matrilocal/avunculocal residence practices provide significant insights into how these societies were organized.

Cacicazgos *(Chiefdoms)*

In the course of the development of neo-evolutionary studies in archaeology, "chiefdoms" were highlighted in the 1980s as the most widespread expression of social formations prior to the advent of "states" (Earle 1987, 2011; Johnson and Earle 1987; Pauketat 2007; Service 1975). The *cacicazgo* was the first chiefdom identified in the Americas (Oberg 1955), and it thus attracts attention as a disciplinary legacy (Redmond and Spencer 1994). On Hispaniola, *cacicazgos* were regionally integrated social and economic territories. The documents suggest a three-tiered hierarchy composed of paramount *caciques* (*matunherí*) who ruled large territories, regional *caciques* who ruled a number of villages, and village headmen.

The indigenous political organization was described in detail, especially with regard to how it differed from European polities. However, there has been some confusion because the written accounts were based on Spanish concepts (e.g., Curet 2002, 2003). Hispaniola was described as a "giant beast" divided into five major provinces, with each divided in two. The "head" was to the east (rising sun) and the "anus" to the west (Harris 1994). These provinces (*cacicazgos*) were ruled by chiefs (*caciques*), who reportedly had power of life and death over their followers (Keegan 2007). The identification of *caciques* was crucial for the Spanish Conquest. It allowed a small group of invaders to isolate a few individuals who could extract tribute for the Spanish from their followers, and to organize *encomiendas*. At the time of the Spanish Conquest, two *caciques* (Caonabó and Behecchio), allied through marriage, are reported to have been paramount *caciques* (*matunherí*) who together ruled most of Hispaniola (Keegan

2007). In opposition to the *cacique* was the *behique*, a shaman or healer who communicated with the spirits through drug-induced trances (*cohoba*), conducted healing ceremonies, and represented the anti-cultural (supernatural) "Other." It has been suggested that *behiques* also served as leaders. However, shamans typically reinforce their status by distancing themselves from other people and cultural norms.

Caribbean chiefdoms have been addressed from four perspectives. Keegan and colleagues employed cross-cultural evidence to examine the social transformations that would account for the sociopolitical organization described by the Spanish (Ensor 2013; Keegan, 1997b, 2007; Keegan et al. 1998). Although they use the term "chiefdom," their concern is with the social construction of polities. Second, Deagan has approached the issue from a historical perspective by addressing the interactions between the Spanish and indigenous communities in Hispaniola (Deagan 2010; Deagan and Cruxent 2002). Third, Crock (2000), Hofman (Hofman et al. 2007), and Keegan (2007) all emphasize mobility, exchange, and control of resources on islands that exhibit organizational complexity, but that otherwise would be considered peripheral. Finally, archaeologists working in Puerto Rico have emphasized material correlates of chiefdoms (e.g., D'Altroy and Earle 1985; Johnson and Earle 1987) to propose an evolutionary sequence for the development of hierarchy (social inequalities) and the rise of chiefdoms (Curet and Stringer 2010; Siegel 2010).

Puerto Rico is unique in the widespread occurrence of stone-lined plazas beginning around AD 900. The largest occur in two complexes that are not associated with domestic structures (i.e., Tibes and Caguana), while smaller courts are found within habitation sites (Torres 2013). The majority of the structures are rectangular, which has led to their association with the soccerlike game (*batey*) described by the Spanish, although there are some circular stone-lined courts, and a star-shaped court at Tibes. It has been suggested that stone-lined courts reflect contacts with Central America that extend back at least 1,000 years (Rodríguez Ramos 2013; Wilson 2007).

One interpretation is that the two main ceremonial centers reflect the monumental architecture expected for chiefdom-level societies (Curet and Oliver 1998; Curet and Stringer 2010; Oliver 2009; Rouse 1992; Siegel 2010). There are several problems with this interpretation (Chapter 5). First, these structures involve the arrangement of stones in a manner that does not require substantial labor, and thus are not "monumental" (Torres et al. 2014). Second, the largest occur in isolated locations between communities, which is more similar to the neutral tribal meeting/battle grounds in highland New Guinea (Rubel and Rosman 1978). Third, smaller versions of these courts occur within villages where they reflect an opposition that is more parsimoniously interpreted as the dialectic between ancestors and affines (Helms 1998), versus the distinction between elites and commoners. Finally, these stone-courts, plazas, or ball courts are substantially different from those observed in Hispaniola and Cuba in terms of their size and layout (Wilson 2007) where the majority of the Spanish descriptions were recorded.

Because these structures appear centuries prior to the generally accepted 13th-century date for the earliest expression of "Taíno" culture, it is understandable that they would be viewed as instrumental in the evolutionary trajectory (Siegel 2010). In contrast, we here propose that Boca Chica pottery originated in the eastern Dominican Republic and spread into Puerto Rico through the incorporation of the inhabitants of this island whose local practices were encapsulated in a wider social formation. This is evident in the relatively sparse frequency of Chicoid pottery at most of these sites. The broader issue is whether classifying such structures as evidence for chiefdoms advances our understanding (Pauketat 2007; Torres 2013).

Mythology and Religion

There is one account of indigenous mythology and religion that was collected by Friar Ramón Pané in 1494 among the Macorix of northern Hispaniola. It is not possible to discuss his report in detail here (Arrom 1974; Stevens-Arroyo 1988). It is worth noting that this account has been used to interpret the indigenous beliefs (Arrobui 1975; Oliver 2009) and the evolution of these beliefs from a South American source. Yet, because this is the only contemporary account of native religion, it is assumed that it accurately reflects "Taíno" beliefs, and by extension, their supposedly Saladoid predecessors (Siegel 2010).

A related effort to justify the unilinear development and singular expression of indigenous chiefdoms has adopted an essentialist paradigm that uses mythology/religion as the most encompassing definition of "culture." As with language, it has been assumed that communities that share similar beliefs or worldviews can be classified as belonging to one culture. This perspective appeals to a psychic unity, a shared Pan-Amazonian worldview, to establish the unification of communities living at the northern limits of the Caribbean Sea, and (perhaps) genetically related (Martínez-Cruzado 2013) peoples living in lowland South America, from whom they are separated by more than 2,500 years (cf. Heckenberger 2005; Siegel 2010). History is thus compressed into a singular moment of structuralist conformity (Lévi-Strauss 1963).

Based on the Pané account, the Macorix had both mythological origins and a pantheon that directly affected their daily life. Their origins myths are associated with two caves in the central Dominican Republic: *Cacibajagua*, whence the "People" came, and *Amayaúna*, the cave of "no importance" from which everyone else ("Others") originated (Stevens-Arroyo 1988). The identification of caves as the portals to the Otherworld accounts for the decoration of caves with pictographs and petroglyphs as well as the deposit of ritual artifacts (e.g., wooden platters, *duhos*), and human burials.

The supernatural control of their daily existence was in the hands of *cemís*, who embodied a balance between good and ill. For example, too little rainfall and the crops would wither, but too much rainfall (*huracán*) and the crops would rot. Survival depended on a delicate balance of these dual forces. José

Oliver (2009) provides an excellent discussion of *cemíism* (translated as "sweetness"), but he does so by using Puerto Rican archaeology and Hispaniolan ethnohistory. As he acknowledges, the physical manifestations of *cemís* in Puerto Rico are distinct from those recovered from Hispaniola (except, perhaps, in the southeastern Dominican Republic). The term *cemí* is used to describe both the spirits and their physical manifestations as idols made from wood, bone, pottery, shell, cotton, etc. (Bercht et al. 1997; Kerchache 1994).

When we consider the distribution of three-pointed stones, stone collars, wooden seats (*duhos*), shell masks (*guaízas*), ball courts (*bateys*), stone-lined courts, circular plazas, houses, settlement organization, burial practices, and so forth, we observe significant differences across the Caribbean (e.g., McGinnis 1997; Ostapkowicz 1998, 2015; Walker 1993, 1997). Three-pointed stones, elbow stones, and stone collars are found primarily in the eastern Dominican Republic and Puerto Rico, although the first, in small number, have been found as far south as Trinidad. Wooden stools are found primarily in the Greater Antilles and Bahamas. They are considered to be the seats of chiefs, which makes their high incidence in the Bahamas puzzling (Ostapkowicz 2015). Roe (1997) notes that wooden statues and pottery figurines give the impression of an individual who is dying, or "wasting away," which suggests that death is the pathway to communication with the spirits. The association of death with the physical body may account for the production of human bone pectorals in the Dominican Republic (Roe 1991).

Oliver (2009) sets the agenda by recognizing that, to appropriately use Spanish descriptions, we need more empirical, archaeological evidence to define the relationships between the indigenous communities of Hispaniola and those of Puerto Rico (Curet 2003; Sinelli 2013). Furthermore, the key question is: To what degree does mythology, and our *etic* interpretations of *emic* beliefs, structure daily practice? One of the most comprehensive studies of Amazonian mythology demonstrated that mythology is dynamic and continuously open to reinterpretations and expressions (Roe 1982); the same symbols have different meanings in different contexts. Ongoing research is focused on distinguishing these contexts.

Demography

The total population at the time of the European encounters is the subject of substantial debate. Estimates for Hispaniola range from 60,000 to 14 million inhabitants (Cook and Borah 1971; Henige 1978; Keegan 1992a, 1992b; Rosenblatt 1976; Wilson 1990), and it is quite possible that there were one million individuals living on the island (Keegan 2007). The linchpin is the census of Indios on Hispaniola that supposedly was taken in 1496 (Cook and Borah 1971). This *repartimiento* reported 1,200,000 Indios on Hispaniola. However, it is not certain that such a census was taken, who was counted (i.e., only men above the age of fifteen who could be pressed into labor), and whether the census included the entire island, because the few European colonial settlements effectively controlled only a small portion across the center of the island at this time. Moreover, the degree to which statistical manipulations of demographic tendencies accurately reflect population trends has been questioned (i.e., what David Henige [1978] called "History as Higher Mathematics"; cf. Zambardino 1978). Here again, the documentary evidence is open to interpretation, manipulation, and debate.

It is reported that there was widespread famine and population decline on Hispaniola that began in 1496 (Cook and Borah 1971; Wilson 1990). European diseases, to which the indigenous populations lacked immunity, contributed to the disruption of food production. Swine flu may have been the main pathogen. Pigs were introduced on Columbus's second voyage in 1493, and as many as one-half of the more than 1,500 men on this expedition fell ill, and many of them died (Morison 1942). Smallpox also has been implicated, and this disease did have a devastating effect on Native American populations. However, the smallpox pandemic did not begin until 1517. Some historians absolve Columbus of responsibility for the decimation of the indigenous population because he unwittingly introduced diseases for which there were no local immunities; and the germ theory of disease transmission would not exist for another 350 years. Nevertheless, harsh treatment, outright brutality, forced labor and tribute payments, suppression of religious beliefs, imposition of European monogamy (*contra* indigenous practice in which *caciques* had multiple "wives" in order to cement social and political relations with multiple communities), and enslavement conducted in the name of Christian conversion, all contributed to the decimation of indigenous communities (see Las Casas 1552; Valcárcel Rojas 2016).

In the recent past, some scholars concluded that the indigenous population was driven to extinction. However, despite European efforts to suppress indigenous practices and beliefs, the enslavement of entire communities, and the devastating effects of introduced diseases, some individuals escaped to remote locations on many of the islands. During the early colonial period, the Spanish held only tenuous control over relatively small areas. The communities established by these "Maroons" were later joined by escaped slaves (Agorsah 1994; La Rosa Corzo 2003, 2005, 2010). Kofi Agorsah (2013) has called the Maroons the original "freedom fighters." The remnants of their communities only recently have received archaeological attention, so their stories are incompletely known. Nevertheless, some Maroon communities have survived to the present. The same is true for descendants of the Kalinago, who have continuously maintained independent enclaves in Central America (called Garifuna) and Dominica.

Finally, the analysis of mitochondrial DNA (mtDNA) from modern individuals with a Caribbean ancestry has revealed a high incidence (perhaps as high as 60%) of Native American mtDNA haplogroups (Martínez-Cruzado 2010, 2013). The evidence suggests that many individuals today are genetically descended from an indigenous woman, because mtDNA is transmitted only through the mother's line. One complication is that the Spanish began to import enslaved Indios from smaller neighboring islands and the mainland within a decade of their arrival (Granberry 1980–1981). The idea that indigenous societies were driven to extinction is a myth.

Early Colonial European Chroniclers and the French Missionaries

The Lesser Antilles first became known to Europeans through Columbus's conversations with the indigenous populations of the Greater Antilles (Allaire 2013; Curet 2005; Oliver 2009; Petitjean Roget 2015; Rouse 1992). They told Columbus of their fear of the man-eating Carib allegedly living to the southeast and continually raiding their settlements (Hofman et al. 2008; Oliver 2009; Petitjean Roget 2015). This fueled prejudice by the Europeans, who held misconceptions about distant, unfamiliar peoples based on preconceived (late-medieval) ideas about a "fantastic insular world" (Hulme 1986; Milbrath 1989; Rainbird 1999). Spain had designs mainly on the Greater Antilles, considering the Lesser Antilles initially a nuisance and later as a source of slaves. The Spaniards' lack of interest in the *islas inútiles* and their subsequent failed ventures at settlement allowed other European nations to colonize the Lesser Antilles.

Some 150 years passed before European nations started to occupy the Lesser Antilles despite fierce indigenous resistance from the Carib or Kalinago, who claimed origin from the South American mainland and asserted themselves aggressively—particularly between Tobago and St. Kitts (Allaire 1977, 2013; Boomert 1986, 1995; Figueredo 1974 ; Sued-Badillo 1995; Whitehead 1995:105). A pattern of exchange developed in the late 16th century between European nations and the Carib that would culminate in the cultivation of tobacco by the latter for sale to passing traders. Carib society was characterized by considerable local autonomy and several levels of political authority. Early documents refer to Carib villages as comprising a series of houses, typically a men's house and a number of family dwellings (e.g., Breton 1665/1666, 1978; Hofman et al. 2015). Eighteenth-century sources are testimony to European encroachment and the demise of the indigenous population, describing hamlets or single households dispersed across the landscape (Labat 1722). By this time, a major demographic decline had reduced the Carib presence in the islands dramatically. Carib populations of St. Kitts, Guadeloupe, and Martinique were no longer existing or were completely marginalized. Meanwhile, Carib communities on other islands were absorbing an increasing number of escaped African slaves, leading to the rise of a Black Carib ethnic identity, alongside the communities that were purely Kalinago. After several wars with the English, the Black Carib were deported from St. Vincent to Central America in 1797, where they are still known as Garifuna (Gonzalez 1988). Descendants of the Carib survive to this day throughout the Lesser Antilles, notably on Dominica, St. Vincent and Trinidad (Bommert 2016; Hofman and Hoogland 2012).

One hundred and fifty years of colonialism undoubtedly changed the structure of Lesser Antillean society completely. The impact upon indigenous island culture by indigenous communities from South America and the Greater Antilles, and later by Africans and Europeans, cannot be underestimated (Sued Badillo 2003; Reid 2009; Whitehead 1995). A fascinating corpus of early colonial documents from the late 15th to early 18th centuries has been left by European chroniclers; among them, French missionaries who provide detailed descriptions of Carib culture and society (e.g., Anonyme de Carpentras 2002; Breton 1665/1666, 1978; Chanca 1988; Coppier 1645; De Laet 1931–37; Du Tertre 1667–1671; Labat 1722; Nicholl 1605; Rochefort 1665). The extraction of ethnographic information on Carib society that is compatible with the archaeological data is extremely interesting and involves data on village locations and layouts, environmental settings, subsistence adaptations, sociopolitical organization, exchange, warfare, religious beliefs, crafts, and lore. Caribbean archaeologists have used this information disparately and non-recursively over the past decades.

Kaleidoscope: The Final Turn

The final image of Caribbean archaeology typically is called Taíno and Carib and still taught in schools across the islands. Although these often are portrayed as fossilized images, they are in fact reflections of continuously moving parts. The perspective one obtains is based on the parameters used to define our perceptions. Starting with European descriptions, we create imaginations that appear in ways that often are different from those created when starting from archaeology (Curet 2014; Wilson 2007). The conclusions of different historians and different archaeologists often vary in significant ways. The challenge is to assemble diverse data and perspectives in logical frameworks that contribute to our understanding of Caribbean life.

We recognize that the use of ceramic series as a proxy for cultural identities raises problems. Rouse (1992) viewed the various styles, subseries, and series as following a single line of development, and this perspective served as a critical method for assembling cultural order. As a natural progression, more recent studies have identified significant differences within and between these categories that suggest that pottery *series* reflect completely distinct ceramic traditions. Saladoid, Ostionoid, Meillacoid, Chicoid, and Palmetto ware are, at different times, contemporaneous. They reflect the specific selections of technology and style, and thus approximate one perception of local and regional identities. These styles maintain their identity even under situations of blending, sharing, and copying. In this regard, they reflect the processes of transculturation more so than earlier themes of replacement and acculturation (Dominguez 1978). Because these pottery series were based on different traditions, we need to ask what other aspects of their cultural and social practices also were different. Our point is that Taíno and Carib cannot be viewed as singular expressions. Caribbean social formations were assembled through the integration of previously distinct, albeit interacting, communities.

Regional transformations included various changes in technological and economic practices, but the most significant were social transformations. For example, new economies and social formations spread rapidly across the islands in the company of Ostionoid and Meillacoid pottery. The inhabitants of the eastern Dominican Republic lived in an arid and semi-marginal location relative to their neighbors, yet they managed to establish some of the largest villages and an elaborate iconography. The eastern Dominican Republic was the interface between Hispaniola Meillacoid and Puerto Rican Ostionoid. The final precolonial social formation emerged on the Mona Passage, where these two distinct societies collided. In other words, communities in the eastern Dominican Republic expanded their opportunities by co-opting the territory of their neighbors through warfare, exchange, and marriage, strategies that Heckenberger (2002, 2005, 2013) suggests comprised a pan-Arawak *ethos*.

A final question is, to what degree can a pan-Arawak ethos be applied more generally to the Caribbean? Encompassed in that question is the degree to which particular practices described by the Spanish can be taken as representative of a singular Antillean culture. There are environmental differences and local dietary practices across the region, but neither of these is sufficient to account for the widely shared cultural practices. The bottom line is: How is the chaos of daily life, ecology and economy, politics and social organization structured to create a sense of community?

The differences we observe in "Taíno" result from the adoption or imposition of a new level of social hierarchy on existing cultural practices. Puerto Rican societies maintained their unique characteristics based on Saladoid and Archaic Age foundations, while in Hispaniola and Cuba, they expressed their Meillacoid and Archaic Age roots. In conclusion, there was no "Taíno." We can highlight particular belief systems and different material expressions isolated in space and time, but the social formations incorporated distinct communities and allowed them to maintain their distinctiveness, while producing regional political economies. Caribbean societies developed specific adaptations to particular environments and social circumstances. Different communities and societies had different historical trajectories and distinct material expressions. In addition, they were in contact with the surrounding mainland and other islands, with which they exchanged materials, people, and ideas. Our goal has been to highlight and to sort through the diverse expressions that define their identities. This perspective involves embracing diversity and emphasizing the processes responsible for a multivalent Caribbean. An important component of which is the heightened participation of professionals and students from the islands.

European authors represented island life as exotic, despite the fact that many of them also lived on islands. Literary treatments vacillated between islands as Utopia (Columbus identified Trinidad as the Garden of Eden ["Earthly Paradise"] on his third voyage) and Hell (e.g., see Rainbird 1999, 2007; for a discussion of islands in European literature). Today, the islands remain exotic in the minds of the millions of tourists who visit annually. To accommodate these visitors, the past is rapidly being replaced by modern development (Hofman and Hoogland 2016; Siegel and Righter 2011; Siegel et al. 2013). The tendency has been to homogenize the islands to provide these visitors with an aseptic experience. It would be a shame to do the same to the past.

REFERENCES

Agorsah, E. K. 1993. An objective chronological scheme for Caribbean history and archaeology. *Social and Economic Studies* 21:119–147.

Agorsah, E. K., Ed. 1994. *Maroon heritage: Archaeological, ethnographic and historical perspectives*. Mona, Jamaica: University of the West Indies Press.

Agorsah, E. K. 2013. In *The Oxford handbook of Caribbean archaeology*, edited by W. F. Keegan, C. L. Hofman, and R. Rodríguez Ramos, pp. 97–108. New York: Oxford University Press.

Alcina Franch, J. 1983. La cultura Taína como sociedad de transición entre los niveles tribal y de jefaturas. In *La Cultura Taína*, pp. 69–80. Madrid: Biblioteca del V Centenario.

Alegría, R. E. 1979. Apuntes para el estudio de los caciques de Puerto Rico. *Revista del Instituto de Cultura Puertoriqueña* 85:25–41.

Alegría, R. E. 1983. *Ball courts and ceremonial plazas in the West Indies*. Yale University Publications in Anthropology No. 79. New Haven, CT: Yale University Press.

Allaire, L. 1977. "Later prehistory in Martinique and the Island Carib: Problems in ethnic identification." Ph.D. dissertation, Yale University. Ann Arbor: University Microfilms.

Allaire, L. 1987. Some comments on the ethnic identity of the Taíno-Carib frontier. In *Ethnicity and culture*, edited by R. Auger, M. F. Glass, S. MacEachern, and P. H. McCartney, pp. 127–133. Calgary: Archaeological Association, University of Calgary.

Allaire, L. 1990. Prehistoric Taíno interaction with the Lesser Antilles: The view from Martinique. Paper presented at the 55th Annual Meeting of the Society for American Archaeology, Las Vegas.

Allaire, L. 1991. Understanding Suazey. In *Proceedings of the XIII International Congress for Caribbean Archaeology*, edited by E. N. Ayubi and J. B. Haviser, pp. 715–728. Willemstad, Curaçao.

Allaire, L. 1994. Historic Carib site discovered. *University of Manitoba St. Vincent Archaeological Project Newsletter* 1 (1994): 1–3.

Allaire, L. 1996. Visions of cannibals: Distant islands and distant lands in Taíno world image. In *The Lesser Antilles in the age of European expansion*, edited by R. Paquette and S. Engerman, pp. 33–49. Gainesville: University Press of Florida.

Allaire, L. 2003. Agricultural societies in the Caribbean: The Lesser Antilles. In *General history of the Caribbean. Volume I: Autochthonous societies*, edited by J. Sued-Badillo, pp. 195–227. Paris: UNESCO Publications.

Allaire, L. 2013. Ethnohistory of the Caribs. In *The Oxford handbook of Caribbean archaeology*, edited by W. F. Keegan, C. L. Hofman, and R. Rodríguez Ramos, pp. 97–108. New York: Oxford University Press.

Allaire, L., and M. Mattioni. 1983. Boutbois et le Godinot: Deux gisements acéramiques de la Martinique. In *Proceedings of the IX International Congress for Caribbean Archaeology*, pp. 27–38. Montreal, Canada.

Allsworth-Jones, P. 2008. *Pre-Columbian Jamaica.* Tuscaloosa: University of Alabama Press.

Allsworth-Jones, P., M. Bogle-Douglas, and K. W. Wesler. 2007. Defining the Montego Bay Style: A re-consideration of R. L. Vanderwal's work in Jamaica. Paper presented at the XXI Congress of the International Association for Caribbean Archaeology, University of the West Indies, St. Augustine, Trinidad.

Allsworth-Jones P., and K. W. Wesler. 2012. *The Taíno settlement at Guayguata: Excavations in St. Mary's Parish, Jamaica.* Oxford: British Archaeological Reports International Series.

Alonso, E. M. 1995. *Fundamentos para la historia del Guanahatabey de Cuba.* Havana: Editorial Academia.

Ammerman, A. J., and L. L. Cavalli-Sforza. 1973. A population model for the diffusion of early farming in Europe. In *The explanation of culture change: Models in prehistory*, edited by C. Renfrew, pp. 674–678. Gloucester Crescent: Duckworth.

Amodio, E. 1999. Los caníbales mutantes: Etapas de la transformación etnica de los Caribes durante la época colonial. *Boletin Americas* 49:9–29.

Anctzak, A., and M. Anctzak. 2006. *Los ídolos de las islas prometidas: Arqueología prehispanicá del Archipélago de los Roques.* Caracas, Venezuela: Editoral Equinoccio.

Anctzak, A. T., J. B. Haviser, M. L. P. Hoogland, et al. In press. Early Horticulturalists of the Southern Caribbean. In *The archaeology of Caribbean and Circum-Caribbean farmers (5000 BC–AD 1500)*, edited by B. Reid. Gainesville: University Press of Florida.

Anonyme de Carpentras. 1990. Un filibustier français dans la mer des Antilles en 1618/1620. Paris: Réédition Seghers.

Antón, S. C. 2008. Human remains from the Río Tanamá Sites AR-38 and AR-39. In *A multidisciplinary approach to site testing and data recovery at two village sites AR-38 and AR-39 on the lower Río Tanamá, municipality of Arecibo, Puerto Rico. Volume 1: Final report*, edited by L. A. Carlson, pp. 149–190. Newberry, FL: Southeastern Archaeological Research, Inc.

Armstrong, D. V. 1978. "Archaic shellfish gatherers of St. Kitts, Leeward Islands: A case study in subsistence and settlement patterns." Master's thesis, Dept. of Anthropology, U.C.L.A.

Armstrong, D. V. 1980. Shellfish gatherers of St. Kitts. A study of archaic subsistence and settlement patterns. In *Proceedings of the VIII Congress of the International*

Association for Caribbean Archaeology, pp. 152–167. Tempe, Arizona: Arizona State University.

Arrobui, J. J. 1975. *Mitología y artes prehispánicas de las Antillas*. Mexico: Siglo XXI Editores.

Arrom, J. J., Ed. 1974. *Fray Ramón Pané, "Relación acerca de las antigüedades de los Indios": El primer tratado escrito en América*. Mexico: Siglo XXI Editores.

Arrom, J. J. 1980. *Estudios de lexicologia Antillana*. Havana: Centro de Estudios del Caribe Casa de las Americas.

Arts, J. 1999. "Morel I Revisited: A study of Huecan and Cedrosan Saladoid Ceramics found at the site of Morel, Guadeloupe, French West Indies." Master's thesis, Faculty of Archaeology. Leiden, Leiden University.

As, A. van, L. Jacobs, and C. L. Hofman. 2008. In search of potential clay sources used for the manufacture of the Pre-Columbian pottery of El Cabo, Eastern Dominican Republic. *Leiden Journal of Pottery Studies* 24:55–74.

Atiles Bido, G., and A. L. Belando. 2006. *El sitio arqueologico la punta de Bayahibe: Primeros agricultores tempranos de las Antillas asentados en la costa sureste de la isla de Santo Domingo*. Santo Domingo: Editora de Revistas.

Atkinson, L-G., Ed. 2006. *The earliest inhabitants: The dynamics of the Jamaican Taíno*. Kingston, Jamaica: University of the West Indies Press.

Atkinson, L-G. 2009. Sacred landscapes: Imagery, iconography, and ideology in Jamaican rock art. In *Rock art of the Caribbean*, edited by M. H. Hayward, L-G. Atkinson, and M. A. Cinquino, pp. 41–57. Tuscaloosa: University of Alabama Press.

Ayubi, E. N. 1990. The study of aesthetic aspects of the pre-Columbian pottery of Aruba, Curaçao and Bonaire. In *Proceedings of the XI International Congress for Caribbean Archaeology*, pp. 128–140. San Juan, Puerto Rico.

Bahamas Archaeological Team. 1984. *Archaeology in the Bahamas*. Report for 1982/1983, Nassau, Bahamas.

Baisre, J. A. 2010. Setting a baseline for Caribbean fisheries. *Journal of Island and Coastal Archaeology* 5:120–147.

Baisre, J. A. 2013. Shifting baselines and the extinction of the Caribbean monk seal. *Conservation Biology* 27:927–935.

Barbotin, P. M. 1987 *Archéologie Antillaise: Arawaks et Caraïbes*. Pointe-à-Pître: Parc nat. Guadeloupe.

Barse, W. 2009. The early Ronquín paleosol and the Orinocan ceramic sequence. *Bulletin of the Peabody Museum of Natural History* 501:85–98.

Bartone, R. N., and J. Crock. 1991. Flaked stone industries at the early Saladoid Trants Site, Montserrat, West Indies. In *Proceedings of the XIV Congress of the International Association for Caribbean Archaeology*, edited by A. Cummins and P. King, pp. 124–146. Barbados: Barbados Museum and Historical Society.

Bate, E. 2011. "Technology and Spanish contact: Analysis of artifacts from the Long Bay Site, San Salvador Island, the Bahamas." Ph.D. dissertation, Department of Anthropology, Indiana University, Bloomington.

Beeker, C. D., G. W. Conrad, and J. W. Foster. 2002. Taíno use of flooded caverns in the East National Park Region, Dominican Republic. *Journal of Caribbean Archaeology* 3:1–26.

Beets, C. J., S. R. Troelstra, P. M. Grootes, et al. 2006. Climate and pre-Columbian settlement at Anse à la Gourde, Guadeloupe, northeastern Caribbean. *Geoarchaeology* 21 (3): 271–280.

Bérard, B. 2004. *Les premières occupations agricoles de l'Arc Antillais, migrations et insularité*. BAR International Series 1299. Oxford: Archaeopress.

Bérard, B. 2008. Lithic technology, One of the ways to complexity for Caribbean archaeology. In *Crossing the borders: New methods and techniques in the study of archaeological materials from the Caribbean*, edited by C. L. Hofman, M. L. P. Hoogland, and A. L. van Gijn, pp. 90–100. Tuscaloosa: University of Alabama Press.

Bérard, B. 2013. The Saladoid. In *The Oxford handbook of Caribbean archaeology*, edited by W. F. Keegan, C. L. Hofman, and R. Rodríguez Ramos, pp. 184–197. New York: Oxford University Press.

Bercht, F., E. Brodsky, J. A. Farmer, and D. Taylor, Eds. 1997. *Taíno: Pre-Columbian art and culture from the Caribbean*. New York: The Monacelli Press.

Berman, M. J., J. Febles, and P. L. Gnivecki. 2005. The organization of Cuban archaeology: Context and brief history. In *Dialogues in Cuban archaeology*, edited by L. A. Curet, S. L. Dawdy, and G. la Rosa Corzo, pp. 41–61. Tuscaloosa: University of Alabama Press.

Berman, M. J., and P. L. Gnivecki. 1995. The colonization of the Bahama archipelago: A reappraisal. *World Archaeology* 26:421–441.

Berman, M. J., P. L. Gnivecki, and M. P. Pateman. 2013. The Bahama archipelago. In *The Oxford handbook of Caribbean archaeology*, edited by W. F. Keegan, C. L. Hofman, and R. Rodríguez Ramos, pp. 264–280. New York: Oxford University Press.

Berman, M. J., and C. D. Hutcheson. 2000. Impressions of a lost technology: A study of Lucayan Taíno basketry. *Journal of Field Archaeology* 27:417–435.

Berman, M. J., and D. M. Pearsall. 2008. At the crossroads: Starch grain and phytolith analyses in Lucayan prehistory. *Latin American Antiquity* 11:219–239.

Berman, M. J., D. M. Pearsall, and A. S. Middleton. 2012. "Crop dispersal and Lucayan tool use in the central Bahamas. Evidence from starch grain, phytolith, macrobotanical, and artifact studies." Manuscript in possession of the authors, cited with permission.

Berman, M. J., A. K. Sievert, and T. R. Whyte. 1999. Form and function of bipolar lithic artifacts from the Three Dog Site, San Salvador, Bahamas. *Latin American Antiquity* 10:415–432.

Blancaneaux, I. 2009. *Contribution à l'étude de la disparition de la culture saladoïde aux petites antilles. Corrélation préhistorique posible entre climat et culture*. Ph.D. dissertation, Université des Antilles et de la Guyane and Université Paris I, Panteón Sorbonne.

Boas, F. 1940. *Race, language and culture*. Chicago: University of Chicago Press.

Boestra, E. H. J. 1982. *De precolumbiaanse bewoners van Aruba, Curaçao en Bonaire*. Netherlands Antilles: De Walburg Pers.

Bonnissent, D. 2003. *St. Martin, Etang Rouge—lot 401*. Bilan Scientifique, Direction Regionale des Affaires Culturelles de la Guadeloupe: 39–43.

Bonnissent, D. 2008. «Archéologie précolombienne de l'île de Saint-Martin, Petites Antilles (3300 BC - 1600 AD).» Ph.D. dissertation, Université Aix-Marseille I.

Bonnissent, D. 2013. Les gisements précolombiens de la Baie Orientale. Campements du Mésoindien et du Néoindien sur l'île de Saint-Martin (Petites Antilles). *Documents d'archéologie française, Editions de la Maison des sciences de L'homme.* Paris.

Bonnissent, D., P. Bertran, A. Chancerel, and T. Romon. 2001. Le gisement précéramique de la Baie Orientale à Saint-Martin (Petites Antilles), résultats préliminaires. *Proceedings of the XIX Congress of the International Association for Caribbean Archaeology,* Aruba.

Booden, M. A., R. G. A. M. Panhuysen, M. L. P. Hoogland, H. de Jong, G. R. Davies, and C. L. Hofman. 2008. Tracing human mobility with 87Sr/86Sr at Anse à la Gourde, Guadeloupe. In *Crossing the borders. New methods and techniques in the study of archaeological materials from the Caribbean,* edited by C. L. Hofman, M. L. P. Hoogland, and A. L. van Gijn, pp. 214–225. Tuscaloosa: University Alabama Press.

Boomert, A. 1983. The Saladoid occupation of Wonotobo Falls, western Suriname. In *Proceedings of the IX International Congress for the Study of the Pre-Columbian Cultures of the Lesser Antilles.*

Boomert, A. 1986. The Cayo complex of St. Vincent: Ethnohistorical and archaeological aspects of the Island Carib problem. *Anthropológica* 66:3–68.

Boomert, A. 1987. Gifts of the Amazons: "Green stone" pendants and beads as items of ceremonial exchange in Amazonia and the Caribbean. *Anthropológica* 67:33–54.

Boomert, A. 1995. Island Carib archaeology. In *Wolves from the sea: Readings in the anthropology of the native Caribbean,* edited by N. H. Whitehead, pp. 23–36. Leiden: KITLV Press.

Boomert, A. 2000. *Trinidad, Tobago, and the Lower Orinoco interaction sphere: An archaeological/ethnohistorical study.* Leiden: Universiteit Leiden.

Boomert, A. 2003. Raptorial birds as icons of shamanism in the prehistoric Caribbean and Amazonia. In *Proceedings of the XIX Congress of the International Association for Caribbean Archaeology,* edited by L. Alofs and R. A. C. F. Dijkhoff, pp. 121–157. Publication of the Museo Arqueologico Aruba 9, Government of Aruba, Oranjestad.

Boomert, A. 2004. Koriabo and the polychrome tradition: The late-prehistoric era between the Orinoco and Amazon mouths. In *The Late Ceramic Age in the Eastern Caribbean,* edited by A. Delpuech and C. L. Hofman, pp. 251–268. BAR International Series. Oxford: Archaeopress.

Boomert, A. 2006. Between the mainland and the Islands: The Amerindian cultural geography of Trinidad. *Antropologando* 5 (15): 149–179.

Boomert, A. 2009. Searching for Cayo in Dominica. In *Proceedings of the XXIII Congress of the International Association for Caribbean Archaeology.*

Boomert, A. 2011. From Cayo to Kalinago. In *Communities in contact: Essays in archaeology, ethnohistory and ethnography of the Amerindian Circum-Caribbean,* edited by C. L. Hofman and A. van Duijvenbode, pp. 291–306. Leiden: Sidestone Press.

Boomert, A. 2013. Gateway to the mainland: Trinidad and Tobago. In *The Oxford handbook of Caribbean archaeology,* edited by W. F. Keegan, C. L. Hofman, and R. Rodríguez Ramos, pp. 141–154. New York: Oxford University Press.

Boomert, A. 2016. *The indigenous peoples of Trinidad and Tobago from the first settlers until today*. Leiden: Sidestone Press.

Boomert, A., and A. J. Bright. 2007. Island archaeology: In search of a new horizon. *Island Studies Journal* 21:3–26.

Boomert, A., and C. L. Hofman. 2016. Glossary. In *Saba's first inhabitants. A story of 3300 years of Amerindian occupation prior to European contact (1800 BC–AD 1492)*, edited by C. L. Hofman and M. L. P. Hoogland, pp. 110–111. Leiden: Sidestone Press.

Boucher, P. P. 1992. *Cannibal encounters: Europeans and Island Caribs, 1492–1764*. Baltimore: Johns Hopkins University Press.

Bourne, E. G. 1906. Columbus, Ramón Pané and the beginnings of American anthropology. *Proceedings of the American Antiquarian Society* 17:310–348.

Bradford, M. A. C. 2002. "Caribbean perspectives on settlement patterns: The Windward Island study." Ph.D. dissertation, Department of Anthropology, University of Iowa.

Braudel, F. 1997. *Les ambitions de l'histoire. Les écrits de Fernand Braudel*, edited by R. de Ayala and P. Braudel. Paris: Fallois.

Braun, D. P. 1983. Pots as tools. In *Archaeological hammers and theories*, edited by J. A. Moore and A. S. Keene. Atlanta: Elsevier.

Breton, R. 1665/1666. *Dictionnaire caraïbe-français*. Paris: Gilles Bouquet.

Bright, A. J. 2011. *Blood is thicker than water: Amerindian intra- and inter-insular relationships and social organization in the pre-Colonial Windward Islands*. Leiden: Sidestone Press.

Brill, R. H., I. L. Barnes, S. S. C. Tong, E. C. Joel, and M. J. Murtaugh. 1987. Laboratory studies of some European artifacts excavated on San Salvador Island. In *Proceedings of the First San Salvador Conference*, edited by D. Gerace, pp. 247–294. San Salvador: College Center of the Finger Lakes.

Brinton, D. 1871. The Arawack language of Guiana and its linguistic and ethnological relations. *Transactions of the American Philosophical Society* 14:427–444.

Brown, P. 1964. Enemies and affines. *Ethnology* 3:335–356.

Brown, P. 1972. *The Chimbu: A study of change in the New Guinea highlands*. Cambridge: Schenkman.

Budinoff, L. 1991. An osteological analysis of the human burials recovered from an early ceramic site on the north coast of Puerto Rico. In *Proceedings of the XII Congress of the International Association for Caribbean Archaeology*, edited by L. S. Robinson, pp. 117–134. Martinique.

Bullbrook, J. A. 1953. On the excavation of a shell mound at Palo Seco, Trinidad, B.W.I. *Yale University Publications in Anthropology*, Number 50. New Haven: Yale University Press.

Bullen, R. P. 1964. The archaeology of Grenada, West Indies. *Contributions of the Florida State Museum, Social Sciences*, no. 11. Gainesville.

Bullen, R. P., and A. K. Bullen. 1968. Barbados Archaeology: 1966. In *Proceedings of the Second International Congress for the Study of Pre-Columbian Cultures in the Lesser Antilles*, pp. 134–144. Barbados Museum, Barbados.

Bullen, R. P., and A. K. Bullen. 1972. Archaeological investigations on St. Vincent and the Grenadines, West Indies. *The William L. Bryant Foundation, American Studies Number 8*. Orlando, Florida.

Bullen, R. P., and A. K. Bullen. 1973. Stratigraphic tests at two sites on Guadeloupe. In *Proceedings of the IV International Congress for the Study of Pre-Columbian Cultures of the Lesser Antilles*, pp. 192–195. Castries, St. Lucia: St. Lucia Archaeological and Historical Society.

Bullen, R. P., and A. K. Bullen. 1974. Tests at Hacienda Grande, Puerto Rico. *Boletin Informativo*, Vol. 1, special edition. San Juan: Fundación Arquelógica, Anthropológica e Historica de Puerto Rico.

Bullen, R. P., A. K. Bullen, and E. Branford. 1973. The Giraudy site, Beane Field, St. Lucia. In *Proceedings of the IV International Congress for the Study of Pre-Columbian Cultures in the Lesser Antilles*, pp. 199–215. Castries, St. Lucia: St. Lucia Archaeological and Historical Society.

Bullen, R. P., and M. Mattioni. 1972. Some ceramic variations at Vivé, Martinique. *International Congress of Americanists* 401:224–230.

Bullen, R. P., and F. W. Sleight. 1963. The Krum Bay site: A preceramic site on St. Thomas, United States Virgin Islands. *The William L. Bryant Foundation, American Studies Number 5*. Orlando, Florida.

Burney, D. A., and L. P. Burney. 1994. Holocene charcoal stratigraphy from Laguna Tortuguero, Puerto Rico, and the timing of human arrival on the island. *Journal of Archaeological Science* 21:273–281.

Butt, A. J. 1977. The Akawaio Shaman. In *Carib-speaking Indians: Culture, society, and language*, edited by E. B. Basso, pp. 43–65. Tucson: University of Arizona Press.

Callaghan, R. T. 1990a. Possible pre-ceramic connections between Central America and the Greater Antilles. In *Proceedings of the XI Congress of the International Association for Caribbean Archaeology*, edited by G. Pantel Tekakis, I. Vargas Arenas. and M. Sanoja Obediente, pp. 65–71. San Juan, Puerto Rico.

Callaghan, R. T. 1990b. "Mainland origins of the preceramic cultures of the Greater Antilles." Ph.D. dissertation, University of Calgary, Alberta, Canada.

Callaghan, R. T. 2001. Ceramic age seafaring and interaction potential in the Antilles: A computer simulation. *Current Anthropology* 42:308–313.

Callaghan, R. T. 2003. Comments on the mainland origins of the preceramic cultures of the Greater Antilles. *Latin American Antiquity* 14:323–338.

Callaghan, R. T. 2007. Survival of a traditional Carib watercraft design element. In *Proceedings of the XXI Congress of the International Association for Caribbean Archaeology*, pp. 739–746. University of the West Indies, Trinidad and Tobago.

Callaghan, R. T. 2008. On the question of the absence of Archaic Age sites on Jamaica. *Journal of Island and Coastal Archaeology* 3:54–71.

Callaghan, R. T. 2010. Crossing the Guadeloupe passage in the Archaic Age. In *Island shores, distant pasts*, edited by S. M. Fitzpatrick and A. Ross, pp. 127–147. Gainesville: University Press of Florida.

Callaghan, R. T. 2013. Archaeological views of Caribbean seafaring. In *The Oxford handbook of Caribbean archaeology*, edited by W. F. Keegan, C. L. Hofman, and R. Rodríguez Ramos, pp. 283–295. New York: Oxford University Press.

Carbone, V. A. 1980. The paleoecology of the Caribbean area. *The Florida Anthropologist* 33:99–119.

Carlson, L. A. 1993. "Strings of command: Manufacture and utilization of shell beads among the Taíno Indians of the West Indies," M.A. thesis, Department of Anthropology, University of Florida, Gainesville.

Carlson, L. A. 1999. "Aftermath of a feast: Human colonization of the southern Bahamian Archipelago and its effects on the indigenous fauna." Ph.D. dissertation, Department of Anthropology, University of Florida, Gainesville.

Carlson, L. A. 2007. Cursory versus complete: Contrasting two zooarchaeology data analysis approaches at the St. Catherine's Site MAY-17 in Trinidad. In *Proceedings of the XXI Congress of the International Association for Caribbean Archaeology*, edited by B. Reid, H. Petitjean Roget, and L. A. Curet, pp. 445–458. University of the West Indies, St. Augustine.

Carlson, L. A., Ed. 2008. *A multidisciplinary approach to site testing and data recovery at two village sites AR-38 and AR-39 on the lower Río Tanamá, municipality of Arecebo, Puerto Rico.* Volume 1: Final report. Newberry, FL: Southeastern Archaeological Research, Inc.

Carlson, L. A. 2010. Phase I cultural resource survey of the Corktree Development Area, Grand Turk, Turks and Caicos Islands, B.W.I. Jonesville, FL: Southeastern Archaeological Research, Inc.

Carlson, L. A., and A. Cordell. 2011. Mangrove-edge activity areas. In *Phase III data recovery investigations at three prehistoric archaeological sites CE-11, CE-32, and CE-33, municipality of Ceiba, Naval Activity Puerto Rico*. Volume 1: Final report, edited by L. A. Carlson and J. M. Torres, pp. 169–233. Newberry, FL: Southeastern Archaeological Research, Inc.

Carlson, L. A., and W. F. Keegan. 2004. Prehistoric resource depletion in the prehistoric northern West Indies. In *Voyages of discovery: The archaeology of islands*, edited by S. M. Fitzpatrick, pp. 85–107. Westport, CT: Praeger Publishers.

Carlson, L. A., and J. M. Torres. 2008. Ceramic analysis. In *A multidisciplinary approach to site testing and data recovery at two village sites AR-38 and AR-39 on the lower Río Tanamá, municipality of Arecebo, Puerto Rico*. Volume 1: Final report, edited by L. A. Carlson, pp. 287–334. Newberry, FL: Southeastern Archaeological Research, Inc.

Carlson, L. A., and J. M. Torres, Eds. 2011. *Phase III data recovery investigations at three prehistoric archaeological sites CE-11, CE-32, and CE-33, municipality of Ceiba, Naval Activity, Puerto Rico*. Volume 1: Final report. Newberry, FL: Southeastern Archaeological Research, Inc.

Carr, C. 2006. Rethinking interregional Hopewellian "interaction." In *Gathering Hopewell: Society, ritual and ritual interaction*, edited by C. Carr and T. D. Case, pp. 575–623. New York: Springer.

Carr, C., and T. D. Case, Eds. 2006. *Gathering Hopewell: Society, ritual and ritual interaction*. New York: Springer.

Cassá, R. 1992. *Los Indios de las Antillas*, Madrid: Editorial MAPFRE.

Castanha, T. 2011. *The myth of indigenous Caribbean extinction: Continuity and reclamation in Borikén Puerto Rico*. New York: Palgrave Macmillan.

Castellanos, R. 1981. La plaza de Chacuey, un instrumento astronomico megalitico. *Boletin del Museo del Hombre Dominicano* 16:31–40.

Castellanos, N., M. Pino, G. Izquierdo, and G. Baena. 2001. Estudio arqueológico del sitio La Escondida del Bucuey, San Luis, provincia de Santiago de Cuba. *El Caribe Arqueológico* 5:96–105.

Chanca, D. A. 2003. *Letter of Dr. Chanca on the second voyage of Columbus.* Milwaukee: Wisconsin Historical Society.

Chanlatte Baik, L. 1981. *La Hueca y Sorcé Vieques, Puerto Rico: Primeras migraciones agroalfareras Antillanas.* Santo Domingo: Taller.

Chanlatte Baik, L. A. 1983. Sorcé-Vieques: Climax cultural del Igneri y su participación en los procesos socioculturales Antillanos. *Proceedings of the IX International Congress for the Study of the Pre-Columbian Cultures of the Lesser Antilles*, pp. 73–95. Santo Domingo, Dominican Republic.

Chanlatte Baik, L. A. 2013. Huecoid culture and the Antillean agroalfarero farmer-potter period. In *The Oxford handbook of Caribbean archaeology*, edited by W. F. Keegan, C. L. Hofman, and R. Rodríguez Ramos, pp. 171–183. New York: Oxford University Press.

Chanlatte Baik, L., and Y. Narganes Storde. 1990. *La nueva arqueología de Puerto Rico, su proyección en Las Antillas.* República Dominicana: Taller.

Chanlatte Baik, L., and Y. Narganes Storde. 2002. *La cultura Saladoide en Puerto Rico.* Río Piedras, Puerto Rico: Museo de Historia, Anthropología y Arte.

Charlevoix, P., and J. de Francisco. 1977. *Historia de las isla Española o de Santo Domingo 1730*, 2 vols. Santo Domingo: Editoria de Santo Domingo.

Cherry, J. F., K. Ryzewski, and T. P. Leppard. 2012. Multi-period landscape survey and site risk assessment on Montserrat, West Indies. *The Journal of Island and Coastal Archaeology* 7:282–302.

Clarke, D. L. 1968. *Analytical archaeology.* London: Methuen & Co. Ltd.

Clerc, E. 1964. Le peuplement précolombien des Antilles et ses vestiges en Guadeloupe. *Bulletin de la Société d'Histoire de la Guadeloupe* 22:18–31.

Clerc, E. 1968. Sites précolombiens de la Grand-Terre de Guadeloupe. In *Proceedings of the Second International Congress for the Study of Pre-Columbian Cultures in the Lesser Antilles*, pp. 47–60. Barbados: Barbados Museum.

Clerc, E. 1970. Archaeological research in Guadeloupe. *Parallèles* 36–37:89–97.

Cobb, C. R. 2000. *From quarry to cornfield.* Tuscaloosa: University of Alabama Press.

Cody, A. 1991a. From the site of Pearls, Grenada: Exotic lithics and radiocarbon dates. In *Proceedings of the XIII International Congress for Caribbean Archaeology*, edited by E. N. Ayubi and J. B. Haviser, pp. 589–604. Reports of the Archaeological-Anthropological Institute of the Netherlands Antilles, No. 9, Curaçao.

Cody, A. 1991b. Distribution of exotic stone artifacts through the Lesser Antilles: Their implications for prehistoric interaction and exchange. In *Proceedings of the XIV Congress of the International Association for Caribbean Archaeology*, edited by A. Cummins and P. King, pp. 204–226. Barbados: Barbados Museum and Historical Society.

Colten, R. H., and B. Worthington. 2014. Faunal remains from the Archaic and Archaic Ceramic Site of Vega del Mar, Cuba. *Journal of Caribbean Archaeology* 14:1–28.

Coll y Toste, C. 1907. *Prehistoria de Puerto Rico*. Sociedad Económica de Amigos del País.

Conrad, G. W., J. W. Foster, and C. D. Beeker. 2001. Organic artifacts from Mantanial de la Aleta, Dominican Republic: Preliminary observations and interpretations. *Journal of Caribbean Archaeology* 2:1–20.

Cook, S. F., and W. Borah. 1971. The aboriginal population of Hispaniola. In *Essays in population history. Vol. 1: Mexico and the Caribbean*, edited by S. F. Cook and W. Borah, pp. 376–410. Berkeley: University of California Press.

Cooper, J. 2007. "Island interaction in the prehistoric Caribbean: An archaeological case study from Northern Cuba." Ph.D. dissertation. University College London, London.

Cooper, J. 2010. Modelling mobility and exchange in pre-Columbian Cuba: GIS led approaches to identifying pathways and reconstructing journeys from the archaeological record. *Journal of Caribbean Archaeology, Special Publication 3*, edited by C. L. Hofman, and A. J. Bright, pp. 122–137.

Cooper, J. 2013. The climatic context for pre-Columbian archaeology in the Caribbean. In *The Oxford handbook of Caribbean archaeology*, edited by W. F. Keegan, C. L. Hofman, and R. Rodríguez Ramos, pp. 47–58. New York: Oxford University Press.

Cooper, J., and R. Boothroyd. 2011. Living islands of the Caribbean: A view of relative sea level change from the water's edge. In *Communities in contact: Essays in archaeology, ethnohistory and ethnography of the American Circum-Caribbean*, edited by C. L. Hofman and A. Duijvenbode, pp. 393–406. Leiden: Sidestone Press.

Cooper, J., R. Valcárcel Rojas, and J. Calvera Rosés. 2010. Recent archaeological fieldwork from the region around Los Buchillones, an indigenous site on the north-central Cuban coast. In *Beyond the blockade: New currents in Cuban archaeology*, edited by S. Kepecs, A. Curet, and G. de la Rosa, pp. 89–105. Tuscaloosa: University of Alabama Press.

Coppa, A., A. Cucina, B. F. Chiarelli, F. Luna Calderon, and D. Mancinelli. 1995. Dental anthropology and paleodemography of the Precolumbian populations of Hispaniola from the third millennium BC to the Spanish contact. *Human Evolution* 10:153–167.

Coppier, G. 1645. *Histoire et voyage des Indes Occidentales, et de plusieurs autres regions maritimes, and esloignées: Diuisé en deux liures*. A. Lyon: Iean Huguetan.

Cordell, A. 1998. Possible manufacturing origins of Ostionoid pottery from the Bahamas. Paper presented at the 55th annual meeting of the Southeastern Archaeological Conference, Greenville, South Carolina.

Cosculluela, J. A. 1946. Prehistoric cultures of Cuba. *American Antiquity* 12:10–18.

Costin, C. L. 1991. Craft specialization: Issues in defining, documenting, and explaining the organization of production. *Archaeological Method and Theory* 1991:1–56.

Craton, M., and G. Saunders. 1992. *Islanders in the stream: A history of the Bahamian people. Volume one: From aboriginal times to the end of slavery*. Athens, GA: University of Georgia Press.

Crespo-Torres, E. 2000. "Estudio comparativo biocultural entre dos poblaciones prehistóricas de las isla de Puerto Rico: Punta Candelero y Paso del Indio." Ph.D. dissertation, Instituto de Investigaciones Antropológicas, Universidad Autónoma de México.

Crespo-Torres, E. F., H. L. Mickleburgh, and R. Varcárcel-Roja. 2013. The study of pre-Columbian human remains in the Caribbean archipelago: From descriptive osteology to a bioarchaeological approach. In *The Oxford handbook of Caribbean archaeology*, edited by W. F. Keegan, C. L. Hofman, and R. Rodríguez Ramos, pp. 436–451. New York: Oxford University Press.

Crock, J. G. 1995. The Forest North site and post-Saladoid settlement in Anguilla. In *Proceedings of the XVIth Congress of the International Association for Caribbean Archaeology, Part 1*: 74–87, Guadeloupe: Conseil Régional de la Guadeloupe.

Crock, J. G. 2000. "Interisland interaction and the development of chiefdoms in the eastern Caribbean." Ph.D. dissertation, University of Pittsburgh. Ann Arbor: University Microfilms.

Crock, J. G., and J. B. Petersen. 1999. *A long and rich cultural heritage: The Anguilla archaeology project, 1992–1998*. Report for the Anguilla Archaeological and Historical Society, the Valley, Anguilla, British West Indies.

Crock, J. G., and J. B. Petersen. 2001. Stratified sites and storm events: The formation and destruction of beach sites in Anguilla, West Indies. *Proceedings of the XIX Congress of the International Association of Caribbean Archaeology*. Publications of the Archaeological Museum Aruba 9, pp. 204–213.

Crock, J. G., J. B. Petersen, and N. Douglas. 1995. Preceramic Anguilla: A view from the Whitehead's Bluff site. *Proceedings of the XV Congress of the International Association for Caribbean Archaeology. Puerto Rico 1993*, pp. 283–292. San Juan: Centro de Estudios Avanzados de Puerto Rico y el Caribe.

Cunningham, R. L. 1997. The biological impacts of 1492. In *The indigenous people of the Caribbean*, edited by S. M. Wilson, pp. 31–35. Gainesville: University Press of Florida.

Curet, L. A. 1992. "The development of chiefdoms in the Greater Antilles: A regional study of the Valley of Maunabo, Puerto Rico." Ph.D. dissertation, Department of Anthropology, Arizona State University, Tempe.

Curet, L. A. 1996. Ideology, chiefly power, and material culture: An example from the Greater Antilles. *Latin American Antiquity* 7:114–131.

Curet, L. A. 1997. Technological changes in prehistoric ceramics from eastern Puerto Rico: An exploratory study. *Journal of Archaeological Science* 246:497–504.

Curet, L. A. 2002. The chief is dead, long live . . . who? Descent and succession in the protohistoric chiefdoms of the Greater Antilles. *Ethnohistory* 49:259–280.

Curet, L. A. 2003. Issues on the diversity and emergence of middle-range societies of the ancient Caribbean: A critique. *Journal of Archaeological Research* 11:1–42.

Curet, L. A. 2004. Island archaeology and units of analysis in the study of ancient Caribbean societies. In *Voyages of discovery: The archaeology of islands*, edited by S. M. Fitzpatrick and A. Ross, pp. 187–202. Westport, CT: Praeger.

Curet, L. A. 2005. *Caribbean paleodemography: Population, culture history, and sociopolitical processes in ancient Puerto Rico*. Tuscaloosa: University of Alabama Press.

Curet, L. A. 2011. Irving Rouse's contribution to American archaeology: The case of migration. In *Islands at the crossroads: Migration, seafaring, and interaction in the Caribbean*, edited by L. A. Curet and M. W. Hauser, pp. 13–21. Tuscaloosa: University of Alabama Press.

Curet. L. A. 2014. The Taíno: Phenomena, concepts and terms. *Ethnohistory* 61:467–495.

Curet, A. L., S. L. Dawdy, and G. La Rosa, Eds. 2005. *Dialogues in Cuban archaeology.* Tuscaloosa: University of Alabama Press.

Curet, L. A., and M. W. Hauser, Eds. 2011. *Islands at the crossroads: Migration, seafaring, and interaction in the Caribbean.* Tuscaloosa: University of Alabama Press.

Curet, L. A., and J. R. Oliver. 1998. Mortuary practices, social development, and ideology in precolumbian Puerto Rico. *Latin American Antiquity* 9:217–239.

Curet, L. A., and L. Stringer, Eds. 2010. *Tibes: People, power, and sacred place at the ceremonial center of Tibes, Puerto Rico, ritual at the center of the cosmos.* Tuscaloosa: University of Alabama Press.

Curet, L. A., and J. M. Torres. 2010. Plazas, bateys, and ceremonial centers: The social and cultural context of Tibes in the ancient history of Puerto Rico. In *Tibes: People, power, and ritual at the center of the cosmos,* edited by L. A. Curet and L. M. Stringer, pp. 261–286. Tuscaloosa: University of Alabama Press, Alabama.

Curtis, J. H., M. Brenner, and D. A. Hodell. 2001. Climate change in the Circum-Caribbean late Pleistocene to present and implications for regional biogeography. In *Biogeography of the West Indies: Patterns and perspectives,* edited by C. A. Woods and F. E. Sergile, pp. 35–54. Washington, DC: CRC Press.

Curtis, J. H., and D. A. Hodell. 1993. An isotopic and trace element study of ostracods from Lake Miragoane, Haiti: A 10,500-year record of paleosalinity and paleotemperature changes in the Caribbean. In *Climate change in continental isotopic records,* edited by P. K. Swart, K. C. Lohmann, J. McKenzie, and S. Savin, pp. 135–152. Washington DC: American Geophysical Union Geophysical Monograph Series, 78.

Cusick, J. G. 1989. "Change in pottery as a reflection of social change: A study of Taíno pottery before and after contact at the site of En Bas Saline, Haiti." Master's thesis, University of Florida, Gainesville.

Cusick, J. G. 1991. Culture change and pottery change in a Taíno village. In *Proceedings of the XIII International Congress for Caribbean Archaeology,* pp. 446–461, Curaçao.

D'Altroy, T., and T. Earle. 1985. Staple finance, wealth finance, and storage in the Inca political economy. *Current Anthropology* 26:187–206.

Dacal Moure, R. 1978. *Artefactos de concha en las comunidades aborigenes Cubanas.* Centro de Informacion Cientifica y Tecnica. Havana: Universidad de la Habana.

Dacal Moure, R. 2004. The recurrent forms in Tanki Flip. In *The archaeology of Aruba: The Tanki Flip site,* edited by A. H. Versteeg and S. Rostain, pp. 159–188. Aruba: Publications of the Archaeological Museum.

Dacal Moure, R., and M. Rivero de la Calle. 1984. *Arqueología aborigen de Cuba.* Havana: Editorial Gente Nueva.

Dacal Moure, R., and M. Rivero de la Calle. 1996. *Art and archaeology of pre-Columbian Cuba.* Translated by D. H. Sandweiss, edited by D. H. Sandweiss and D. R. Watters. Pittsburgh: University of Pittsburgh Press.

Davies, E. L., C. W. Brott, and D. L. Weide. 1969. *The western lithic co-tradition.* San Diego, CA: San Diego Museum Papers Number 6.

Davila, O. 1978. Analysis of the lithic materials of the Savanne Carree No. 2 site, Ft. Liberté region, Haiti. *Boletin del Museo del Hombre Dominicano* 10:201–226.

Davis, D. D. 1982. Archaic settlement and resource exploitation in the Lesser Antilles: Preliminary information from Antigua. *Caribbean Journal of Science* 17:107–122.

Davis, D. D. 1988a. Calibration of the Ceramic Period chronology for Antigua, West Indies. *Southeastern Archaeology* 7:52–60.

Davis, D. D. 1988b. Coastal biogeography and human subsistence: Examples from the West Indies. *Archaeology of Eastern North America* 16:177–185.

Davis, D. D. 1992. Rumor of cannibals. *Archaeology* January/February:49.

Davis, D. D. 1993. Archaic blade production on Antigua, West Indies. *American Antiquity* 58:688–697.

Davis, D. D. 1996. Revolutionary archaeology in Cuba. *Journal of Archaeological Method and Theory* 3:159–188.

Davis, D. D. 2000. *Jolly Beach and the pre-Ceramic occupation of Antigua, West Indies*. Yale University Publications in Anthropology, Number 84. New Haven, CT: Yale University Press.

Davis, D. D., and R. C. Goodwin. 1990. Island Carib origins: Evidence and non-evidence. *American Antiquity* 55:37–48.

Davis, D. D., and K. Oldfield. 2003. Archaeological reconnaissance of Anegada, British Virgin Islands. *Journal of Caribbean Archaeology* 4:1–11.

Davis, E. W. 1985. *The serpent and the rainbow*. New York: Simon & Schuster.

Deagan, K. 1987. Initial encounters: Arawak responses to European contact at the En Bas Saline site, Haiti. In *Proceedings of the First San Salvador Conference*, edited by D. Gerace, pp. 341–359. San Salvador: College Center of the Finger Lakes.

Deagan, K. 1989. The search for La Navidad, Columbus's 1492 settlement. In *First encounters*, edited by J. T. Milanich and S. Milbrath, pp. 41–54. Gainesville: University Press of Florida.

Deagan, K., Ed. 1995. *Puerto Real: The archaeology of a sixteenth-century Spanish town in Hispaniola*. Gainesville: University Press of Florida.

Deagan, K. 2004. Reconsidering Taíno social dynamics after Spanish conquest: Gender and class in culture contact studies. *American Antiquity* 69:597–626.

Deagan, K. 2010. Cuba and Florida: Entwined histories of historical archaeologies. In *Beyond the blockade: New currents in Cuban archaeology*, edited by S. Kepecs, L. A. Curet, and G. La Rosa, pp. 16–25. Tuscaloosa: University of Alabama Press.

Deagan, K., and J. M. Cruxent. 2002. *Archaeology at La Isabela: America's first European town*. New Haven: Yale University Press.

de Booy, T. 1912. Lucayan remains in the Caicos Islands. *American Anthropologist* 14:81–105.

de Booy, T. 1913a. Lucayan artifacts from the Bahamas. *American Anthropologist* 15:1–7.

de Booy, T. 1913b. Certain kitchen-middens in Jamaica. *American Anthropologist* 15:425–434.

deFrance, S. D. 2013. Zooarchaeology in the Caribbean: Current research and future prospects. In *The Oxford handbook of Caribbean archaeology*, edited by W. F. Keegan, C. L. Hofman, and R. Rodríguez Ramos, pp. 378–390. New York: Oxford University Press.

deFrance, S. D., W. F. Keegan, and L. A. Newsom. 1996. The archaeobotanical, bone isotope, and zooarchaeological records from Caribbean sites in comparative perspective. In *Case studies in environmental archaeology*, edited by E. J. Reitz, L. A. Newsom, and S. J. Scudder, pp. 289–304. New York: Plenum Press.

de Laet, J. 1931–1937. *Iaerlyck verhael*, 4 vols. *Haia* 1937 (1931): 152.

de Waal, M. S. 2006. "Pre-Columbian social organisation and interaction interpreted through the study of settlement patterns. An archaeological case-study of the Pointe des Châteaux, La Désirade and les Iles de la Petite Terre Micro-Region, Guadeloupe, French West Indies." Ph.D. dissertation, Leiden University.

Delpuech, A., C. L. Hofman, and M. L. P. Hoogland. 1999. Anse à la Gourde, St. François. In *Bilan scientifique*, pp. 28–31. Basse Terre: Service Régionale des Affaires Culturelles de la Guadeloupe, DRAC.

Delpuech, A. 2004. Espaces naturels et territories amérindiens dans la Caraïbe orientale. In *Late Ceramic Age societies in the Eastern Caribbean*, edited by A. Delpuech and C. L. Hofman, pp. 3–16. BAR International Series. Oxford: Archaeopress.

Delpuech, A., and C. L. Hofman, Eds. 2004. *The Late Ceramic Age in the eastern Caribbean*. BAR International Series. Oxford: Archaeopress.

Delpuech, A., C. L. Hofman, and M. L. P. Hoogland. 2001. Excavations at the site of Anse à la Gourde, Guadeloupe. Organization, history and environmental setting. In: *Proceedings of the XVIII Congress of the International Association for Caribbean Archaeology*, pp. 156–161. Guadeloupe.

Derrida, J. 1967. *Of grammatology*. Baltimore: Johns Hopkins University Press.

DeWolf, M. W. 1953. Excavations in Jamaica. *American Antiquity* 18:230–238.

Dijkhoff, R. A. C. F. 1997. "Tanki Flip: An early Urumaco site in Aruba." Master's thesis, Faculty of Archaeology, Leiden University, Leiden.

Dijkhoff, R. A. C. F., and M. S. Linville. 2007. *The archaeology of Aruba: The marine shell heritage*. Aruba: Archaeological Museum of Aruba.

Divale, W. 1974. Migration, external warfare and matrilocal residence. *Behavior Science Research* 9:75–133.

Domínguez, L. 1978. La transculturacion en Cuba. *Cuba Arqueologica*, pp. 33–50.

Domínguez, L. 1991. *Arqueología del centro-sur de Cuba*. Havana: Editorial Academia.

Doran, E., Jr. 1958. The Caicos conch trade. *Geographical Review* 48:388–401.

Dorst, M. C. 2006. *Preliminary research report: Excavation of the Amerindian SAN-1 site at Manzanilla, Trinidad February 2006*. National Archaeological Committee of Trinidad and Tobago, St. Augustine.

Dorst, M. C. 2008. *The pre-Columbian SAN-1 site, Manzanilla, Trinidad, Preliminary Research Report, Fieldwork October 2007*. National Archaeological Committee of Trinidad and Tobago, St. Augustine.

Douglas, N. 1991. Recent Amerindian finds on Anguilla. In *Proceedings of the XIII International Congress for Caribbean Archaeology*, edited by A. N. Ayubi and J. B. Haviser. Reports of the Anthropological and Archaeological Institute of the Netherlands Antilles, Number 9, Curaçao.

Drewett, P. L. 1991. *Prehistoric Barbados*. Wales: Archetype Publications Ltd.

Drewett, P. L. 2004. Post-Saladoid society on Barbados. In *Late Ceramic Age societies in the Eastern Caribbean*, edited by A. Delpuech and C. L. Hofman, pp. 215–230. BAR International Series. Oxford: Archaeopress.

Dreyfus, S. 1992. Indian America: Island Caribs. In *The Christopher Columbus encyclopedia*, edited by S. A. Bedini, pp. 349–351. New York: Simon & Schuster.

Dubelaar, C. N. 1995. *The petroglyphs of the Lesser Antilles, the Virgin Islands and Trinidad.* Amsterdam: Foundation for Scientific Research in the Caribbean Region.

DuChemin, G. R. 2013. "Animal use and community in pre-Columbian Puerto Rico: Zooarchaeology of the Río Portugués." Ph.D. dissertation, University of Florida, Gainesville.

Duerden, J. E. 1897. Aboriginal remains in Jamaica. *Journal of the Institute of Jamaica*, vol. 2, no. 4.

Duijvenbode, A. van. 2014. Forming identities: An overview of intentional cranial modification in the Caribbean. In *Proceedings of the XXIV Congress of the International Association for Caribbean Archaeology*, pp. 39–51.

Duijvenbode, A. van 2017. "Facing Society." Ph.D. dissertation, Leiden University.

Dunn, O., and J. E. Kelley, Jr., Eds. 1989. *The* diario *of Christopher Columbus's first voyage to America 1492–1493*, abstracted by Bartolomé de las Casas. Norman: University of Oklahoma Press.

du Tetre, J. B. 1667–1671. *Histoire des Antilles habitées par les François.* Paris.

Earle, T. K. 1987. Chiefdoms in archaeological and ethnohistorical perspective. *Annual Review of Anthropology* 16:279–308.

Earle, T. K. 2011. Chiefs, chieftaincies, chiefdoms, and chiefly confederacies. *Social Evolution and History* 10:27–54.

Ember, M. 1974. The conditions that may favor avunculocal residence. *Behavior Science Review* 9:203–209.

Ensor, B. E. 2000. Social formations, *modo de vida*, and conflict in archaeology. *American Antiquity* 65:15–42.

Ensor, B. E. 2003. "Crow-Omaha marital alliances and social transformations: Archaeological case studies on the Taíno, Hohokam, and Archaic Lower Mississippi Valley." Ph.D. dissertation, University of Florida, Gainesville.

Ensor, B. E. 2011. Kinship theory in archaeology: From critiques to the study of transformations. *American Antiquity* 76:203–227.

Ensor, B. E. 2013a. Kinship and social organization in the pre-Hispanic Caribbean. In *The Oxford handbook of Caribbean archaeology*, edited by W. F. Keegan, C. L. Hofman, and R. Rodríguez Ramos, pp. 84–96. New York: Oxford University Press.

Ensor, B. E. 2013b. *Crafting prehispanic Maya kinship.* Tuscaloosa: University of Alabama Press.

Ensor, B. E. 2013c. *The archaeology of kinship.* Tempe: University of Arizona Press.

Espenshade, C. T. 2000. Reconstructing household vessel assemblages and site duration at an early Ostionoid site from south-central Puerto Rico. *Journal of Caribbean Archaeology* 1:1–22.

Espenshade, C. T. 2011. *The cultural landscape of Jácana: Archaeological investigations of Site PO-29, Municipio de Ponce, Puerto Rico: Volume I.* Stone Mountain, Georgia: New South Associates.

Faber Morse, B. 2004. At the onset of complexity: Late Ceramic Age developments in St. Croix. In *Late Ceramic Age societies in the Eastern Caribbean*, edited by A. Delpuech and C. L. Hofman, pp. 183–193. BAR International Series. Oxford: Archaeopress.

Febles, J. 1982. *Estudio tipológico y technógico del material de piedra tallada del sitio arqueológico Caminar I, Matanzas, Cuba.* Havana: Editorial Academia.

Febles, J. 1991. Estudio comparativo de las industrias de la piedra tallada de Aguas Verdes Baracoa y Playitas, Matanzas: Probable relación de estas industrias con otras del S.E. de los Estados Unidos. In *Arqueología de Cuba y Otras áreas Antillanas*, edited by J. Febles and A. V. Rives, pp. 312–371. Havana: Editorial Academia.

Fewkes, J. W. 1907. *The aborigines of Puerto Rico and neighboring islands.* Twenty-fifth Annual Report of the American Bureau of Ethnology, pp. 1–220. Washington, DC: U.S. Government Printing Office.

Fewkes, J. W. 1922. *A prehistoric island culture of the Americas.* Thirty-fourth Annual Report of the American Bureau of Ethnology, pp. 35–281. Washington, DC: U.S. Government Printing Office.

Figueredo, A. 1974. History of Virgin Islands archaeology. *Journal of the Virgin Islands Archaeological Society* 1:1–6.

Figueredo, A. E. 2015. Manioc dethroned and maize triumphant: Interpretations on the ethnohistory and archaeology of the Bahamas with sundry notes on relations of production. *Journal of Caribbean Archaeology* 15:120–134.

Fitzpatrick, S. M. 2006. A critical approach to ^{14}C dating in the Caribbean: Using chronometric hygiene to evaluate chronological control and prehistoric settlement. *Latin American Antiquity* 17:389–418.

Fitzpatrick, S. M. 2011. Verification of an Archaic Age occupation on Barbados, southern Lesser Antilles. *Radiocarbon* 53:595.

Fitzpatrick, S. M. 2013. The southward route hypothesis. In *The Oxford handbook of Caribbean archaeology*, edited by W. F. Keegan, C. L. Hofman, and R. Rodríguez Ramos, pp. 198–204. New York: Oxford University Press.

Fitzpatrick, S. M. 2015. The Pre-Columbian Caribbean: Colonization, population dispersal, and island adaptations. *Paleoamerica* 1:305–331

Fitzpatrick, S. M., M. Kappers, Q. Kaye, et al. 2009. Precolumbian settlements on Carriacou, West Indies. *Journal of Field Archaeology* 343:247–266.

Fitzpatrick, S. M., and W. F. Keegan. 2007. Human impacts and adaptations in the Caribbean islands: An historical ecology approach. *Earth and Environmental Science Transactions of the Royal Science of Edinburgh* 981:29–45.

Fitzpatrick, S. M., W. F. Keegan, and K. Sullivan Sealey. 2008. Human impacts on marine environments in the West Indies during the middle to late Holocene. In *Ancient human impacts on global marine environments*, edited by T. Rick and J. Erlandson, pp. 147–165. Berkeley: University of California Press.

Ford, R. I., Ed. 1985. Prehistoric food production in North America. *University of Michigan Museum of Anthropology, Anthropological Papers Number 75.* Ann Arbor, Michigan.

Fortuna, L. 1978. Analisis polinico de Sanate Abajo. *Boletin del Museo del Hombre Dominicano* 10:125–130.

Fosberg, F. R. 1963. *Man's place in the island ecosystem.* Honolulu: Bishop Museum Press.

Fouéré, P., S. Bailon, D. Bonnissent. 2011. Casperre de Marie-Galante: Grotte du Morne Rita. *Bilan scientifique* 34–37.

Fouéré, P., S. Bailon, D. Bonnissent. 2015. La grotte de Morne Rita, Capesterre de Marie-Galante Guadeloupe: Nouvelles données. Paper presented at the XXVI Congress of the International Association for Caribbean Archaeology. Sint Maarten.

Fuess, M. T., J. Donahue, D. R. Watters, and D. Nicholson. 1991. A report on thin section petrography of the ceramics from Antigua, northern Lesser Antilles: Methods and theory. In *Proceedings of the XIV Congress of the International Association for Caribbean Archaeology*, edited by A. Cummins and P. King, pp. 11–24. Barbados: Barbados Museum and Historical Society.

Fuson, R. H. 1983. The diario de Colón: A legacy of poor transcription, translation, and interpretation. *Terrae Incognitae* 15:51–75.

Fuson, R. H. 1987. *The log of Christopher Columbus.* Camden, ME: International Marine Publishing.

Galloway, P. K., Ed. 1989. *The Southeastern Ceremonial Complex: Artifacts and analysis.* Lincoln: University of Nebraska Press.

García Goyco, O., and C. Solís Magaña. 1999. *Informe de fin de obras, proyecto arqueológico Paso del Indio, Vega Baja, Puerto Rico.* San Juan, PR: Instituto de Cultura Puertorriqueña.

Garcia-Casco, A., S. Knippenberg, R. Rodríguez Ramos. 2013. Pre-columbian jadeitite artifacts from the Golden Rock site, St. Eustatius, Lesser Antilles, with special reference to jadeitite artifacts from Elliot's, Antigua: Implications for potential source regions and long-distance exchange networks in the greater Caribbean. *Journal of Archaeological Science* 408:3153–3169.

Garrow, P. H., C. H. J. McNutt, G. G. Weaver, and J. R. Oliver. 1995. *La Iglesia de Maraguez PO-39: Investigation of a local ceremonial center on the Cerrillos River Valley, Ponce, Puerto Rico.* Atlanta: Garrow and Associates.

Gerace, D. T., and J. Winter. 2015. Bahamian clays and their processing into Palmetto Ware ceramics: An experimental archaeology project. *Journal of Caribbean Archaeology* 15:22–36.

Gijn, A. L. van. 1993. Flint exploitation on Long Island, Antigua, West Indies. *Analecta Praehistorica Leidensia* 26:183–197.

Gijn, A. L. van, and H. Kelly. 2008. Understanding the function of coral tools from Anse a la Gourde: An experimental approach. In *Crossing the borders: New methods and techniques in the study of archaeological materials from the Caribbean*, edited by C. L. Hofman, M. L. P. Hoogland, and A. L. van Gijn, pp. 115–124. Tuscaloosa: University Alabama Press.

Giovas, C. M., and S. M. Fitzpatrick. 2014. Prehistoric migration in the Caribbean: Past perspectives, new models and the ideal free distribution of West Indian colonization. *World Archaeology* 46:569–589.

Giovas, C. M., M. J. LeFebvre, and S. M. Fitzpatrick. 2012. New records for prehistoric introduction of neotropical mammals to the West Indies: Evidence from Carriacou, Lesser Antilles. *Journal of Biogeography* 393:476–487.

Godo, P. 1997. El problema del protoagricola de Cuba: Discusión y perspectivas. *El Caribe Arqueológico* 2:19–29.

Godo, P. 2005. Mythical expressions in the ceramic art of agricultural groups in the prehistoric Antilles. In *Dialogues in Cuban archaeology*, edited by L. A. Curet, S. L. Dawdy, and G. la Rosa Corzo, pp. 147–162. Tuscaloosa: University of Alabama Press.

González, N. M. 1988. *Sojourners of the Caribbean: Ethnogenesis and ethnohistory of the Garifuna*. Urbana: University of Illinois Press.

Goodwin, R. C. 1978. The Lesser Antilles Archaic: New data from St. Kitts. *Journal of the Virgin Islands Archaeological Society* 5:6–16.

Goodwin, R. C. 1979. "The prehistoric cultural ecology of St. Kitts, West Indies: A case study in Island Archaeology." Ph.D. dissertation, Arizona State University, Tempe.

Goodwin, R. C., and J. B. Walker. 1975. *Villa Taina de Boqueron*. San Juan: Inter-American University Press.

Granberry, J. 1956. The cultural position of the Bahamas in Caribbean archaeology. *American Antiquity* 22:128–134.

Granberry, J. 1979–1981. Spanish slave trade in the Bahamas, 1509–1530: An aspect of the Caribbean pearl industry, 3 parts. *Journal of the Bahamas Historical Society*, Vols. 1, 2, and 3.

Granberry, J. 1991. Lucayan toponyms. *Journal of the Bahamas Historical Society* 13:3–12.

Granberry, J. 2013. Indigenous languages of the Caribbean. In *The Oxford handbook of Caribbean archaeology*, edited by W. F. Keegan, C. L. Hofman, and R. Rodríguez Ramos, pp. 61–69. New York: Oxford University Press.

Granberry, J., and G. S. Vescelius. 2004. *Languages of the pre-Columbian Antilles*. Tuscaloosa: The University of Alabama Press.

Granberry, J., and J. Winter. 1995. Bahamian ceramics. In *Proceedings of the XV International Congress for Caribbean Archaeology*, edited by R. E. Alegría and M. Rodríguez, pp. 3–14. Centro de Estudios Avanzados de Puerto Rico y el Caribe, San Juan.

Gross, J. M. 1976. The Archaic Period of the Virgin Islands: New investigations. In *Proceedings of the XVI International Congress for the Study of Pre-Columbian Cultures of the Lesser Antilles*, pp. 232–238. Pointe á Pitre, Guadeloupe: Société d'Histoire de la Guadeloupe.

Grouard, S. 2001. «Subsistance, systèmes techniques et gestion territoriale en mileu insulaire antillais précolombien. Exploitation des vertébrés et des crustacées aux époques Saladoïdes et Troumassoïdes de Guadeloupe 400 av. J.C. à 1500 ap. J.C.» Ph.D. dissertation. Université de Paris X-Nanterre, Paris.

Grouard, Sandrine. 2002. Subsistance et mode de vie des premiers habitants de Guadeloupe (500 av.–1500 ap. J.-C.). *Préhistoires Méditerranéennes* 10–11: 191–213.

Grouard, S., S. Perdikaris, and K. Debue. 2013. Dog burials associated with human burials in the West Indies during the early pre-Columbian Ceramic Age (500 BC–600 AD). *Anthropozoologica* 48:447–465.

Guarch Delmonte, G. M. 1972a. *Excavaciones en el extremo oriental de Cuba*. Serie Arqueologica, No. 1, Havana, Cuba.

Guarch Delmonte, G. M. 1972b. *La ceramica Taina de Cuba*. Serie Arqueologica No. 2. Havana, Cuba.

Guarch Delmonte, G. M. 1974. *Ensayo de reconstrucción etno-histórica del Taíno de Cuba*. Serie Arqueologica No. 4. Havana, Cuba.

Guarch Delmonte, G. M. 1990. *Estructura para las comunidades aborígenes de Cuba*, Holguín, Cuba: Ediciones Holguín.

Guerrero, J. G. 1981. Dos plazas indigenas y el poblado de Cotubanama, Parque Nacional del Este. *Boletin del Museo del Hombre Dominicano* 16:13–30.

Gustave, S., M. Habau, P. Belhache, J. Fabre, C. Ney, and M. Schvoerer. 1991. Composition élémentaire d'une série de tessons recueillis sur les sites prehistoriques de Vive et du Diamant Martinique. In *Proceedings of the XIV Congress of the International Association for Caribbean Archaeology*, edited by A. Cummins and P. King, pp. 40–48. Barbados: Barbados Museum and Historical Society.

Gutiérrez, M., and J. Rodríguez. 2009. The use of the style category in Puerto Rico: Moving towards a reevaluation of the concept. *Bulletin of the Peabody Museum of Natural History* 501:119–145.

Hackenberger, S. 1991. Archaeological test excavation of Buccament valley rockshelter, St. Vincent: Preceramic stone tools in the Windwards Island, and the early peopling of the eastern Caribbean. *Proceedings of the XIII Congress of the International Association for Caribbean Archaeology*, pp. 86–91. Curaçao.

Hamburg, T. 1999. Part two: Anse des Pères. Pottery. In *Archaeological investigations on St. Martin, Lesser Antilles. The sites of Norman Estate, Anse des Pères and Hope Estate with a contribution to the 'La Hueca problem'*, edited by C. L. Hofman and M. L. P. Hoogland, pp. 73–85. Leiden: Archaeological Studies Leiden University.

Hardy, M. D. 2008. "Saladoid economy and complexity on the Arawakan frontier." Ph.D. dissertation, Department of Anthropology, Florida State University, Tallahassee.

Harlow, G. E., A. R. Murphy, D. J. Hozjan, C. N. de Mille, and A. A. Levinson. 2006. Pre-Columbian jadeite axes from Antigua, West Indies. *Canadian Mineralogist* 44:305–321.

Harrington, M. R. 1921. *Cuba before Columbus*. Indian Notes and Monographs, vols. I and II. Heye Foundation. New York: Museum of the American Indian.

Harris, M. H., and R. Hinds. 1995. Pottery from Maxwell, Barbados. In *Proceedings of the XV Congress of the International Association for Caribbean Archaeology*, edited by R. E. Alegría, and M. Rodríguez, pp. 511–522. San Juan: Centro de Estudios Avanzados de Puerto Rico y el Caribe.

Harris, P. O'B. 1973. Preliminary report on Barwari Trace. In *Proceedings of the IV International Congress for the Study of Pre-Columbian Cultures of the Lesser Antilles*. Castries, St. Lucia: St. Lucia Archaeological and Historical Society.

Harris, P. O'B. 1976. The preceramic period in Trinidad. In *Proceedings of the First Puerto Rican Symposium of Archaeology*, edited by L. S. Robinson, pp. 33–65. Santurce, Puerto Rico.

Harris, P. O'B. 1983. Antillean axes/adzes: Persistence of an Archaic tradition. In *Proceedings of the IX International Congress for the Study of the Pre-Columbian Cultures of the Lesser Antilles*, pp. 257–290. Montreal, Canada: Centre de Recherches Caraïbes.

Harris, P. O'B. 1991. A paleo-Indian stemmed point from Trinidad, West Indies. In *Proceedings of the XIV Congress of Caribbean Archaeologists*, edited by A. Cummins and P. King, pp. 73–93. Barbados: Barbados Museum and Historical Society.

Harris, P. O'B. 1994. "Nitaíno and Indians: A preliminary ethnographic outline of contact Hispaniola." Master's thesis, University of Florida, Gainesville.

Haviser, J. B. 1987. *Amerindian cultural geography on Curacao*. Amsterdam: Foundation for Cultural Cooperation.

Haviser, J. B. 1989. Preliminary results of test excavations at the Hope Estate Site, St. Martin. In *Proceedings of the XIII International Congress for Caribbean Archaeology*, edited by E. N. Ayubi and J. B. Haviser, pp. 647–666. Willemstad, Curaçao.

Haviser, J. B. 1991. *The first Bonaireans*. Reports of the Archaeological-Anthropological Institute of the Netherlands Antilles, number 9. Willemstad, Curaçao.

Haviser, J. B. 1997. Settlement strategies in the early ceramic age. In *The indigenous people of the Caribbean*, edited by S. M. Wilson, pp. 57–69. Gainesville: University Press of Florida.

Hayes, D. 2013. Phase II test excavations Kronprindsens Gade archaeological site. CRM report, St. Croix.

Hayward, M. H., L-G. Atkinson, and M. A. Cinquino, Eds. 2009. *Rock art of the Caribbean*. Tuscaloosa: University of Alabama Press.

Hayward, M. H., L-G. Atkinson, and M. A. Cinquino, with contributions by G. Richard. 2013. Rock art of the Caribbean. In *The Oxford handbook of Caribbean archaeology*, edited by W. F. Keegan, C. L. Hofman, and R. Rodríguez Ramos, pp. 486–503. New York: Oxford University Press.

Heckenberger, M. J. 2002. Rethinking the Arawakan diaspora: Hierarchy, regionality, and the Amazonian "Formative." In *Comparative Arawakan histories: Rethinking language family and culture area in Amazonia*, edited by J. D. Hill and F. Santos-Granero, pp. 99–122. Urbana: University of Illinois Press.

Heckenberger, M. J. 2005. *The ecology of power: Culture, place, and personhood in the southern Amazon, AD 1000–2000*. New York: Routledge.

Heckenberger, M. 2013. The Arawak diaspora: Perspectives from South America. In *The Oxford handbook of Caribbean archaeology*, edited by W. F. Keegan, C. L. Hofman, and R. Rodríguez Ramos, pp. 111–125. New York: Oxford University Press.

Helms, M. W. 1998. *Access to origins*. Austin: University of Texas Press.

Henige, D. 1978. On the contact population of Hispaniola: History as higher mathematics. *Hispanic American Historical Review* 58:217–237.

Henige, D. 1991. *In search of Columbus: The sources for the first voyage*. Tempe: University of Arizona Press.

Henocq, C., and F. Petit. 1995. Baie Rouge, gisement archéologique tardif de l'île de St. Martin. *Proceedings of the XVI Congress of the International Association for Caribbean Archaeology*, pp. 316–332. Basse Terre, Guadeloupe: Conseil Regional de la Guadeloupe.

Hernández Aquino, L. 1977. *Diccionario de voces indigenas de Puerto Rico*. Puerto Rico: Editorial Cultural.

Higman, B. W. 2011. *A concise history of the Caribbean*. New York: Cambridge University Press.

Higuera-Gundy, A. 1991. "Antillean vegetational history and paleoclimate recon-structed from the paleolimnological record of Lake Miragoane, Haiti." Ph.D. dis-sertation, University of Florida, Gainesville.

Higuera-Gundy, A., M. Brenner, D. A. Hodell, J. H. Curtis, B. W. Leyden, and M. W. Binford. 1999. A 10,500 ¹⁴C-yr record of climate and vegetation change from Haiti. *Quaternary Research* 52:159–170.

Hill, J. D., and F. Santos-Granero. 2002. *Comparative Arawakan histories: Rethinking language family and culture area in Amazonia.* Illinois: University of Illinois Press.

Hinds, R., and M. H. Harris. 1995. Pottery from Mustique. In *Proceedings of the XV Congress of the International Association for Caribbean Archaeology*, edited by R. E. Alegría and M. Rodríguez, pp. 459–470. San Juan: Centro de Estudios Avanzados de Puerto Rico y el Caribe.

Hodder, I. 1979. Social and economic stress and material culture patterning. *American Antiquity* 14:446–454.

Hoffman, C. A., Jr. 1967. "Bahama prehistory: Cultural adaptation to an island envi-ronment." Ph.D. dissertation, University of Arizona. Ann Arbor: University Microfilms.

Hoffman, C. A., Jr. 1979. The ceramic typology of the Mill Reef site, Antigua, Leeward Islands. *Journal of the Virgin Islands Archaeological Society* 7:35–51.

Hoffman, C. A., Jr. 1987. The Long Bay Site, San Salvador. *American Archaeology* 6:97–102.

Hofman, C. L. 1993. "In search of the native population of pre-Columbian Saba AD 400–1450. Part one. Pottery styles and their interpretations." Ph.D. dissertation, Leiden University, Leiden.

Hofman, C. L. 1995. Three late prehistoric sites in the periphery of Guadeloupe: Grande Anse, Les Saintes and Morne Cybèle 1 and 2, La Désirade. In *Proceedings of the XVI Congress of the International Association for Caribbean Archaeology*, edited by G. Richard, pp. 156–167. Basse Terre: Conseil Régionale de la Guadeloupe.

Hofman, C. L. 1999. The pottery. In *Archaeological investigations on St. Martin, the sites of Anse des Pères, Norman Estate and Hope Estate. With a contribution to the La Hueca problem, Part three: Hope Estate*, edited by C. L. Hofman and M. L. P. Hoogland, pp. 149–188. Leiden: ASLU.

Hofman, C. L. 2008. Indianenverhalen. *Het kwetsbare verleden van de Antillen.* Leiden: Universiteit Leiden Open Access.

Hofman, C. L. 2012. *Anse Trabaud commune de Sainte-Anne, Martinique: Reconstruction d'un village amérindien. Son insertion dans le réseau d'echanges Antillais entre 600 et 1200 après J.-C.* Leiden: Rapport de prospection thématique avec sondages.

Hofman, C. L. 2013. The post-Saladoid in the Lesser Antilles AD 600/800–1492. In *The Oxford handbook of Caribbean archaeology*, edited by W. F. Keegan, C. L. Hofman, and R. Rodríguez Ramos, pp. 205–220. New York: Oxford University Press.

Hofman, C. L., and I. Auguiste. 2013. Kalinago connections: Archaeology and legacy of colonial encounters in the Lesser Antilles. Paper presented at the 78th annual meeting of Society for American Archaeology, Honolulu, Hawaïi.

Hofman, C. L., and E. M. Branford. 2009. Lavoutte revisited: Preliminary results of the 2009 rescue excavations at Cas-En-Bas, St. Lucia. Paper presented at the

XXIII Congress of the International Association for Caribbean Archaeology. Jolly Beach, Antigua.

Hofman, C. L., and A. J. Bright. 2010. Toward a pan-Caribbean perspective of pre-colonial mobility and exchange. Preface to a special volume of the *Journal of Caribbean Archaeology*. *Journal of Caribbean Archaeology*, Special Number 3:i–iii.

Hofman, C. L., A. J. Bright, A. Boomert, and S. Knippenberg. 2007. Island rhythms: The web of social relationships and interaction networks in the Lesser Antillean archipelago between 400 BC and AD 1492. *Latin American Antiquity* 183:243–268.

Hofman, C. L., A. J. Bright, and M. L. P. Hoogland. 2006. Archipelagic resource mobility. Shedding light on the 3000 years old tropical forest campsite at Plum Piece, Saba, Northern Lesser Antilles. *Journal of Island and Coastal Archaeology* 12:145–164.

Hofman, C. L., A. J. Bright, and R. Rodríguez Ramos. 2010. Crossing the Caribbean Sea. Towards a holistic view of pre-colonial mobility and exchange. *Journal of Caribbean Archaeology* Special Number 3:1–18.

Hofman, C. L., A. Boomert, A. J. Bright, M. L. P. Hoogland, S. Knippenberg, and A. V. Samson. 2011. Ties with the homelands: Archipelagic interaction and the enduring role of the South and Central American Mainlands in the pre-Columbian Lesser Antilles. In *Islands at the crossroads: Migration, seafaring, and interaction in the Caribbean*, edited by L. A. Curet and M. W. Hauser, pp. 13–21. Tuscaloosa: University of Alabama Press.

Hofman, C. L., and E. B. Carlin. 2010. The ever-dynamic Caribbean: Exploring new approaches to unravelling social networks in the pre-colonial and early colonial periods. In *Linguistics and archaeology in the Americas: The historization of language and society*, edited by E. B. Carlin and S. Van De Kerke, pp. 107–122. Leiden: Brill.

Hofman, C. L., A. Delpuech, M. L. P. Hoogland, and M. S. de Waal. 2004. Late Ceramic Age survey of the northeastern islands of the Guadeloupean archipelago. In *Late Ceramic Age societies in the eastern Caribbean*, edited by A. Delpuech and C. L. Hofman, pp. 159–182. BAR International Series. Oxford: Archaeopress.

Hofman, C. L., and A. van Duijvenbode, Eds. 2011. *Communities in contact: Essays in archaeology, ethnohistory and ethnography of the Amerindian Circum-Caribbean*. Leiden: Sidestone Press.

Hofman, C. L., and M. L. P. Hoogland. 1991. The later prehistory of Saba, N.A.: The settlement site of Kelbey's Ridge 1300–1450 A.D. In *Proceedings of the XIII Congress of the International Association for Caribbean Archaeology*, edited by E. N. Ayubi, and J. B. Haviser, pp. 477–492. Willemstad, Curaçao.

Hofman, C. L., and M. L. P. Hoogland, Eds. 1995. *Archaeological investigations on St. Martin 1993: The sites of Norman Estate, Hope Estate, Anse des Peres*. Guadeloupe: Direction Régionale des Affaires Culturelles de Guadeloupe.

Hofman, C. L., and M. L. P. Hoogland. 2003. Plum Piece, evidence for Archaic seasonal occupation on Saba, northern Lesser Antilles around 3300 BP. *Journal of Caribbean Archaeology* 4:12–27.

Hofman, C. L., and M. L. P. Hoogland. 2004. Social dynamics and change in the northern Lesser Antilles. In *Late Ceramic Age societies in the eastern Caribbean*, edited by A. Delpuech and C. L. Hofman, pp. 47–58. BAR International Series. Oxford: Archaeopress.

Hofman, C. L., and M. L. P. Hoogland. 2011. Unravelling the multi-scale networks of mobility and exchange in the pre-colonial Circum-Caribbean. In *Communities in contact: Essays in archaeology, ethnohistory and ethnography of the Amerindian Circum-Caribbean*, edited by C. L. Hofman and A. van Duijvenbode, pp. 15–43. Leiden: Sidestone Press.

Hofman, C. L., and M. L. P. Hoogland. 2012. Caribbean encounters: Rescue excavations at the early colonial Island Carib site of Argyle, St. Vincent. *Analecta Praehistorica Leidensia* 43–44: 63–76.

Hofman, C. L., and M. L. P. Hoogland. 1999. *Archaeological investigations on St. Martin (Lesser Antilles). The sites of Norman Estate, Anse des Pères, and Hope Estate. With a contribution to the 'La Hueca problem'.* Leiden: ASLU 4.

Hofman, C. L., and M. L. P. Hoogland. 2015a. Beautiful tropical islands in the Caribbean Sea. Human responses to floods and droughts and the indigenous archaeological heritage of the Caribbean. In *Water and heritage: Material, conceptual and spiritual connections*, edited by W. J. H. Willems and H. Schaik, pp. 99–119. Leiden: Sidestone Press.

Hofman, C. L., and M. L. P. Hoogland. 2015b. Investigaciones arqueológicas en los sitios El Flaco (Loma de Guayacanes) y La Luperona (UNIJICA). Informe preliminary, *Boletín del Museo del Hombre Dominicano* 46 (42): 61–74.

Hofman C.L. , and M.L.P. Hoogland. 2016. Connecting Stakeholders: Collaborative preventive archaeology projects at sites affected by natural and/or human impacts. *Caribbean Connections* 5(1): 1–31.

Hofman, C. L., M. L. P. Hoogland, and A. Delpuech. 1999. New perspectives on a Huecan Saladoid assemblage on Guadeloupe: The case of Morel I. In *Archaeological investigations on St. Martin Lesser Antilles. The sites of Norman Estate, Anse des Pères and Hope Estate. With a contribution to the 'La Hueca problem,'* edited by C. L. Hofman and M. L. P. Hoogland, pp. 303–312. Leiden: ASLU.

Hofman, C. L., M. L. P. Hoogland, and A. Delpuech. 2001. Spatial organization at a Troumassoid settlement, the case of Anse à la Gourde, Guadeloupe. *Proceedings of the XIX Congress of the International Association for Caribbean Archaeology*, pp. 124–131.

Hofman, C. L., M. L. P. Hoogland, A. Delpuech, et al. 1999. *Guadeloupe, Le Moule, site précolombien de Morel, n97117001. Fouilles archéologiques de 1999.* Guadeloupe: Direction Régionale des Affaires Culturelles.

Hofman, C. L., M. L. P. Hoogland, H. L. Mickleburgh, J. E. Laffoon, M. F. Field, D. A. Weston, and M. H. Field. 2012. Life and death at Lavoutte, Saint Lucia, Lesser Antilles. *Journal of Field Archaeology* 37:209–225.

Hofman, C. L., M. L. P. Hoogland, and B. Roux. 2015. Reconstruire le táboüi, le manna et les pratiques funéraires au village caraïbe d'Argyle, Saint-Vincent. In *À la recherche du Caraïbe perdu: Les populations amérindiennes des Petites Antilles de l'époque précolombienne à la période coloniale*, edited by B. Grunberg, pp. 41–50. Paris: L'Harmattan.

Hofman, C. L., M. L. P. Hoogland, A. L. van Gijn, Eds. 2008. *Crossing the borders: New methods and techniques in the study of archaeological materials from the Caribbean.* Tuscaloosa: University of Alabama Press.

Hofman, C. L., M. L. P. Hoogland, and W. F. Keegan. 2004. *Archaeological reconnaissance at St. Lucia, West Indies. Preliminary report.* Report prepared for the Archaeological and Historical Society, St. Lucia. Florida Museum of Natural History and Leiden University, Gainesville/Leiden. www.flmnh.ufl.edu/caribarch/slucia.

Hofman, C. L., and L. Jacobs. 2001. The dynamics of technology, function and style: A study of Early Ceramic Age pottery from the Caribbean. *Newsletter of the Department of Pottery Technology* 18–19:7–44. Leiden: Leiden University.

Hofman, C. L., A. A. A. Mol, M. L. P. Hoogland, and R. Valcarcel Rojas. 2014. Stage of encounters: Migration, mobility and interaction in the pre-colonial and early colonial Caribbean, *World Archaeology* 46 (4): 590–609.

Hofman, C. L., A. A. A. Mol., R. Rodríguez Ramos, and S. Knippenberg. 2014. Networks set in stone: Archaic-Ceramic interaction in the early prehistoric northeastern Caribbean. In *Archéologie Caraïbe,* edited by B. Bérard and C. Losier, Taboui Series No. 2, pp. 119–132. Leiden: Sidestone Press.

Hofman, C. L., R. Rodriguez Ramos, and J. Pagán Jiménez. In press. The "Neolithization" of the northeastern Caribbean: Mobility and social interaction. In *Early farming in the Caribbean,* edited by B. Reid. Gainesville: University Presses of Florida.

Holdren, A. C. 1998. "Raiders and traders: Caraïbe social and political networks at the time of European contact and colonization in the Eastern Caribbean." Ph.D. dissertation. University of California, Los Angeles.

Honeychurch, L. 1995. *The Dominica story—A history of the island.* London: Macmillan.

Honychurch, L. 2000. *Caribbean people.* Oxford: Nelson Thornes.

Hoogland, M. L. P. 1996. "In search of the native population of pre-Columbian Saba AD 400–1450. Part two. Settlements in their natural and social environment." Ph.D. dissertation, Leiden University, Leiden.

Hoogland, M. L. P., and C. L. Hofman. 1993. Kelbey's Ridge 2, a 14th century Taíno settlement on Saba, Netherlands Antilles. In *The end of our third decade. Papers written on the occasion of the 30th anniversary of the Institute of Prehistory,* edited by C. Bakels, pp. 163–181. *Analecta Praehistorica Leidensia* 26 vol. 2, Leiden.

Hoogland, M. L. P., and C. L. Hofman. 1999. Expansion of the Taíno cacicazgos towards the Lesser Antilles. *Journal de la Société des Américanistes* 85:93–113.

Hoogland, M. L. P., and C. L. Hofman. 2011. Archaeological investigations at Spanish Water, Curaçao. *Proceedings of the XXIII International Association for Caribbean Archaeology,* pp. 631–639. Antigua.

Hoogland, M. L. P., and C. L. Hofman. 2013. From corpse taphonomy to mortuary behavior in the Caribbean: A case study from the Lesser Antilles. In *The Oxford handbook of Caribbean archaeology,* edited by W. F. Keegan, C. L. Hofman, and R. Rodríguez Ramos, pp. 452–469. New York: Oxford University Press.

Hoogland, M. L. P., and C. L. Hofman. 2015. Archaeological assessment in compliance with the Valetta Treaty. Spanish Water, Curacao. In *Managing our past into* the future: Archaeological heritage management in the Dutch Caribbean, edited by C. L. Hofman and J. B. Haviser, pp. 183–194. Leiden: Sidestone Press.

Hoogland, M. L. P., C. L. Hofman, and A. Boomert. 2011. Argyle, St. Vincent: New insights into the Island Carib occupation of the Lesser Antilles. Paper presented at the XXIV Congress of the International Association for Caribbean Archaeology. Martinique.

Hoogland, M. L. P., C. L. Hofman, H. Hooghiemstra, and M. H. Field. 2015. Under the mangrove: Coastal dynamics and deeply buried deposits at the site of Anse Trabaud, Martinique. Paper presented at the XXVI Congress of the International Association for Caribbean Archaeology. St. Martin.

Hoogland, M. L. P., C. L. Hofman, and R. G. A. M. Panhuysen. 2010. Island dynamics: Evidence for mobility and exchange at the site of Anse á la Gourde, Guadeloupe. In *Island shores, distant pasts. Archaeological and biological approaches to the pre-Columbian settlement of the Caribbean*, edited by A. H. Ross and F. M. Fitzpatrick, pp. 148–162. Gainesville: University Press of Florida.

Hoogland, M. L. P., T. Romon, and P. Brasselet. 1999. Troumassoid burial practices at the site of Anse à la Gourde, Guadeloupe. *Proceedings of the XVIII Congress of the International Association for Caribbean Archaeology*, pp. 173–178. Guadeloupe.

Howard, R. R. 1950. "The archaeology of Jamaica and its position in relation to Circum-Caribbean culture." Ph.D. dissertation, Yale University, New Haven.

Howard, R. R. 1956. The archaeology of Jamaica: A preliminary survey. *American Antiquity* 22:45–59.

Howard, R. R. 1965. New perspectives on Jamaican archaeology. *American Antiquity* 31:250–255.

Hulme, P. 1986. *Colonial encounters: Europe and the native Caribbean, 1492–1797.* London: Methuen.

Hulme, P. 1988. Chiefdoms of the Caribbean. *Critiques of Anthropology* 8:105–118.

Hulme, P., and N. L. Whitehead, 1992. *Wild majesty: Encounters with Caribs from Columbus to the present day, an anthology.* Oxford: Oxford University Press.

Hutcheson, C. D. 2015. The impressions of Long Bay: Basketry impressed ceramics from the Long Bay Site, San Salvador, Bahamas. *Journal of Caribbean Archaeology* 15:37–61.

Irwin, G. 1992. *The prehistoric exploration and colonization of the Pacific.* Cambridge: Cambridge University Press.

Jardines Macías, J., and J. Calvera Roses. 1999. Estructuras de viviendos aborígenes en Los Buchillones. *El Caribe Arqueológico* 3:44–52.

Jiménez Santander, J. 2012. Censo de sitios arqueológicos aborigenes de Cuba. Havana: Departamento de Arqueología, Instituto Cubano de Anthropología, CITMA.

Johnson, A., and T. K. Earle. 1987. *The evolution of human society: From forager group to agrarian state.* Stanford, CA: Stanford University Press.

Johnson, S. M. 2002. *Les petroglyphes des Petites Antilles Meridionales: Contextes physique et culturel.* Oxford: BAR International Series 1051.

Jones O'Day, S. 2002. Late prehistoric Lucayan occupation and subsistence on Middle Caicos Island, Northern West Indies. *Caribbean Journal of Science* 38:1–10.

Jordan, F. M., R. D. Gray, S. J. Greenhill, and R. Mace. 2009. Matrilocal residence is ancestral in Austronesian societies. *Proceedings of the Royal Society B: Biological Sciences*, 276, 1664:1957–1964.

Jouravleva, I. 2002. Origen de la alfarería de las comunidades protoagroalfareras de la región central de Cuba. *El Caribe Arqueológico* 6:35–43.

Jouravleva, I., and N. González. 2000. *Nuevos resultados acerca de la cerámica de Arroyo del Palo*. Havana: Centro de Antropología.

Joyce, R. A., and S. D. Gillespie, Eds. 2000. *Beyond kinship: Social and material reproduction in house societies*. Philadelphia: University of Pennsylvania Press.

Judge, J. 1986. Where Columbus found the New World. *National Geographic Magazine* 170:566–599.

Keegan, L. T., W. F. Keegan, L. A. Carlson and C. Altes. 2011. Shell Net Weights from Florida and Puerto Rico. In R. Murphy (ed.), *Proceedings of the XXIII Congress of the International Association for Caribbean Archaeology*, Antigua.

Keegan, W. F. 1985. "Dynamic horticulturalists: Population expansion in the prehistoric Bahamas." Ph.D. dissertation, Department of Anthropology, UCLA. University Microfilms.

Keegan, W. F. 1986a. The optimal foraging analysis of horticultural production. *American Anthropologist* 88:92–107.

Keegan, W. F. 1986b. The ecology of Lucayan Arawak fishing practices. *American Antiquity* 51:816–825.

Keegan, W. F. 1989a. Creating the Guanahatabey (Ciboney): The modern genesis of an extinct culture. *Antiquity* 63:373–379.

Keegan, W. F. 1989b. Transition from a terrestrial to a maritime economy: A new view of the crab/shell dichotomy. In *Early ceramic population lifeways and adaptive strategies in the Caribbean*, edited by P. E. Siegel, pp. 119–128. Oxford: BAR International Series 506.

Keegan, W. F. 1992. *The people who discovered Columbus*. Gainesville: University Press of Florida.

Keegan, W. F. 1994. West Indian Archaeology. 1. Overview and foragers. *Journal of Archaeological Research* 2:255–284.

Keegan, W. F. 1995. Modeling dispersal in the prehistoric West Indies. *World Archaeology* 26:400–420.

Keegan, W. F. 1996a. Columbus was a cannibal: Myths and the first encounters. In *The Lesser Antilles in the age of European expansion*, edited by R. Paquette and S. Engerman, pp. 17–32. Gainesville: University Press of Florida.

Keegan, W. F. 1996b. West Indian archaeology 2. After Columbus. *Journal of Archaeological Research* 2:265–294.

Keegan, W. F. 1997. *Bahamian archaeology: Life in the Bahamas and Turks and Caicos before Columbus*. Nassau: Media Publishing.

Keegan, W. F. 1999. The archaeology of farming systems. *Encyclopedia of Life Support Systems, Archaeology*, vol. 1. UNESCO, eolss.net.

Keegan, W. F. 2000a. West Indian Archaeology. 3. Ceramic age. *Journal of Archaeological Research* 8:135–167.

Keegan, W. F. 2000b. History and culture of food and drink in the Americas, Section V.D.2. The Caribbean, including northern South America and eastern Central America: Early history. In *The Cambridge world history of food and nutrition*, edited by K. Kipple and K. C. Ornelas, pp. 1260–1277. Cambridge: Cambridge University Press.

Keegan, W. F. 2001. Archaeological investigations on Ile à Rat, Haiti: Avoid the –OID. In *Proceedings of the XVIII International Congress for Caribbean Archaeology*, pp. 233–239. St. Georges, Grenada.

Keegan, W. F. 2004. Islands of chaos. In *The Late Ceramic Age in the eastern Caribbean*, edited by A. Delpuech and C. L. Hofman, pp. 33–46. Oxford: British Archaeological Reports.

Keegan, W. F. 2006a. All in the family—descent and succession in the protohistoric chiefdoms of the Greater Antilles: A comment on Curet. *Ethnohistory* 53:383–392.

Keegan, W. F. 2006b. Archaic influences in the origins and development of Taíno societies. *Caribbean Journal of Science* 42:1–10.

Keegan, W. F. 2007. *Taíno Indian myth and practice*. Gainesville: University Press of Florida.

Keegan, W. F. 2009. Central plaza burials in Saladoid Puerto Rico: An alternative perspective. *Latin American Antiquity* 20:375–385.

Keegan, W. F. 2010. Demographic imperatives for island colonists. In *The global origins and development of seafaring*, edited by A. Anderson, J. H. Barrett, and K. V. Boyle, pp. 171–178. Cambridge: MacDonald Institute.

Keegan, W. F. 2013. The "Classic" Taínos. In *The Oxford handbook of Caribbean archaeology*, edited by W. F. Keegan, C. L. Hofman, and R. Rodríguez Ramos, pp. 70–83. New York: Oxford University Press.

Keegan, W. F. 2015. Mobility and disdain: Columbus and cannibals in the land of cotton. *Ethnohistory* 62:1–15.

Keegan, W. F., and L.-G. Atkinson. 2006. The development of Jamaican prehistory. In *The earliest inhabitants: The dynamics of the Jamaican Taíno*, edited by L.-G. Atkinson, pp. 13–33. Kingston, Jamaica: University of the West Indies Press.

Keegan, W. F., and L. A. Carlson. 2008. *Talking Taíno*. Tuscaloosa: University of Alabama Press.

Keegan, W. F., and J. de Bry. 2015. Archaeological reconnaissance of the Jumentos Cays. In *Proceedings of the XX Congress for Caribbean Archaeology*. San Juan, Puerto Rico.

Keegan, W. F., and M. J. DeNiro. 1988. Stable carbon- and nitrogen-isotope ratios of bone collagen used to study coral-reef and terrestrial components of prehistoric Bahamian diet. *American Antiquity* 53:320–336.

Keegan, W. F., and J. M. Diamond. 1987. Colonization of islands by humans: A biogeographical perspective. In *Advances in archaeological method and theory*, Vol. 10, edited by M. B. Schiffer, pp. 49–92. San Diego: Academic Press.

Keegan, W. F., S. M. Fitzpatrick, K. Sullivan Sealey, M. LeFebvre, and P. T. Sinelli. 2008. The role of small islands in marine subsistence strategies: Case studies from the Caribbean. *Human Ecology* 36:635–654.

Keegan, W. F., C. L. Hofman, and M. L. P. Hoogland. 2002. Archaeological reconnaissance of Saint Lucia, West Indies, 4-28-2002 to 5-19-2002. http://www.flmnh.ufl.edu/caribarch/slucia2002.htm

Keegan, W. F., C. L. Hofman, and R. Rodríguez Ramos, Eds. 2013. *The Oxford handbook of Caribbean archaeology*. New York: Oxford University Press.

Keegan, W. F., and M. D. Maclachlan. 1989. The evolution of avunculocal chief-doms: A reconstruction of Taíno kinship and politics. *American Anthropologist* 91:613–630.

Keegan, W. F., M. D. Maclachlan, and B. Byrne. 1998. Social foundations of the Taíno caciques. In *Chiefdoms and chieftaincy in the Americas*, edited by E. Redmond, pp. 217–244. Gainesville: University Press of Florida.

Keegan, W. F., R. Portell, and J. Slapsinsky. 2003. Changes in invertebrate taxa at two pre-Columbian sites in southwestern Jamaica. *Journal of Archaeological Science* 30:1607–1617.

Keegan, W. F., and R. Rodríguez Ramos. 2004. Sin rodeos. *El Caribe Arqueologico* 8:8–13.

Keehnen, F. W. M. 2011. Conflicting cosmologies: The exchange of brilliant objects between the Taíno of Hispaniola and the Spanish. In *Communities in contact: Essays in archaeology, ethnohistory and ethnography of the Amerindian Circum-Caribbean*, edited by C. L. Hofman and A. van Duijvenbode, pp. 253–268. Leiden: Sidestone Press.

Keen, B., Trans. 1959. *The life of Admiral Christopher Columbus by his son Ferdinand*. New Brunswick, NJ: Rutgers University Press.

Kepecs, S., L. A. Curet, and G. la Rosa Corzo, Eds. 2010. *Beyond the blockade: New currents in Cuban archaeology*. Tuscaloosa: University of Alabama Press.

Kerchache, J. 1994. *L'Art Taíno*. Paris: Paris-Musées.

Knight, V. J., Jr. 2010. La Loma del Convento: Its centrality to current issues in Cuban archaeology. In *Beyond the blockade: New currents in Cuban archaeology*, edited by S. Kepecs, L. A. Curet, and G. la Rosa Corzo, pp. 26–46. Tuscaloosa: University of Alabama Press.

Kimura, B. K., M. J. LeFebvre, S. D. deFrance, H. I. Knodel, M. S. Turner, N. S. Fitzsimmons, S. M. Fitzpatrick, C. J. Mulligan. 2016. Origin of pre-Columbian guinea pigs from Caribbean archeological sites revealed through genetic analysis. *Journal of Archaeological Science*: Reports 5:442–452.

Kirby, I. A. E. 1974. The Cayo pottery of St. Vincent: A pre-Calivigny series. In *Proceedings of the V International Congress for the Study of the Pre-Columbian Cultures of the Lesser Antilles*, pp. 61–64. Antigua Archaeological Society, Antigua.

Kirch, P. V. 1997. Microcosmic histories: Island perspectives on global change. *American Anthropologist* 991:30–42.

Kirch, P. V. 2000. *On the road of the winds: An archaeological history of the Pacific islands before European contact*. Berkeley: University of California Press.

Knippenberg, S. 1995. "Norman Estate and Anse des Pères: Two pre-Columbian sites on Saint Martin." Master's thesis, Leiden University, Leiden.

Knippenberg, S. 1999. Part one: Methods and strategies. In *Archaeological investigations on St. Martin Lesser Antilles. The sites of Norman Estate, Anse des Pères and Hope Estate with a contribution to the 'La Hueca problem'*, edited by C. L. Hofman and M. L. P. Hoogland, pp. 25–34. Leiden: ASLU.

Knippenberg, S. 2001. Flint collecting strategies on Long Island. Paper presented at the XIX Congress of the International Association for Caribbean Archaeology, Aruba.

Knippenberg, S. 2004. Distribution and exchange of lithic materials: Three pointers and axes from St. Martin. In *Late Ceramic Age societies in the eastern Caribbean*, edited by A. Delpuech and C. L. Hofman, pp. 121–138. BAR International Series. Oxford: Archaeopress.

Knippenberg, S. 2006. "Stone artefact production and exchange among the northern Lesser Antilles." Ph.D. dissertation, Leiden University, Leiden.

Knippenberg, S. 2011. Much to choose from. The use and distribution of siliceous stone in the Lesser Antilles. In *Communities in contact. Essays in archaeology, ethnohistory and ethnography of the Amerindian Circum-Caribbean*, edited by C. L. Hofman and A. Duijvenbode, pp. 171–185. Leiden: Sidestone Press.

Knippenberg, S. 2013. L'apport de matières lithiques exogènes dans la Martinique précolombienne et leur place dans les réseaux d'échanges précolombiens au sein de la Caraïbe. In *Martinique, Terre Amérindienne. Une approche pluridisciplinair*, edited by B. Bérard, pp. 205–221. Leiden: Sidestone Press.

Knippenberg, S., and J. J. P. Zijlstra. 2008. Chert sourcing in the northern Lesser Antilles. The use of geochemical techniques in discriminating chert materials. In *Crossing the borders: New methods and techniques in the study of archaeological materials of the Caribbean*, edited by C. L. Hofman, M. L. P. Hoogland, and A. L. van Gijn. Tuscaloosa: University of Alabama Press.

Koski-Karell, D. A. 2002. "Prehistoric northern Haiti: Settlement in diachronic ecological context." Ph.D. dissertation, Catholic University of America, Washington, DC.

Kozlowski, J. 1974. *Preceramic cultures in the Caribbean*. Zeszyty Naukowe Uniwerstytetu Jagiellonskiego, vol. 386, Prace Archeologiczne, Zezyt 20, Kraków.

Kozlowski, J. 1980. In search of the evolutionary pattern of the preceramic cultures of the Caribbean. *Boletin del Museo del Hombre Dominicano* 9:61–79.

Krieger, H. W. 1931. Aboriginal Indian pottery of the Dominican Republic. *United States National Museum, Bulletin 156*, Washington, DC.

Labat, J. B. 1722. *Nouveau voyages aux iles de L'Amerique*. Paris.

Laffoon, J. E. 2012. "Patterns of paleomobility in the ancient Antilles: An isotopic approach." Ph.D. dissertation. Leiden University, Leiden.

Laffoon, J. E. 2013. Paleomobility research in Caribbean contexts: New perspectives from isotope analysis. In *The Oxford handbook of Caribbean archaeology*, edited by W. F. Keegan, C. L. Hofman, and R. Rodríguez Ramos, pp. 418–435. New York: Oxford University Press.

Laffoon J. E. 2016. Human mobility and dietary patterns in precolonial Puerto Rico: integrating multiple isotope data. In *Cuban Archaeology In The Caribbean*, edited by I. Roksandic, pp. 147–167. Florida Museum Of Natural History: Ripley P. Bullen Series. Gainsville: University Press of Florida.

Laffoon, J. L., M. L. P. Hoogland, G. R. Davies, and C. L. Hofman. 2016. Human dietary assessment in the pre-colonial Lesser Antilles: New stable isotope evidence from Lavoutte, Saint Lucia. *Journal of Archaeological Science Reports* 5:168–180.

Laffoon, J. E., E. Plomp, G. R. Davies, M. L. P. Hoogland, and C. L. Hofman. 2013. The movement and exchange of dogs in the prehistoric Caribbean: An isotopic investigation. *International Journal of Osteoarchaeology* 25:454–465.

Laffoon, J. E., R. Rodríguez Ramos, L. A. Chanlatte Baik, et al. 2014. Long-distance exchange in the precolonial Circum-Caribbean: A multi-isotope study of animal tooth pendants from Puerto Rico. *Journal of Anthropological Archaeology* 35:220–233.

Laffoon, J. E., R. Calcárcel Rojas, and C. L. Hofman. 2013. Oxygen and carbon isotope analysis of human dental enamel from the Caribbean: Implications for investigating individual origins. *Archaeometry* 55:742–765.

Laguer Díaz, C. A. 2013. The construction of an identity and the politics of remembering. In *The Oxford handbook of Caribbean archaeology*, edited by W. F. Keegan, C. L. Hofman, and R. Rodríguez Ramos, pp. 557–567. New York: Oxford University Press.

Lammers-Keijsers, Y. M. J. 2008. *Tracing traces from present to past: A functional analysis of pre-Columbian shell and stone artefacts from Anse à la Gourde and Morel, Guadeloupe, FWI.* Leiden: Leiden University Press.

Lane, C. S., S. P. Horn, and K. H. Orvis. 2008. The earliest evidence of Ostionoid maize agriculture from the interior of Hispaniola. *Caribbean Journal of Science* 44:43–52.

La Rosa Corzo, G. 2003. *Runaway slave settlements in Cuba: Resistance and repression.* Chapel Hill: University of North Carolina Press.

La Rosa Corzo, G. 2005. Subsistence of Cimarrones: An archaeological study. In *Dialogues in Cuban archaeology*, edited by L. A. Curet, S. L. Dawdy, and G. la Rosa Corzo, pp. 163–180. Tuscaloosa: University of Alabama Press.

La Rosa Corzo, G. 2010. The archaeology of escaped slaves: Utensils for resistance. In *Beyond the blockade: New currents in Cuban archaeology.* Edited by S. Kepecs, L. A. Curet, and G. la Rosa Corzo, pp. 126–142. Tuscaloosa: University of Alabama Press.

Las Casas, B. de. 1552. *Brevísima relación de la destrucción de las Indias.* http://www.ciudadseva.com/textos/otros/brevisi.htm

Las Casas, B. de. 1951. *Historia de las Indias.* 3 volumes, edited by A. Millares Carlo. Mexico City: Fondo de Cultura Económica.

Las Casas, B. de. 1992. *Apologética historia sumaria III.* España: Alianza Editorial.

Lathrap, D. W. 1970. *The upper Amazon.* Great Britain: Thames and Hudson.

Lee, J. W. 1991. Dr. James W. Lee's articles and papers published in *Archaeology Jamaica*. *Archaeology Jamaica*, new series 3:11–12.

LeFebvre, M. J., and S. D. deFrance. 2014. Guinea pigs in the pre-Columbian West Indies. *Journal of Island and Coastal Archaeology* 9:16–44.

Lenik, S, 2012. Carib as a colonial category: Comparing ethnohistoric and archaeological evidence from Dominica, West Indies. *Ethnohistory* 591:79–107.

Lévi-Strauss, C. 1963. *Structural anthropology.* New York: Basic Books.

Lévi-Strauss, C. 1969. *The elementary structures of kinship.* Boston: Beacon Press.

Lévi-Strauss, C. 1982. *The way of the masks.* Seattle: University of Washington Press.

Linares, O. 1976. "Garden hunting" in the Amazon tropics. *Human Ecology* 4:331–349.

Littman, S. B. 2001. Quaternary sea level change in the Caribbean: The implications for archaeology. In *Proceedings of the XIX International Congress for Caribbean*

Archaeology, pp. 59–65. Oranjestad: Publications of the Archaeological Museum of Aruba.

Longley, G. C. 1914. Kitchen middens of Jamaica. *American Museum Journal* 14:296–298.

Lovén, S. 1932. *Stone dart points from the district of Old Harbour, Jamaica*. Göteborg.

Lovén, S. 1935. *Origins of the Tainan culture, West Indies*. Göteborg: Erlanders Boktryckerie Aktiebolag.

Lundberg, E. 1980. Old and new problems in the study of Antillean aceramic traditions. In *Proceedings of the VIII International Congress for the Study of Pre-Columbian Cultures of the Lesser Antilles*, pp. 131–138. Anthropological Papers 22. Tempe: Arizona State University.

Lundberg, E. R. 1985. Interpreting the cultural associations of aceramic deposits in the Virgin Islands. *Journal of Field Archaeology* 12:201–212.

Lundberg, E. R. 1989. "Preceramic procurement patterns at Krum Bay, Virgin Islands." Ph.D. dissertation, University of Illinois, Urbana-Champaign.

Lundberg, E. R. 1991. Interrelationships among preceramic complexes of Puerto Rico and the Virgin Islands. In *Proceedings of the XIII International Congress for Caribbean Archaeology*, edited by E. N. Ayubi and J. B. Haviser, pp. 73–85. Willemstad, Curaçao.

Lundberg, E., E. C. Richter, and M. D. Caesar. 1992. The Late Ceramic age in the Northern Virgin Islands. Paper presented at the 57th Annual Meeting of the Society for American Archaeology. Pittsburgh.

MacArthur, R. H., and E. O. Wilson. 1967. *The theory of island biogeography*. Princeton, NJ: Princeton University Press.

Macintyre, M. 1983. Warfare and the changing context of "Kune" on Tubetube. *The Journal of Pacific History* 18:11–34.

MacNutt, F. A., Trans. 1970. *De Orbe Novo* [P. Martyr D'Anghiera, 1493–1525]. New York: Burt Franklin.

Maclachlan, M. D., and W. F. Keegan. 1990. Archeology and the ethno-tyrannies. *American Anthropologist* 92:1011–1013.

MacNeish, R. S., and A. Nelken-Turner. 1983. *Final annual report of the Belize Archaeological Research Reconnaissance*. Center for Archaeological Studies, Boston University, Boston.

MacNutt, F. A. 1912. *Peter Martyr d'Anghera*. Translation of Peter Martyr's *De Orbe Novo*. New York: Burt Franklin.

Malaizé, B., P. Bertran, P. Carbonel. 2011. September hurricanes and climate in the Caribbean during the past 3700 years B.P. *The Holocene* 216:911–924.

Malinowski, B. 1922. *Argonauts of the western Pacific*. New York: E.P. Dutton & Co.

Malinowski, B. 1935. *Coral gardens and their magic*. London: George Allen and Unwin.

Mann, C. J. 1986. Composition and origin of material in pre-Columbian pottery, San Salvador Island, Bahamas. *Geoarchaeology* 1:183–194.

Martias, R. 2005. «Saint-Martin, Etang Rouge 3. Lot 411 97150 Guadeloupe, les Terres Basses.» Rapport de diagnostic Inrap, DRAC Guadeloupe, non publié.

Martin, J. A. 2012. *Island Caribs and French settlers in Grenada: 1498–1763*. Grenada: Grenada National Museum Press.

Martínez Arango, F. 1997. *Los aborígenes de la cuenca de Santiago de Cuba.* Miami: Ediciones Universal.

Martínez-Cruzado, J. 2010. The history of Amerindian mitochondrial DNA lineages in Puerto Rico. In *Island shores, distant pasts: Archaeological and biological approaches to the Pre-Columbian settlement of the Caribbean,* edited by S. M. Fitzpatrick and A. H. Ross, pp. 54–80. Gainesville: University of Florida Press.

Martínez-Cruzado, J. 2013. The DNA evidence for the human colonization and spread across the Americas: Implications for the peopling of the Caribbean. In *The Oxford handbook of Caribbean archaeology,* edited by W. F. Keegan, C. L. Hofman, and R. Rodríguez Ramos, pp. 470–485. New York: Oxford University Press.

Martir de Angleria, P. 1989. *Decadas del Nuevo Mundo,* 2 vols. Santo Domingo: Sociedad Dominicana de Bibliofilos, Inc.

Matthiessen, P. 1975. *Far Tortuga: A novel.* New York: Random House.

Mattioni, M., and R. P. Bullen. 1970. A chronological chart for the Lesser Antilles. In *Proceedings of the III International Congress for the study of pre-Columbian cultures of the Lesser Antilles,* pp. 1–3. St. George, Grenada.

McGinnis, S. A. 1997. "Ideographic expression in the Precolumbian Caribbean." Ph.D. dissertation, Department of Anthropology, University of Texas at Austin, Austin.

McKusick, M. 1959. "The Distribution of ceramic styles in the Lesser Antilles, West Indies." Ph.D. dissertation, Yale University. Ann Arbor: University Microfilms.

McKusick, M. 1960. Aboriginal canoes in the West Indies. *Yale University Publications in Anthropology* 70:3–11.

Meggers, B. J. 1996. *Amazonia: Man and culture in a counterfeit paradise.* Washington, DC: Smithsonian Institution Press.

Meggers, B. J., C. Evans, and E. Estrada. 1965. *Early formative period of coastal Ecuador: The Valdivia and Machalilla phases.* Washington, DC: Smithsonian Institution.

Michener, J. 1988. *Caribbean.* Knopf, New York.

Mickleburgh, H. L. 2013. "Reading the dental record: A dental anthropological approach to foodways, health and disease, and crafting in the pre-Columbian Caribbean." Ph.D. dissertation, Faculty of Archaeology, Leiden University, Leiden.

Mickleburgh, H. L., and J. R. Pagan-Jimenez. 2012. New insights into the consumption of maize and other food plants in the pre-Columbian Caribbean from starch grains trapped in human dental calculus. *Journal of Archaeological Science* 39 (7): 2468–2478.

Milanich, J. T., Ed. 1984. *McKeithen Weeden Island: The culture of northern Florida, AD 200–900.* New York: Academic Press.

Milanich, J. T., and S. Milbrath, Eds. 1989. *First encounters.* Gainesville: University Press of Florida.

Milbrath, S. 1989. Old World meets New: Views across the Atlantic. In *First encounters,* edited by J. T. Milanich and S. Milbrath, pp. 183–210. Gainesville: University Press of Florida.

Milne, G. A., and M. C. Peros. 2013. Data–model comparison of Holocene sea-level change in the circum-Caribbean region. *Global and Planetary Change* 107:119–131.

Miner Solá, E. 2002. *Diccionario Taíno illustrado.* Puerto Rico: Ediciones Servilibro.

Mitchell, S. W. 1984. Late Holocene tidal creek-lake transitions, Long Island, Bahamas. Addendum to *Proceedings of the Second Symposium on the Geology of the Bahamas*, edited by J. W. Teeter, pp. 1–28. San Salvador, Bahamas: College Center of the Finger Lakes Bahamian Field Station.

Mitchell, S. W., and W. F. Keegan. 1987. Reconstruction of the coastlines of the Bahama Islands in 1492. *American Archaeology* 6:88–96.

Mol, A. A. A. 2007. *Costly giving, giving Guaízas: Towards an organic model of the exchange of social valuables in the Late Ceramic Age Caribbean.* Leiden: Sidestone Press.

Mol, A. A. A. 2013. Studying pre-Columbian interaction networks: Mobility and exchange. In *The Oxford handbook of Caribbean archaeology*, edited by W. F. Keegan, C. L. Hofman, and R. Rodríguez Ramos, pp. 329–346. New York: Oxford University Press.

Mol, A. A. A. 2014. *The connected Caribbean: A socio-material network approach to patterns of homogeneity and diversity in the pre-colonial period.* Leiden: Sidestone Press.

Mol, A. A. A., M. L. P. Hoogland, and C. L. Hofman. 2015. Remotely local: Ego networks of late pre-Colonial (AD 1000–1450) Saba northeastern Caribbean. *Journal of Archaeological Method and Theory* 22:275–305.

Montane, M. J. C. 1981. Sociedades igualitarias y modo de produccion. *Boletín de Antropología Americana* 3:71–89.

Moore, C. 1982. Investigation of preceramic sites on Ile à Vache, Haiti. *The Florida Anthropologist* 35:186–199.

Moore, C. 1991. Cabaret: Lithic workshop sites in Haiti. In *Proceedings of the XIII Congress of the International Association for Caribbean Archaeology.* Willemstad, Curaçao.

Moore, C. 1998. "Archaeology in Haiti." Unpublished manuscript cited with the permission of the author.

Moore, J. 2001. Evaluating five models of human colonization. *American Anthropologist* 103:395–408.

Morales Santos, L. 2010. New early tradition stone tools industries in Cuba. In *Dialogues in Cuban archaeology*, edited by L. A. Curet, S. L. Dawdy, and G. la Rosa Corzo, pp. 47–69. Tuscaloosa: University of Alabama Press.

Morgan, G. S. 1993. Quaternary land vertebrates of Jamaica. *Geological Society of America Memoirs* 182:417–442.

Morgan, G. S., and C. A. Woods. 1986. Extinction and the zoogeography of West Indian land mammals. *Biological Journal of the Linnean Society* 28:167–203.

Morison, S. E. 1942. *Admiral of the Ocean Sea.* Boston: Little, Brown.

Morison, S. E. 1963. *Journals and other documents on the life and voyages of Christopher Columbus.* New York: Heritage Press.

Morsink, J. 2006. "Re-constructing constructions: Quotidian life and social practice at Anse à la Gourde." Master's thesis, Leiden University, Leiden.

Morsink, J. 2011. Social continuity in the Caribbean past: A Maison perspective on cultural continuity. *Caribbean Connections* 12:3–12.

Morsink, J. 2012. "The power of salt: A holistic approach to salt in the prehistoric Circum-Caribbean region." Ph.D. dissertation, Department of Anthropology, University of Florida, Gainesville.

Morsink, J. 2013. Exchange as a social contract: A perspective from the microscale. In *The Oxford handbook of Caribbean archaeology*, edited by W. F. Keegan, C. L. Hofman, and R. Rodríguez Ramos, pp. 312–328. New York: Oxford University Press.

Morsink, J. 2015. Spanish-Lucayan interaction: Continuity of native economies in early historic times. *Journal of Caribbean Archaeology* 15:102–119.

Moscoso, F. 1981. "The development of tribal society in the Caribbean." Ph.D. dissertation, SUNY at Binghamton. Ann Arbor: University Microfilms.

Moscoso, F. 1986. *Tribu y clase en el Caribe antiguo*. San Pedro de Macoris, Dominican Republic: Universidad Central del Este.

Murdock, G. P. 1949. *Social structure*. New York: Macmillan.

Murphy, A. R. 1999. "The prehistory of Antigua, Ceramic Age: Subsistence, settlement, culture and adaptation within an insular environment." Ph.D. dissertation, University of Calgary, Calgary.

Myers, R. A. 1984. Island Carib cannibalism, *Nieuwe West-Indische Gids* 158: 147–184.

Narganes Storde, Y. M. 1991b. Los restos faunísticos del sitio de Puerto Ferro, Vieques, Puerto Rico. In *Proceedings of the XIV Congress of the International Association for Caribbean Archaeology*, edited by A. Cummins and P. King, pp. 94–114. Barbados: Barbados Museum and Historical Society.

Narganes Storde, Y. M. 1995. La lapidaria de la Hueca, Vieques, Puerto Rico. In *Proceedings of the XV International Congress for Caribbean Archaeology*, edited by R. Alegría and M. Rodríguez, pp. 141–151. San Juan: Centro de Estudios Avanzados de Puerto Rico y el Caribe.

Newsom, L. A. 1993. "Native West Indian plant use." Ph.D. dissertation, Department of Anthropology, University of Florida, Gainesville.

Newsom, L. A., and K. A. Deagan. 1994. *Zea mays* in the West Indies: The archaeological and early historic record. In *Corn and culture in the prehistoric New World*, edited by S. Johannessen and C. A. Hastorf, pp. 203–217. Boulder, CO: Westview Press.

Newsom, L. A., and E. S. Wing. 2004. *On land and sea: Native American uses of biological resources in the West Indies*. Tuscaloosa: University of Alabama Press.

Nicholl, J. 1605. *An houre glasse of Indian newes. Or a ... discourse shewing, the ... miseries ... indured by 67 Englishmen, which were sent for a supply to the planting in Guiana, in the year 1605, etc.* London: British Library.

Nicholson, D. V. 1976. The importance of sea level changes in Caribbean archaeology. *Journal of the Virgin Islands Archaeological Society* 3:19–23.

Nicholson, D. V. 1983. *The Story of the Arawaks in Antigua and Barbuda*. St. John: Antigua Archaeological Society.

Nieuwenhuis, C. 2008. The significance of wear and residue studies: An example from Plum Piece, Saba. In *Crossing the borders. New methods and techniques in the study of archaeological materials from the Caribbean*, edited by C. L. Hofman, M. L. P. Hoogland, and A. L. van Gijn, pp. 125–136. Tuscaloosa: Alabama University Press.

Nieweg, D. 2000. "Shells in archaeology. Archaeological shell on Trinidad and Guadeloupe: Two case studies." Master's thesis,. Leiden University, Leiden.

Noble, G. K. 1965. *Proto-Arawakan and its descendants*. Bloomington: Indiana University Publications in Anthropology and Linguistics, no. 38.

Nodine, B. 1990. Aceramic populations in the Lesser Antilles: Evidence from Antigua, West Indies. Paper presented at the 55th annual meeting of the Society for American Archaeology, Las Vegas.

Nokkert, M., A. Brokke, S. Knippenberg, and T. Hamburg. 1995. An Archaic occupation at Norman Estate, St. Martin. In *Proceedings of the XVI Congress of the International Association for Caribbean Archaeology, Guadeloupe*, pp. 333–351. Guadeloupe: Conseil Regional de l'Archeologie de la Guadeloupe.

Oberg, K. 1955. Types of social structure among the lowland tribes of South and Central America. *American Anthropologist* 57:472–487.

O'Day, S. J. 2002. Late prehistoric Lucayan occupation and subsistence on Middle Caicos Island, Northern West Indies. *Caribbean Journal of Science* 38:1–10.

O'Day S. J., and W. F. Keegan. 2001. Expedient shell tools from the Northern West Indies. *Latin American Antiquity* 12:1–17.

Olazagasti, I. 1997. The material culture of the Taíno Indians. In *The indigenous people of the Caribbean*, edited by S. M. Wilson, pp. 131–139. Gainesville: University Press of Florida.

Oliver, J. 1995. The archaeology of Lower Camp site, Culebra Island: Understanding variability in peripheral zones. In *Proceedings of the XV International Congress for Caribbean Archaeology*, edited by R. Alegría and M. Rodríguez, pp. 485–500. San Juan: Centro de Estudios Avanzados de Puerto Rico y el Caribe.

Oliver, J. R. 1998. *El centro ceremonial Caguana, Puerto Rico*. Oxford: British Archaeological Reports.

Oliver, J. R. 1999. The La Hueca Complex in Puerto Rico and the Caribbean: Old problems, new perspectives, possible solutions. In *Archaeological investigations on St. Martin, Lesser Antilles: The sites of Norman Estate, Hope Estate, and Anse des Peres*, edited by C. L. Hofman and M. L. P. Hoogland, pp. 253–297. Leiden: ASLU.

Oliver, J. R. 2000. Gold symbolism among Caribbean chiefdoms: Of feathers, Çibas and Guanín power among Taíno elites. In *Pre-Columbian gold in South America: Technology style, and iconography*, edited by C. McEwan, pp. 196–219. London: British Museum Press.

Oliver, J. R. 2005. The proto-Taíno monumental cemis of Caguana. In *Ancient Borinquen*, edited by P. E. Siegel, pp. 230–284. Tuscaloosa: University of Alabama Press.

Oliver, J. R. 2009. *Caciques and cemí idols: The web spun by Taíno rulers between Hispaniola and Puerto Rico*. Tuscaloosa: University Alabama Press.

Olsen, F. 1974. *On the trail of the Arawaks*. Norman: University of Oklahoma Press.

Olsen, F. 1976. Preceramic findings in Antigua. *Proceedings of the first Puerto Rican Symposium in Archaeology*, pp.85–94. San Juan: Fundacion Archeológica, Antropológica y Historia de Puerto Rico.

Ortega, E., and J. G. Guerrero. 1985. El complejo litico de la cordillera, las grandes puntas especializadas y su relacion con los modos de vida preagroalfareros en la prehistoria de Santo Domingo. In *Proceedings of the X International Congress for the Study of the Pre-Columbian Cultures of the Lesser Antilles*, pp. 311–334. Montreal: Centre de Recherches Caraïbes.

Ortiz, F. 1983. *Contrapunto Cubano del azúcar y el tabaco*. Havana: Editorial de Ciencias Sociales.

Ortíz Aguilú, J., E. J. Maiz, J. Sued-Badillo, and T. R. Sara. 2001. Palo Hincado, Puerto Rico: New insights from ongoing investigations. Paper presented at the XIX Congress of the International Association for Caribbean Archaeology, Aruba.

Ortiz Aguilú, J. J., J. Rivera Meléndez, A. Príncipe Jácome, M. Mélendez Maiz, and M. Lavergne Colberg. 1991. Intensive agriculture in pre-Columbian West Indies: The case for terraces. In *Proceedings of the XIV Congress of the International Association for Caribbean Archaeology*, edited by A. Cummins and P. King, pp. 278–285. Barbados: Barbados Museum and Historical Society.

Osgood, C. 1942. The Ciboney culture of Cayo Redondo, Cuba. *Yale University Publications in Anthropology*, number 25. New Haven: Yale University Press.

Ostapkowicz, J. M. 1998. "Taíno wooden sculpture: Duhos, rulership, and the visual arts in the 12th–16th century Caribbean." Ph.D. dissertation, School of World Art Studies, University of East Anglia, Norwich, UK.

Ostapkowicz, J. 2015. "Either a piece of domestic furniture of the Indians or one of their Gods": The study of Lucayan duhos. *Journal of Caribbean Archaeology* 15:120–134.

Oviedo y Valdés, G. F. de. 1959. *Historia general y natural de las Indias*, vols. 1–2. Madrid: Ediciones Atlas.

Oyuela-Caycedo, A., and R. M. Bonzani. 2005. *San Jacinto 1: A historical ecological approach to an Archaic site in Colombia*. Tuscaloosa: University of Alabama Press.

Pagán-Jiménez, J. R. 2008. Envisioning ancient human plant use at the Río Tanamá site 2, AR-39, through starch analysis of lithic and clay griddle implements. In *A multidisciplinary approach to the data recovery at two village sites on the Río Tanamá*, edited by L. Carlson, pp. 241–257. Jonesville, FL: SEARCH, Inc.

Pagán Jiménez, J. R. 2011. Early phytocultural processes in the pre-colonial antilles: A pan-Caribbean survey for an ongoing starch grain research. In *Communities in contact: Essays in archaeology, ethnohistory and ethnography of the Amerindian Circum-Caribbean*, edited by C. L. Hofman and A. Van Duijvenbode, pp. 87–117. Leiden: Sidestone Press.

Pagán-Jiménez, J. R. 2013. Human–plant dynamics in the precolonial Antilles: A synthetic update. In *The Oxford handbook of Caribbean archaeology*, edited by W. F. Keegan, C. L. Hofman, and R. Rodríguez Ramos, pp. 391–406. New York: Oxford University Press.

Pagán-Jiménez, J. R., and R. Rodríguez Ramos. 2008. Towards the liberation of archaeological praxis in a "postcolonial colony" of a "postcolonial" world: The case of Puerto Rico. In *Post-colonialism and archaeology*, edited by M. Liebman, and U. Z. Rizvi. Lanham, MD: AltaMira Press.

Pagán-Jiménez, J. R., R. Rodríguez-Ramos, B. A Reid, M. van den Bel, and C. L. Hofman. 2015. Early dispersals of maize and other food plants into the Southern Caribbean and Northeastern South America. *Quaternary Science Reviews* 123:231–246.

Paine, R. R. 1989. Model life table fitting by maximum likelihood estimation: A procedure to reconstruct paleodemographic characteristics from skeletal age distributions. *American Journal of Physical Anthropology* 79:51–61.

Pajón, J. M., I. Hernándea, P. P. Godo. 2007. Proyecto "Reconstrucción Paleoclimática y Paleoambiental de Sectores Claves de Cuba y el Caribe": Contribución a los estudios de poblamiento y asentamientos de sitios arqueológicos en Cuba." In *Memorias del Segundo Seminario Internacional de Arqueologiá* CD-ROM, edited by R. Arrazcaeta. Havana: Gabinete de Arqueología de la Oficina del Historiador de la Cuidad de Havana.

Pantel, A. G. 1976. Progress Report and Analysis: Barrera-Mordán Complex, Azua, Dominican Republic. In *Proceedings of the XVI International Congress for the Study of Pre-Columbian Cultures of the Lesser Antilles*, pp. 253–257. Guadeloupe: Société d'Histoire de la Guadeloupe.

Pantel, A. G. 1988. "Precolumbian flaked stone assemblages in the West Indies." Ph.D. dissertation, University of Tennessee. Ann Arbor: University Microfilms.

Pauketat, T. R. 2007. *Chiefdoms and other archaeological delusions*. Lanham, MD: AltaMira Press.

Pearsall, D. 1989. *Paleoethnobotany: A handbook of procedures*. New York: Academic Press.

Pekka Helminen, J. 1988. ¿Eran cannibales los Caribes? Fray Bartolomé de las Casas y el cannibalismo. *Revista de Historia de America* 105:147–158.

Peros, M. C., E. Graham, and A. M. Davis. 2006. Stratigraphic investigations at Los Buchillones, a coastal Taíno site in north-central Cuba. *Geoarchaeology* 21:403.

Pendergast, D. M., E. Graham, R. J. Calvera, and M. J. Jardines. 2002. The house in which they dwelt: The excavation and dating of Taíno wooden structures at Los Buchillones, Cuba. *Journal of Wetland Archaeology* 21:61–75.

Persons, A. B. 2013. "Pottery, people, and place: Examining the emergence of political authority in Late Ceramic Age Cuba." Ph.D. dissertation, Department of Anthropology, University of Alabama, Tuscaloosa.

Pestle, W. J. 2013. Stable isotope analysis of paleodiet in the Caribbean. In *The Oxford handbook of Caribbean archaeology*, edited by W. F. Keegan, C. L. Hofman, and R. Rodríguez Ramos, pp. 407–417. New York: Oxford University Press.

Petersen, J. B. 1996. Archaeology of Trants. Part 3. Chronological and settlement data. *Annals of the Carnegie Museum* 654:323–361.

Petersen, J. B. 1997. Taíno, Island Carib, and prehistoric Amerindian economics in the West Indies: Tropical forest adaptations to island environments. In *Indigenous people of the Caribbean*, edited by S. M. Wilson, pp. 118–130. Gainesville: University Press of Florida.

Petersen, J. B., and J. G. Crock. 1999. Late Saladoid to late prehistoric occupation in Anguilla: Site setting, chronology and settlement hierarchy. In *Proceedings of XVIII Congress of the International Association for Caribbean Archaeology*, edited by G. Richard, pp. 124–135. St. George's, Grenada.

Petersen, J. B., C. L. Hofman, and L. A. Curet. 2004. Time and culture: Chronology and taxonomy in the eastern Caribbean and the Guianas. In *Late Ceramic Age societies in the eastern Caribbean*, edited by A. Delpuech and C. L. Hofman, pp. 17–32. Oxford: BAR.

Petitjean Roget, H. 1981. Les populations amérindiennes: Aspects de la préhistoire Antillaise. In *l'Historial Antillais vol. 1, Guadeloupe et Martinique: Des îles aux hommes, Pointe-à-Pitre*, edited by J. L. Bonniol, pp. 77–152. French Guiana: Société Dajani.

Petitjean Roget, H. 1995. Les Calebasses Peintes, la potterie et l'arc en ciel chez les Caraïbes Insulaires. *Proceedings of the XVI Congress of the International Association for Caribbean Archaeology, Basse-Terre, Guadeloupe.*

Petitjean Roget, H. 2001. Contribution à l'etude du Troumassoïde et du Suazoïde AD 600–1200: Une hypothèse sur les causes de la régression du Saladoïde aux Petites Antilles. In *Proceedings of the XVIII International Congress for Caribbean Archaeology*, edited by G, Richard, pp. 227–238. St. George's, Grenada.

Petitjean Roget, H. 2005. Une collection archéologique des Petites Antilles entre au Musée Régional d'Histoire et d'Ethnographie de la Martinique. *La Revue du Louvre et des musées de France* 2: 37–46.

Petitjean Roget, H. 2013. A la recherché des paroles perdues: Essai d'interpretation des mots Turey, Nucay, Caona et Tuob. Paper presented at the XXV Congress of the International Association for Caribbean Archaeology, July 15–20, 2013, San Juan, Puerto Rico.

Petitjean Roget, H. 2015. Taíno et Kalina. Paper presented at the International Congress of the International Association for Caribbean Archaeology. Basse-Terre: Guadeloupe.

Petitjean Roget, J. 1970. Archeology in Martinique. *Parallèlès* 36–37:48–67.

Pino, M. 1970. *Excavaciones en Cueva Funche.* Serie Espeleologica y Carsologica, No. 11. Havana.

Pino, M. 1995. *Actualización de fechados radiocarbónicas de sitios arqueológicos de Cuba hasta Diciembre de 1993.* Havana: Editorial Academia.

Plomp, E. 2011. "Neither human nor beast. The role of the dog in Pre-Columbian Caribbean societies." Unpublished BA-thesis, Leiden University.

Pregill, G. K., D. W. Steadman, and D. R. Watters. 1994. Late Quaternary vertebrate faunas of the Lesser Antilles: Historical components of Caribbean biogeography. *Bulletin of the Carnegie Museum of Natural History* 30:1–51.

Price, R. 1966. Caribbean fishing and fisherman: A historical sketch. *American Anthropologist* 68:1363–1383.

Quitmyer, I. 2003. Zooarchaeology of Cinnamon Bay, St. John, U.S. Virgin Islands: Pre-Columbian overexploitation of animal resources. In Zooarchaeology: Papers to honor Elizabeth S. Wing, edited by F. W. King and C. M. Porter. *Bulletin of the Florida Museum of Natural History* 44:131–158.

Rafinesque, C. S. 1836. *The American Nations; or, Outlines of their general history, ancient and modern.* Philadelphia: N.p.

Rainbird, P. 1999. Islands out of time: Toward a critique of island archaeology. *Journal of Mediterranean Archaeology* 12:216–260.

Rainbird, P. 2007. *The archaeology of islands.* Cambridge: Cambridge University Press.

Rainey, F. G. 1940. Porto Rican archaeology. Scientific survey of Porto Rico and the Virgin Islands. Volume XVIII—Part 1. New York: New York Academy of Sciences.

Rainey, F. G. 1941. Excavations in the Ft. Liberté Region, Haiti. *Yale University Publications in Anthropology*, nos. 23–24. New Haven.

Rainey, F., and J. J. Ortiz Aguilú. 1983. "Bois Neuf: The archaeological view from west central Haiti." Unpublished manuscript in possession of the author.

Rappaport, R. 1968. *Pigs for the ancestors: Ritual in the ecology of a New Guinea people.* New Haven: Yale University Press.

Redmond, E. M., and C. S. Spencer. 1994. The cacicazgo: An indigenous design. In *Caciques and their people: A volume in honor of Ronald Spores,* edited by J. Marcus and J. F. Zeitlin, pp. 189–225. Anthropological Papers, No. 89, Ann Arbor: Museum of Anthropology, University of Michigan.

Reichard, A. 1904. Archaeological discoveries in Jamaica. *Globus* 86, Braunschweig.

Reichel-Dolmatoff, G. 1965. Excavaciones arqueológicas en Puerto Hormiga Departamento de Bolívar. *Antropología 2.* Bogotá: Universidad de los Andes.

Reid, B. A. 2009. *Myths and realities of Caribbean history.* Tuscaloosa: University of Alabama Press.

Reid, B. A., and R. Grant Gilmore III, Eds. 2014. *Encyclopedia of Caribbean archaeology.* Florida: University Press of Florida.

Reitz, E. J. 1989. "Vertebrate fauna from Krum Bay, St. Thomas, Virgin Islands." Ph.D. dissertation. University of Illinois, Urbana-Champagne. Ann Arbor: University Microfilms.

Reitz, E. J. 1994. Archaeology of Trants, Montserrat. Part 2. Vertebrate fauna. *Annals of the Carnegie Museum* 63:297–313.

Reitz, E. J., and J. A. Dukes. 1995. Use of vertebrate resources at Trants, a Saladoid site on Montserrat. In *Proceedings of the XV Congress of the International Association for Caribbean Archaeology,* pp. 201–208. San Juan, Puerto Rico.

Renfrew, C., and J. F. Cherry, Eds. 1986. *Peer polity interaction and socio-political change.* New York: Cambridge University Press.

Rey Bettancourt, E., and F. García Rodríguez. 1988. Simultud entre los artifactos lithicos dellajano oriente de Asia y de Cuba. *Annuario de Arqueología 1988,* pp. 1–13. Havana: Academia de Ciencias de Cuba.

Rice, P. R. 1987. *Pottery analysis: A sourcebook.* Chicago: University of Chicago Press.

Richard, G. 1994. Premier indice d'une occupation précéramique en Guadeloupe continentale. *Journal de la Société des Américanistes* 80:241–242.

Richards, A. 2006. The impact of land-based development on Taíno archaeology in Jamaica. In *The earliest inhabitants: The dynamics of the Jamaican Taíno,* edited by L.-G. Atkinson, pp. 75–86. Kingston: University of the West Indies Press.

Righter, E. 1997. The ceramics, art, and material culture of the early Ceramic period in the Caribbean Islands. In *The indigenous people of the Caribbean,* edited by S. M. Wilson, pp. 70–79. Gainesville: University Press of Florida.

Righter, E. 2002. *The Tutu archaeological village site: A multidisciplinary case study in human adaptation.* London: Routledge.

Righter, E., M. K. Sandford, and L. Sappelsa. 1995. Bioarchaeological investigations at the Tutu archaeological village site, St. Thomas, USVI: A preliminary report. Paper presented at the XV Congress of the International Association for Caribbean Archaeology, Puerto Rico.

Riley, T. J. 1987. Ridged-field agriculture and the Mississippian economic pattern. In *Emergent horticultural economies of the eastern woodlands,* edited by W. F. Keegan, pp. 295–304. Southern Illinois University, Center for Archaeological Investigations, Occasional Paper 7, Carbondale.

Riley, T. J., R. Edging, and J. Rosen. 1990. Cultigens in prehistoric eastern North America. *Current Anthropology* 31:525–541.

Rímoli, R. O., and J. Nadal. 1980. Cerámica temprana de Honduras del Oeste. *Boletín del Museo del Hombre Dominicano* 15:17–79.

Rivera-Collazo, I. C. 2011a. The ghost of Caliban: Island archaeology, insular archaeologists, and the Caribbean. In *Islands at the crossroads: Migration, seafaring, and interaction in the Caribbean*, edited by L. A. Curet and M. W. Hauser, pp. 22–40. Tuscaloosa: University of Alabama Press.

Rivera-Collazo, I. C. 2011b. Palaeoecology and human occupation during the mid-Holocene in Puerto Rico: the case of Angostura. In *Communities in contact*, edited by C. L. Hofman and A. van Duijvenbode, pp. 407–421. Leiden: Sidestone Press.

Rives, A., and J. Febles. 1988. Approximacíon a una metódica Interpretative de los ajuares de sílex de las communidades aborígenes de Cuba. *Anuario de arqueología* 1988, pp. 14–27. Havana: Academia de Ciencias.

Robiou-Lamarche, S. 1994. *Encuentro con la mitología Taína*. San Juan, Puerto Rico: Editorial Punto y Coma.

Robiou-Lamarche, S. 2002. Osa Major: La idealización del huracán de Mesoamérica a las Antillas. *El Caribe Arqueológico* 6:86–93.

Rochefort, C. de. 1665. *Histoire naturelle et morale des îles Antilles de l'Amérique; Avec un vocabulaire caraïbe*. 2nd edition. Rotterdam: Arnout Leers.

Rodríguez Álvarez, Á. 2003. "Astronomía en la prehistoria de Puerto Rico: Caguana y Tibes, antiguos observatorios precolombinos." Ph.D. dissertation, University de Valladoid, Spain.

Rodríguez López, M. 1989. The zoned incised crosshatch ZIC ware of early precolumbian Ceramic Age sites in Puerto Rico and Vieques Island. In *Early ceramic population lifeways and adaptive strategies in the Caribbean*, edited by P. E. Siegel, pp. 637–671. Oxford: BAR International Series 506.

Rodríguez López, M. 1990. Arqueología del Río Loiza. In *Proceedings of the XI International Congress for Caribbean Archaeology*, edited by G. Pantel Tekakis, I. Vargas Arenas, and M. Sanoja Obediente, pp. 287–294. San Juan, Puerto Rico.

Rodríguez López, M. 1991. Arqueología del Punta Candelero, Puerto Rico. In *Proceedings of the XIII International Congress for Caribbean Archaeology*, edited by E. N. Ayubi and J. B. Haviser, pp. 605–627. Willemstad, Curaçao.

Rodríguez López, M. 1992. Diversidad cultural tardía en la prehistoria del este de Puerto Rico. Paper presented at the 57th Annual Meeting of the Society for American Archaeology. Pittsburgh.

Rodríguez López, M. 1997. Religious beliefs of the Saladoid People. In *The indigenous people of the Caribbean*, edited by S. M. Wilson, pp. 80–87. Gainesville: University Press of Florida.

Rodríguez Ramos, R. 1999. Lithic reduction trajectories at La Hueca and Punta Candalero sites, Puerto Rico: A preliminary report. In *Proceedings of the XVIII International Congress for Caribbean Archaeology*, pp. 251–261. St. Georges, Grenada.

Rodríguez Ramos, R. 2001. "Lithic reduction trajectories at La Hueca and Punta Candelero Sites, Puerto Rico." Unpublished Master's thesis, Department of Anthropology, Texas A&M University, College Station, Texas.

Rodríguez Ramos, R. 2005. The function of the edge-ground cobble put to the test: An initial assessment. *Journal of Caribbean Archaeology* 5:1–22.

Rodríguez Ramos, R. 2008. From the Guanahatabey to the "Archaic" of Puerto Rico: The non-evident evidence. *Ethnohistory* 553:393–415.

Rodriguez Ramos, R. 2010. *Rethinking Puerto Rican precolonial history*. Tuscaloosa: University of Alabama Press.

Rodriguez Ramos, R. 2013. Isthmo-Colombian engagements. In *The Oxford handbook of Caribbean archaeology*, edited by W. F. Keegan, C. L. Hofman, and R. Rodríguez Ramos, pp. 155–170. New York: Oxford University Press.

Rodríguez Ramos, R., E. Babilonia, L. A. Curet, and J. Ulloa Hung. 2008. The pre-Arawak pottery horizon in the Antilles: A new approximation. *Latin American Antiquity* 191:47–63.

Rodríguez Ramos, R., J. R. Pagán-Jiménez, and C. L. Hofman. 2013. The humanization of the insular Caribbean. In *The Oxford handbook of Caribbean archaeology*, edited by W. F. Keegan, C. L. Hofman, and R. Rodríguez Ramos, pp. 126–140. New York: Oxford University Press.

Rodríguez Ramos, R., J. M. Torres, and J. R. Oliver. 2010. Rethinking time in Caribbean archaeology. In *Island shores, distant pasts*, edited by S. Fitzpatrick and A. H. Ross, pp. 21–53. Gainesville: University Press of Florida.

Roe, P. G. 1982. *The cosmic zygote*. New Brunswick, NJ: Rutgers University Press.

Roe, P. G. 1985. A preliminary report on the 1980 and 1982 field seasons at Hacienda Grande 12 PSJ-7: Overview of site history, mapping and excavations. In *Proceedings of the X International Congress for the Study of the Pre-Columbian Cultures of the Lesser Antilles*, pp. 151–180. Centre de Recherches Caraïbes, Montreal.

Roe, P. G. 1989. A grammatical analysis of Cedrosan Saladoid vessel form categories and surface decoration: Aesthetic and technical styles in early Antillean ceramics. In *Early ceramic population lifeways and adaptive strategies in the Caribbean*, edited by P. E. Siegel, pp. 267–382. Oxford: BAR International Series 506.

Roe, P, G. 1991. The best enemy is a drilled, defunct and decorative enemy: Human corporeal art (frontal bone pectoral belt ornaments, carved humeri and pierced teeth) in precolumbian Puerto Rico. In *Proceedings of the XIII International Congress for Caribbean Archaeology*, pp. 854–873. Curaçao: Reports of the Anthropological-Anthropological Institute of the Netherland Antilles, No. 9.

Roe, P. G. 1995a. Eternal companions: Amerindian dogs from *tierra firme* to the Antilles. In *Proceedings of the XV International Congress for Caribbean Archaeology*, edited by R. E. Alegría and M. Rodríguez, pp. 155–172. San Juan: Centro de Estudios Avanzados de Puerto Rico y el Caribe.

Roe, P. G. 1995b. Style, society, myth, and structure. In *Style, society, and person*, edited by C. Carr and J. E. Neitzel, pp. 27–76. New York: Plenum Press.

Roe, P. G. 1997. Just wasting away: Taíno shamanism and concepts of fertility. In *Taíno: Pre-Columbian art and culture from the Caribbean*, edited by F. Bercht, E. Brodsky, J. A. Farmer, and D. Taylor, pp. 124–157. New York: The Monacelli Press.

Roe, P. G., A. G. Pantel, and M. B. Hamilton. 1990. Monserrate restudied: The 1978 Centro field season at Luquillo beach: Excavation overview, lithics and physical anthropological remains. In *Proceedings of the XI International Association for Caribbean Archaeology*, pp. 338–369. San Juan, Puerto Rico.

Roksandic, M., C. Arredondo, Y. Chinique des Armas, and S. Armstrong. 2013. Changes in mobility between two levels of Caminar Abajo cemetery, Matanzas,

Cuba: Paleodemographic evidence. Paper presented at the 78th meeting of the Society for American Archaeology, Honolulu, Hawaii.

Roosevelt, A. C. 1990. *Parmana: prehistoric maize and manioc subsistence along the Amazon and Orinoco*. New York: Academic Press.

Roosevelt, A. C., and P. E. Siegel. "Irving Rouse (1913–2006)." *American Anthropologist* 109: 235–237.

Rosenblatt, A. 1976. The population of Hispaniola at the time of Columbus. In *The native population of the Americas in 1492*, edited by W. M. Denevan, pp. 43–66. Madison: University of Wisconsin Press.

Rosman, A., and P. G. Rubel. 1989. Dual organization and its developmental potential in two contrasting environments. In *The attraction of opposites*, edited by D. Maybury-Lewis and U. Almagor, pp. 209–234. Ann Arbor: University of Michigan Press.

Ross, A. H. 2004. Cranial evidence of precontact multiple population expansions in the Caribbean. *Caribbean Journal of Science* 40:291–298.

Roth, L. T. R. 2002. "Total phosphorus use area determination of Lucayan settlements, Middle Caicos, Turks and Caicos Islands, British West Indies." Master's thesis, University of Calgary, Calgary.

Roumain, J. 1943. L'outillage lithique des Ciboney d'Haiti. *Bulletin du Bureau d'Ethnologie, République d'Haiti* 2:22–27.

Rouse, I. 1939. Prehistory in Haiti: A study in method. *Yale University Publications in Anthropology*, No. 21, New Haven.

Rouse, I. 1941. Culture of the Ft. Liberté region, Haiti. *Yale University Publications in Anthropology*, No. 24, New Haven.

Rouse, I. 1942. Archaeology of the Mariabon Hills, Cuba. *Yale University Publications in Anthropology*, No. 26. New Haven.

Rouse, I. 1948a. The Arawak. In *Handbook of South American Indians, vol. 4. The Circum-Caribbean tribes*, edited by J. H. Steward. *Bureau of American Ethnology Bulletin* 143:507–546.

Rouse, I. 1948b. The Carib. In *Handbook of South American Indians, vol. 4. The Circum-Caribbean tribes*, edited by J. H. Steward. *Bureau of American Ethnology Bulletin* 143:547–565.

Rouse, I. 1952. Porto Rican prehistory. Introduction: Excavations in the west and north. In *Scientific survey of Porto Rico and the Virgin Islands. New York Academy of Science* 18:307–460.

Rouse, I. 1964. Prehistory of the West Indies. *Science* 144:499–513.

Rouse, I. 1972. *Introduction to prehistory: A systematic approach.* New York: McGraw-Hill.

Rouse, I. 1977. Pattern and process in West Indian archaeology. *World Archaeology* 9:1–11.

Rouse, I. 1986. *Migrations in prehistory: Inferring population movements from cultural remains*. New Haven: Yale University Press.

Rouse, I. 1989. Peopling and repeopling of the West Indies. In *Biogeography of the West Indies: Past, present and future*, edited by C. A. Woods. Gainesville: Sandhill Crane Press.

Rouse, I. 1992. *The Taínos: The people who greeted Columbus.* New Haven: Yale University Press.

Rouse, I. 1996. History of archaeology in the Caribbean area. In *The history of archaeology: An encyclopedia*, edited by T. Murray. New York: Garland Publishing.

Rouse, I., and R. Alegría. 1990. *Excavations at Maria de la Cruz Cave and Hacienda Grande village site, Loiza, Puerto Rico.* New Haven: Yale University Publications in Anthropology.

Rouse, I., and L. Allaire. 1978. Caribbean. In *Chronologies in New World archaeology,* edited by R. E. Taylor and C. Meighan, pp. 431–481. New York: Academic Press.

Rouse, I., L. Allaire, and A. Boomert. 1985. Eastern Venezuela, the Guinas and the West Indies. Manuscript prepared for an unpublished volume, *Chronologies in South American archaeology,* edited by C. Meighan, pp. 647–666.

Rouse, I., and J. M. Cruxent. 1963. *Venezuelan archaeology.* New Haven: Yale University Press.

Rouse, I., and C. Moore. 1985. Cultural sequence in southwestern Haiti. *Bulletin de Bureau National d'Ethnologie* 1:25–38.

Rouse, I., and B. F. Morse. 1999. *Excavations at the Indian Creek site, Antigua, West Indies.* New Haven: Yale University Publications in Anthropology.

Rubel, P. G., and A. Rosman. 1978. *Your own pigs you may not eat: A comparative study of New Guinea societies.* Chicago: University of Chicago Press.

Sahlins, M. 1976. *Culture and practical reason.* Chicago: University of Chicago Press.

Sale, K. 1990. *The conquest of paradise.* New York: Penguin.

Samson, A. V. M. 2010. *Renewing the house: Trajectories of social life in the Yacayeque community of El Cabo, Higüey, Dominican Republic, A.D. 800 to 1505.* Leiden: Sidestone Press.

Samson, A. V. M. 2013. Household archaeology in the pre-Columbian Caribbean. In *The Oxford handbook of Caribbean archaeology,* edited by W. F. Keegan, C. L. Hofman, and R. Rodríguez Ramos, pp. 363–377. New York: Oxford University Press.

Samson, A. V., and M. L. P. Hoogland. 2007. Residencia Taína: Huellas de asentamiento en El Cabo, República Dominicana. *El Caribe Arqueológico,* 10:93–103.

Sanoja Obediente, M. 1987. Ecología y asentamientos humanos en el noreste de Venezuela. In *Actas del tercer simposio de la Fundación de Arqueología de Caribe,* edited by M. Sanoja Obidiente, pp. 1–10. Washington, D.C.: La Fundacion de Arqueologia del Caribe.

Santos-Granero, F. 2002. The Arawakan matrix: Ethos, language, and history in Native South America. In *Comparative Arawakan histories: Rethinking language family and culture area in Amazonia,* edited by J. D. Hill and F. Santos-Granero, pp. 25–50. Illinois: University of Illinois Press.

Sara, T. R., and W. F. Keegan, Eds. 2004. *Archaeological survey and paleoenvironmental investigations of portions of U.S. Naval Station Guantanamo Bay, Cuba.* Newport News, VA: Geo-Marine, Inc.

Sauer, C. O. 1966. *The early Spanish Main.* Berkeley: University of California Press.

Saunders, N., and D. Gray. 1996. Zemis, trees and symbolic landscapes: Three Taíno carvings from Jamaica. *Antiquity* 70:801–812.

Saxe, A., 1970. "Social dimensions of mortuary practices." Ph.D. dissertation. Ann Arbor: University of Michigan.

Schmidt, M. 1917. *Die Aruaken: Ein beitrag zum problem der kulturverbreitung.* Leipzig, Germany: Veit & Comp.

Scudder, S. 2001. Evidence of sea level rise at the early Ostionan Coralie site GT-3, *c.* AD 700, Grand Turk, Turks and Caicos Islands. *Journal of Archaeological Science* 28:1221–1233.

Scudder, S. 2006. Early Arawak subsistence strategies: The Rodney's House site of Jamaica. In *The earliest inhabitants: The dynamics of the Jamaican Taíno*, edited by L-G. Atkinson, pp. 113–128. Kingston: University of the West Indies Press.

Scudder, S. J., and I. R. Quitmyer. 1998. Evaluation of evidence of pre-Columbian human occupation at Great Cave, Cayman Brac, Cayman Islands. *Caribbean Journal of Science* 34:41–49.

Sealey, N. E. 1985. *Bahamian landscapes.* London: Collins Caribbean.

Sears, W. H., and S. D. Sullivan. 1978. Bahamas archaeology. *American Antiquity* 43:3–25.

Seidemann, R. M. 2001. The Bahamian problem in Florida Archaeology: Oceanographic perspectives on the issue of Pre-Columbian contact. *Florida Anthropologist* 54:4–23.

Serrand, N. 2001a. "Exploitation des invertébrés marins et terrestres par les populations Saladoïdes et Post-Saladoïdes du nord des Petites Antilles 500 B.C.–1200 A.D." Ph.D. dissertation, Université de Paris I, Panthéon Sorbonne.

Serrand, N. 2001b. Long distance transportation of freshwater bivalves Unionidae in the Lesser Antilles during the 1st millennium AD: Example from the Hope Estate Saladoid site St. Martin. In *Proceedings of the XVIII Congress of the International Association for Caribbean Archaeology*, pp. 136–152.

Serrand, N. 2001c. Les rester coquilliers du site précéramique de Baie Oriëntale Saint-Martin, Petites Antilles du Nord: Consommation de mollusques et pro-duction d'outils en coquille—résultats préliminaires. *Proceedings of the XIX Congress of the International Association for Caribbean Archaeology*, pp. 89–101. Aruba.

Serrand, N., and W. F. Keegan. 2004. Preliminary observations on the molluscan assemblage of Medio Cay, Guantanamo Bay, Cuba. In *Archaeological survey and paleoenvironmental investigations of portions of U.S. Naval Station Guantanamo Bay, Cuba*, edited by T. R. Sara and W. F. Keegan, pp. G3–G6. Newport News, VA: Geo-Marine, Inc.

Service, E. R. 1962. *Primitive social organization: An evolutionary perspective.* New York: Random House.

Service, E. R. 1975. *Origins of the state and civilization.* New York: W. W. Norton & Co.

Sherlock, Philip M. 1939. *The aborigines of Jamaica.* Kingston: The Institute of Jamaica.

Shearn, I. 2014. "Pre-Columbian regional community integration in Dominica, West Indies." Ph.D. dissertation, University of Florida, Gainesville.

Siegel, P. E. 1991. Migration research in Saladoid archaeology: A review. *The Florida Anthropologist* 44:79–91.

Siegel, P. E. 1992. "Ideology, power, and social complexity in prehistoric Puerto Rico." Ph.D. dissertation, Department of Anthropology, State University of New York at Binghamton.

Siegel, P. E. 1993. Saladoid survival strategies: Evidence from site locations. In *Proceedings of the XIV Congress of the International Association for Caribbean Archaeology*, pp. 315–337. Barbados.

Siegel, P. E. 1996a. Ideology and culture change in prehistoric Puerto Rico: A view from the community. *Journal of Field Archaeology* 23:313–333.

Siegel, P. E. 1996b. An interview with Irving Rouse. *Current Anthropology* 37:671–689.

Siegel, P. E. 1997. Ancestor worship and cosmology among the Taíno. In *Taíno: Pre-Columbian art and culture from the Caribbean*, edited by F. Bercht, E. Brodsky, J. A. Farmer, and D. Taylor, pp. 106–111. New York: The Monacelli Press.

Siegel, P. E. 1999. Contested places and places of contest: The evolution of social power and ceremonial space in prehistoric Puerto Rico. *Latin American Antiquity* 10:209–238.

Siegel, P. E. 2004. What happened AD 600 in Puerto Rico? Corporate groups, population restructuring, and post-Saladoid social changes. In *Late Ceramic Age societies in the eastern Caribbean*, edited by A. Delpuech and C. L. Hofman, pp. 87–100. Oxford: British Archaeological Series.

Siegel, P. E. 2010. Continuity and change in the evolution of religion and political organization on pre-Columbian Puerto Rico. *Journal of Anthropological Archaeology* 29:302–326.

Siegel, P. E. 2013. Caribbean archaeology in historical perspective. In *The Oxford handbook of Caribbean archaeology*, edited by W. F. Keegan, C. L. Hofman, and R. Rodríguez Ramos, pp. 21–46. New York: Oxford University Press.

Siegel, P. E., C. L. Hofman, B. Bérard, et al. 2013. Confronting Caribbean heritage in an archipelago of diversity: Politics, stakeholders, climate change, natural disasters, tourism and development. *Journal of Field Archaeology* 38:376–390.

Siegel, P. E., J. G. Jones, D. M. Pearsall, et al. 2015. Paleoenvironmental evidence for the first human colonization of the eastern Caribbean. *Quaternary Science Reviews* 129:275–295.

Siegel, P. E., J. G. Jones, D. M. Pearsall, and D. P. Wagner. 2005. Environmental and cultural correlates in the West Indies: A view from Puerto Rico. In *Ancient Borinquen: Archaeology and ethnohistory of native Puerto Rico*, edited by P. E. Siegel, pp. 88–121. Tuscaloosa: University of Alabama Press.

Siegel, P. E., and E. Righter, Eds. 2011. *Protecting heritage in the Caribbean.* Tuscaloosa: University of Alabama Press.

Siegel, P. E., and K. P. Severin. 1993. The first documented prehistoric gold-copper alloy artifact from the West Indies. *Journal of Archaeological Science* 201:67–79.

Silverberg, J., R. L. Vanderwal, and E. S. Wing. 1972. The White Marl site in Jamaica: Report of the 1964 Robert R. Howard excavations. Department of Anthropology, University of Wisconsin, Milwaukee.

Sinelli, P. T. 2010. "Archaeological investigations of two prehistoric sites representing Hispaniolan colonization of Middle Caicos, Turks and Caicos Islands." Ph.D. dissertation, Gainesville.

Sinelli, P. 2013. Meillacoid and the origins of Classic Taíno society. In *The Oxford handbook of Caribbean archaeology*, edited by W. F. Keegan, C. L. Hofman, and R. Rodríguez Ramos, pp. 221–231. New York: Oxford University Press.

Sleight, F. W. 1965. Certain environmental considerations in West Indian archaeology. *American Antiquity* 31:226–231.

Steadman, D. W., and A. V. Stokes. 2002. Changing exploitation of terrestrial vertebrates during the past 3,000 years on Tobago, West Indies. *Human Ecology* 30:339–367.

Steadman, D. W., and S. Jones. 2006. Long-term trends in prehistoric fishing and hunting on Tobago, West Indies. *Latin American Antiquity* 173:316–334.

Steadman, D. W., P. S. Martin, R. D. E. MacPhee, 2005. Asynchronous extinction of late Quaternary sloths on continents and islands. *Proceedings of the National Academy of Sciences* 10233:11763–11768.

Stevens-Arroyo, A. M. 1988. *Cave of the Jagua: The mythological world of the Taínos.* Albuquerque: University of New Mexico Press.

Steward, J. H. 1955. *Theory of culture change.* Urbana: University of Illinois Press.

Steward, J. H., and L. C. Faron. 1959. *Native peoples of South America.* New York: McGraw-Hill.

Stokes, A. V. 1991. "A settlement survey of Nonsuch Bay: Implications for Prehistoric subsistence in the Caribbean." Master's thesis, University of Florida, Gainesville.

Stokes, A. V. 1998. "A biogeographic survey of prehistoric human diet in the West Indies using stable isotopes." Ph.D. dissertation, Department of Anthropology, University of Florida, Gainesville.

Stokes, A. V., and W. F. Keegan. 1996. A reconnaissance for prehistoric archaeological sites on Grand Cayman. *Caribbean Journal of Science* 32:425–430.

Stokes, B. J. 2002. Settlement patterns and the placement of Jamaican Taíno chiefdoms in a Greater Antilles context: Theory and practical method. Paper presented at the Archaeological Society of Jamaica's Symposium Current Research in Jamaican Archaeology, Kingston.

Stouvenot, C., and F. Casagrande. 2015. Recherche des occupations précolumbiennes dans les hauteurs de Capesterre-Belle-Eau Guadeloupe: Rèsultats préliminaires. Paper presented at the XXVI Congress of the International Association for Caribbean Archaeology. Sint Maarten.

Sued-Badillo, J. 1978. *Los Caribes: Realidad o fabula.* Río Piedras, PR: Editorial Antillana.

Sued-Badillo, J. 1979. *La mujer indigena y su sociedad*, 2nd ed. Rio Piedras, PR: Editorial Antillana.

Sued-Badillo, J. 1992. Facing up to Caribbean history. *American Antiquity* 57:599–607.

Sued-Badillo, J., Ed. 2003. *General history of the Caribbean. Volume I: Autochthonous societies.* Paris: UNESCO Publishing.

Sued-Badillo, J. 2007. *Agüeybaná el bravo.* San Juan, PR: Ediciones Puerto.

Sullivan, S. D. 1974. "Archaeological reconnaissance of Eleuthera, Bahamas." Master's thesis, Department of Anthropology, Florida Atlantic University, Boca Raton.

Sullivan, S. D. 1976. *Archaeological reconnaissance of the Turks and Caicos Islands, British West Indies.* Report submitted to the Government of the Turks and Caicos, Grand Turk.

Sullivan, S. D. 1980. An overview of the 1976 to 1978 archaeological investigations in the Caicos Islands. *Florida Anthropologist* 33:94–98.

Sullivan, S. D. 1981. "The colonization and exploitation of the Turks and Caicos Islands." Ph.D. dissertation, University of Illinois at Urbana–Champaign.

Sullivan, S. and G. Freimuth. 2015. Archaeoastronomy of a complex Lucayan site in the Classic Taino tradition. Paper presented at the XXVI International Congress for Caribbean Archaeology, St. Martin.

Sutty, L. 1991. Paleoecological formations in the Grenadines of Grenada and their relationships to preceramic and ceramic settlements: Carriacou. In *Proceedings of the XIII International Congress for Caribbean Archaeology*, edited by E. N. Ayubi and J. B. Haviser, pp. 127–147. Willemstad, Curaçao.

Tabio, E., and J. M. Guarch. 1966. *Excavations en Arroyo del Palo, Mayari, Cuba*. La Havana: Academia de Ciencias de Cuba.

Tabio, E., and E. Rey. 1966. *Prehistoria de Cuba*. Havana: Academia de Ciencias de Cuba.

Taverne, Y., and A. H. Versteeg. 1992. Golden Rock shells. In *The archaeology of St. Eustatius, the Golden Rock site*, edited by A. H. Versteeg and K. Schinkel, pp. 84–92. Publication of the St. Eustatius Historical Foundation, no. 2.

Terrell, J. E., K. M. Kelly, and P. Rainbird. 2001. Foregone conclusions? *Current Anthropology* 42:97–124.

Terrell, J. E., J. P. Hart, S. Barut, N. Cellinese, A. Curet, T. Denham, C. M. Kusimba, K. Latinis, R. Oka, M. E. D. Pohl, K. O. Pope, P. R. Williams, H. Haines, and J. E. Staller. 2003. Domesticated landscapes: The subsistence ecology of plant and animal domestication. *Journal of Archaeological Method and Theory* 10:323–368.

Torres, J. M. 2010. Tibes and the social landscape: Integration, interaction, and the community. In *Tibes: People, power, and ritual at the center of the cosmos*, edited by L. A. Curet and L. M. Stringer, pp. 231–260. Tuscaloosa: University of Alabama Press.

Torres, J. M. 2012. "The social construction of community, polity and place in ancient Puerto Rico AD 600–1200." Ph.D. dissertation, Department of Anthropology, University of Florida, Gainesville.

Torres, J. M. 2013. Rethinking chiefdoms in the Caribbean. In *The Oxford handbook of Caribbean archaeology*, edited by W. F. Keegan, C. L. Hofman, and R. Rodríguez Ramos, pp. 347–362. New York: Oxford University Press.

Torres, J. M., L. A. Curet, S. Rice-Snow, M. Castor, and A. Castor. 2014. Of flesh and stone: Labor investment and regional socio-political implications of plaza/batey construction at the ceremonial center of Tibes A.D. 600–A.D. 1200, Puerto Rico. *Latin American Antiquity* 27:125–151.

Torres, J. M., and R. Rodríguez Ramos. 2008. The Caribbean: A continent divided by water. In *Archaeology and geoinformatics: Case studies from the Caribbean*, edited by B. A. Reid, pp. 13–29. Tuscaloosa: University of Alabama Press.

Torres Etayo, D. 2010. Investigations at Laguna de Limones: Suggestions for a change in the theoretical direction of Cuban archaeology. In *Beyond the blockade: New currents in Cuban archaeology*. Edited by S. Kepecs, L. A. Curet, and G. la Rosa Corzo, pp. 70–88. Tuscaloosa: University of Alabama Press.

Tosteson, H. 2008. Historical context of the Río Grande de Arecibo. In *A multidisciplinary approach to site testing and data recovery at two village sites AR-38 and AR-39 on the lower Río Tanamá, municipality of Arecebo, Puerto Rico. Volume 1: Final report*, edited by L. A. Carlson, pp. 35–50. Newberry, FL: Southeastern Archaeological Research, Inc.

Trincado Fontán, M. N., and J. Ulloa Hung. 1996. Las communidades Meillacoides del littoral sudoriental de Cuba. *El Caribe Arqueológico* 1:74–82.

Tromans, M. A. 1986. "Temporal and spatial analysis of two Antillean Period settlements, Middle Caicos, Turks and Caicos Islands, British West Indies." Master's thesis, Florida Atlantic University, Boca Raton.

Tyler, S. L. 1988. *Two worlds: The Indian encounter with the European, 1492–1509.* Salt Lake City: University of Utah Press.

Ulloa Hung, J. 2005. Approaches to early ceramics in the Caribbean: Between diversity and unilineality. In *Dialogues in Cuban archaeology*, edited by A. L Curet, S. L. Dawdy, and G. La Rosa, pp. 103–124. Tuscaloosa: University of Alabama Press.

Ulloa Hung, J. 2013. "Arqueología en la línea noroeste de La Española: Paisajes, cerámicas e interacciones." Ph.D. dissertation, Leiden University.

Ulloa Hung, J. 2014. *Arqueología en la línea noroeste de La Española. Paisajes, cerámicas e interacciones.* Santo Domingo: Instituto Tecnológico de Santo Domingo.

Ulloa Hung, J., and R. Valcárel Rojas. 1997. Las comunidades apropiadoras ceramistas del sureste de Cuba: Un estudio de su cerámica. *El Caribe Arqueológico* 2:31–40.

Ulloa Hung, J., and R. Valcárel Rojas. 2002. *Cerámica temprana en el centro del oriente de Cuba.* Santo Domingo: Videograph.

Ulloa Hung, J., and R. Valcárcel Rojas. 2013. Archaeological practice, Archaic presence, and interaction in indigenous societies in Cuba. In *The Oxford handbook of Caribbean archaeology*, edited by W. F. Keegan, C. L. Hofman, and R. Rodríguez Ramos, pp. 232–249. New York: Oxford University Press.

Ulloa Hung, J., and R. Valcárcel Rojas 2016. Indígenas e Indios en el Caribe. Presencia, legado y estudio. Santo Domingo: IINTEC.

Ulloa Hung, J., J. M. Vázquez, H. Silva, and R. Valcárcel. 2001. La alfarería temprana del centro-oriente de Cuba: Un análisis arqueométrico. *El Caribe Arqueológico* 5:34–41.

Valcárcel Rojas, R. 2002. *Banes precolombino: La ocupación agricultora.* Holguín, Cuba: Ediciones Holguín.

Valcárcel Rojas, R. 2008. Las sociedades agrícultoras ceramistas en Cuba: Una mirada desde los datos arqueológicos y ethnohistóricos. *El Caribe Arqueológico* 11:2–19.

Valcárcel Rojas, R. 2012. "Interaccion colonial en un pueblo de Indios encomendados. El Chorro de Maita, Cuba." Ph.D. dissertation, Leiden University, The Netherlands.

Valcárcel Rojas, R. 2016. *Colonial interaction at El Chorro de Maíta, Cuba.* Gainesville: University Press of Florida.

Valcárcel Rojas, R., J. Cooper, J. Calvera Rosés, O. Brito, and M. Labrada. 2006. Postes en el mar: Excavacíon de una estructura constructiva aborigen en Los Buchillones. *El Caribe Arqueologico* 9:76–88.

Valcarcel Rojas R., M. L. P. Hoogland, and C. L. Hofman. 2014. Indios: Arqueología de una nueva identidad. In *Indios en Holguín*, edited by R. Valcarcel Rojas and H. Perez Concepcion, pp. 20–42. Holguín: Editorial La Mezquita.

Valcárcel Rojas, R., J. E. Laffoon, D. A. Weston, H. L. Mickleburgh, and A. van Duijvenbode. 2011. A diverse approach to a context of diversity. In *Communities in contact: Essays in archaeology, ethnohistory and ethnography of the Amerindian Circum-Caribbean*, edited by C. L. Hofman and A. van Duijvenbode, pp. 225–252. Leiden: Sidestone Press.

Valcárcel Rojas, R., and M. Martinón-Torres. 2013. Metals in the indigenous societies of the insular Caribbean. In *The Oxford handbook of Caribbean archaeology*, edited by W. F. Keegan, C. L. Hofman, and R. Rodríguez Ramos, pp. 504–522. New York: Oxford University Press.

Valcárcel Rojas, R., M. Martinón-Torres, J. Cooper, and T. Rehren. 2010. Turey treasure in the Caribbean: Brass and Indo-Hispanic contact at El Chorro de Maíta, Cuba. In *Dialogues in Cuban archaeology*, edited by L. A. Curet, S. L. Dawdy, and G. la Rosa Corzo, pp. 106–125. Tuscaloosa: University of Alabama Press.

Valcárcel Rojas, R., C. Rodríguez, L. Pérez, and J. Guarch. 2001. Un contexto apropiador ceramista temprano: Corinthia 3, Holguín, Cuba. *El Caribe Arqueológico* 5:76–88.

Valcárcel Rojas, R., and C. A. Rodríguez Arce. 2005. El Chorro de Maíta: Social inequality and mortuary space. In *Dialogues in Cuban archaeology*, edited by L. A. Curet, S. L. Dawdy, and G. la Rosa Corzo, pp. 125–146. Tuscaloosa: University of Alabama Press.

Valcarcel Rojas R., A. V. M. Samson, and M. L. P. Hoogland. 2013. Indo-Hispanic dynamics: From contact to colonial interaction in the Greater Antilles. *International Journal of Historical Archaeology* 1:18–39.

Valdés, J. J. 1994. Paleogeographic perspectives on the first landfall of Columbus. *Southeastern Geographer* 34:73–91.

Van den Bel, M., and T. Romon. 2010. A Troumassoid site at Trois-Rivières, Guadeloupe, FWI: Funerary practices and house patterns at La Pointe de Grande Anse. *Journal of Caribbean Archaeology* 9:1–17.

Van der Klift, H. M. 1992. Faunal remains of Golden Rock. In *The archaeology of St. Eustatius: The Golden Rock site*, edited by A. H. Versteeg and K Schinkel, pp. 72–84. Publication of the St. Eustatius Historical Foundation, No 2.

Vanderwal, R. 1968. "The prehistory of Jamaica: A ceramic study." Master's thesis, University of Wisconsin-Milwaukee.

Van Soest, M. C. 2000. *Sediment subduction and crustal contamination in the Lesser Antilles island arc: The geochemical and isotopic imprints on recent lavas and geothermal fluids*. Netherlands Research School of Sedimentary Geology, publication number 20000101, Amsterdam.

Varela, C. 1984. *Cristóbal Colón, textos y documentos completos*. Second edition. Madrid: Alianza Editorial.

Vargas Arenas, I. 1995. La arqueología urbana. Paradigma para le creación de una historia alternative de la ciudad de Caracas. *Tierra Firme. Revista de Historia y Ciencias Sociales* 51 (33): 315–37.

Vargas Arenas, I., and M. Sanoja Obediente. 1999. Archaeology as a social science: Its expression in Latin America. In *Archaeology in Latin America*, edited by G. Politis and B. Alberti, pp. 57–73. London: Routledge.

Vega, B. 1979. *Los metales y los aborígenes de la Española*. Santo Domingo: Fundación Cultural Dominicana.

Vega, B. 1980. *Los cacicazgos de la Hispaniola.* Santo Domingo: Ediciones Museo del Hombre Dominicano.

Veloz Maggiolo, M. 1972. *Arqueologia prehistorica de Santo Domingo.* Singapore: McGraw-Hill.

Veloz Maggiolo, M. 1991. *Panorama histórico del Caribe precolombino.* Santo Domingo: Edición del Banco Central de la República Dominicana.

Veloz Maggiolo, M. 1993. *La isla de Santo Domingo antes de Colon.* Santo Domingo: Banco Central de la República Dominicana.

Veloz Maggiolo, M. 1997. The daily life of the Taíno people. In *Taíno: Pre-Columbian art and culture from the Caribbean,* edited by F. Bercht, E. Brodsky, J. A. Farmer, and D. Taylor, pp. 34–45. New York: The Monacelli Press.

Veloz Maggiolo, M., J. Gonzáles Colón, and E. Maiz. 1974. El preceramico de Puerto Rico a La Luz de Los Hallazgos de Cayo Cofresi. Paper presented at the 41st International Congress of Americanists, Mexico City.

Veloz Maggiolo, M., and E. Ortega. 1996. Punta Cana y el origen de la agricultura en la isla de Santo Domingo. In *Ponencias del primer seminario de arqueología del Caribe,* edited by M. Veloz Maggiolo and A. Caba Fuentes, pp. 5–11. Dominican Republic: Museo Arqueológico Regional Altos de Chavón.

Veloz Maggiolo, M., E. Ortega, M. Sanoja, and I. Vargas. 1976. Preliminary report on archaeological investigations at El Atajadizo, Dominican Republic. In *Proceedings of the VI International Congress for the Study of Pre-Columbian Cultures of the Lesser Antilles,* pp. 283–294. Société d'Histoire de la Guadeloupe, Pointe á Pitre, Guadeloupe.

Veloz Maggiolo, M., E. Ortega, and A. Caba Fuentes. 1981. *Los modos de vida Meillacoides y sus posibles origenes.* Santo Domingo: Museo del Hombre Dominicano.

Veloz Maggiolo, M., E. Ortega, and F. Luna Calderon. 1991. Los ocupantes tempranos de Punta Cana, República Dominicana. In *Proceedings of the XIV Congress of the International Association for Caribbean Archaeology,* edited by A. Cummins and P. King, pp. 262–277. Barbados Museum and Historical Society, Barbados.

Veloz Maggiolo, M., and A. G. Pantel. 1988. Modo de vida de los recolectores en la arqueología del Caribe parte I. *Boletín de Antropología Americana* 18:149–167.

Veloz Maggiolo, M., and A. G. Pantel. 1989. Modo de vida de los recolectores en la arqueología del Caribe parte II. *Boletín de Antropología Americana* 19:83–117.

Veloz Maggiolo, M., I. Vargas, M. Sanoja, and F. Luna Calderon. 1976. *Arqueologia de Yuma, República Dominicana.* Santo Domingo: Taller.

Veloz Maggiolo, M., and B. Vega. 1982. The Antillean preceramic: A new approximation. *Journal of New World Archaeology* 5:33–44.

Vento Canosa, E., and D. González. 1996. Paleopatologia aborigen de Cuba. *El Caribe Arqueológico* 1:31–38.

Vernon, N. 2007. "Investigations at the Clifton site: A specialized Lucayan site on New Providence Island, the Bahamas." Master's thesis, University of Florida, Gainesville.

Verpoorte, A. 1993. "Stenen op een eiland: Veldverkenning van de vuursteenvoorkomens en werkplaatsen van Long Island, Antigua, West Indies." Master's thesis, Leiden University, Leiden.

Versteeg, A. H. 2000: The Archaeology of St. Eustatius. Available at http://home.wxs. nl/~vrstg/eastern/eustatius/eustatius.htm (accessed 26 September 2005).

Versteeg, A. H., and S. Rostain, Eds. 1995. *The archaeology of Aruba: The Tanki Flip site.* Oranjestad: Archaeological Museum Aruba.

Versteeg, A. H., and K. Schinkel, Eds. 1992. *The archaeology of St. Eustatius: The Golden Rock site.* Publication of the St. Eustatius Historical Foundation, No. 2.

Versteeg, A. H., K. Schinkel, and S. M. Wilson. 1993. Large-scale excavations versus surveys: Examples from Nevis, St. Eustatius and St. Kitts in the northern Caribbean. *Analecta Praehistorica Leidensia* 26:139–161.

Voss, A. 2015. Resultados preliminares de la excavatión de un sitio saladoide en el costa norte de la República Dominicana. In *Proceedings of the Congress of the International Association for Caribbean Archaeology,* pp. 145–157. San Juan, Puerto Rico.

Walker, J. B. 1980. "Analysis and replication of the lithic artifacts from the Sugar Factory Pier site, St. Kitts, West Indies." Master's thesis, Washington State University, Pullman.

Walker, J. B. 1985. A preliminary report on the lithic and osteological remains from 1980, 1981, and 1982 field seasons at Hacienda Grande (12PSj7-5). In *Proceedings of the X International Congress for the Study of Pre-Columbian Cultures of the Lesser Antilles,* pp. 181–224. Montreal: Centre de Recherches Caraïbe.

Walker, J. B. 1993. "Stone collars, elbow stones, and three pointers, and the nature of Taíno ritual and myth." Ph.D. dissertation, Washington State University, Pullman.

Walker, J. B. 1997. Taíno stone collars, elbow stones, and three-pointers. In *Taíno: Pre-Columbian art and culture from the Caribbean,* edited by F. Bercht, E. Brodsky, J. A. Farmer, and D. Taylor, pp. 80–91. New York: The Monacelli Press.

Walker, J. 2005. The Paso del Indio site, Vega Baja, Puerto Rico: A progress report. In *Ancient Borinquen,* edited by P. E. Siegel, pp. 55–87. Tuscaloosa: University of Alabama Press.

Wallace, V. 1992. The socio-cultural life of Arawak Indians of Jamaica: An archaeological evaluation. *Archaeology Jamaica,* new series 6:73–96.

Watlington, F. 2003. The physical environment: Biogeographical teleconnections in Caribbean prehistory. In *General history of the Caribbean: Vol 1: Autochthonous Societies,* edited by J. Sued-Badillo, pp. 30–92. Paris: UNESCO Publishing.

Watson, K. 1988. Amerindian cave art in Jamaica: Mountain River Cave. *Jamaica Journal* 211:13–20.

Watson, P. J., S. A. LeBlanc, and C. L. Redman. 1971. *Explanation in archeology: An explicitly scientific approach.* New York: Columbia University Press.

Watts, D. 1987. *The West Indies: Patterns of development, culture, and environmental change.* Cambridge: Cambridge University Press.

Watters, D. R. 1976. "Caribbean prehistory: A century of research, models, and trends." Master's thesis, University of Nevada, Reno.

Watters, D. R. 1982. Relating oceanography to Antillean archaeology: Implications from Oceania. *Journal of New World Archaeology* 5:3–12.

Watters, D. R. 1997. Maritime trade in the prehistoric eastern Caribbean. In *The indigenous people of the Caribbean,* edited by S. M. Wilson, pp. 88–99, Gainesville: University Press of Florida.

Watters, D. R., J. Donahue, and R. Stuckenrath. 1992. Paleoshorelines and the prehistory of Barbuda, West Indies. In *Paleoshorelines and prehistoric settlement*, edited by L. L. Johnson, pp. 15–52. Boca Raton, Florida: CRC Press.

Watters, D. R., and J. B. Petersen. 1999. Trants, Montserrat: The 1995 field season. In *Proceedings of the XVI Congress of the International Association for Caribbean Archaeology, vol. 2*, pp. 27–39. Guadeloupe.

Watters, D. R., and I. Rouse. 1989. Environmental diversity and maritime adaptations in the Caribbean area. In *Early ceramic population lifeways and adaptive strategies in the Caribbean*, edited by P. E. Siegel, pp. 129–144. Oxford: BAR International Series 506.

Watters, D. R., and R. Scaglion. 1994. Beads and pendants from Trants, Montserrat: Implications for the prehistoric lapidary industry of the Caribbean. *Annals of the Carnegie Museum* 63:215–237.

Weeks, J. M., P. J. Ferbel, and V. Ramírez Zabala. 1996. Rock art at Corral de los Indios de Chacuey, Dominican Republic. *Latin American Indian Literatures Journal* 12:88–97.

Weiss, K. 1973. Demographic models for anthropology. *Memoirs of the Society for American Archaeology* 27:i–186.

Welsch, R. L., J. Terell, and J. A. Nadolski. 1992. Language and culture on the north coast of New Guinea. *American Anthropologist* 94 (3): 568–600.

Wesler, K. 2013. Jamaica. In *The Oxford handbook of Caribbean archaeology*, edited by W. F. Keegan, C. L. Hofman, and R. Rodríguez Ramos, pp. 250–263. New York: Oxford University Press.

West, R. C., and J. P. Augelli. 1976. *Middle America: Its lands and peoples.* Englewood Cliffs, NJ: Prentice Hall.

Weston D. A., and R. Valcárcel Rojas. 2016. Communities in contact: health and paleodemography at El Chorro de Maíta, Cuba. In *Cuban Archaeology In The Caribbean*, edited by I. Roksandic, pp. 83–105. Florida Museum Of Natural History: Ripley P. Bullen Series. Gainsville: University Press of Florida.

Whitehead, Neil L. 1984. "Carib cannibalism." The historical evidence. *Société des Americanistes* 70:69–87.

Whitehead, N. L. 1988. *Lords of the tiger spirit.* Dordrecht: Floris.

Whitehead, N. L. 1995. Ethnic plurality and cultural continuity in the native Caribbean: Remarks and uncertainties as to data and theory. In *Wolves from the sea*, edited by N. L. Whitehead, pp. 91–111. Leiden: KITLV Pres.

Wilbert, J. 1976. To become a maker of canoes: An essay in Warao enculturation. *UCLA Latin American Studies Series and Latin American Studies* 37:303–358.

Wild, K. 2001. Historic and archaeological investigations at Cinnamon Bay, St. John, U.S. Virgin Islands. In *Proceedings of the XVIII International Congress for Caribbean Archaeology*, pp. 304–310. St. George: Grenada.

Willey, G. R. 1976. . The Caribbean preceramic and related matters in summary perspectives. *First Puerto Rico symposium on archaeology*, edited by L. Sickler Robinson, pp. 1–9. San Juan: Fundacion Arqueologica, Anthropologica, e Historica de Puerto Rico

Willey, G. R., and P. Phillips. 1958. *Method and theory in American archaeology.* Chicago: University of Chicago Press.

Willey, G. R., and J. A. Sabloff. 1974. *A history of American archaeology*. Chicago: University of Chicago Press.

Wilson, S. M. 1989. The prehistoric settlement pattern of Nevis, West Indies. *Journal of Field Archaeology* 16:427–450.

Wilson, S. M. 1990. *Hispaniola: The chiefdoms of the Caribbean in the early years of European contact*. Tuscaloosa: University of Alabama Press.

Wilson, S. M. 1993. The cultural mosaic of the indigenous Caribbean. *Proceedings of the British Academy* 81:37–66.

Wilson, S. M., Ed. 1997. *The indigenous people of the Caribbean*. Gainesville: University Press of Florida.

Wilson, S. M. 2007. *The archaeology of the Caribbean*. Cambridge: Cambridge University Press.

Wilson, S. M., H. B. Iceland, and T. R. Hester. 1998. Preceramic connections between Yucatan and the Caribbean. *Latin American Antiquity* 9:342–352.

Wilson, S. M., and L. Kozuch. 2006. *The prehistory of Nevis, a small island in the Lesser Antilles*. New Haven: Yale University Press.

Wing, E. S. 1993. The realm between wild and domestic. In *Skeletons in her cupboard: Festschrift for Juliet Clutton-Brock*, edited by A. S. Clason, E. Payne, and H. P. Uerpmann, pp. 243–250. Oxford: Oxbow Monograph.

Wing, E. S. 1996. Vertebrate remains excavated from the sites of Spring Bay and Kelbey's Ridge, Saba, Netherlands Antilles. Appendix 2 in M. L. P. Hoogland, "In search of the native population of pre-Columbian Saba. Part Two. Settlements in their natural and social environment." Ph.D. dissertation. Leiden University.

Wing, E. S. 2001. Native American use of animals in the Caribbean. In *Biogeography of the West Indies: Patterns and perspectives*, edited by C. A. Woods and F. E. Sergile, pp. 481–518. Boca Raton: CRC Press.

Wing, E. S. 2008. Pets and camp followers in the West Indies. In *Case studies in environmental archaeology*, 2nd edition, edited by E. J. Reitz, C. M. Scarry, and S. J. Scudder, pp. 405–426. New York: Springer.

Wing, E. S., and E. J. Reitz. 1982. Prehistoric fishing communities of the Caribbean. *Journal of New World Archaeology* 5:13–32.

Wing, E. S., and S. J. Scudder. 1983. Animal exploitation by prehistoric people living on a tropical marine edge. In *Animals and archaeology: 2. Shell middens, fishes and birds*, edited by C. Grigson and J. Clutton-Brock, pp. 197–210. Oxford: B.A.R. International Series No. 183.

Wing, E. S., and S. R. Wing. 1995. Prehistoric Ceramic Age adaptation to varying diversity of animal resources along the West Indian archipelago. *Journal of Ethnobiology* 15:119–148.

Winter, J. 1991. A multiple Lucayan burial from New Providence, Bahamas. In *Proceedings of the XII Congress of the International Association for Caribbean Archaeology*, edited by L. S. Robinson, pp. 153–162. Martinique.

Winter, J., and M. Gilstrap. 1991. Preliminary results of ceramic analysis and the movements of populations into the Bahamas. In *Proceedings of the XII Congress of the International Association for Caribbean Archaeology*, edited by L. S. Robinson, pp. 371–386. Martinique.

Woods, C. A. 1989. *Biogeography of the West Indies, past, present and future.* Gainesville, FL: Sandhill Crane Press.

Woods, C. A., and F. E. Sergile. 2001. *Biogeography of the West Indies: Patterns and perspectives.* Washington, DC: CRC Press.

Yafa, S. H. 2005. *Big cotton: How a humble fiber created fortunes, wrecked civilizations, and put America on the map.* New York: Viking Press.

Zambardino, R. A. 1978. Critique of David Henige's "On the contact population of Hispaniola: History as higher mathematics." *Hispanic American Historical Review* 58:700–708.

Zucchi, A. 1990. La serie Meillacoide y sus relaciones con la cuenca del Orinoco. In *Proceedings of the X International Congress for Caribbean Archaeology,* pp. 272–286. Puerto Rico: Fundacion Arqueologica, Anthropologica, e Historica de Puerto Rico.

Zucchi, A. 1991. Prehispanic connections between the Orinoco, the Amazon and the Caribbean area. In *Proceedings of the XIII International Congress for Caribbean Archaeology,* edited by E. N. Ayubi and J. B. Haviser, pp. 202–220. Willemstad, Curaçao.

Zucchi, A. 2002. A new model of the northern Arawakan expansion. In *Comparative Arawakan histories: Rethinking language family and culture area in Amazonia,* edited by J. D. Hill, pp. 199–222. Urbana: University of Illinois Press.

Zucchi, A., and K. Tarble. 1984. Los Cedeñoides: Un nuevo grupo prehispánico del Orinoco medio. *Acta Científica Venezolana* 35:293–309.

INDEX

Sand Hill site (Belize) 26
Sandy Hill site (Anguilla) 215
San Jacinto site (Colombia) 116
San Juan, Puerto Rico 65
San Juan de Maguana, Dominican
    Republic 141
San Salvador, Bahamas 171, 173, 179,
    182, 239
Sans Souci site (St. Vincent) 234
Santa Isabel site (Puerto Rico) 103, 147
Santa María 138–139, 141
Santana Sarmiento site (Cuba) 164
Santiago de Cuba, Cuba 156, 157–158
Sauteurs Bay site (Grenada) 234
Savanne Carree No. 2 site (Haiti) 32
Savanne Suazey site (Grenada) 222
Scudder, Sylvia 25, 191
sea level 3, 25, 29, 39, 63, 75, 106, 133,
    171, 173, 184, 192, 199, 203, 204, 217,
    226, 230
seasonal cycles 8, 9, 29, 34, 39, 43, 48,
    71–72, 85, 107, 154, 171–172, 174–175,
    183–186, 199, 205–208
Seaview site (Barbuda) 211
Seboruco site (Cuba) 28
Seboruco-Mordán Culture 28, 33, 152
sediment analysis 29, 42, 44, 92, 106,
    168, 173, 178, 184–185, 194, 201
settlement clusters 96–97, 107–108, 114,
    144, 161, 163
settlement pairs 127, 136–137, 146, 148,
    159, 161, 163, 182, 251–252
Service Régional de l'Archéologie 216
shaman (*behique*) 80, 109, 214, 238, 253
Sheffield Scientific School, Yale
    University 18
Shell Culture 84, 86
shell tools 31, 33, 34–35, 82, 158, 168, 193,
    194, 205, 206–207, 208, 220
  atlatl spurs 73, 76
  celts 73, 203
  cups/plates 42, 158
  gouges 38, 38n, 42, 76, 158
  hammers 46, 76
  hoes 76
  net gauges 76, 133

scrapers, bivalve 73, 76, 159, 161, 193,
    194, 224
Siegel, Peter 174
Sierra de Baharuco mountains 6
Sierra Maestra mountains, Cuba 6, 156
Silk Cotton tree 55
Silver Sands site (Barbados) 211
Sinelli, Peter 174
sitios de habitación 156–157
Sleight, Frederick 44
smallpox 256
Smith Gut site (St. Eustatius) 202
social distance 51, 59, 102
social organization 29, 43, 55, 57,
    77–78, 93, 96–99, 128, 136–137, 161,
    169, 229, 245, 251–252, 259
  band level 28–29, 93
  conical clan 100
  formation 51, 117, 137–138, 146,
    253–254, 259
  headmen 112, 252
  hierarchy 57, 77, 93, 137–138, 161, 173,
    225, 253, 259
  heterarchy 93, 112
  landscapes 112, 213, 215, 234, 237
  memory 237
  networks 51, 103, 135, 145, 208, 224–225,
    238, 252
  tribal level 93, 100
  chiefdoms 60, 93, 106–107, 112, 137,
    138, 149, 162, 195, 252–254
  reproduction 96
  transformation 20, 136–137, 138,
    253, 259
Solutrian blades 23
Sophia Bay (Dominica) 234
Sorcé site (Vieques Island) 53, 66–67,
    79, 94, 127, 211
Soroya 8
South America 2, 4–5, 6–9, 11–13, 15, 24,
    27–29, 35–38, 43, 48, 51–55, 59,
    62–63, 68, 73–74, 76, 78–79,
    81–82, 93, 99, 116–117, 125, 144,
    148–149, 164, 191, 197, 201, 207,
    209–211, 215, 228–229, 232, 235,
    240, 254, 257–258

Terres Basses, St. Martin 203
The Bottom (Saba) 215–216
The Level site (Saba) 203
Three Dog site (Bahamas) 171, 179–180
Tibes Ceremonial Center (Puerto
    Rico) 93, 96, 100–103, 109–112, 158,
    166, 237, 253
timespacescapes 23
time-space systematics 11, 16–18, 72, 155
Toa Baja, Puerto Rico 88
Tobago 3, 5, 37, 39–40, 48, 53, 197,
    200–201, 207, 212, 232–233, 257
Torres, Joshua 7, 87, 96–97, 110, 112
tourism xv, xvi, 244, 260
traditions 19, 25–27, 32, 38, 41–42, 47,
    55, 58, 62–63, 68, 71, 81, 86, 116,
    126, 137, 152, 154, 156, 180, 232–233,
    258–259
transculturation xvi, 44, 117, 148, 151,
    155, 258
Trants site (Montserrat) 53, 61, 63–65,
    81, 209, 211
tribute 146, 252, 256
Trincado Fontán, Daniel 156–157
Trinidad 3, 5, 9, 15, 27, 33–37, 41, 48, 53,
    66, 144, 147, 197, 200–201, 207,
    212, 255, 258, 260
Trobriand Islands 99–100
troglodytes 29
Trois-Riviéres, Guadeloupe 80–81
Trou David sites (St. Martin) 201
Troumassée River, St. Lucia 221
Troumassoid xvi, 19, 215–218, 238
    pottery series 215, 217
    Mamoran subseries 215, 217
    Troumassan subseries 221
    Troumassée A 215
    Troumassée B 221
    Suazan subseries 215, 217, 222
Turks & Caicos Islands xvi, 4, 6, 86,
    119–120, 126, 132, 170–186
Turks Bank 173–174
Tutu site (St. Thomas) 93–94

Ulloa Hung, Jorge 45–46, 125–126, 127,
    156–157, 159

underwater excavations 167, 168, 171
University of the West Indies 187–188
UNESCO 36
United States Army Corps of
    Engineers 83, 89
United States Navy 83
Upper Blake's (Montserrat) 203
use-wear studies 32, 206
Utuado, Puerto Rico 104, 109, 111

Valcárcel Rojas, Roberto 157n, 158, 159,
    161–164, 169
Valdivia site (Ecuador) 116
Vega Baja, Puerto Rico 39
Vega Real, Dominican
    Republic 146
Velázquez, Diego 47
Veloz Maggiolo, Marcio 28, 30–31,
    36–37, 41, 116–117, 122, 148
Venezuela 4, 19, 27, 33, 35, 38, 41–42,
    52–53, 61, 67, 116, 135, 148, 168, 174,
    186, 197
    llanos 135
Vescelius, Gary 109
Vespucci, Amerigo 239n2
Vieques Island 40, 53, 59, 63, 66, 79,
    87, 92, 104, 127, 136, 209–211
Vieille Case site (Dominica) 213
viewscapes 7, 10, 58, 126, 173
Vignier III site (Haiti) 24
Villa ClaraProvince, Cuba 152
Virgin Gorda (BVI) 6
Virgin Islands 3, 4, 6, 13, 40, 44, 58–59,
    84, 88, 104, 134, 140–141, 202
vomit spatula 140, 143, 167, 177
voodoo 177
voyaging 8, 10, 26–27, 38–39, 55, 116
    computer simulations 26–27,
    38–39, 57, 59
    corridors 10, 116
    long-distance 8, 27, 55
    shadow 10

Waal, Maike de 230
Wai Wai 93
Walker's Rest site (Dominica) 234

warfare 77, 99–100, 106–107, 124, 143, 146, 241, 257–259
watercraft
  rafts 27, 55
  sails 27, 54–55
Watters, David xvi, 61, 63
wattle-and-daub structure 140
Weeden Island, Florida 165
wellheads, broken pots 75
West Indies, defined 23
Westmoreland Parish, Jamaica 192
West Palm Beach, Florida 6, 170
Whitehead's Bluff site (Anguilla) 201, 203, 208
Whitelands Formation xv, 183
White Marl site (Jamaica) 190–191
white-on-red painting (WOR) 53, 64, 70, 210, 225
Windward Islands 14–15, 37–38, 54, 59, 63, 201, 207, 212, 215215, 221–222, 233–234, 240
Windward Point Bay, Anguilla 203

Windwardside site (Saba) 213
Winter, John 178
Wonotobo Falls site (Suriname) 210
World Heritage site 36

Yale Caribbean Program 187
Yambou River, St. Vincent 235–236
Yaguajay cluster 162–163
Yayael 245
Yayel site (Cuba) 159
Yocahu 80, 242
Yucatan Channel 25
Yucatan Peninsula 25–27

Zagers, Carl 204
Zapata, Cuba 33
Zenú Culture (Colombia) 164
zombie 177
zoned-incised-crosshatch (ZIC) 64, 66–67, 70, 210
Zucchi, Alberta 116–117, 148

CPSIA information can be obtained
at www.ICGtesting.com
Printed in the USA
BVHW041545280720
584738BV00001B/1

9 780190 605254